Grand Blue Dreaming 9

PRESENTED BY KENJI INOUE & KIMITAKE YOSHIOKA

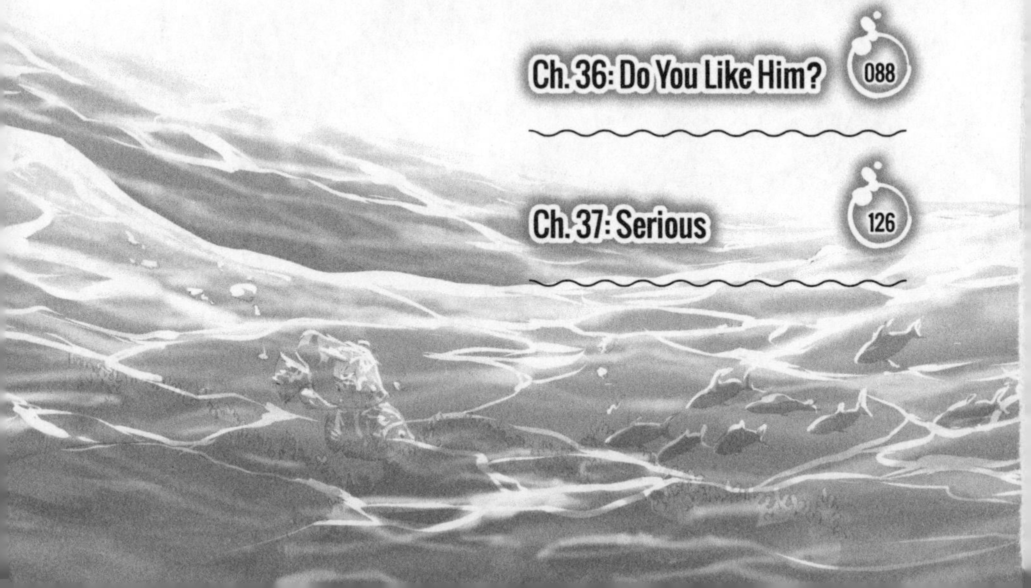

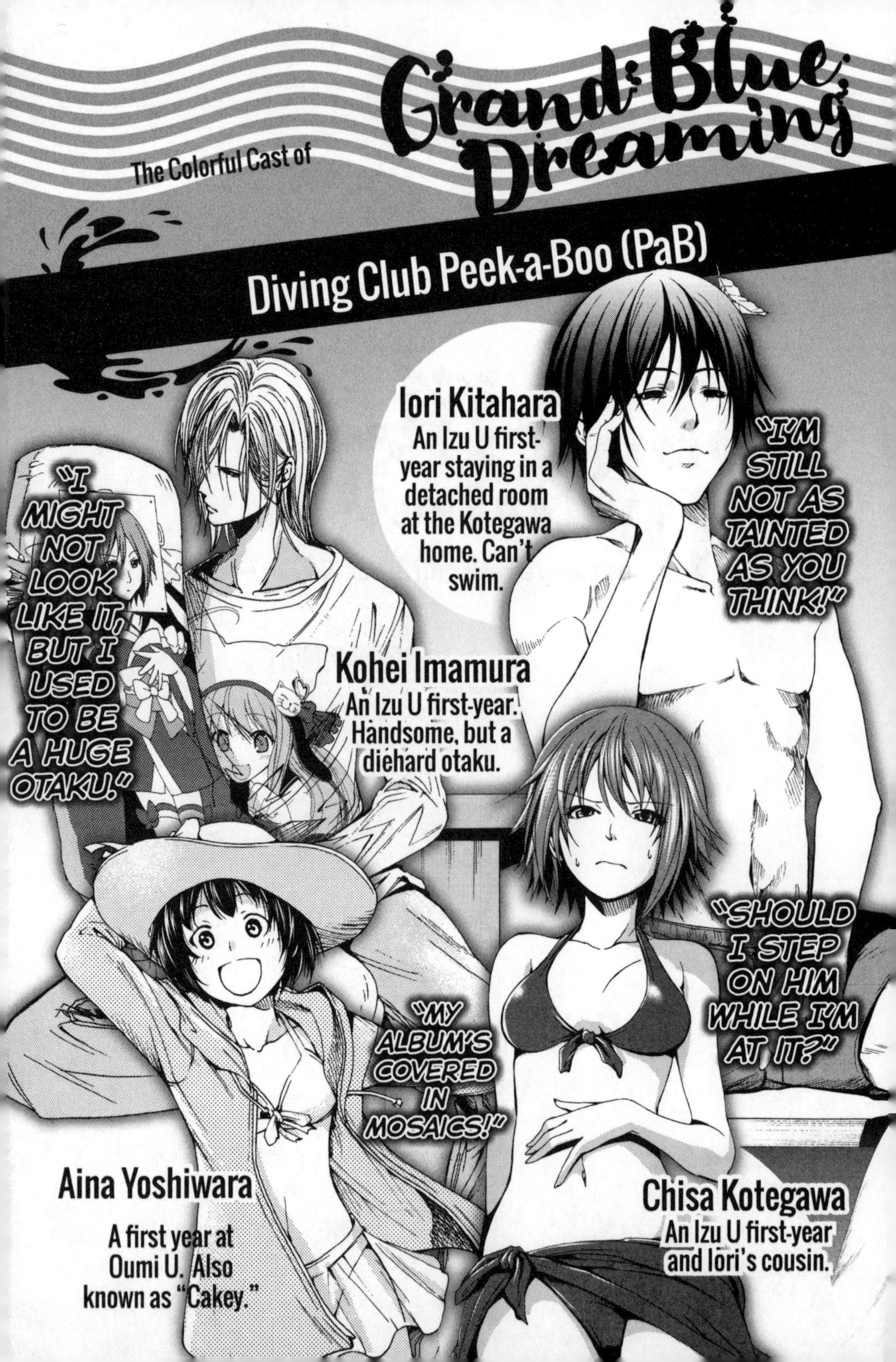
The Colorful Cast of
Grand Blue Dreaming
Diving Club Peek-a-Boo (PaB)
Iori Kitahara
An Izu U first-year staying in a detached room at the Kotegawa home. Can't swim.
"I'M STILL NOT AS TAINTED AS YOU THINK!"
Kohei Imamura
An Izu U first-year. Handsome, but a diehard otaku.
"I MIGHT NOT LOOK LIKE IT, BUT I USED TO BE A HUGE OTAKU."
Chisa Kotegawa
An Izu U first-year and Iori's cousin.
"SHOULD I STEP ON HIM WHILE I'M AT IT?"
Aina Yoshiwara
A first year at Oumi U. Also known as "Cakey."
"MY ALBUM'S COVERED IN MOSAICS!"

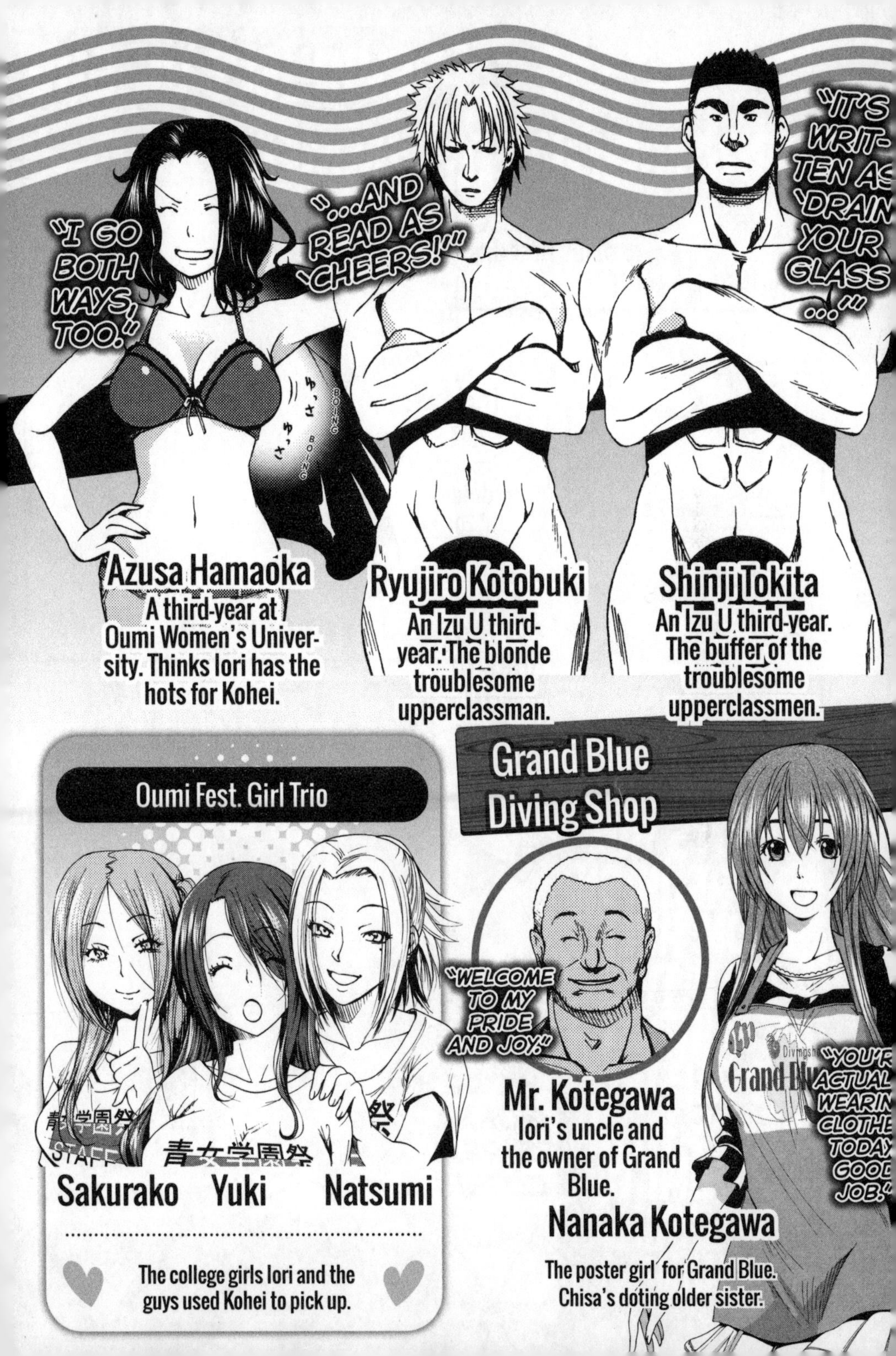

“IT'S WRIT-TEN AS 'DRAIN YOUR GLASS...'”
Shinji Tokita
An Izu U third-year. The buffer of the troublesome upperclassmen.
“...AND READ AS 'CHEERS!'”
Ryujiro Kotobuki
An Izu U third-year. The blonde troublesome upperclassman.
“I GO BOTH WAYS, TOO.”
ゆっさ BOING
ゆっさ BOING
Azusa Hamaoka
A third-year at Oumi Women's University. Thinks Iori has the hots for Kohei.
Grand Blue Diving Shop
“YOU'R ACTUAL WEARIN CLOTHE TODAY GOOD JOB.”
Grand Blu
Nanaka Kotegawa
The poster girl for Grand Blue. Chisa's doting older sister.
“WELCOME TO MY PRIDE AND JOY.”
Mr. Kotegawa
Iori's uncle and the owner of Grand Blue.
Oumi Fest. Girl Trio
青女学園祭
STAFF
Sakurako
Yuki
Natsumi
The college girls Iori and the guys used Kohei to pick up.

PREVIOUSLY ON GBD

A PRANK-FILLED SUMMER CAMP ♥

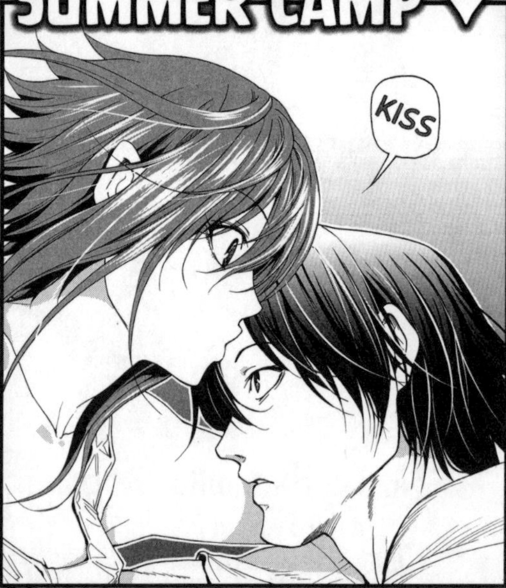
KISS

When Iori shows up to his first day of work in high spirits...

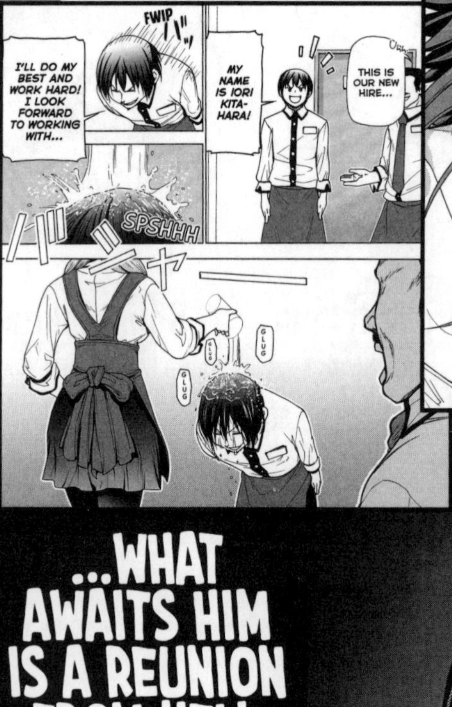
THIS IS OUR NEW HIRE...
MY NAME IS IORI KITA-HARA!
FWIP
I'LL DO MY BEST AND WORK HARD! I LOOK FORWARD TO WORKING WITH...
SPSHHH
GLUG
GLUG
GLUG

...WHAT AWAITS HIM IS A REUNION FROM HELL WITH THE ROTTEN BITCH HE BUTTED HEADS WITH AT OUMI U, SAKURAKO-CHAN!

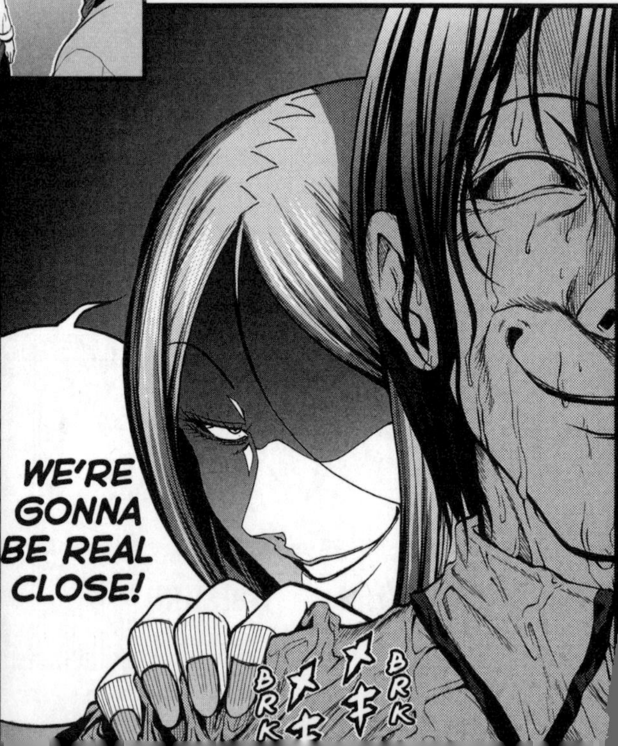
WE'RE GONNA BE REAL CLOSE!
BRK
BRK

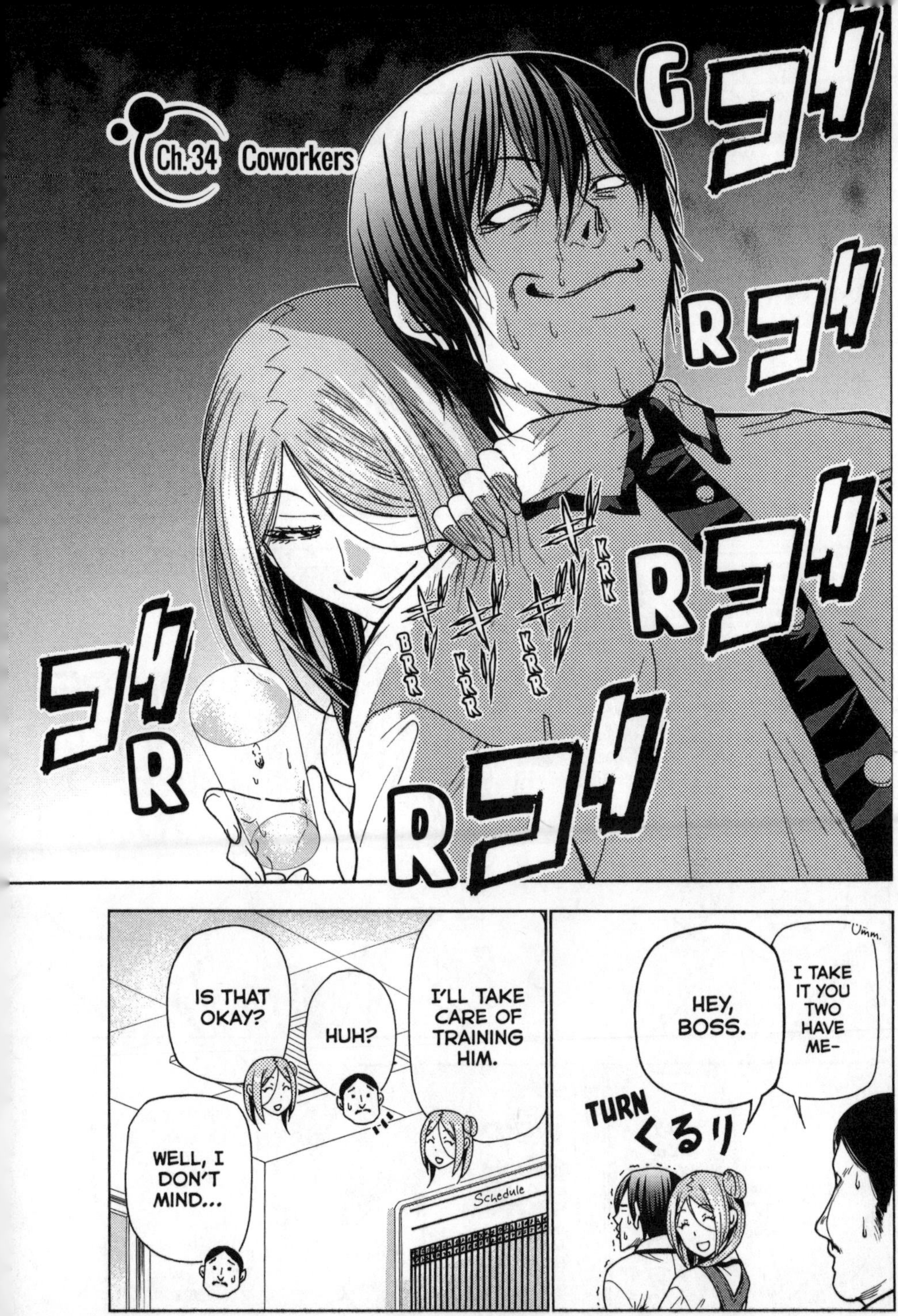
Ch.34 Coworkers
Gコク
Rコク
Rコク
KRK
KRR
KRR
BRR
Rコク
コクR
Umm.
I TAKE IT YOU TWO HAVE ME-
HEY, BOSS.
TURN くるり
I'LL TAKE CARE OF TRAINING HIM.
HUH?
IS THAT OKAY?
WELL, I DON'T MIND...
Schedule

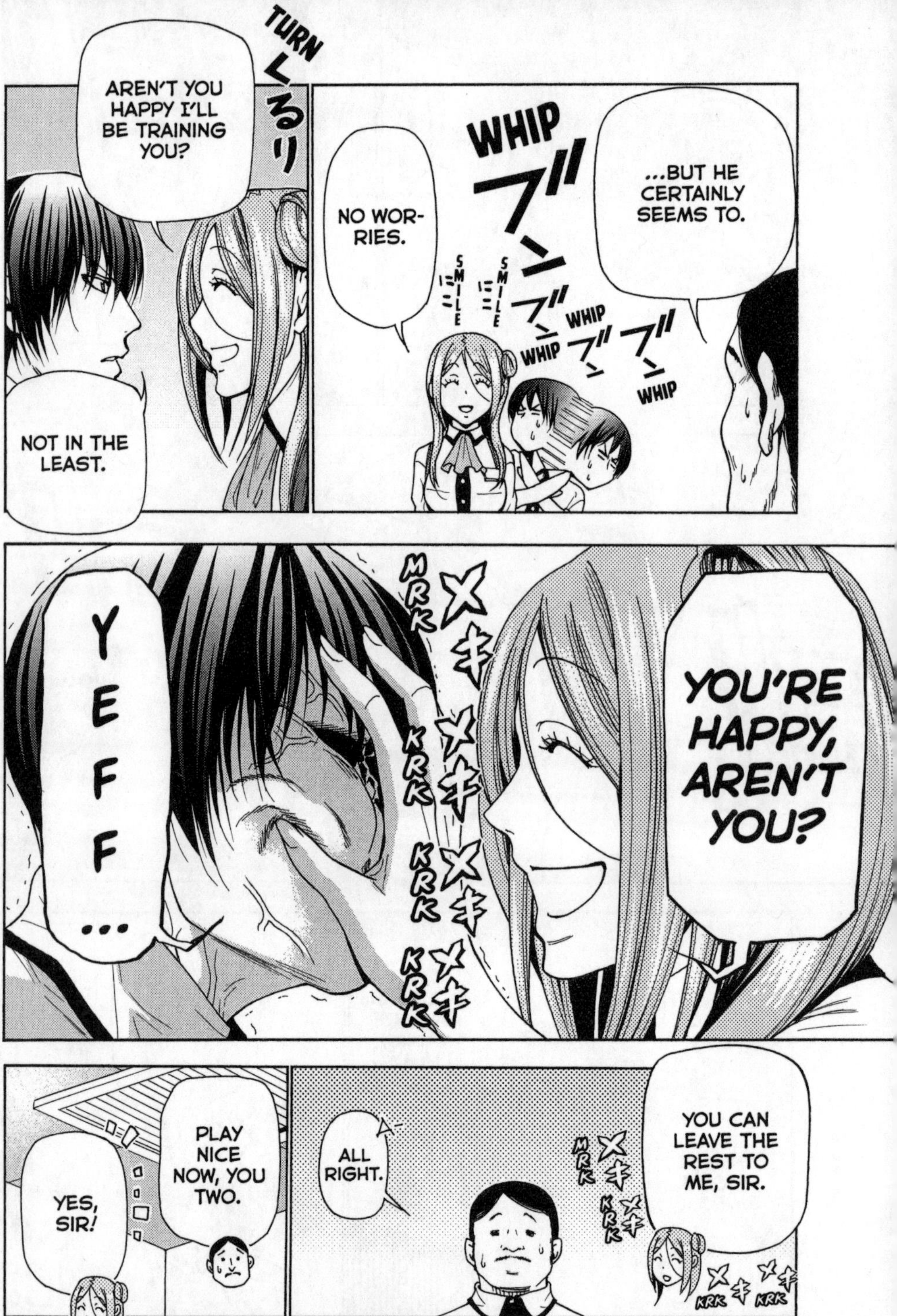
...BUT HE CERTAINLY SEEMS TO.
WHIP WHIP WHIP WHIP
NO WORRIES.
SMILE SMILE
TURN
AREN'T YOU HAPPY I'LL BE TRAINING YOU?
NOT IN THE LEAST.
YOU'RE HAPPY, AREN'T YOU?
MRK KRK KRK KRK
YEFF...
YOU CAN LEAVE THE REST TO ME, SIR.
MRK KRK KRK KRK
ALL RIGHT.
PLAY NICE NOW, YOU TWO.
YES, SIR!

HRRR
ぎぎぎRぎ

...YES,
MA'AM.

YOU
STAY
PUT.

CHAK
ガチャ

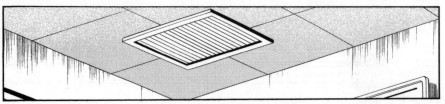

YOU'RE TO
ADDRESS
ME AS SAKU-
RAKO-SAMA
FROM NOW
ON.

と゛
DA

ん゛っ
DAM

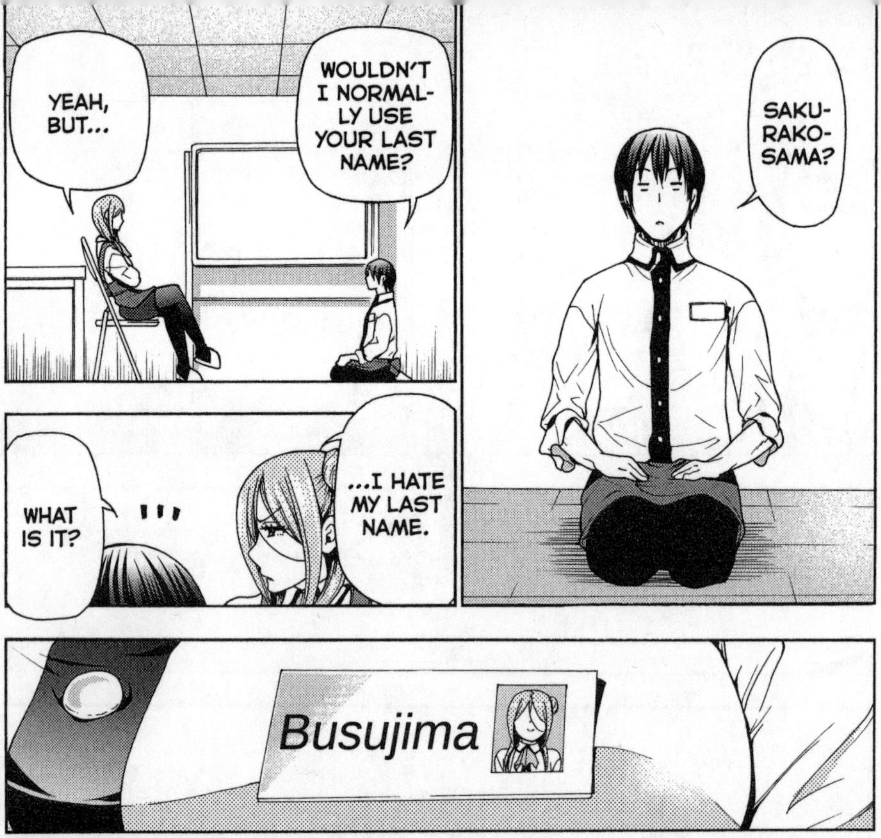
SAKU-RAKO-SAMA?
WOULDN'T I NORMAL-LY USE YOUR LAST NAME?
YEAH, BUT...
...I HATE MY LAST NAME.
WHAT IS IT?
Busujima

*Busu means ugly in Japanese.

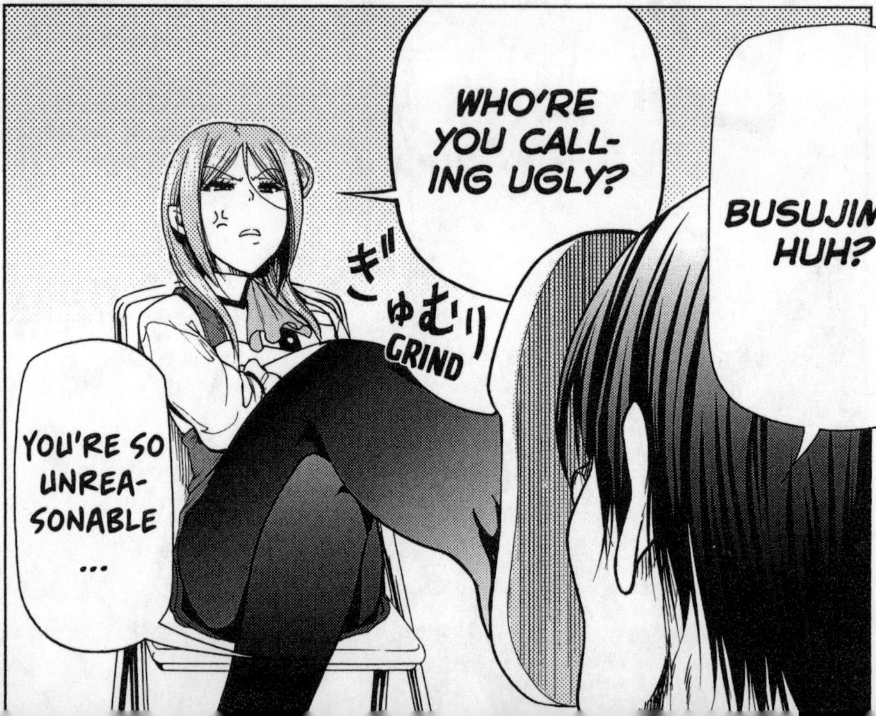
BUSUJIMA, HUH?
WHO'RE YOU CALL-ING UGLY?
ぎゅむり
GRIND
YOU'RE SO UNREA-SONABLE ...

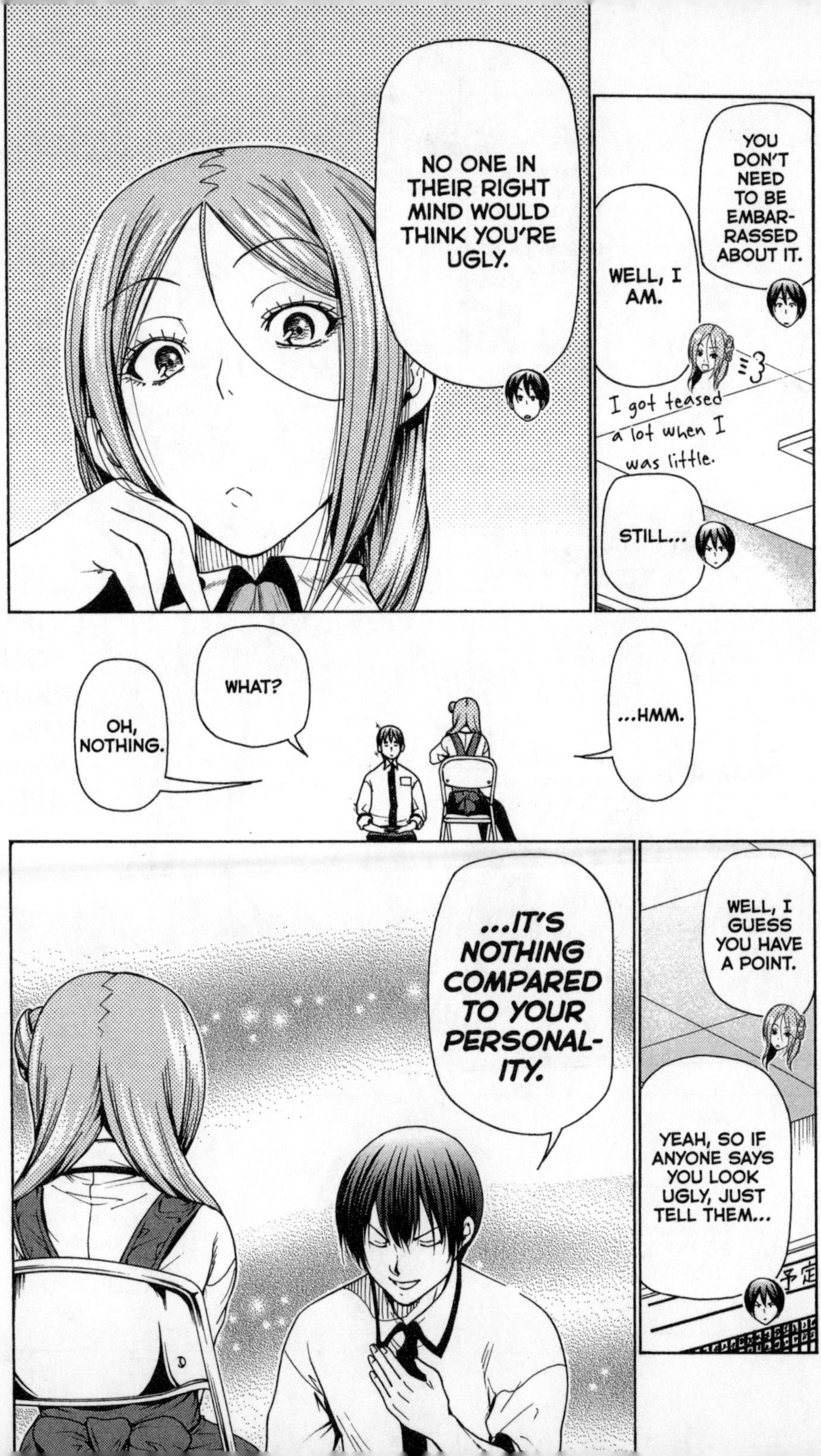
YOU DON'T NEED TO BE EMBARRASSED ABOUT IT.
WELL, I AM.
I got teased a lot when I was little.
STILL...
NO ONE IN THEIR RIGHT MIND WOULD THINK YOU'RE UGLY.
...HMM.
WHAT?
OH, NOTHING.
WELL, I GUESS YOU HAVE A POINT.
YEAH, SO IF ANYONE SAYS YOU LOOK UGLY, JUST TELL THEM...
...IT'S NOTHING COMPARED TO YOUR PERSONALITY.

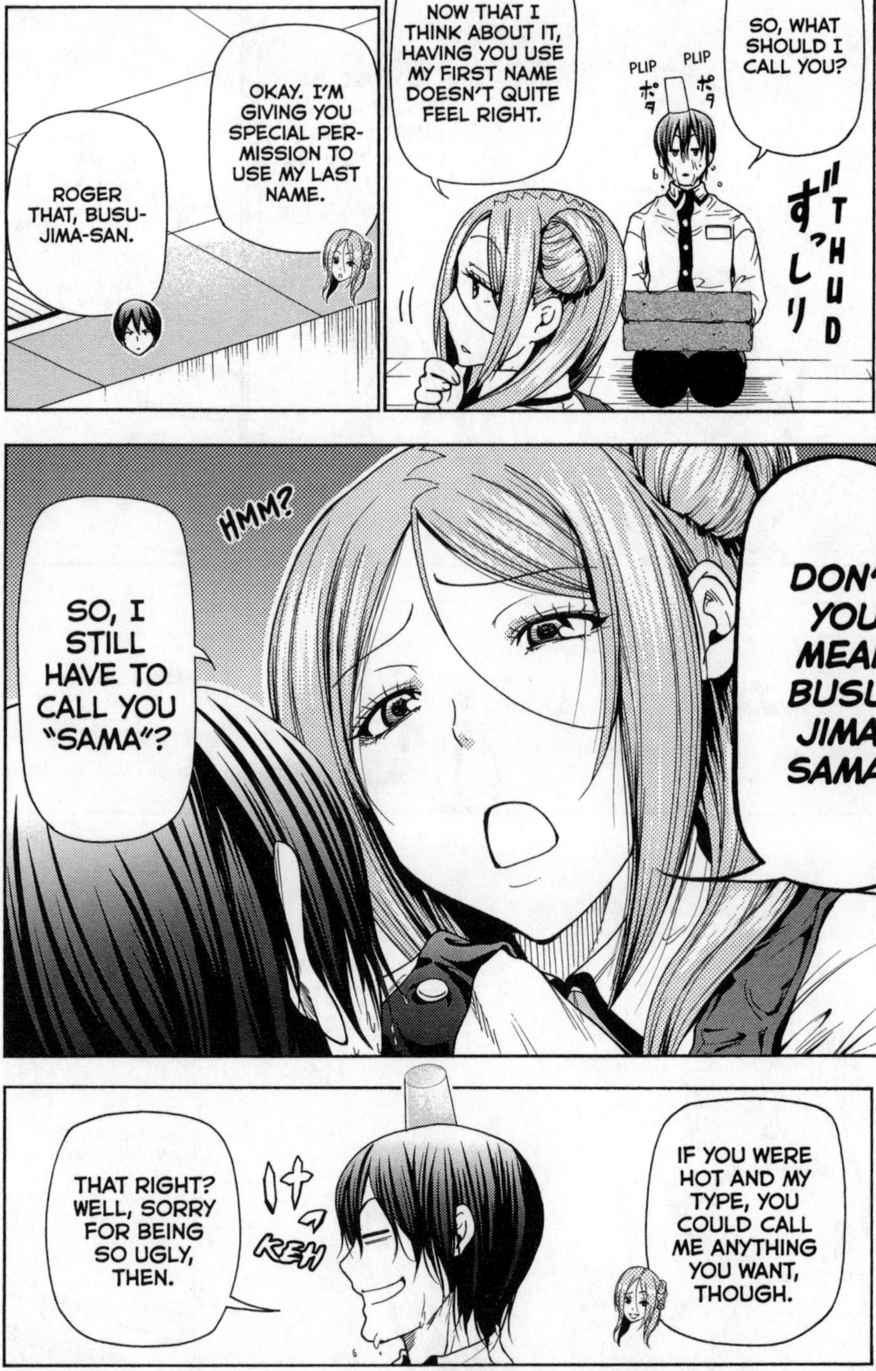
SO, WHAT SHOULD I CALL YOU?
PLIP PLIP
ポタ ポタ
ずっしり
THUD
NOW THAT I THINK ABOUT IT, HAVING YOU USE MY FIRST NAME DOESN'T QUITE FEEL RIGHT.
OKAY. I'M GIVING YOU SPECIAL PER-MISSION TO USE MY LAST NAME.
ROGER THAT, BUSU-JIMA-SAN.
DON'T YOU MEAN BUSU-JIMA-SAMA?
HMM?
SO, I STILL HAVE TO CALL YOU "SAMA"?
IF YOU WERE HOT AND MY TYPE, YOU COULD CALL ME ANYTHING YOU WANT, THOUGH.
ケッ
KEH
THAT RIGHT? WELL, SORRY FOR BEING SO UGLY, THEN.

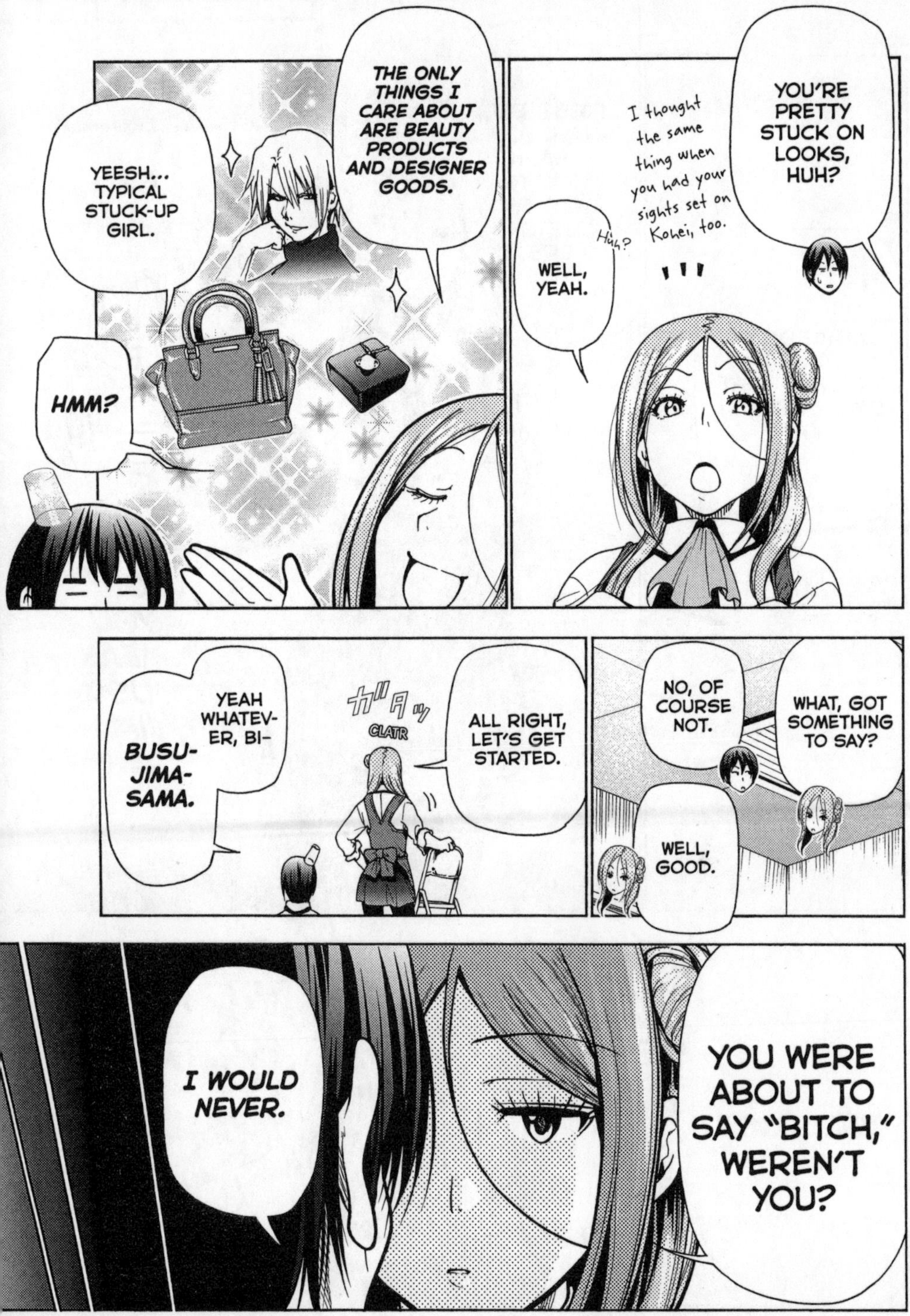
YOU'RE PRETTY STUCK ON LOOKS, HUH?
I thought the same thing when you had your sights set on Kohei, too.
Huh?
WELL, YEAH.
THE ONLY THINGS I CARE ABOUT ARE BEAUTY PRODUCTS AND DESIGNER GOODS.
YEESH... TYPICAL STUCK-UP GIRL.
HMM?
WHAT, GOT SOMETHING TO SAY?
NO, OF COURSE NOT.
WELL, GOOD.
ALL RIGHT, LET'S GET STARTED.
ガタッ
CLATR
YEAH WHATEVER, BI- BUSUJIMA-SAMA.
YOU WERE ABOUT TO SAY "BITCH," WEREN'T YOU?
I WOULD NEVER.

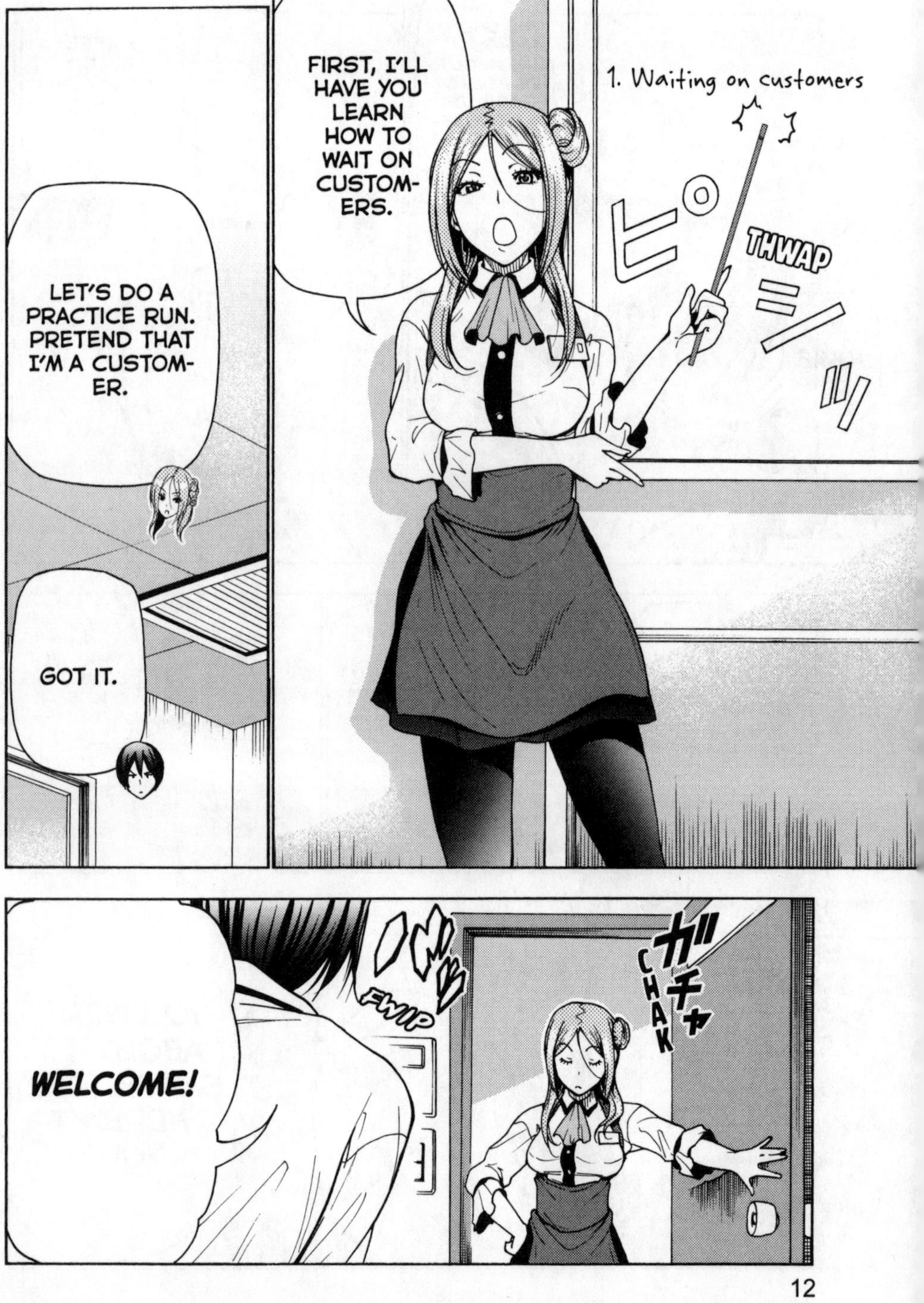
FIRST, I'LL HAVE YOU LEARN HOW TO WAIT ON CUSTOMERS.
1. Waiting on customers
THWAP
LET'S DO A PRACTICE RUN. PRETEND THAT I'M A CUSTOMER.
GOT IT.
CHAK
FWIP
WELCOME!

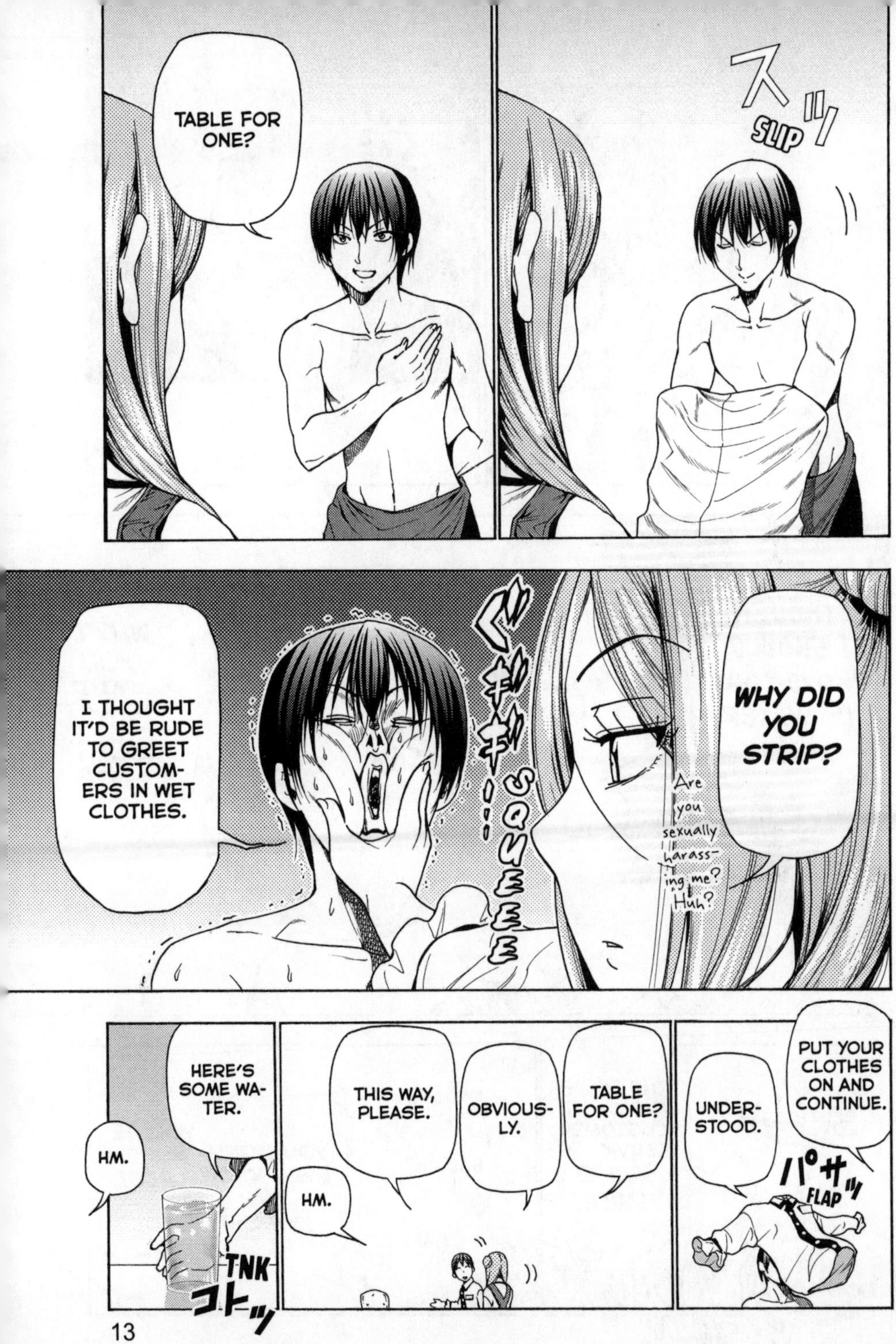

スッ
SLIP
TABLE FOR ONE?
WHY DID YOU STRIP?
Are you sexually harass-ing me? Huh?
ギギギ
SQUEEEE
I THOUGHT IT'D BE RUDE TO GREET CUSTOM-ERS IN WET CLOTHES.
PUT YOUR CLOTHES ON AND CONTINUE.
UNDER-STOOD.
パサッ
FLAP
TABLE FOR ONE?
OBVIOUS-LY.
THIS WAY, PLEASE.
HM.
HERE'S SOME WA-TER.
HM.
TNK
コトッ

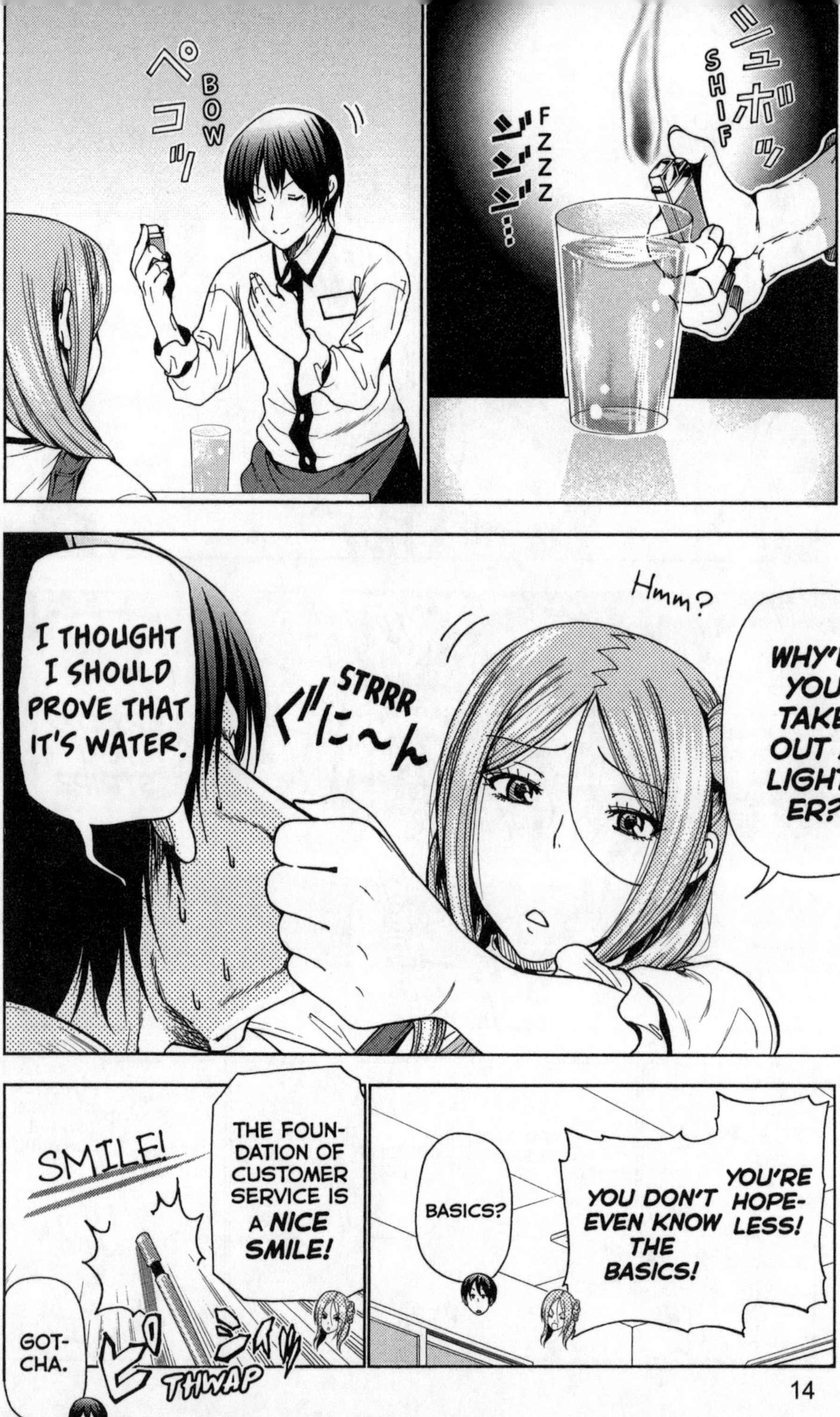
シュボッ
SHIF
ジジジ…
FZZZ
ペコッ
BOW
Hmm?
WHY'D YOU TAKE OUT A LIGHTER?
ぐに～ん
STRRR
I THOUGHT I SHOULD PROVE THAT IT'S WATER.
YOU'RE HOPELESS!
YOU DON'T EVEN KNOW THE BASICS!
BASICS?
THE FOUNDATION OF CUSTOMER SERVICE IS A NICE SMILE!
SMILE!
THWAP
GOTCHA.

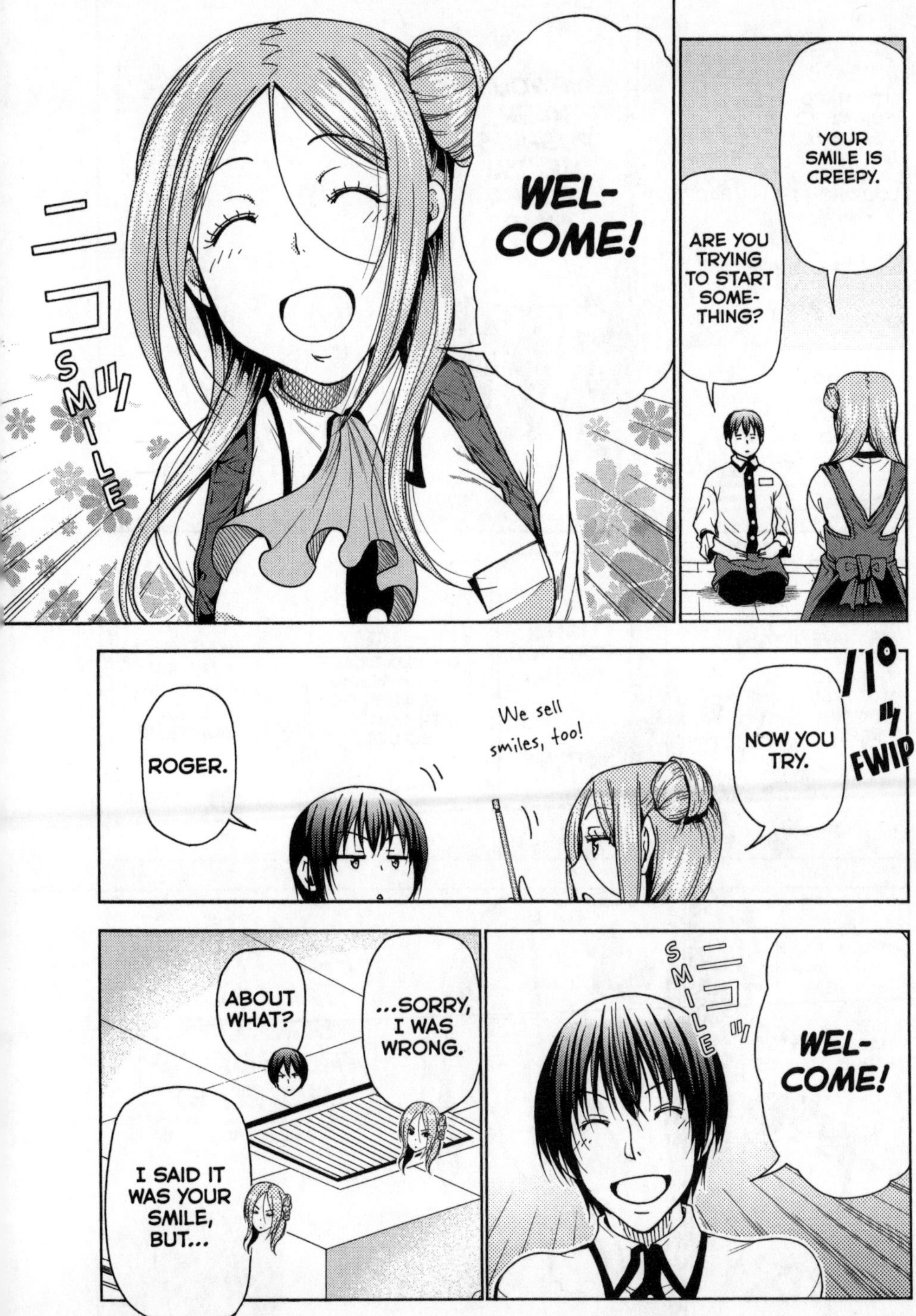
YOUR SMILE IS CREEPY.
ARE YOU TRYING TO START SOME-THING?
ニコッ
SMILE
WEL-COME!
パッ
FWIP
NOW YOU TRY.
We sell smiles, too!
ROGER.
ニコッ
SMILE
WEL-COME!
...SORRY, I WAS WRONG.
ABOUT WHAT?
I SAID IT WAS YOUR SMILE, BUT...

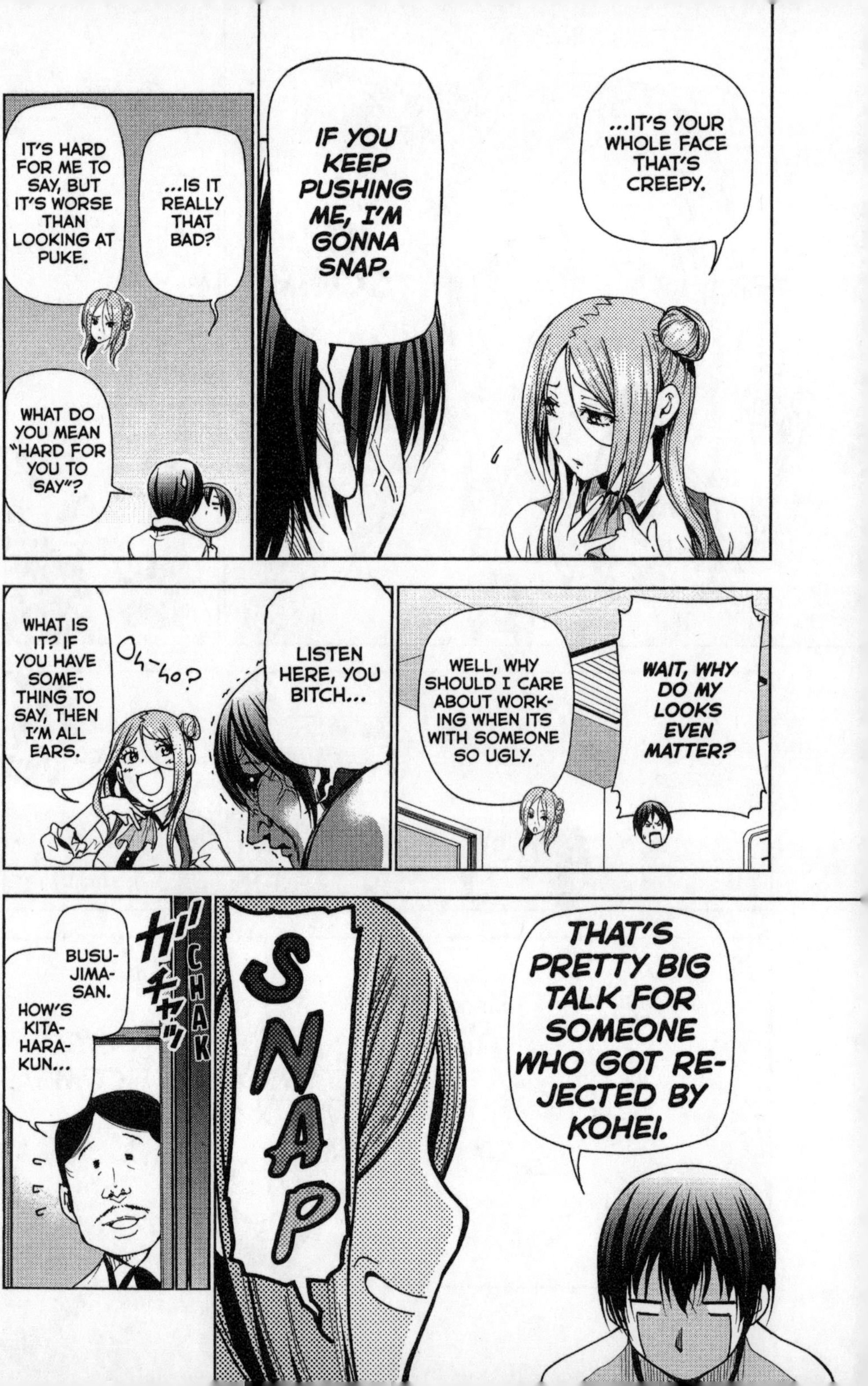
...IT'S YOUR WHOLE FACE THAT'S CREEPY.
IF YOU KEEP PUSHING ME, I'M GONNA SNAP.
...IS IT REALLY THAT BAD?
IT'S HARD FOR ME TO SAY, BUT IT'S WORSE THAN LOOKING AT PUKE.
WHAT DO YOU MEAN "HARD FOR YOU TO SAY"?
WAIT, WHY DO MY LOOKS EVEN MATTER?
WELL, WHY SHOULD I CARE ABOUT WORKING WHEN ITS WITH SOMEONE SO UGLY.
LISTEN HERE, YOU BITCH...
WHAT IS IT? IF YOU HAVE SOMETHING TO SAY, THEN I'M ALL EARS.
THAT'S PRETTY BIG TALK FOR SOMEONE WHO GOT REJECTED BY KOHEI.
SNAP
ガチャッ
CHAK
BUSUJIMA-SAN. HOW'S KITAHARA-KUN...

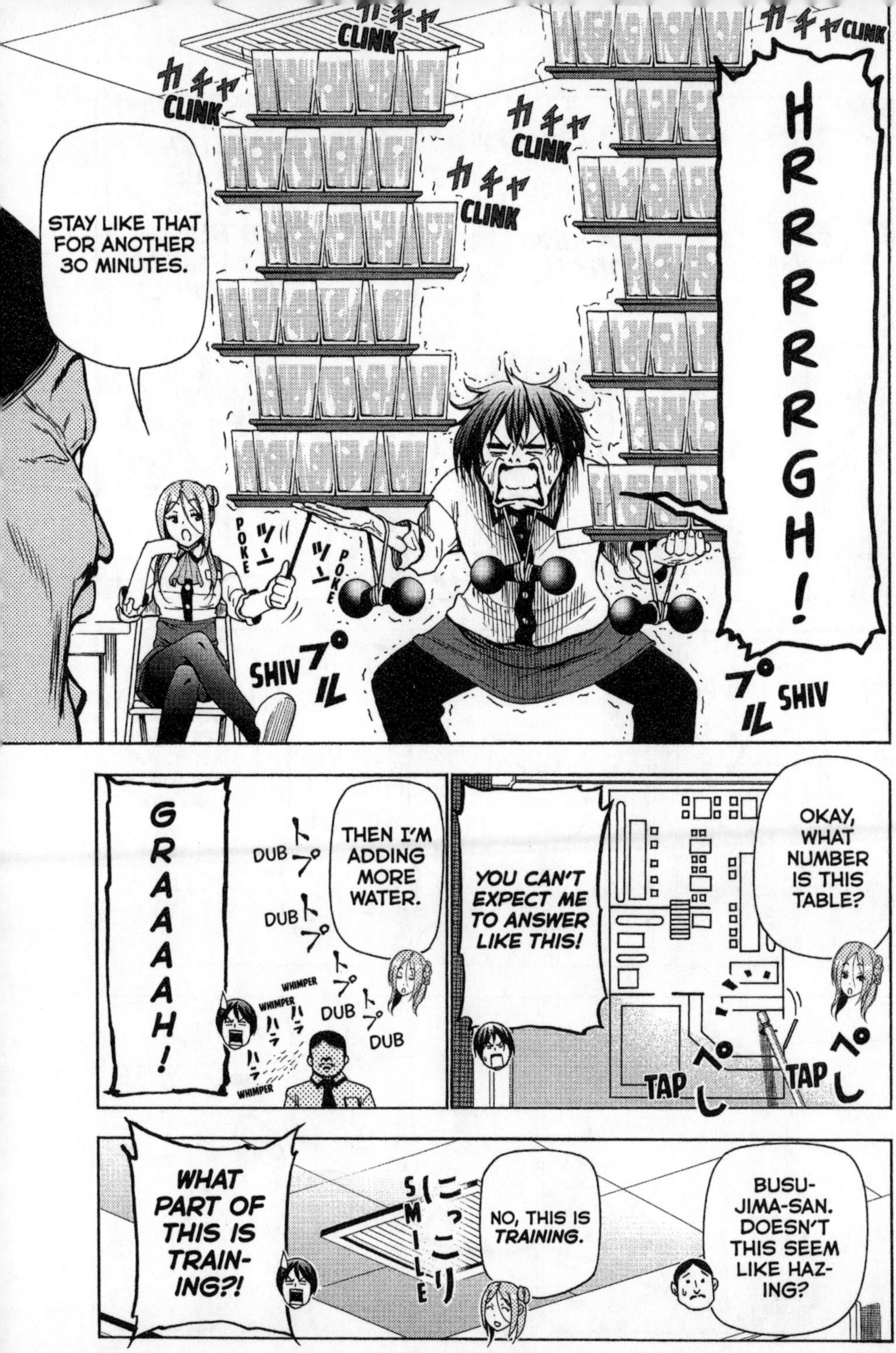
HRRRRGH!
カチャ CLINK
カチャ CLINK
カチャ CLINK
カチャ CLINK
カチャ CLINK
STAY LIKE THAT FOR ANOTHER 30 MINUTES.
ツン POKE
ツン POKE
プル SHIV
プル SHIV
OKAY, WHAT NUMBER IS THIS TABLE?
ぺし TAP
ぺし TAP
YOU CAN'T EXPECT ME TO ANSWER LIKE THIS!
THEN I'M ADDING MORE WATER.
トプ DUB
トプ DUB
トプ DUB
トプ DUB
ハラ WHIMPER
ハラ WHIMPER
ハラ WHIMPER
GRAAAAAH!
BUSU-JIMA-SAN. DOESN'T THIS SEEM LIKE HAZ-ING?
NO, THIS IS *TRAINING.*
にっこり SMILE
WHAT PART OF THIS IS TRAIN-ING?!

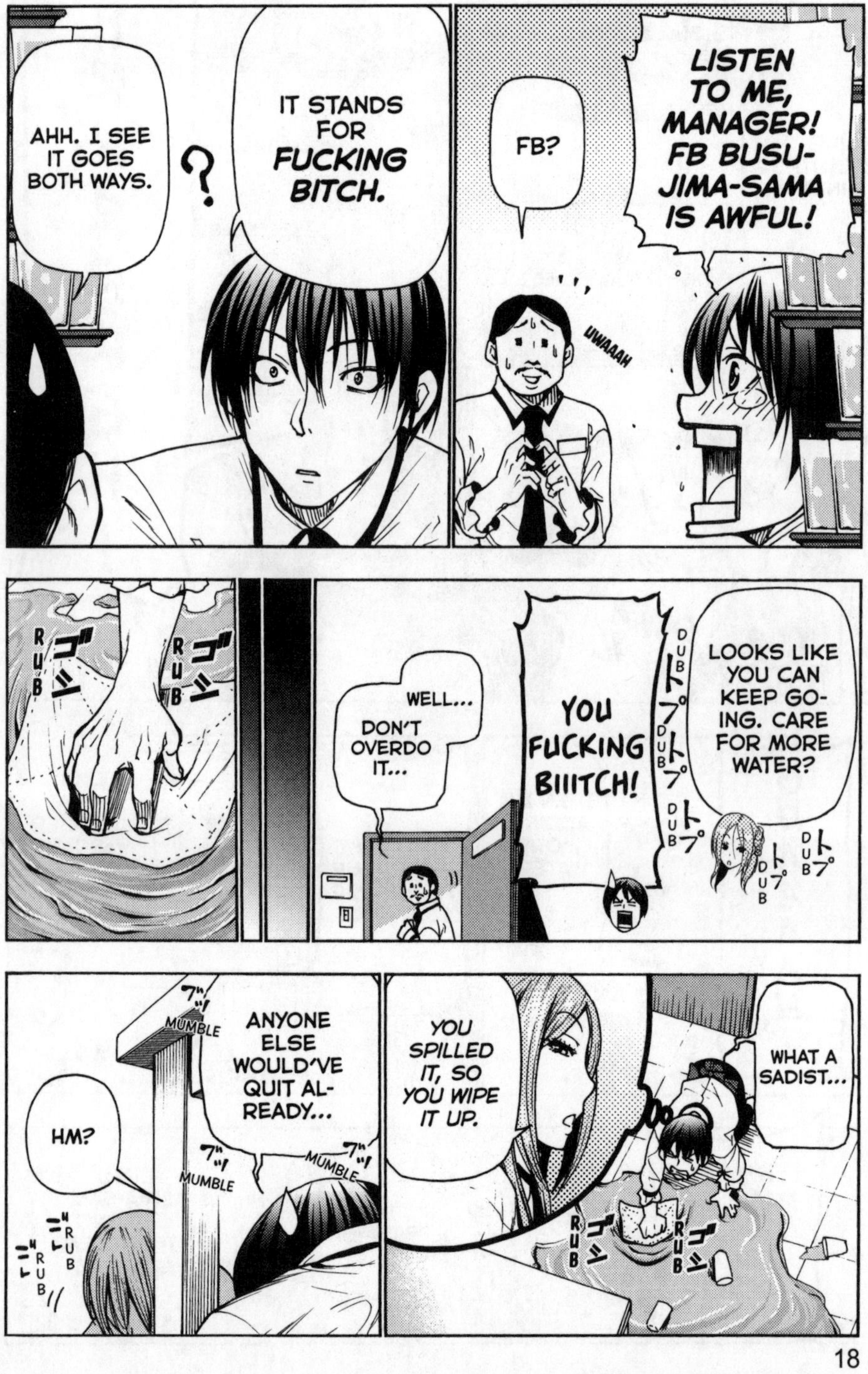
LISTEN TO ME, MANAGER! FB BUSU-JIMA-SAMA IS AWFUL!
FB?
UWAAAH
IT STANDS FOR FUCKING BITCH.
AHH. I SEE IT GOES BOTH WAYS.
LOOKS LIKE YOU CAN KEEP GO-ING. CARE FOR MORE WATER?
DUB DUB
DUB DUB
YOU FUCKING BIIITCH!
WELL... DON'T OVERDO IT...
RUB RUB
WHAT A SADIST...
YOU SPILLED IT, SO YOU WIPE IT UP.
RUB RUB
MUMBLE
ANYONE ELSE WOULD'VE QUIT AL-READY...
MUMBLE MUMBLE
HM?
RUB RUB

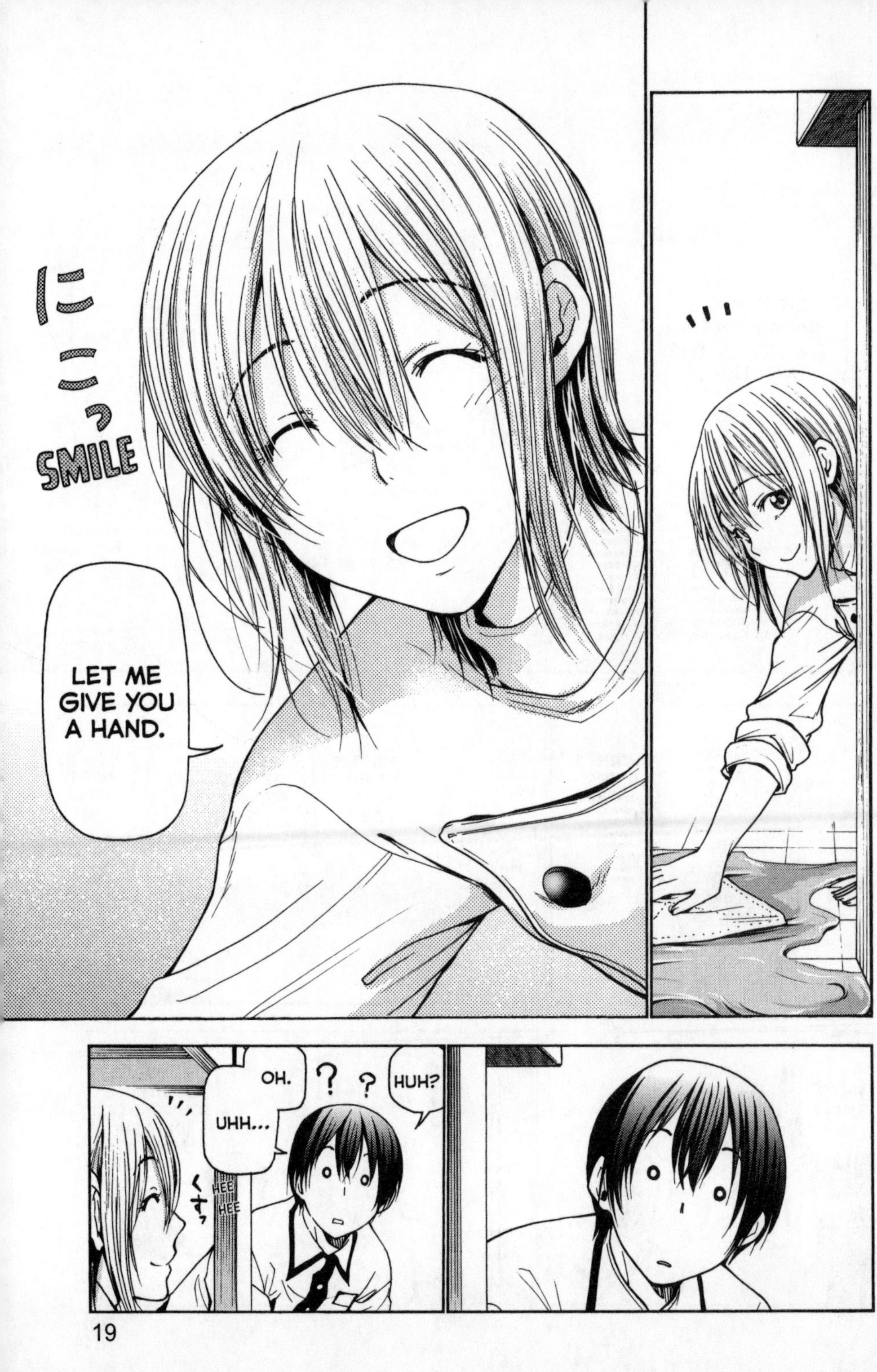
にこっ
SMILE
LET ME GIVE YOU A HAND.
HUH?
? ?
OH.
UHH...
くすっ
HEE HEE

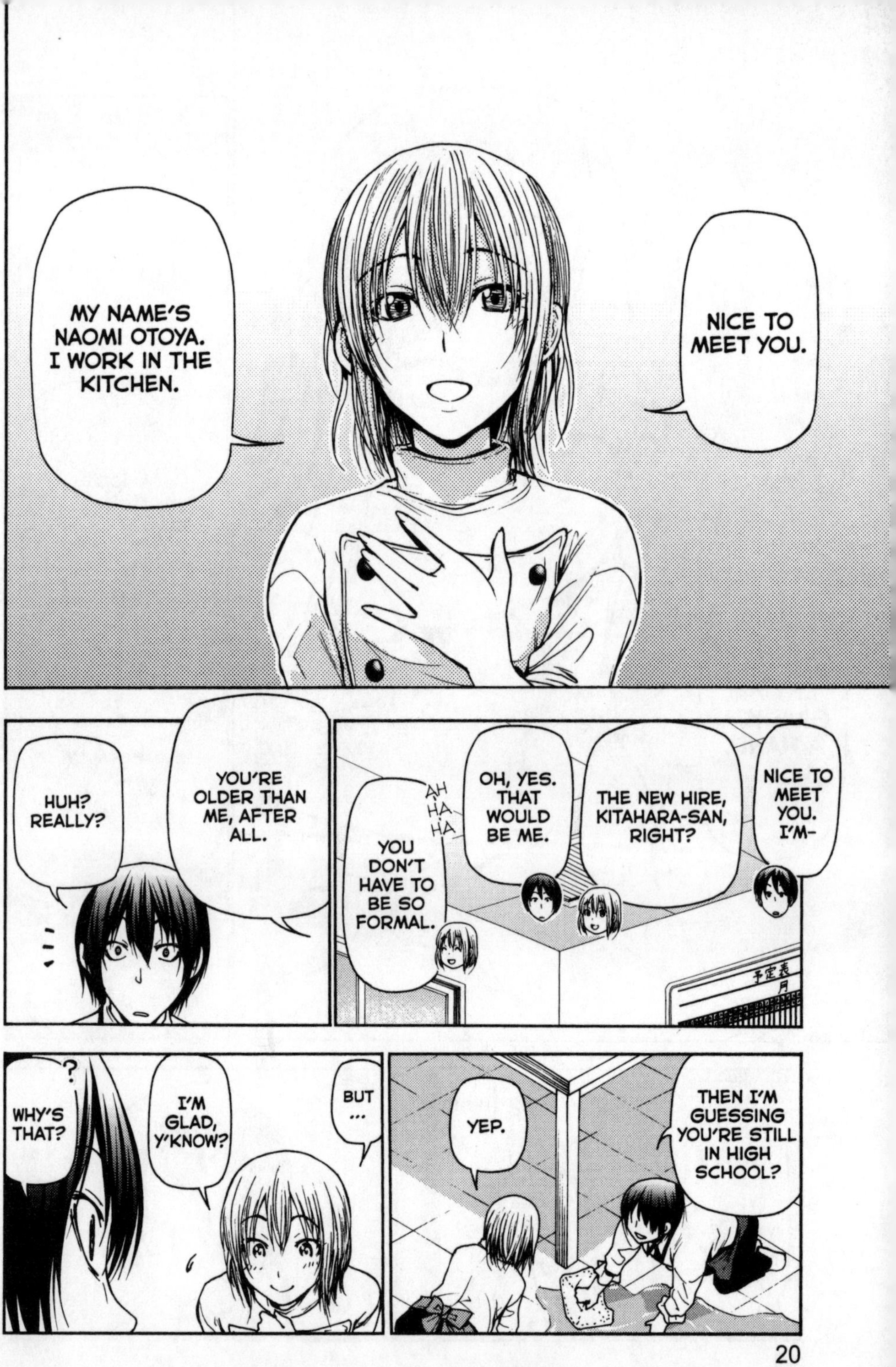
MY NAME'S NAOMI OTOYA. I WORK IN THE KITCHEN.
NICE TO MEET YOU.
NICE TO MEET YOU. I'M-
THE NEW HIRE, KITAHARA-SAN, RIGHT?
OH, YES. THAT WOULD BE ME.
AH HA HA
YOU DON'T HAVE TO BE SO FORMAL.
YOU'RE OLDER THAN ME, AFTER ALL.
HUH? REALLY?
THEN I'M GUESSING YOU'RE STILL IN HIGH SCHOOL?
YEP.
BUT ...
I'M GLAD, Y'KNOW?
WHY'S THAT?
?

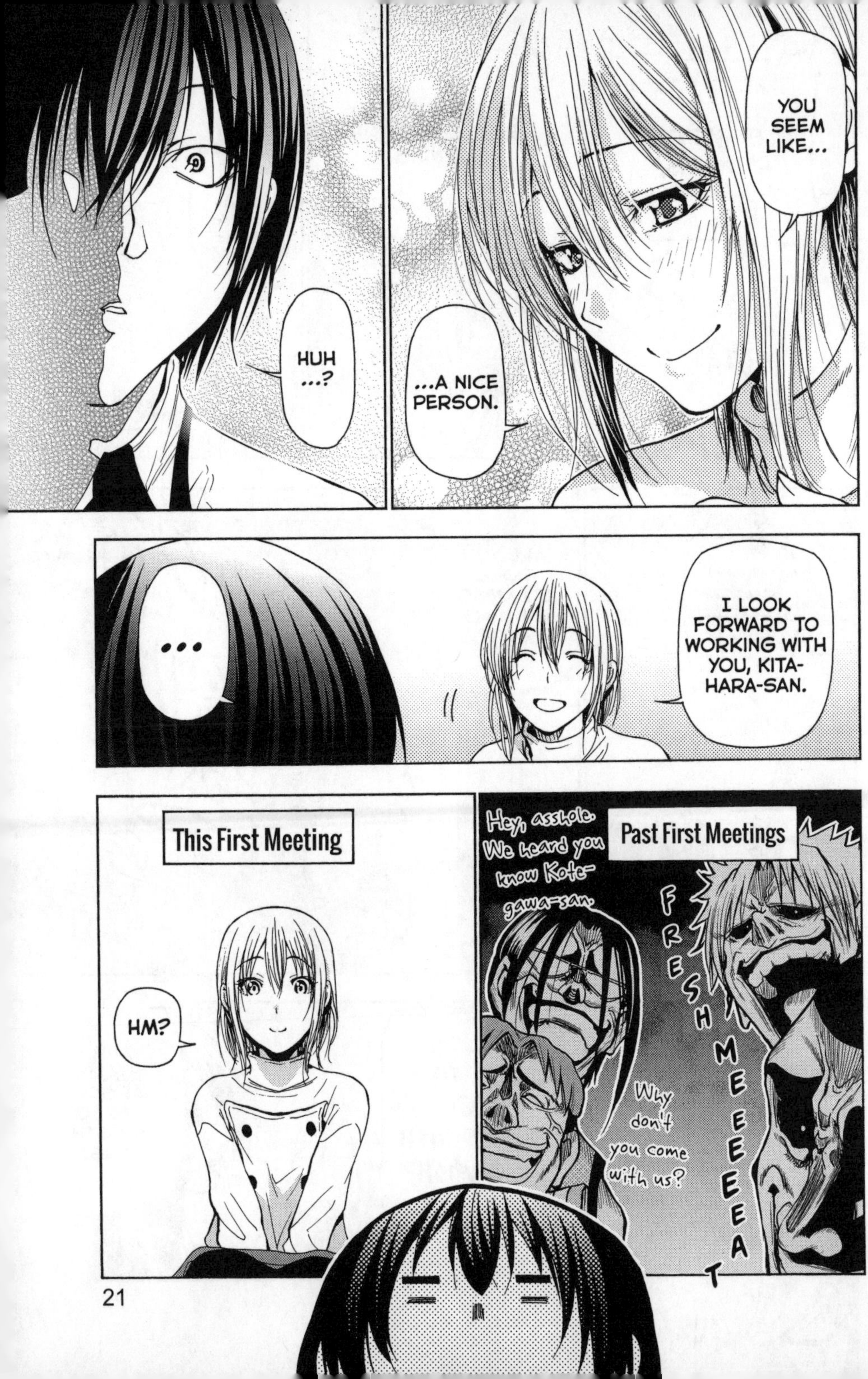
YOU SEEM LIKE...
...A NICE PERSON.
HUH ...?
I LOOK FORWARD TO WORKING WITH YOU, KITA-HARA-SAN.
...
Past First Meetings
Hey, asshole. We heard you know Kote-gawa-san.
FRESH MEEEEEAT
Why don't you come with us?
This First Meeting
HM?

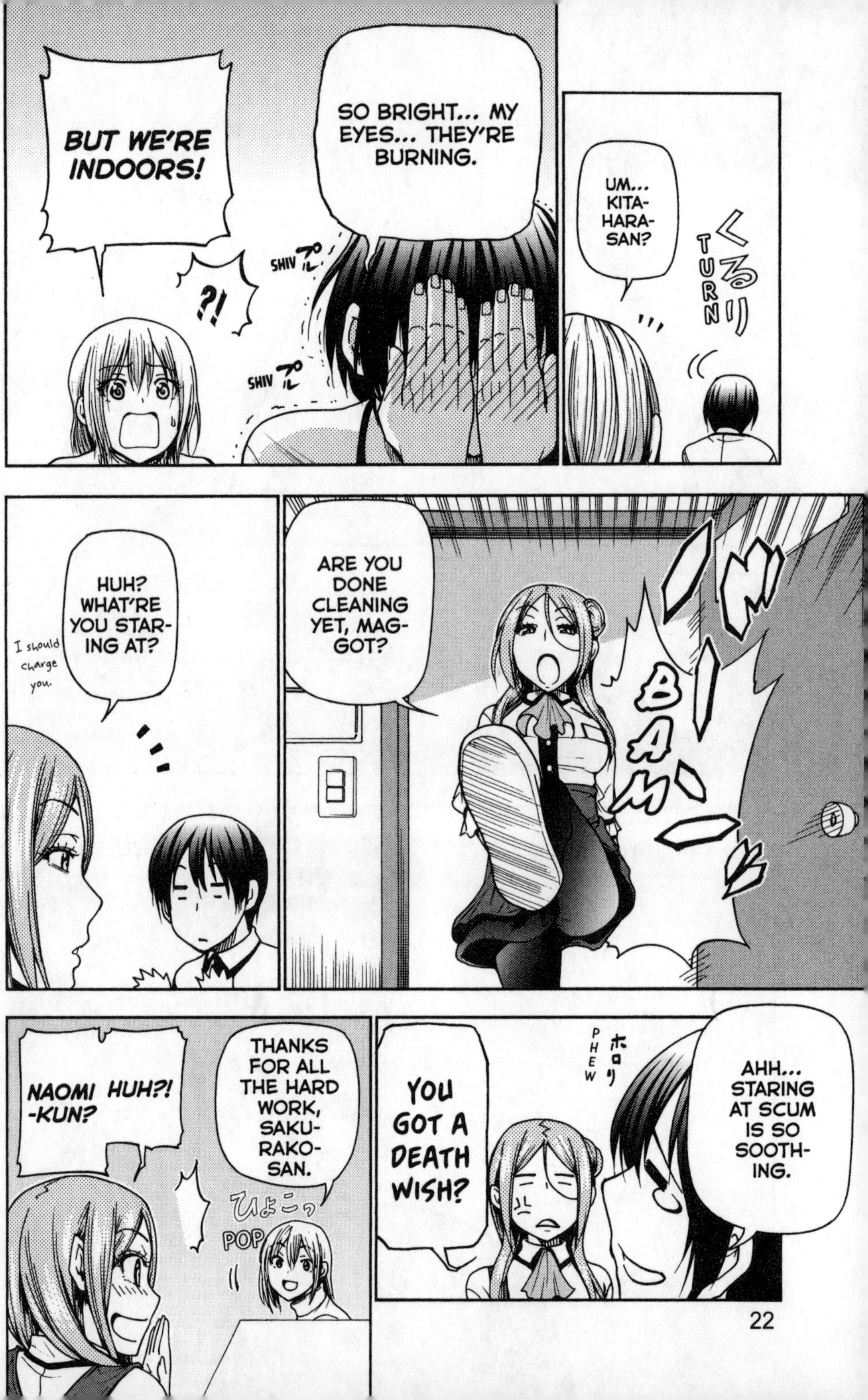
UM... KITA-HARA-SAN?
TURN
SO BRIGHT... MY EYES... THEY'RE BURNING.
SHIV
SHIV
BUT WE'RE INDOORS!
?!
BAM
ARE YOU DONE CLEANING YET, MAG-GOT?
HUH? WHAT'RE YOU STAR-ING AT?
I should charge you.
AHH... STARING AT SCUM IS SO SOOTH-ING.
PHEW
YOU GOT A DEATH WISH?
THANKS FOR ALL THE HARD WORK, SAKU-RAKO-SAN.
POP
NAOMI -KUN?
HUH?!

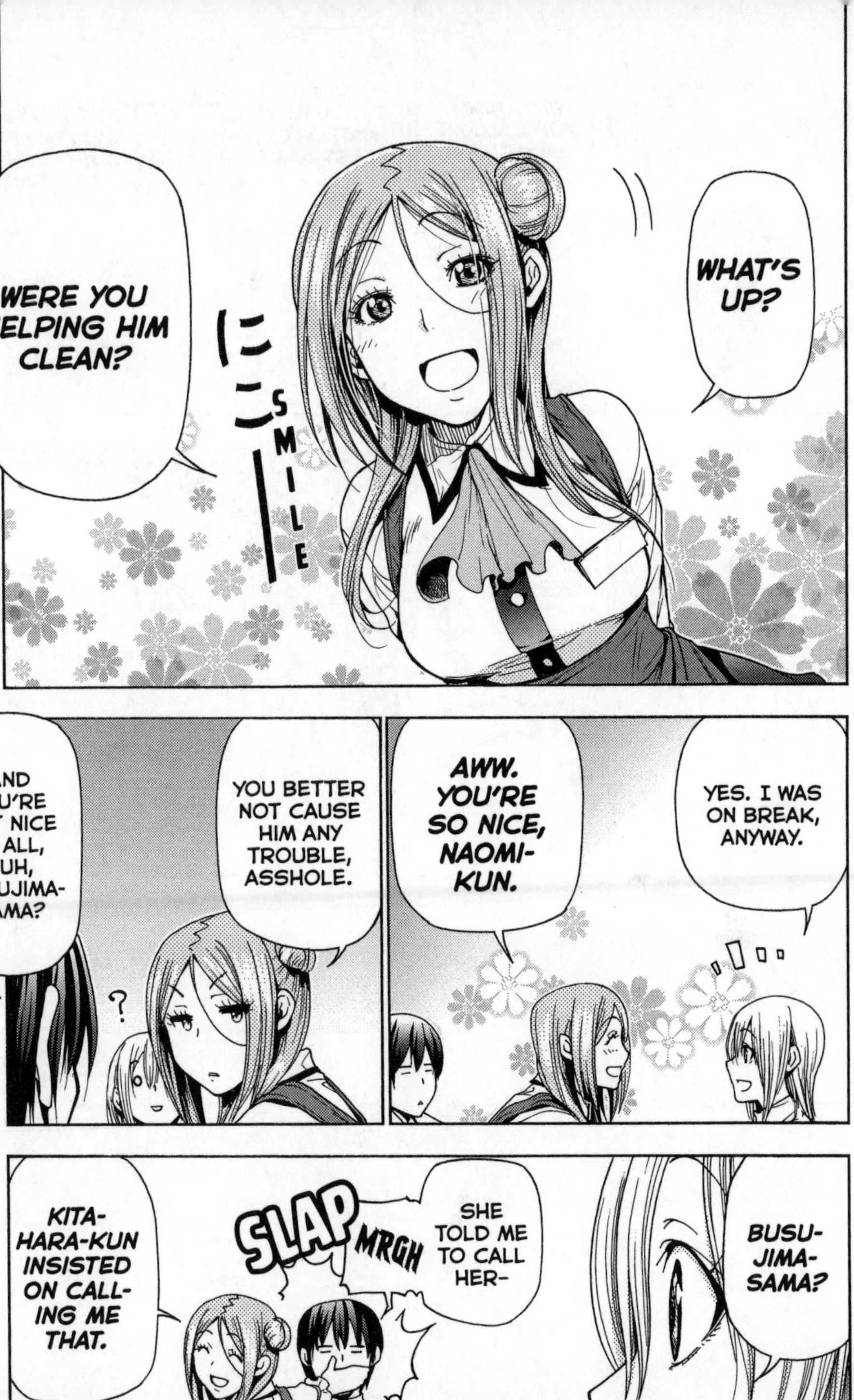
WHAT'S UP?
SMILE
WERE YOU HELPING HIM CLEAN?
YES. I WAS ON BREAK, ANYWAY.
AWW. YOU'RE SO NICE, NAOMI-KUN.
YOU BETTER NOT CAUSE HIM ANY TROUBLE, ASSHOLE.
AND YOU'RE NOT NICE AT ALL, HUH, BUSUJIMA-SAMA?
BUSU-JIMA-SAMA?
SHE TOLD ME TO CALL HER-
MRGH
SLAP
KITA-HARA-KUN INSISTED ON CALL-ING ME THAT.

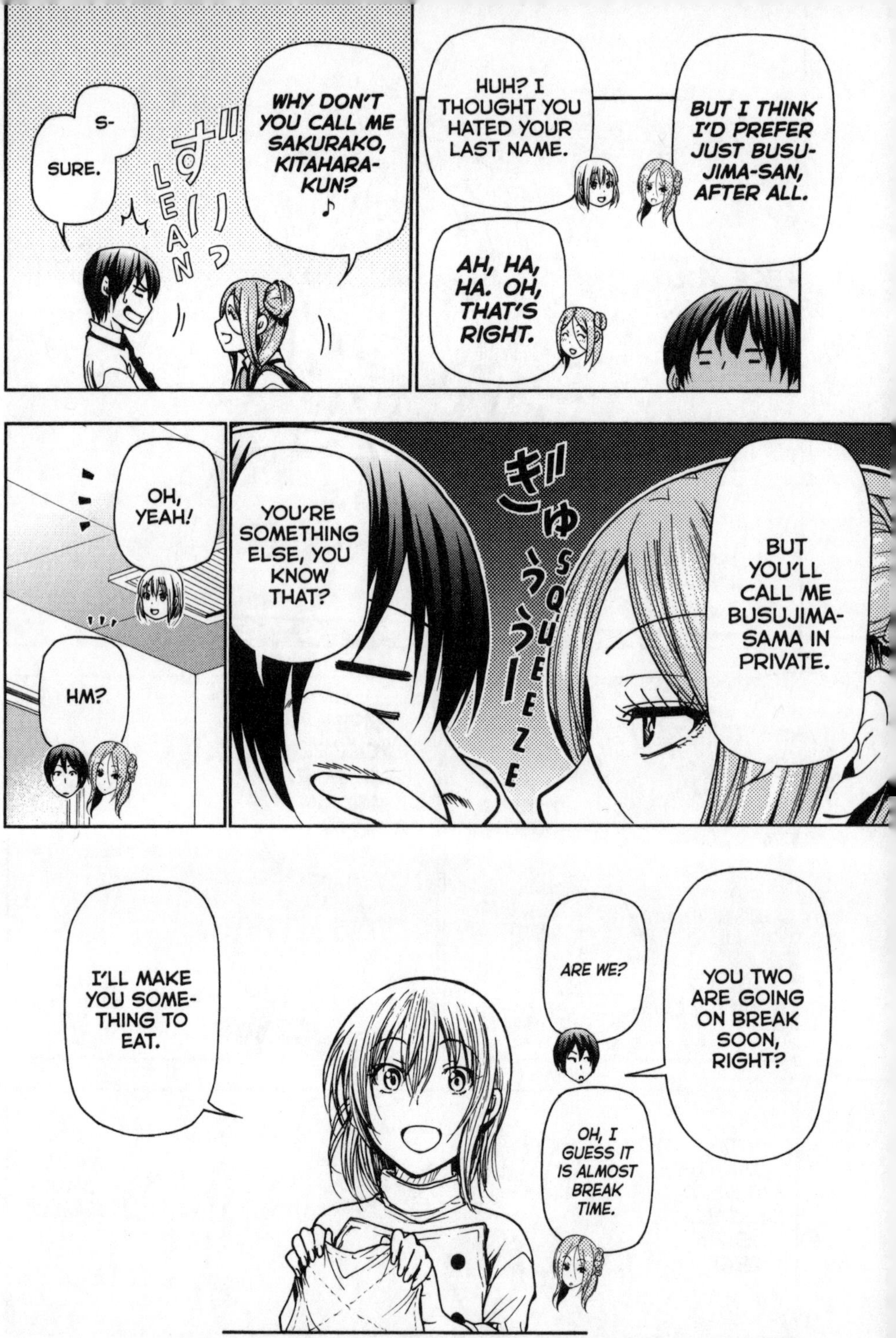
BUT I THINK I'D PREFER JUST BUSUJIMA-SAN, AFTER ALL.
HUH? I THOUGHT YOU HATED YOUR LAST NAME.
AH, HA, HA. OH, THAT'S RIGHT.
WHY DON'T YOU CALL ME SAKURAKO, KITAHARA-KUN? ♪
LEAN
S- SURE.
BUT YOU'LL CALL ME BUSUJIMA-SAMA IN PRIVATE.
SQUEEZE
YOU'RE SOMETHING ELSE, YOU KNOW THAT?
OH, YEAH!
HM?
YOU TWO ARE GOING ON BREAK SOON, RIGHT?
ARE WE?
OH, I GUESS IT IS ALMOST BREAK TIME.
I'LL MAKE YOU SOMETHING TO EAT.

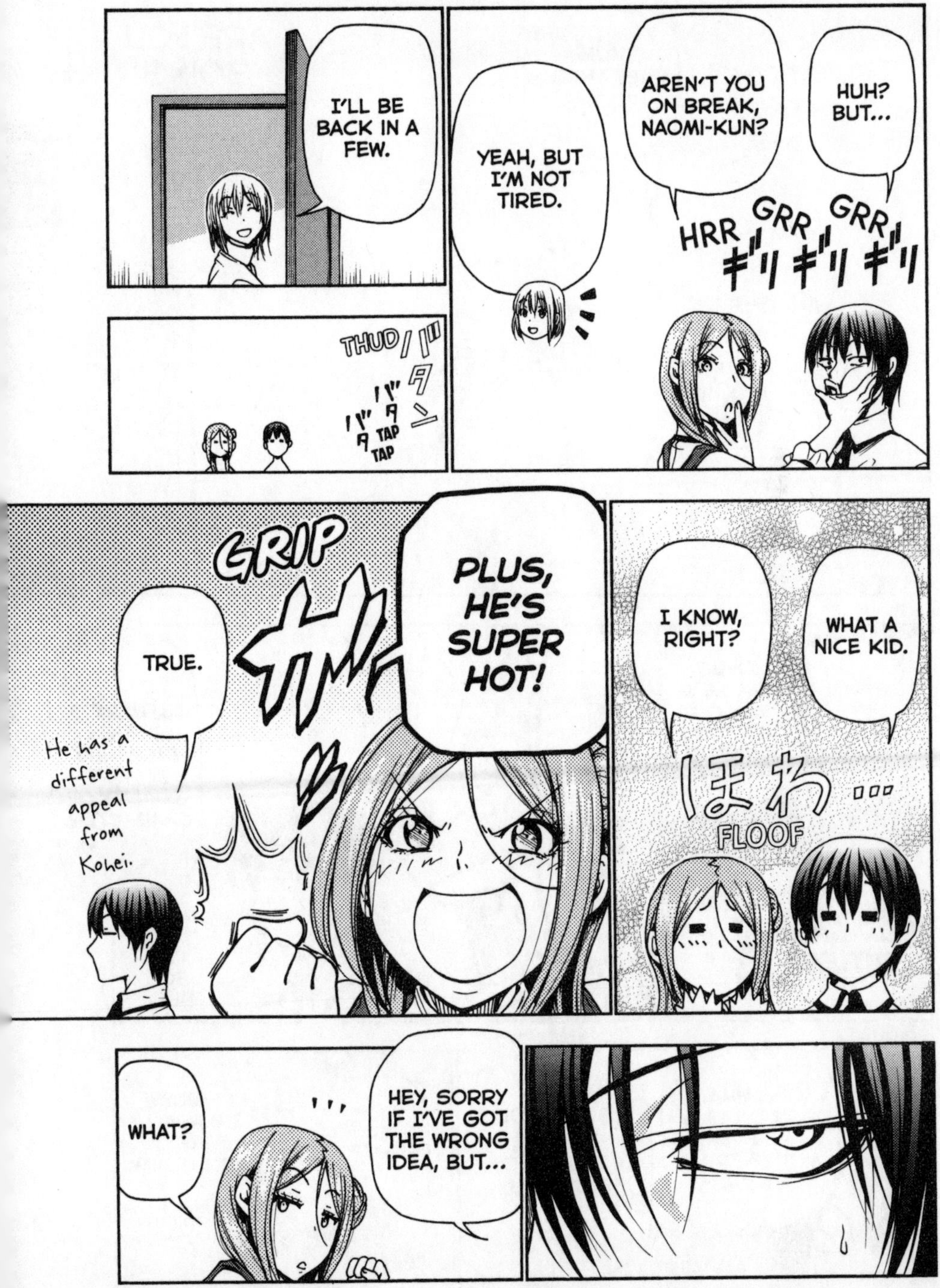
HUH? BUT...
AREN'T YOU ON BREAK, NAOMI-KUN?
HRR GRR GRR
ギリギリギリ
YEAH, BUT I'M NOT TIRED.
I'LL BE BACK IN A FEW.
THUD
バタン
バタバタ
TAP TAP
WHAT A NICE KID.
I KNOW, RIGHT?
ほわ...
FLOOF
PLUS, HE'S SUPER HOT!
GRIP
TRUE.
He has a different appeal from Kohei.
HEY, SORRY IF I'VE GOT THE WRONG IDEA, BUT...
WHAT?

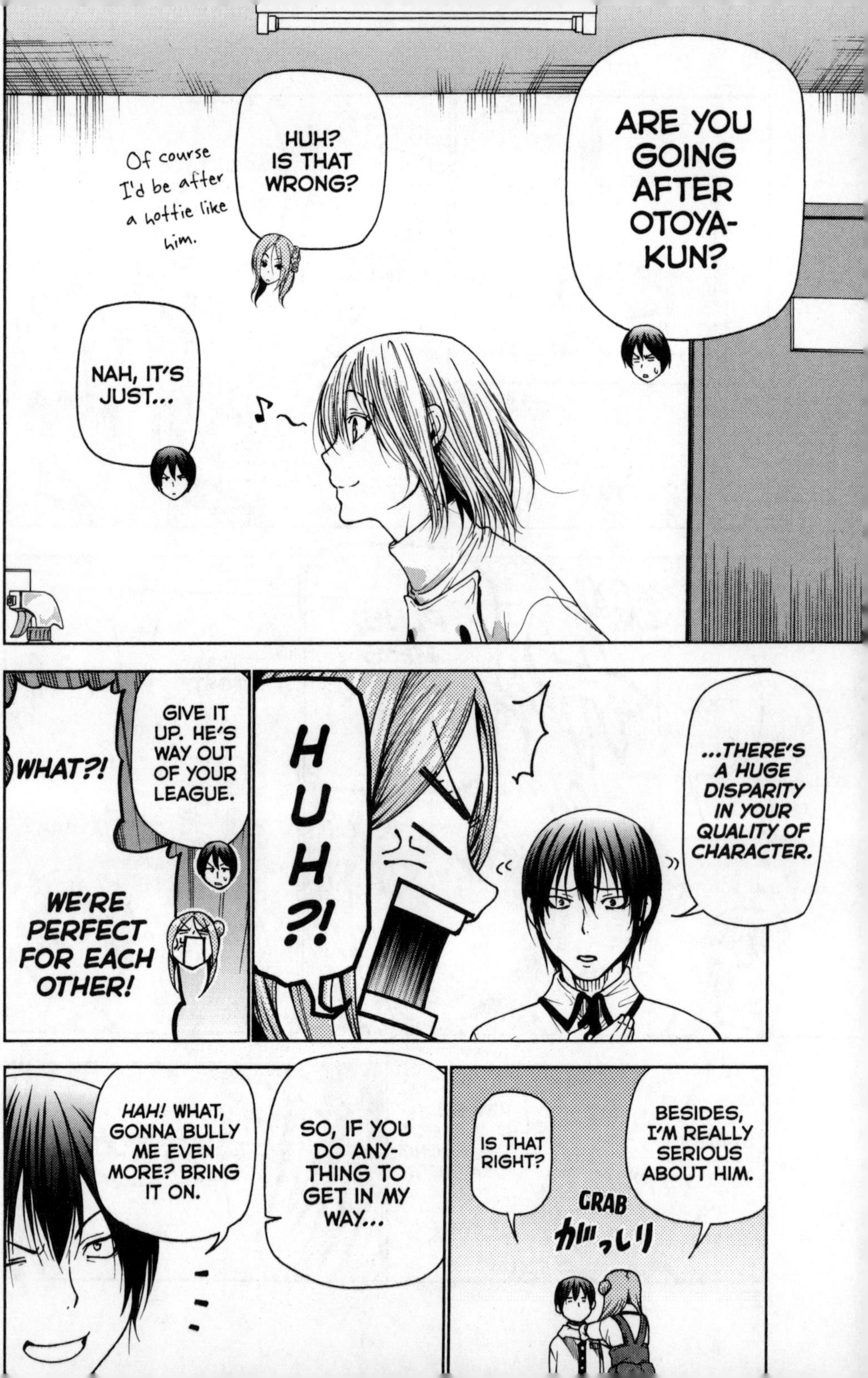
ARE YOU GOING AFTER OTOYA-KUN?
HUH? IS THAT WRONG?
Of course I'd be after a hottie like him.
NAH, IT'S JUST...
...THERE'S A HUGE DISPARITY IN YOUR QUALITY OF CHARACTER.
HUH?!
GIVE IT UP. HE'S WAY OUT OF YOUR LEAGUE.
WHAT?!
WE'RE PERFECT FOR EACH OTHER!
BESIDES, I'M REALLY SERIOUS ABOUT HIM.
IS THAT RIGHT?
GRAB
ガッしり
SO, IF YOU DO ANYTHING TO GET IN MY WAY...
HAH! WHAT, GONNA BULLY ME EVEN MORE? BRING IT ON.
...

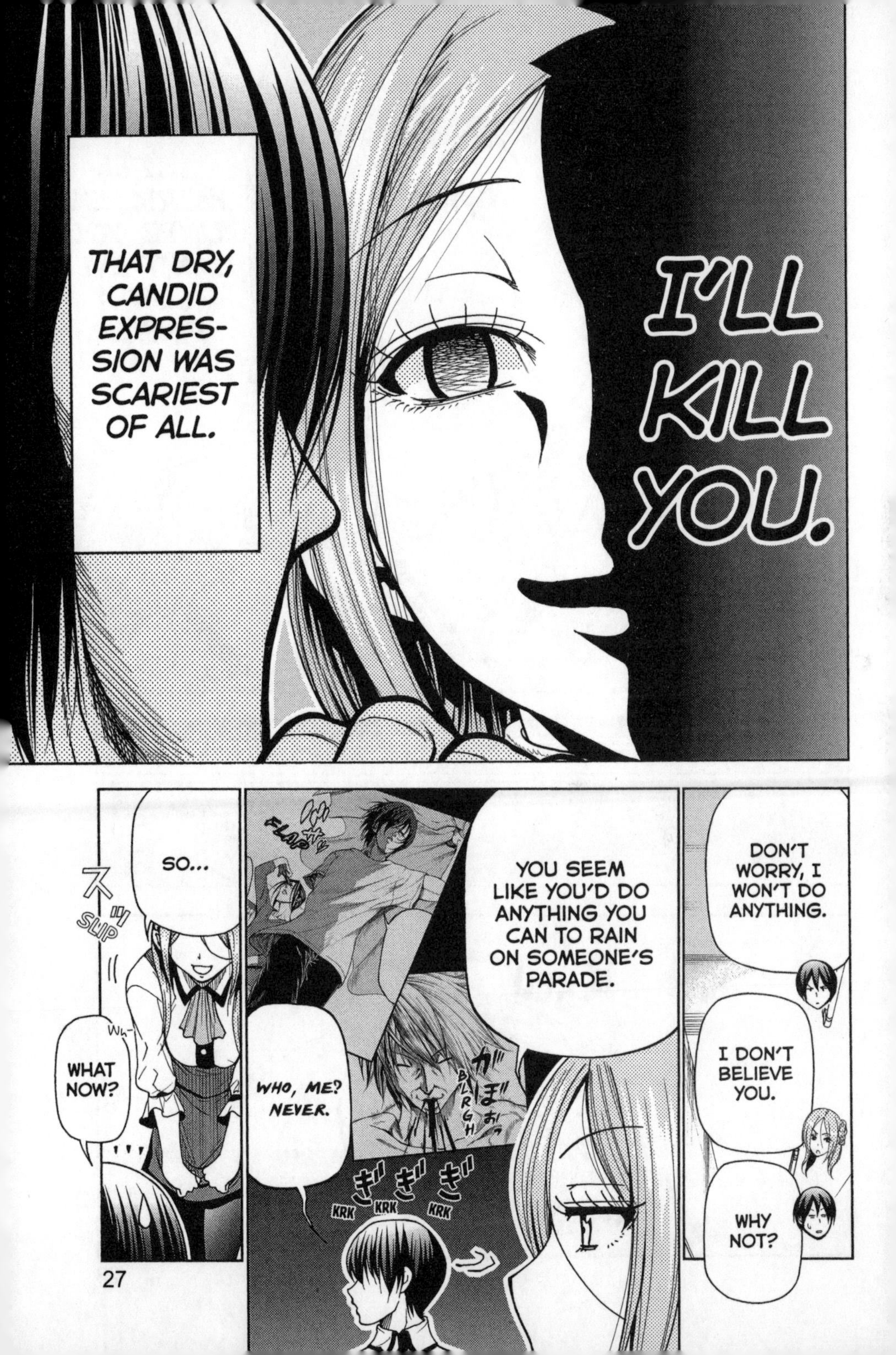
I'LL KILL YOU.
THAT DRY, CANDID EXPRESSION WAS SCARIEST OF ALL.
DON'T WORRY, I WON'T DO ANYTHING.
I DON'T BELIEVE YOU.
WHY NOT?
FLAP
YOU SEEM LIKE YOU'D DO ANYTHING YOU CAN TO RAIN ON SOMEONE'S PARADE.
BLRGH
WHO, ME? NEVER.
KRK KRK KRK
SO...
SLIP
WHAT NOW?

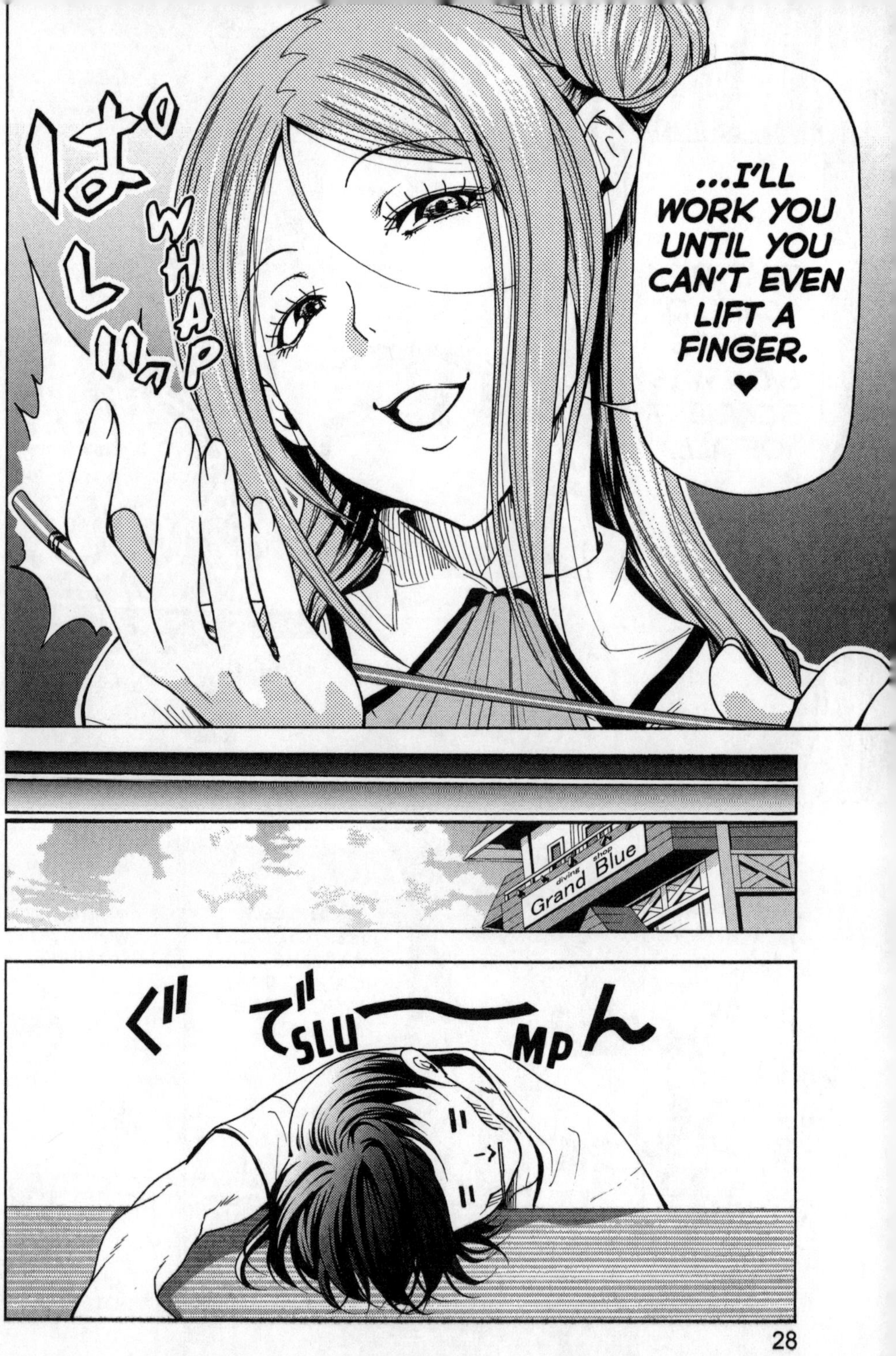
...I'LL WORK YOU UNTIL YOU CAN'T EVEN LIFT A FINGER. ♥
ぱしぃっ
WHAP
diving shop
Grand Blue
ぐでーん
SLUMP

IS WORK ROUGH?
YEAH... IN SO MANY WAYS...
IT'S TIRING AND EMBAR-RASSING...
HUH?
EMBAR-RASS-ING?
OH, I'D BETTER GET GOING.
15:07
SEE YA LATER.
OKAY. TAKE CARE.
SWAY フラ
SWAY フラ
THUD

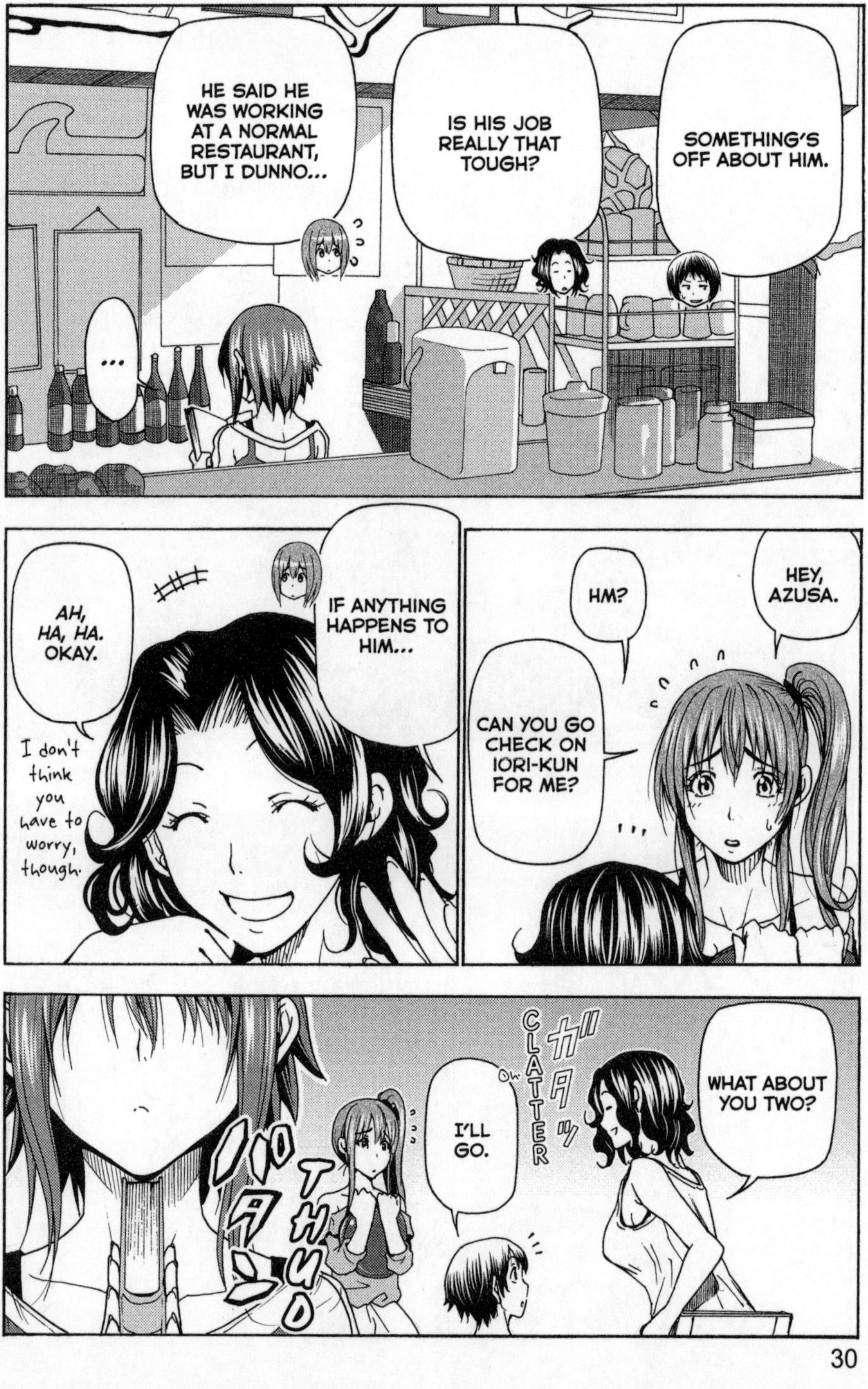
SOMETHING'S OFF ABOUT HIM.
IS HIS JOB REALLY THAT TOUGH?
HE SAID HE WAS WORKING AT A NORMAL RESTAURANT, BUT I DUNNO...
...
HEY, AZUSA.
HM?
CAN YOU GO CHECK ON IORI-KUN FOR ME?
IF ANYTHING HAPPENS TO HIM...
AH, HA, HA. OKAY.
I don't think you have to worry, though.
WHAT ABOUT YOU TWO?
ガタッ
CLATTER
Oh.
I'LL GO.
バタン
THUD

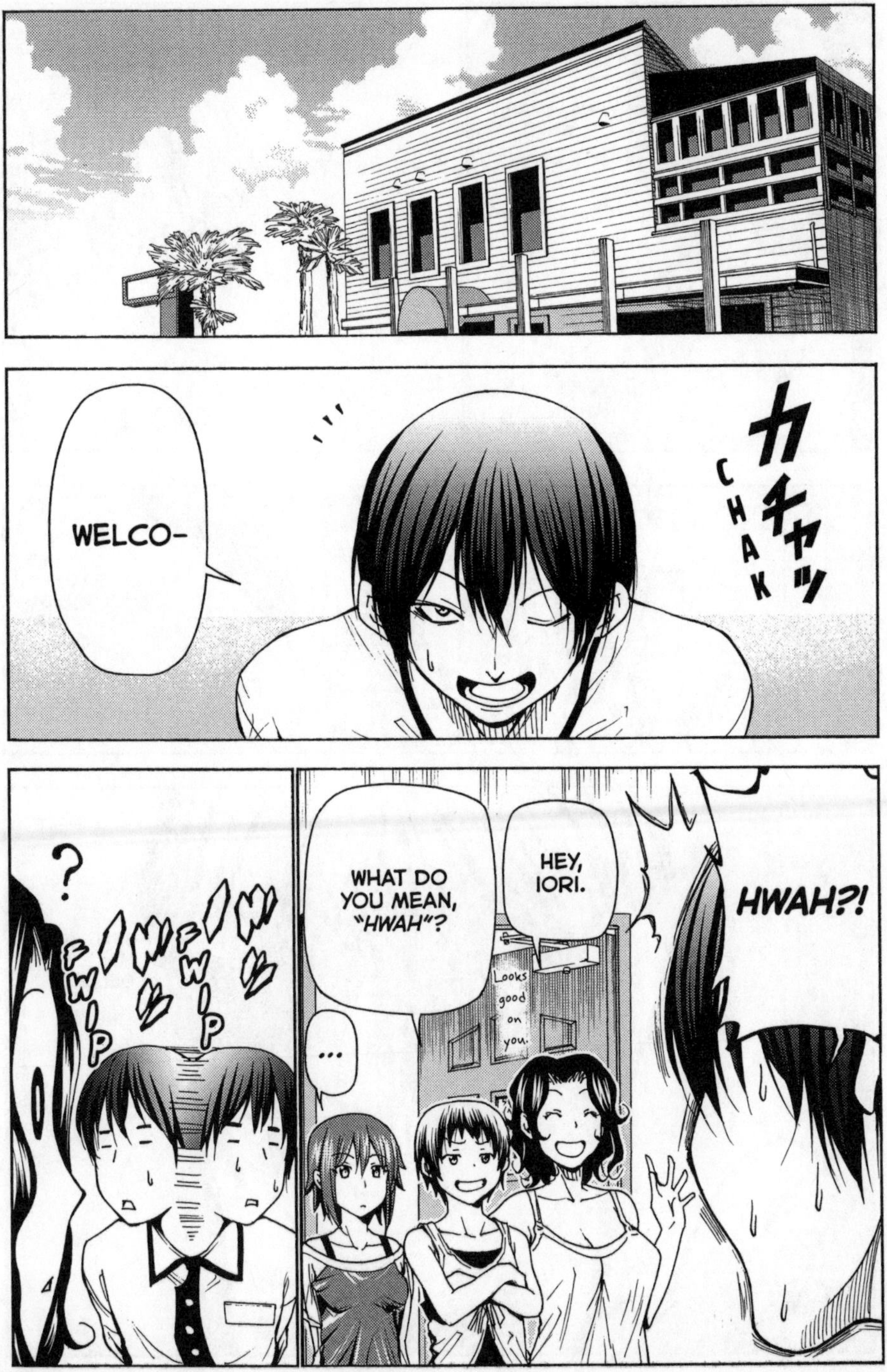

カチャッ
CHAK
WELCO-
HWAH?!
HEY, IORI.
WHAT DO YOU MEAN, "HWAH"?
Looks good on you.
...
?
FWIP
FWIP

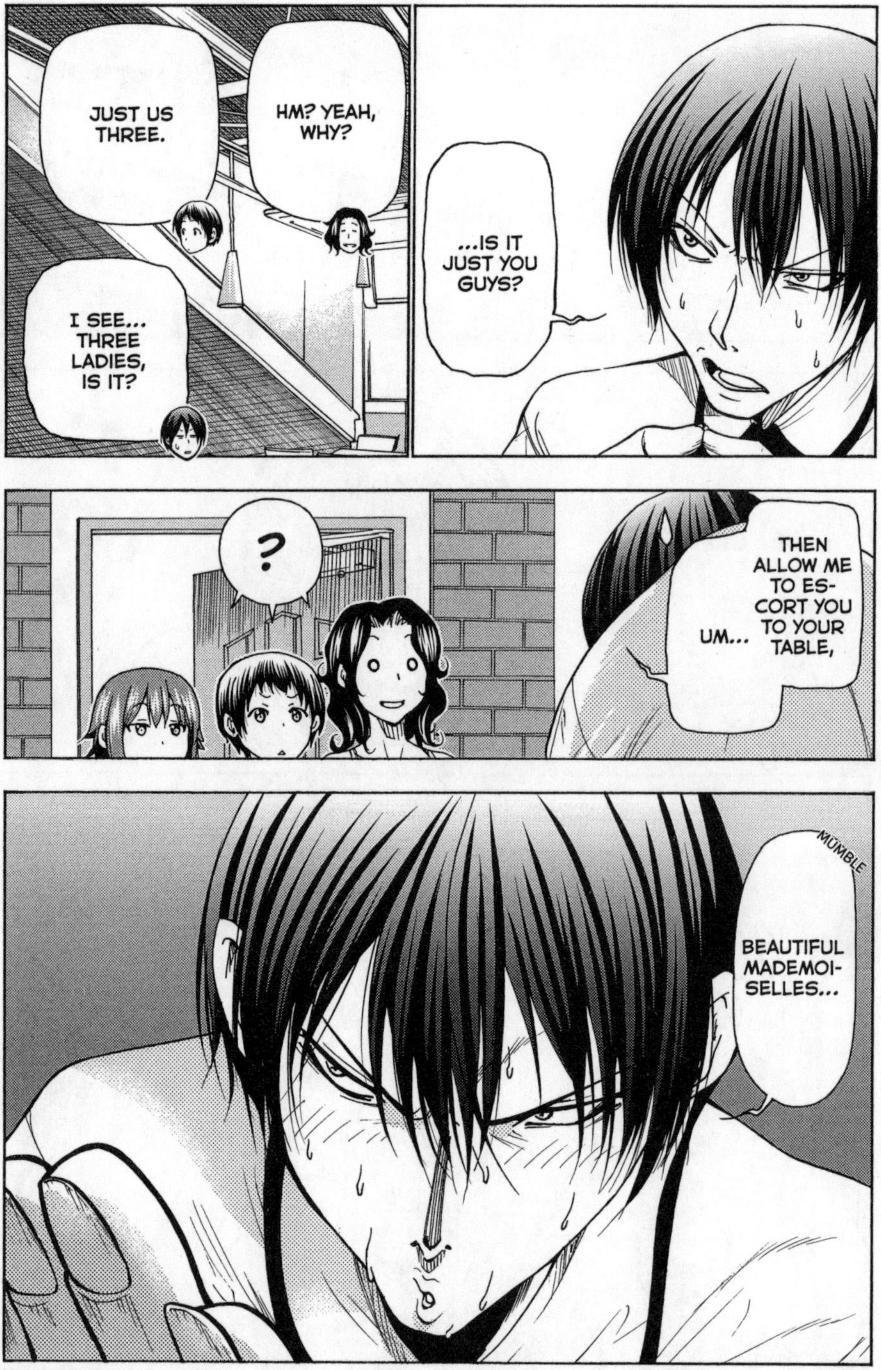
...IS IT JUST YOU GUYS?
HM? YEAH, WHY?
JUST US THREE.
I SEE... THREE LADIES, IS IT?
THEN ALLOW ME TO ES-CORT YOU TO YOUR TABLE,
UM...
?
MUMBLE
BEAUTIFUL MADEMOI-SELLES...

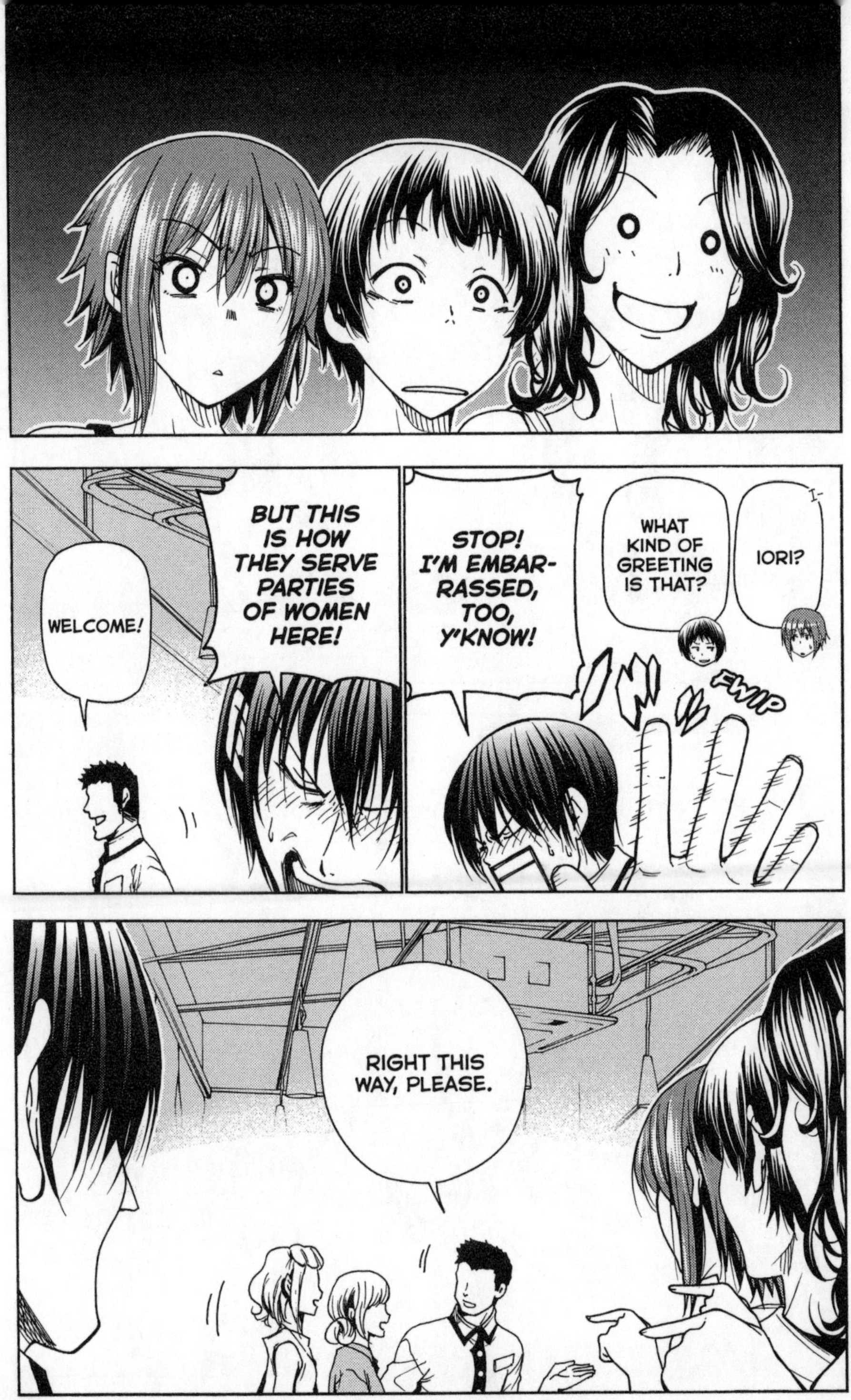
I-
IORI?
WHAT KIND OF GREETING IS THAT?
STOP! I'M EMBARRASSED, TOO, Y'KNOW!
FWIP
BUT THIS IS HOW THEY SERVE PARTIES OF WOMEN HERE!
WELCOME!
RIGHT THIS WAY, PLEASE.

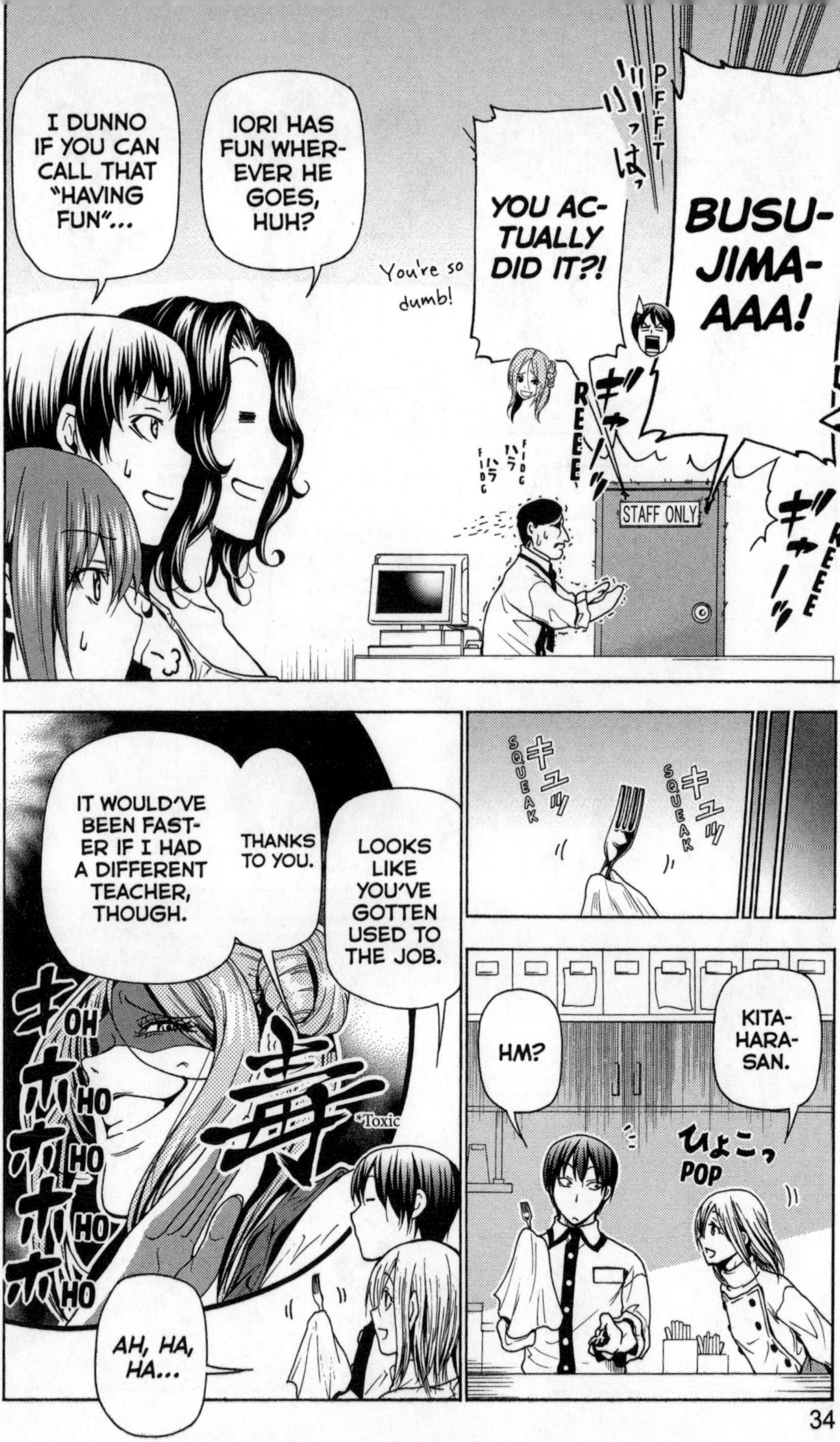
SLAM
ンダーン
BUSU-JIMA-AAA!
ギャーッ
REEE
ぶっは
PFFT
YOU ACTUALLY DID IT?!
ギャーッ
REEE
ハラ ハラ
FIDG FIDG
STAFF ONLY
You're so dumb!
IORI HAS FUN WHEREVER HE GOES, HUH?
I DUNNO IF YOU CAN CALL THAT "HAVING FUN"...
キュッ
SQUEAK
キュッ
SQUEAK
KITA-HARA-SAN.
ひょこっ
POP
HM?
LOOKS LIKE YOU'VE GOTTEN USED TO THE JOB.
THANKS TO YOU.
IT WOULD'VE BEEN FASTER IF I HAD A DIFFERENT TEACHER, THOUGH.
毒
*Toxic
OH HO HO HO HO
AH, HA, HA...

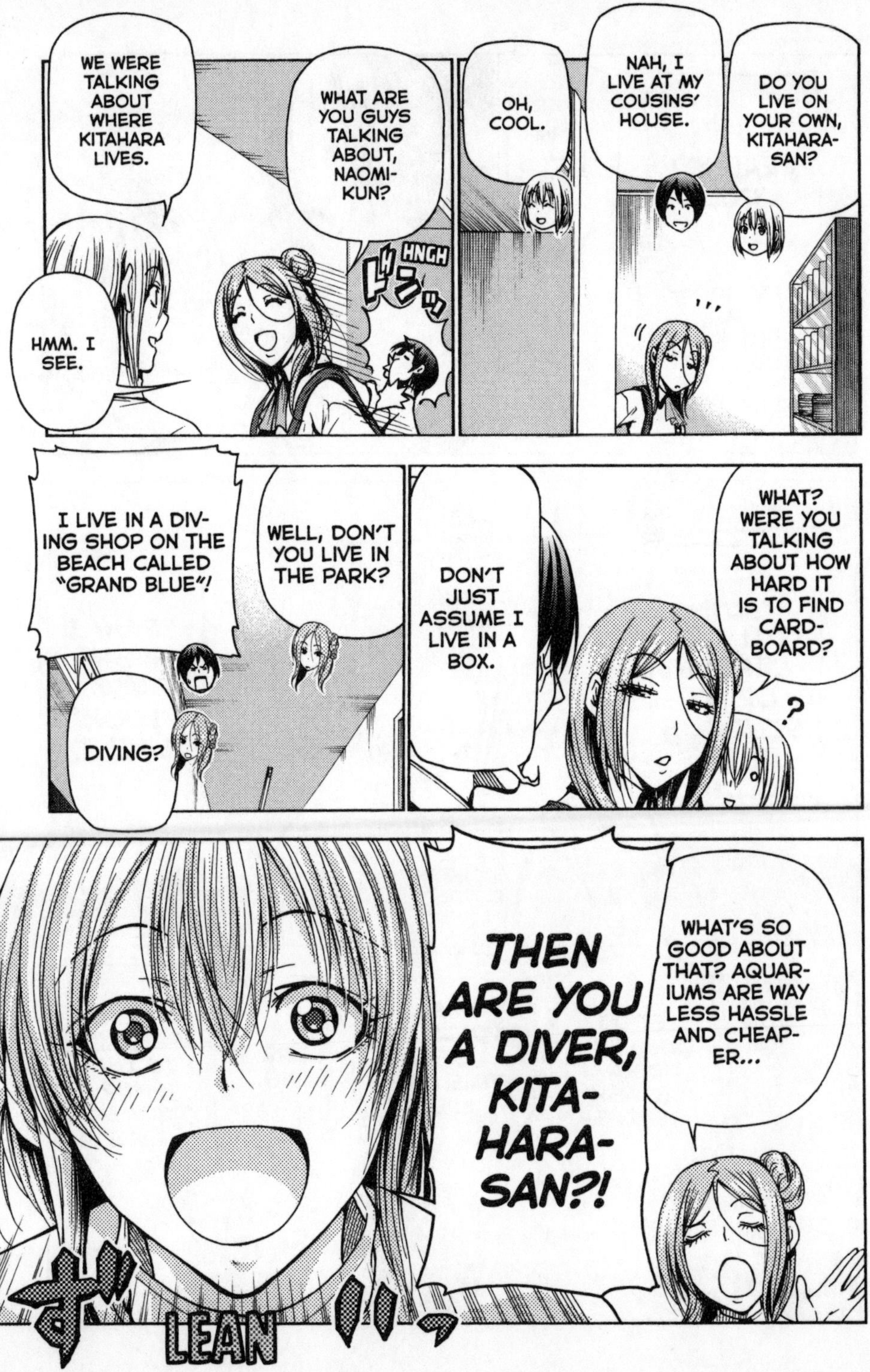
DO YOU LIVE ON YOUR OWN, KITAHARA-SAN?
NAH, I LIVE AT MY COUSINS' HOUSE.
OH, COOL.
WHAT ARE YOU GUYS TALKING ABOUT, NAOMI-KUN?
HNGH
WE WERE TALKING ABOUT WHERE KITAHARA LIVES.
HMM. I SEE.
WHAT? WERE YOU TALKING ABOUT HOW HARD IT IS TO FIND CARDBOARD?
DON'T JUST ASSUME I LIVE IN A BOX.
WELL, DON'T YOU LIVE IN THE PARK?
I LIVE IN A DIVING SHOP ON THE BEACH CALLED "GRAND BLUE"!
DIVING?
WHAT'S SO GOOD ABOUT THAT? AQUARIUMS ARE WAY LESS HASSLE AND CHEAPER...
THEN ARE YOU A DIVER, KITAHARA-SAN?!
LEAN

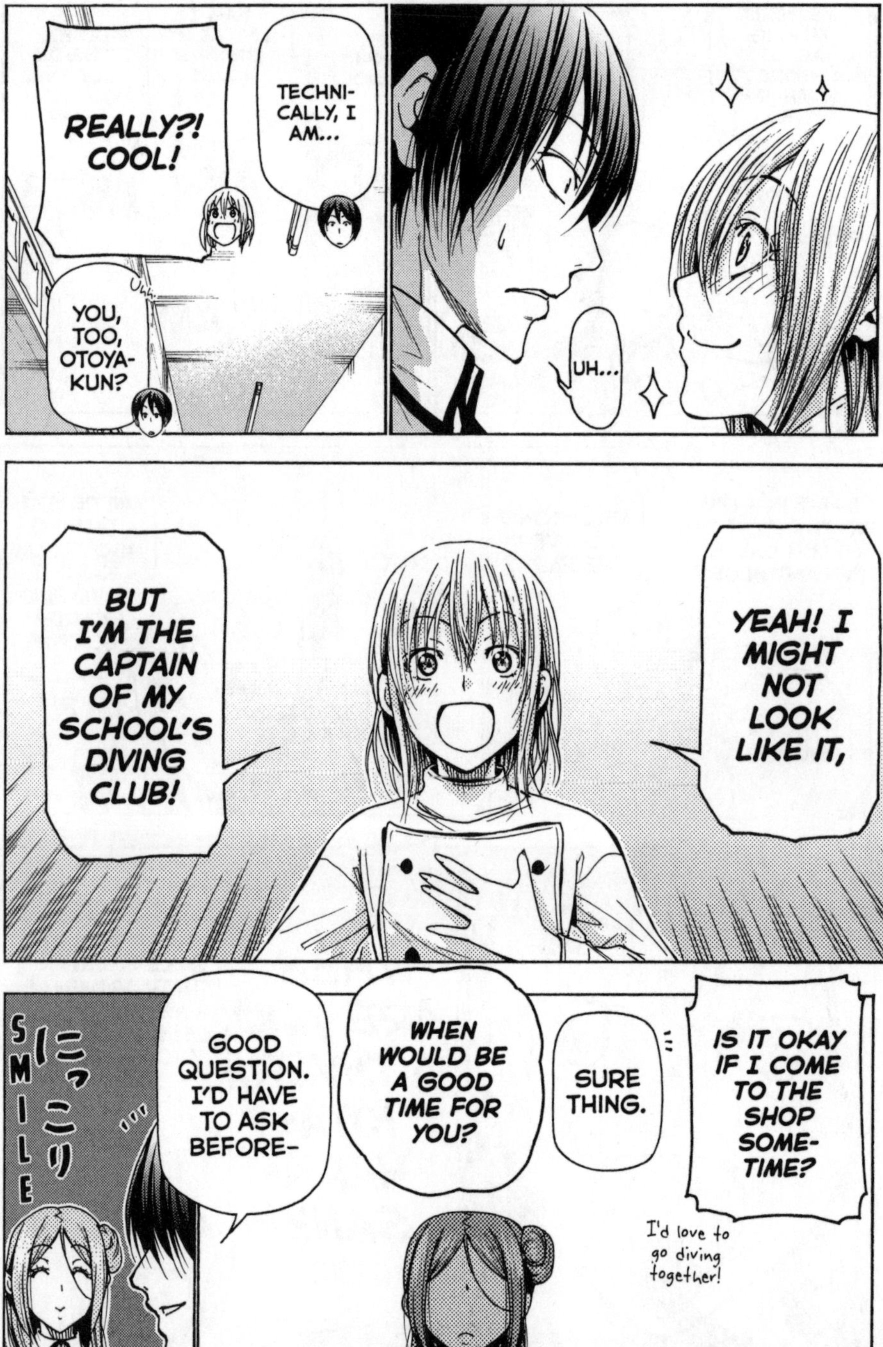
UH...
TECHNICALLY, I AM...
REALLY?! COOL!
Uhh.
YOU, TOO, OTOYA-KUN?
YEAH! I MIGHT NOT LOOK LIKE IT,
BUT I'M THE CAPTAIN OF MY SCHOOL'S DIVING CLUB!
IS IT OKAY IF I COME TO THE SHOP SOMETIME?
I'd love to go diving together!
SURE THING.
WHEN WOULD BE A GOOD TIME FOR YOU?
GOOD QUESTION. I'D HAVE TO ASK BEFORE-
にっこり
SMILE

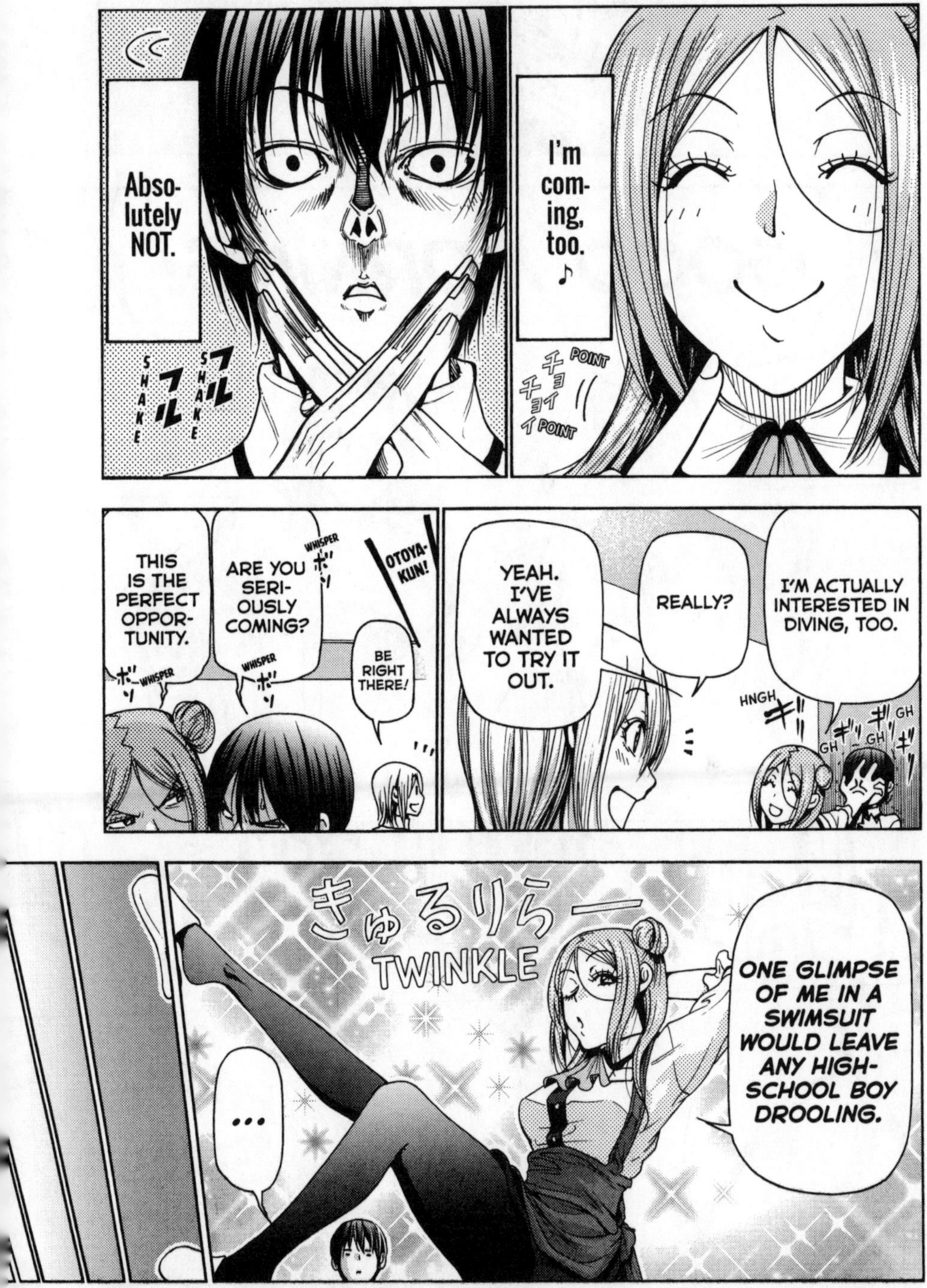
I'm com-ing, too. ♪
チョイ チョイ POINT POINT
Abso-lutely NOT.
フル フル SHAKE SHAKE
I'M ACTUALLY INTERESTED IN DIVING, TOO.
REALLY?
YEAH. I'VE ALWAYS WANTED TO TRY IT OUT.
HNGH ギリ GH GH GH
OTOYA-KUN!
BE RIGHT THERE!
ARE YOU SERI-OUSLY COMING?
ボソ WHISPER
THIS IS THE PERFECT OPPOR-TUNITY.
ボソ WHISPER
ONE GLIMPSE OF ME IN A SWIMSUIT WOULD LEAVE ANY HIGH-SCHOOL BOY DROOLING.
きゅるりらー
TWINKLE
...

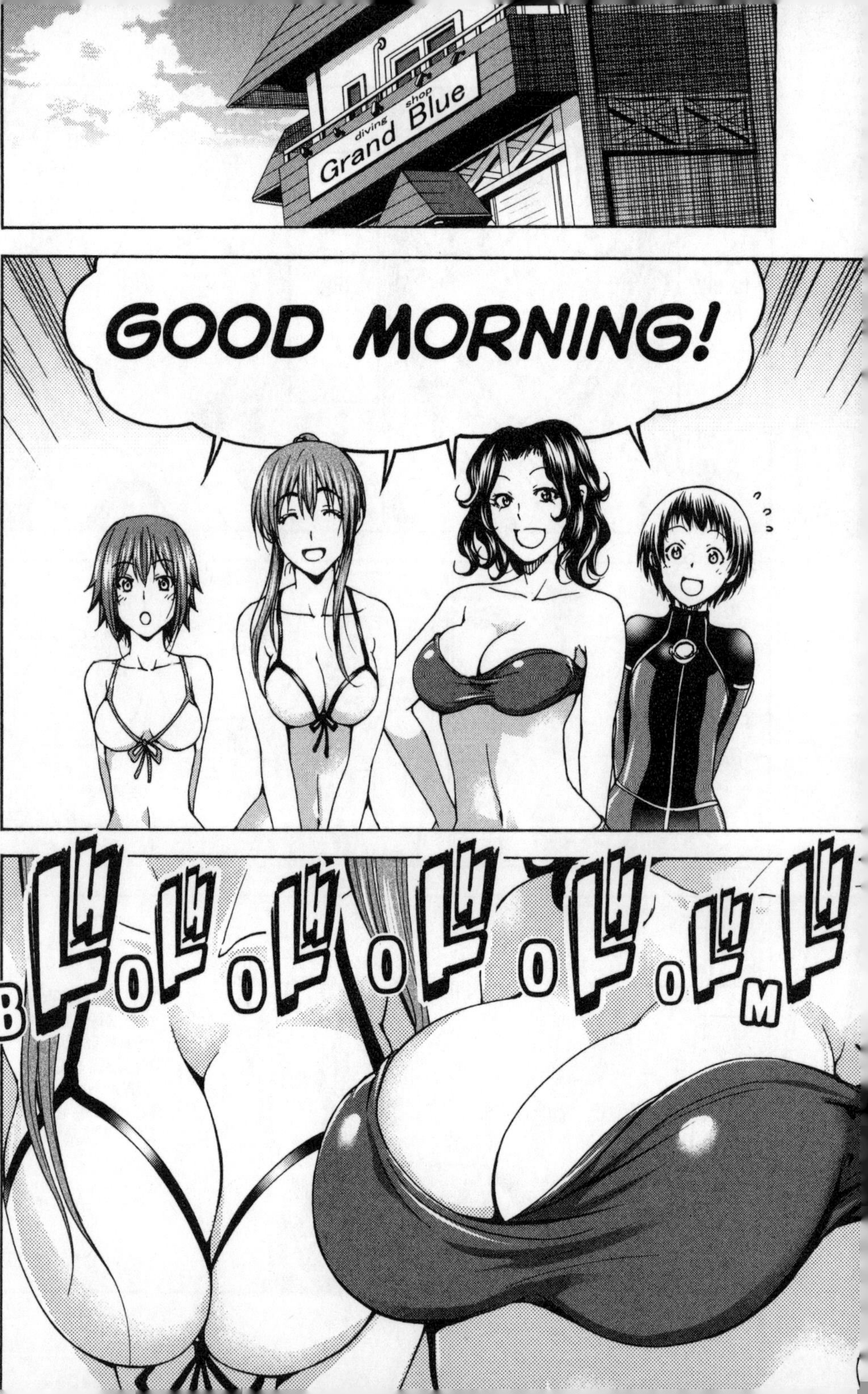
diving shop
Grand Blue
GOOD MORNING!

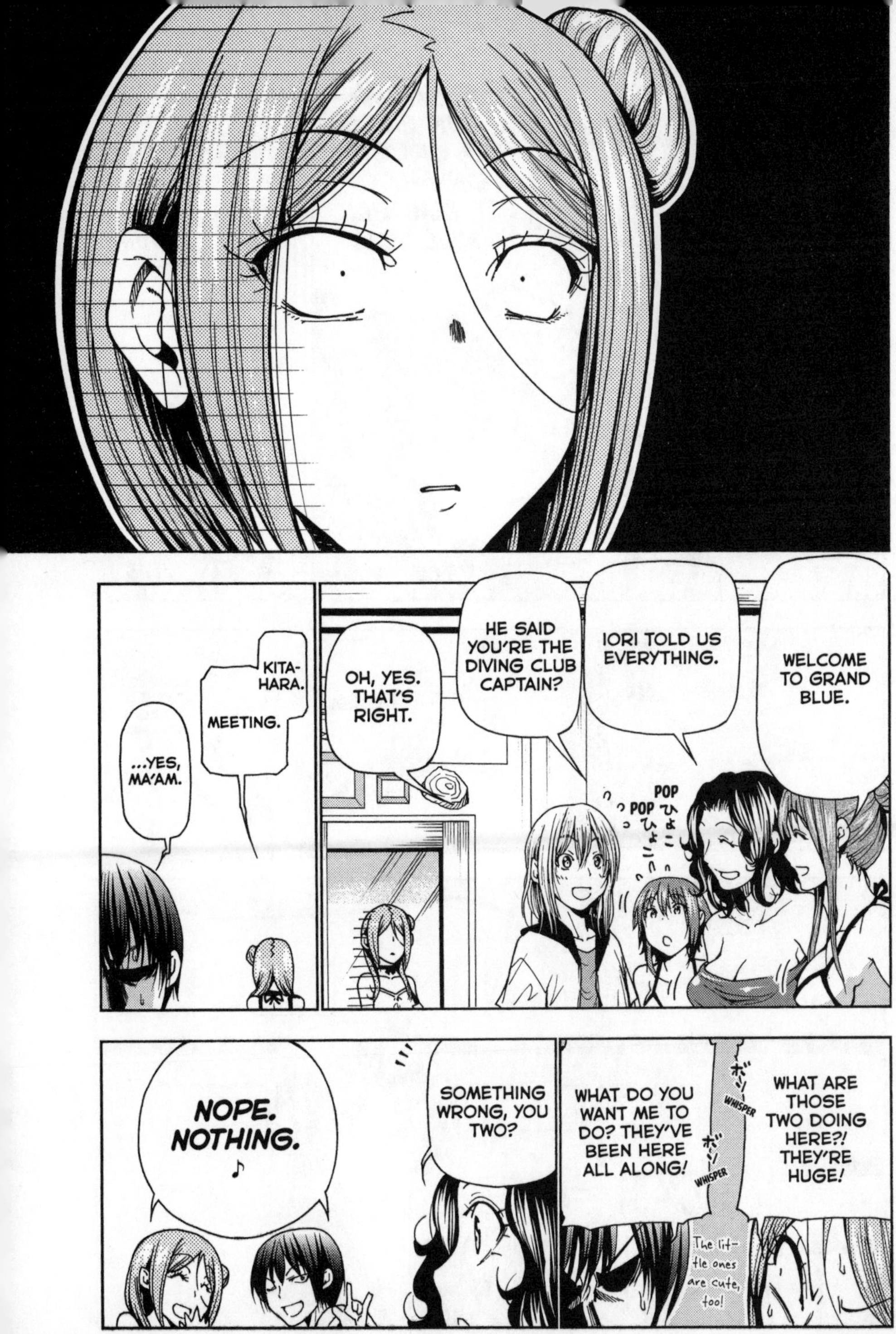
WELCOME TO GRAND BLUE.
IORI TOLD US EVERYTHING.
HE SAID YOU'RE THE DIVING CLUB CAPTAIN?
POP POP ひょこ ひょこ
OH, YES. THAT'S RIGHT.
KITA-HARA.
MEETING.
...YES, MA'AM.
WHAT ARE THOSE TWO DOING HERE?! THEY'RE HUGE!
ボソ WHISPER
WHAT DO YOU WANT ME TO DO? THEY'VE BEEN HERE ALL ALONG!
ボソ WHISPER
The lit-tle ones are cute, too!
SOMETHING WRONG, YOU TWO?
NOPE. NOTHING. ♪

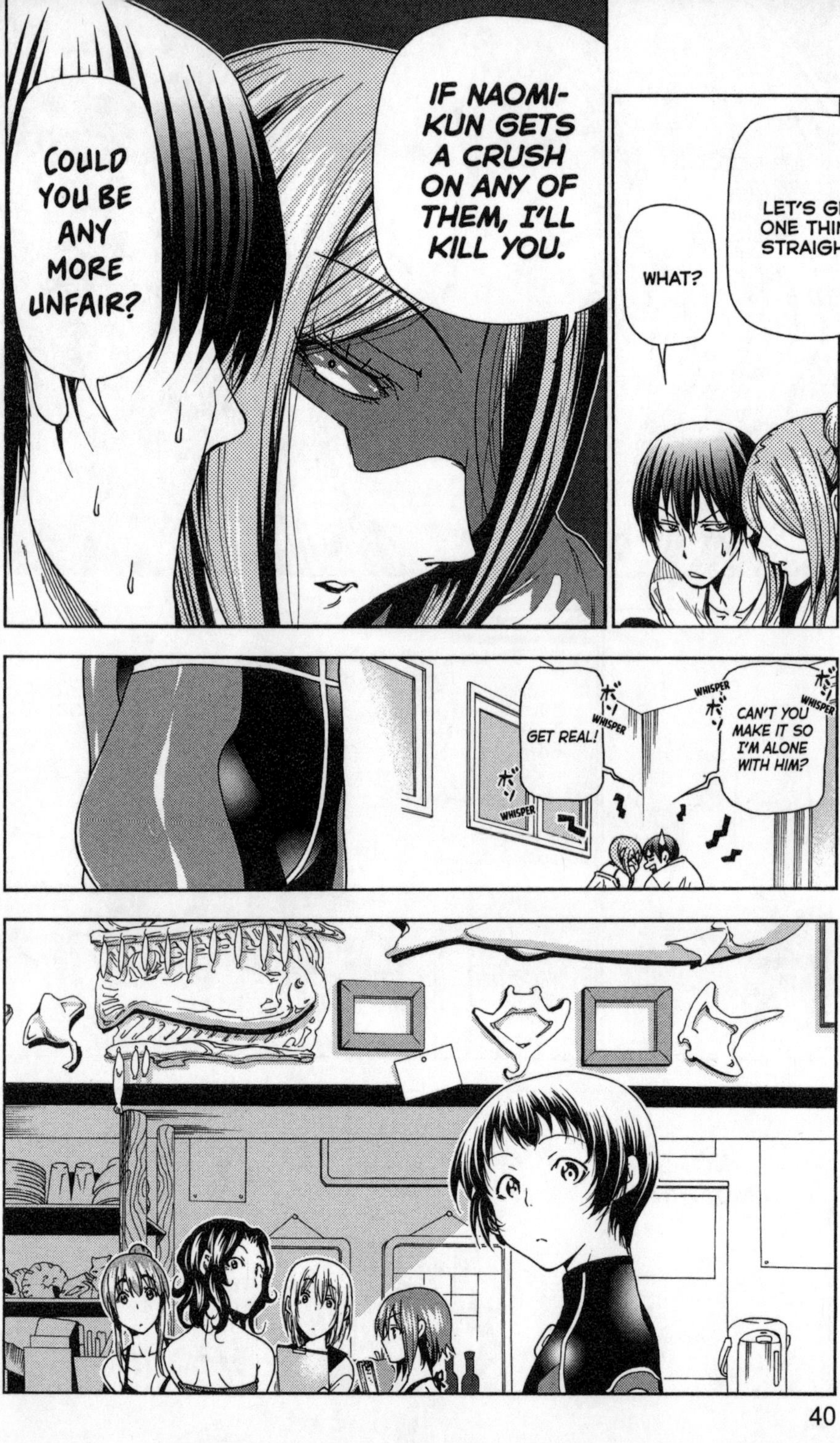
LET'S GET ONE THING STRAIGHT.
WHAT?
IF NAOMI-KUN GETS A CRUSH ON ANY OF THEM, I'LL KILL YOU.
COULD YOU BE ANY MORE UNFAIR?
WHISPER
WHISPER
CAN'T YOU MAKE IT SO I'M ALONE WITH HIM?
WHISPER
GET REAL!
WHISPER

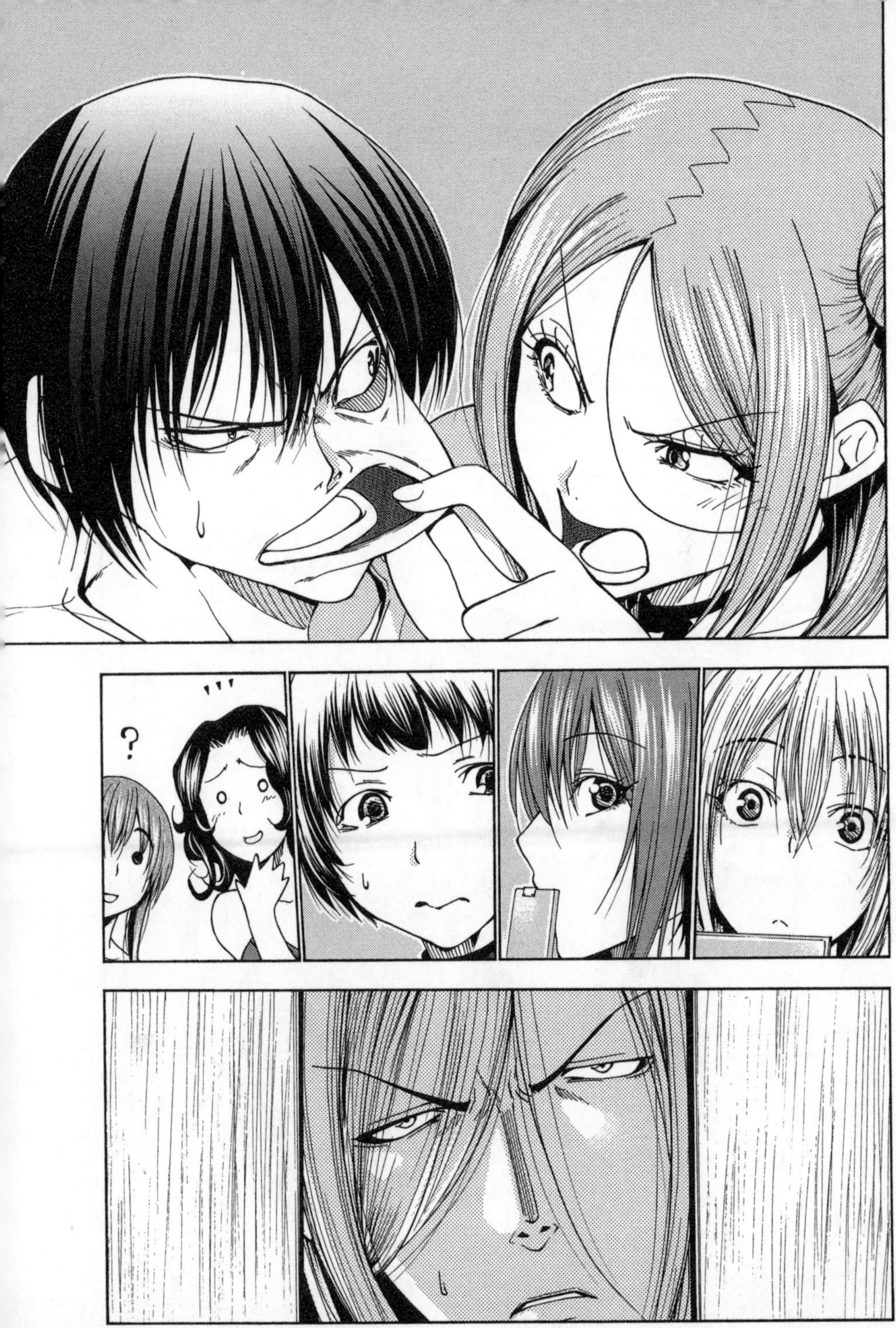
?

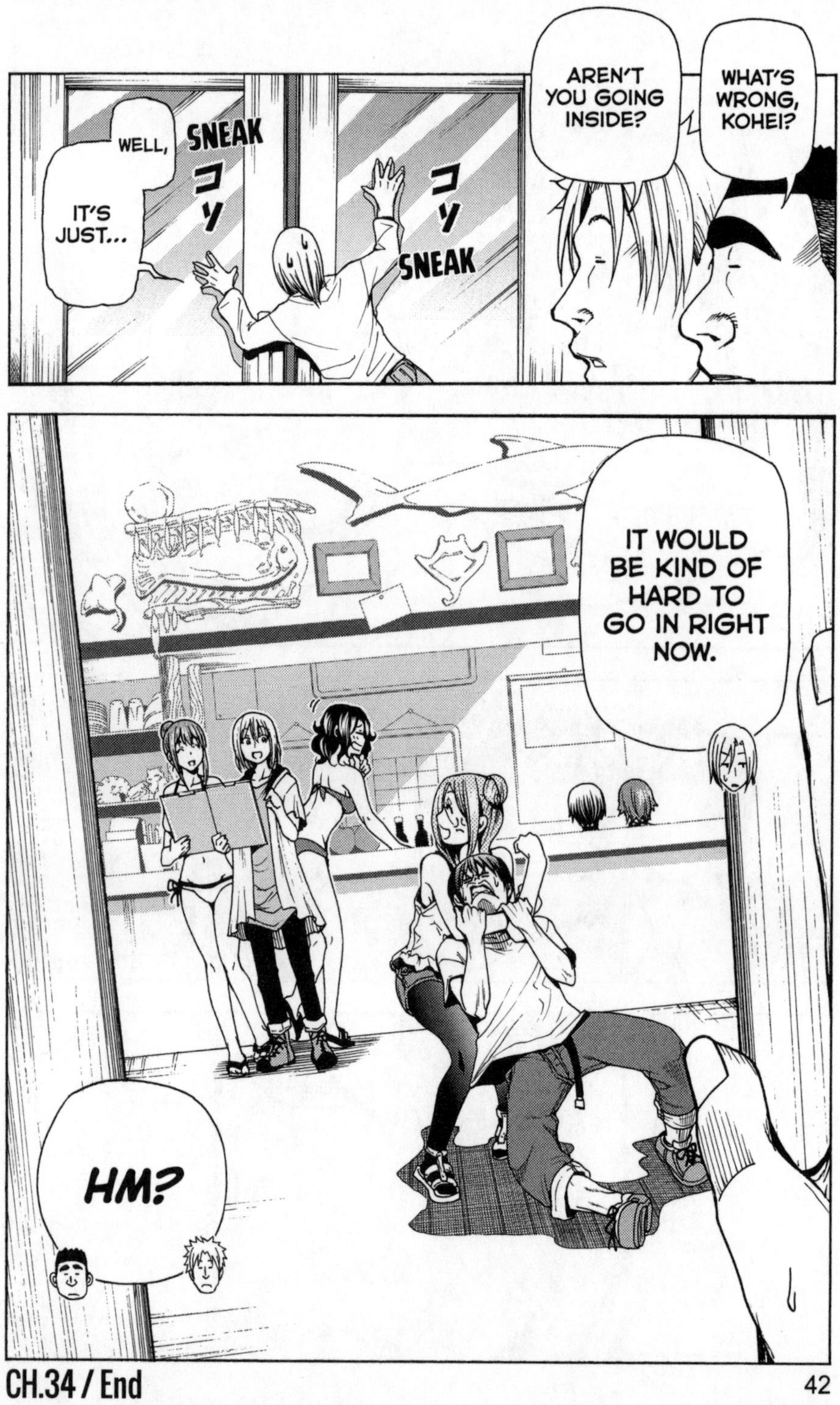
WHAT'S WRONG, KOHEI?
AREN'T YOU GOING INSIDE?
コソ
SNEAK
コソ
SNEAK
WELL,
IT'S JUST...
IT WOULD BE KIND OF HARD TO GO IN RIGHT NOW.
HM?

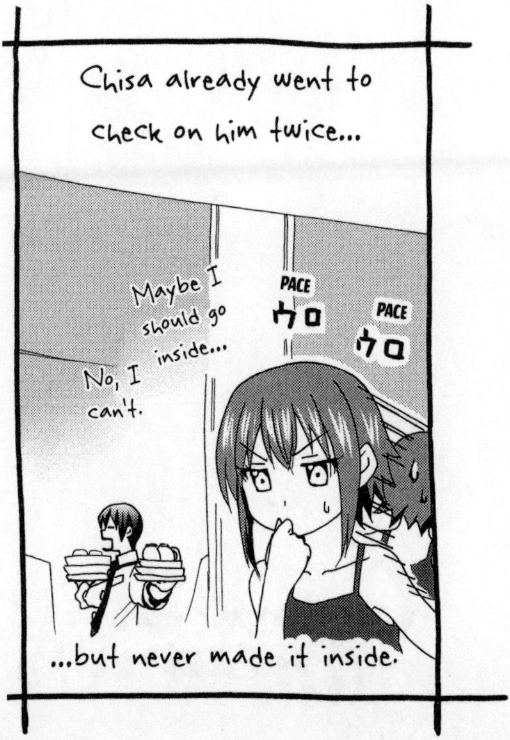
Chisa already went to check on him twice...
PACE ウロ
PACE ウロ
Maybe I should go inside...
No, I can't.
...but never made it inside.

Grand Blue Dreaming

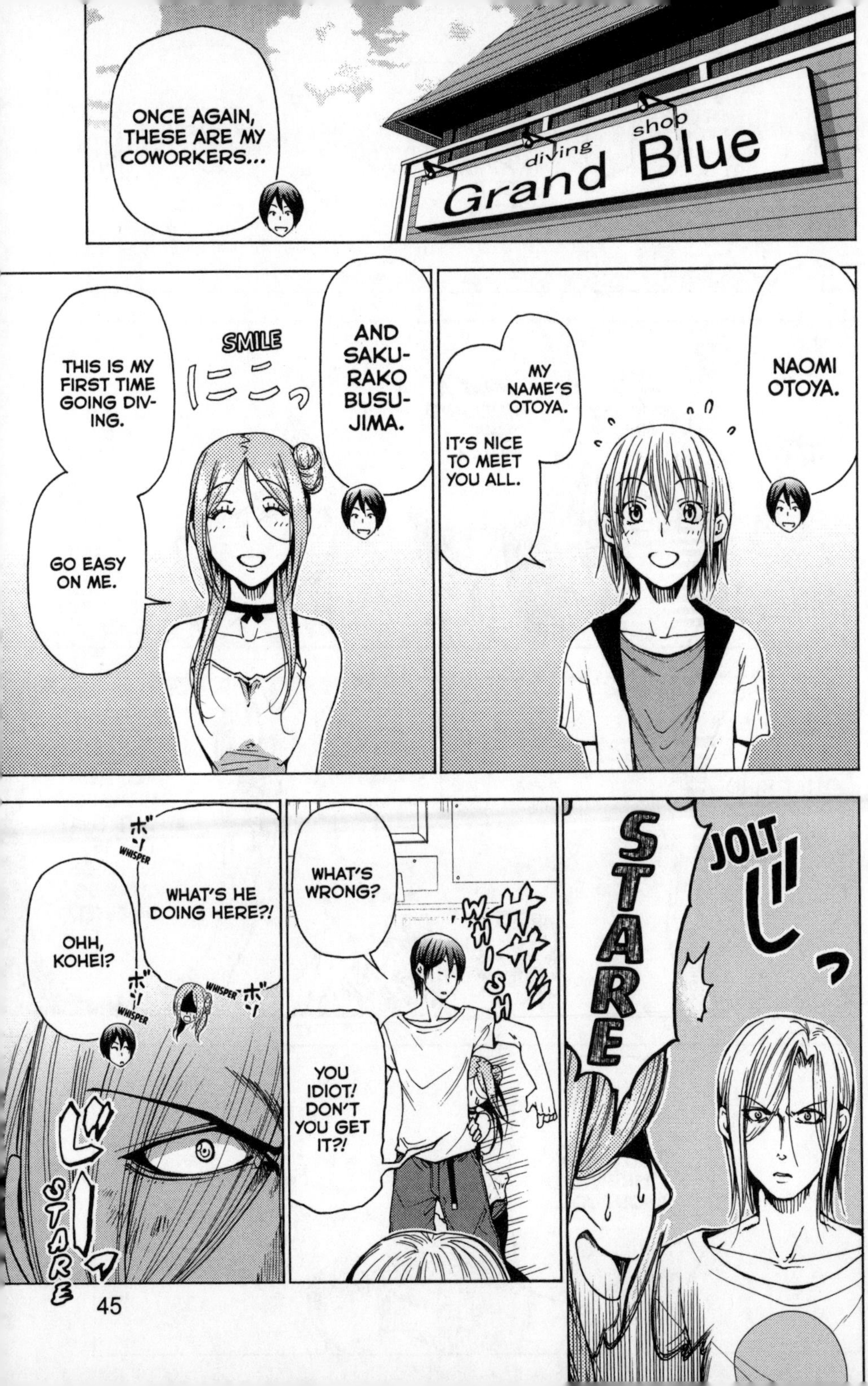
ONCE AGAIN, THESE ARE MY COWORKERS...
diving shop
Grand Blue
NAOMI OTOYA.
MY NAME'S OTOYA.
IT'S NICE TO MEET YOU ALL.
AND SAKU-RAKO BUSU-JIMA.
SMILE
THIS IS MY FIRST TIME GOING DIV-ING.
GO EASY ON ME.
JOLT
STARE
WHAT'S WRONG?
WHISH
YOU IDIOT! DON'T YOU GET IT?!
WHAT'S HE DOING HERE?!
WHISPER
OHH, KOHEI?
WHISPER
WHISPER
STARE

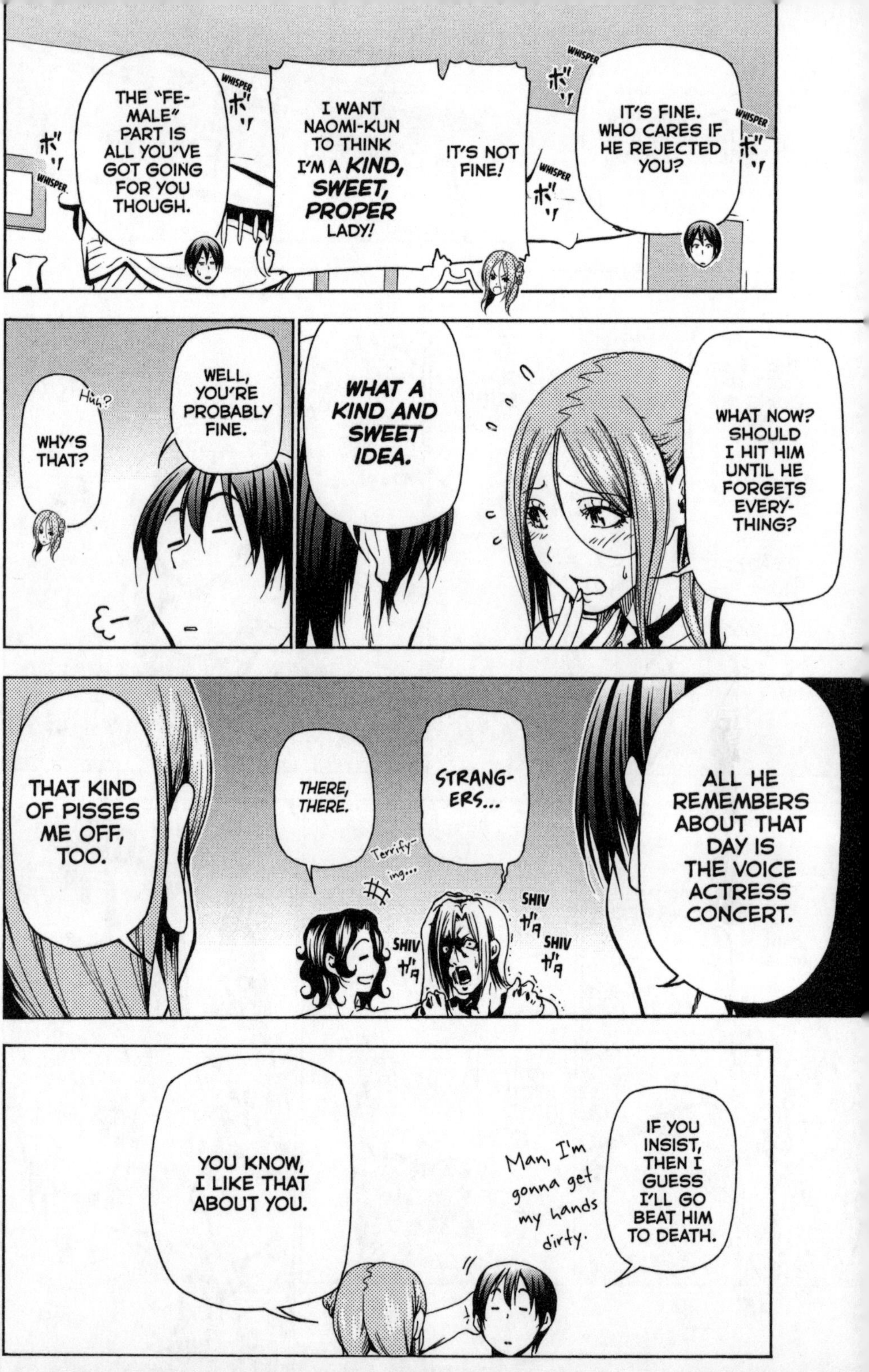
WHISPER
ボソ
IT'S FINE. WHO CARES IF HE REJECTED YOU?
WHISPER
ボソ
WHISPER
ボソ
IT'S NOT FINE!
I WANT NAOMI-KUN TO THINK I'M A KIND, SWEET, PROPER LADY!
WHISPER
ボソ
THE "FE-MALE" PART IS ALL YOU'VE GOT GOING FOR YOU THOUGH.
WHISPER
ボソ
WHAT NOW? SHOULD I HIT HIM UNTIL HE FORGETS EVERY-THING?
WHAT A KIND AND SWEET IDEA.
WELL, YOU'RE PROBABLY FINE.
Huh?
WHY'S THAT?
ALL HE REMEMBERS ABOUT THAT DAY IS THE VOICE ACTRESS CONCERT.
STRANG-ERS...
SHIV
ガタ
SHIV
ガタ
THERE, THERE.
Terrify-ing...
SHIV
ガタ
THAT KIND OF PISSES ME OFF, TOO.
IF YOU INSIST, THEN I GUESS I'LL GO BEAT HIM TO DEATH.
Man, I'm gonna get my hands dirty.
YOU KNOW, I LIKE THAT ABOUT YOU.

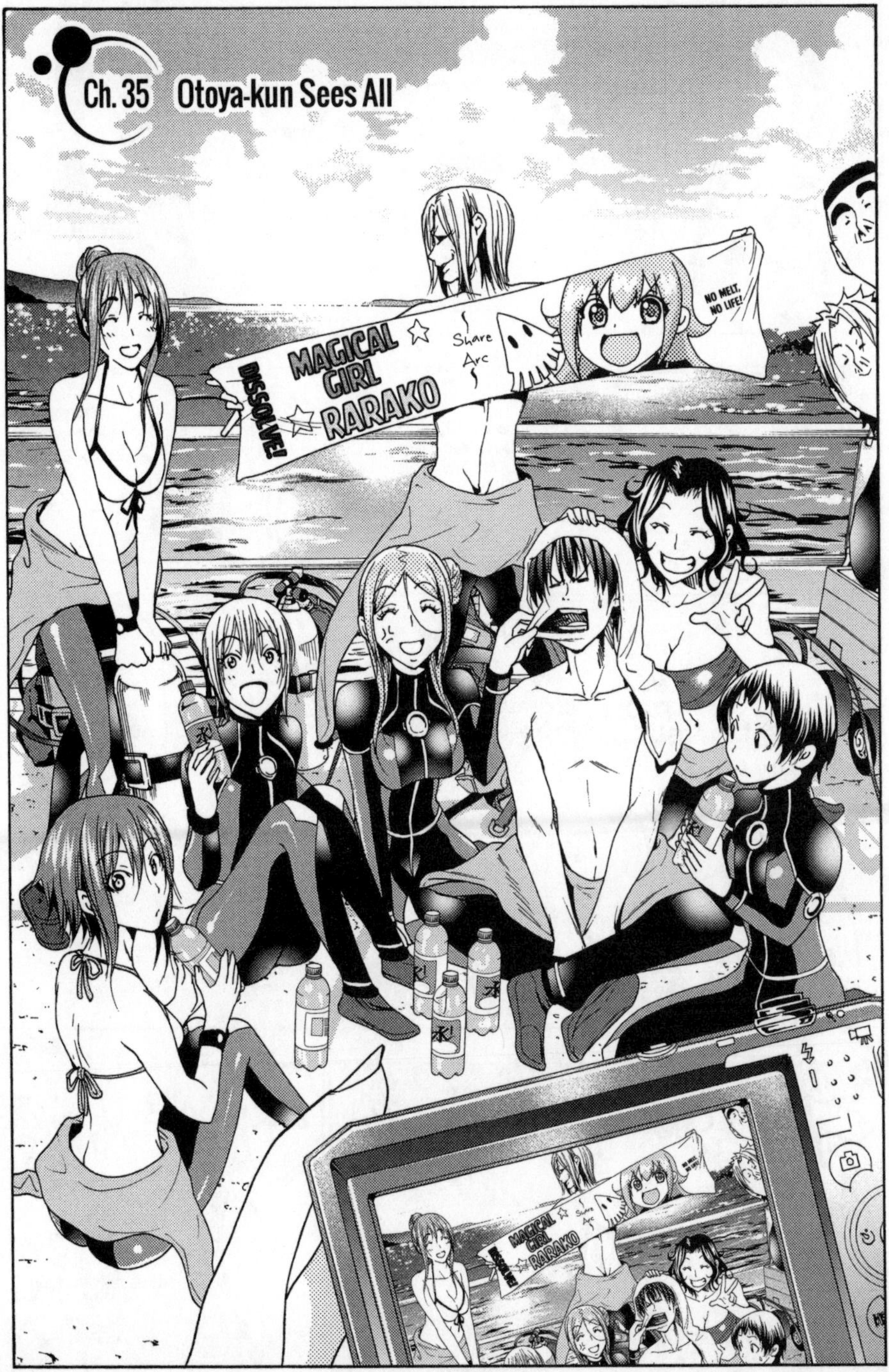
Ch. 35 Otoya-kun Sees All
MAGICAL GIRL RARAKO
DISSOLVE!
Share Arc
NO MELT, NO LIFE!

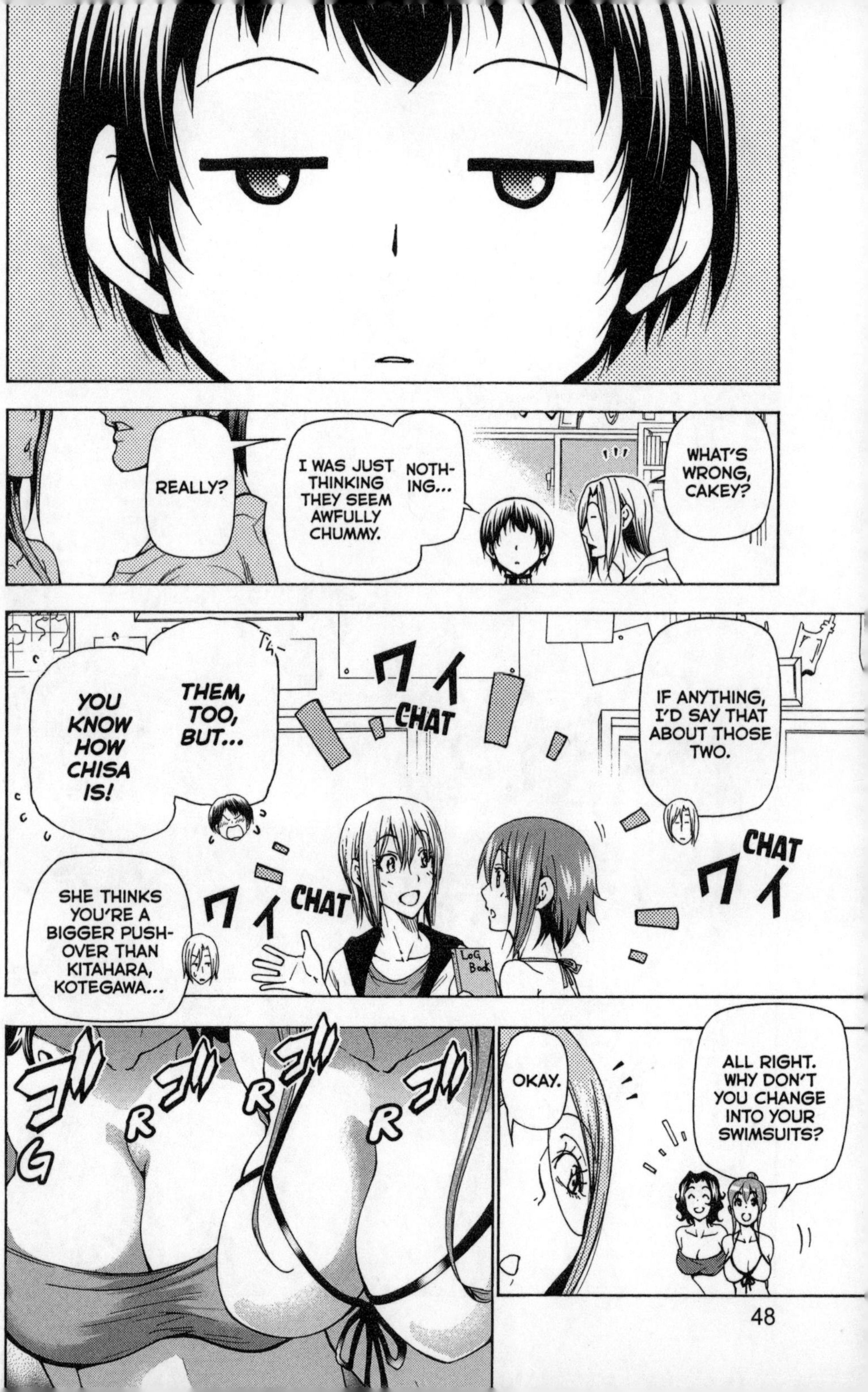
WHAT'S WRONG, CAKEY?
NOTH-ING...
I WAS JUST THINKING THEY SEEM AWFULLY CHUMMY.
REALLY?
IF ANYTHING, I'D SAY THAT ABOUT THOSE TWO.
ワイ CHAT
ワイ CHAT
THEM, TOO, BUT...
YOU KNOW HOW CHISA IS!
ワイ CHAT
SHE THINKS YOU'RE A BIGGER PUSH-OVER THAN KITAHARA, KOTEGAWA...
ALL RIGHT. WHY DON'T YOU CHANGE INTO YOUR SWIMSUITS?
OKAY.
G R R

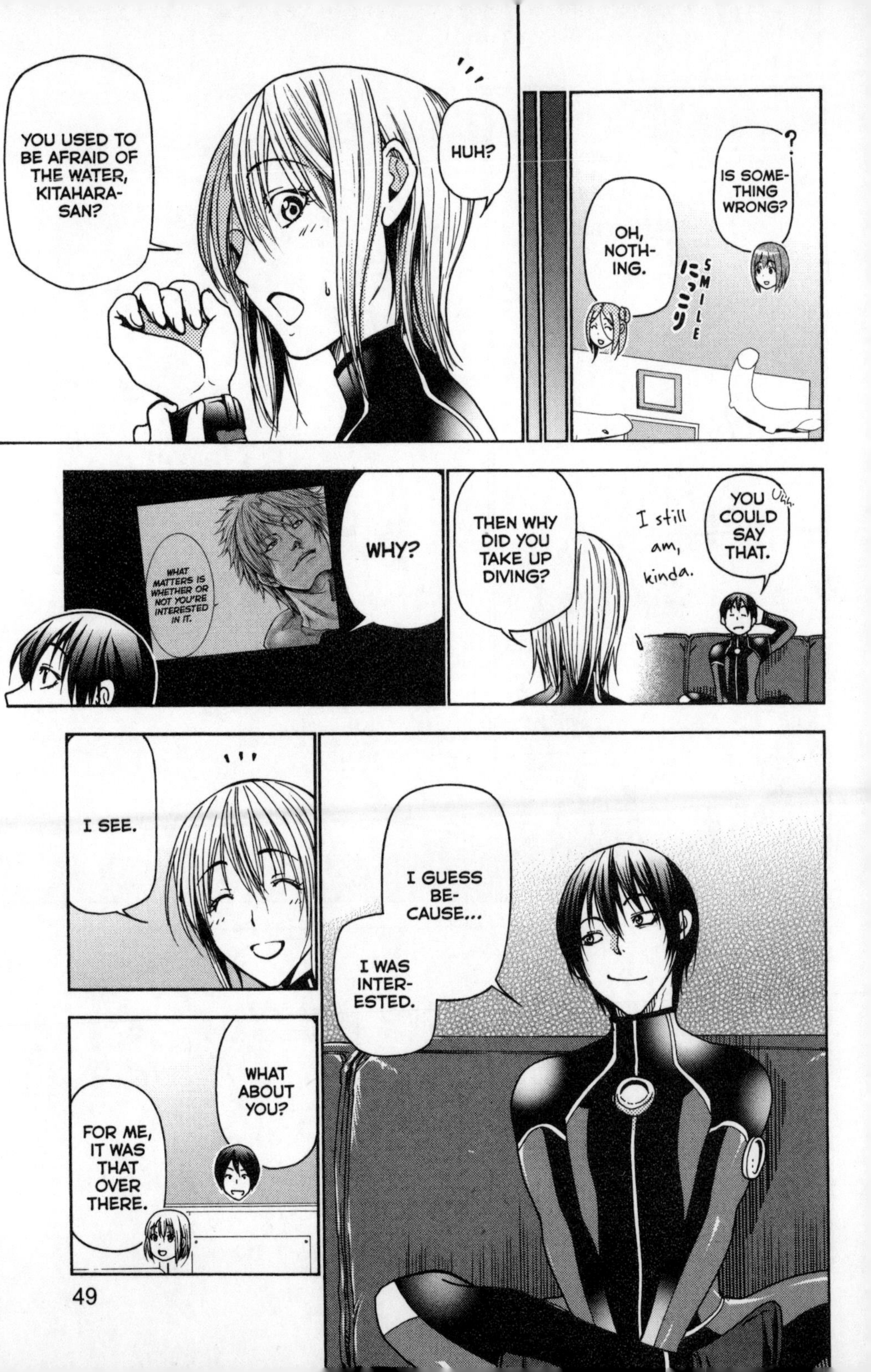
IS SOMETHING WRONG?
OH, NOTHING.
SMILE
にっこり
HUH?
YOU USED TO BE AFRAID OF THE WATER, KITAHARA-SAN?
YOU COULD SAY THAT.
Uhh.
I still am, kinda.
THEN WHY DID YOU TAKE UP DIVING?
WHY?
WHAT MATTERS IS WHETHER OR NOT YOU'RE INTERESTED IN IT.
I GUESS BECAUSE...
I WAS INTERESTED.
I SEE.
WHAT ABOUT YOU?
FOR ME, IT WAS THAT OVER THERE.

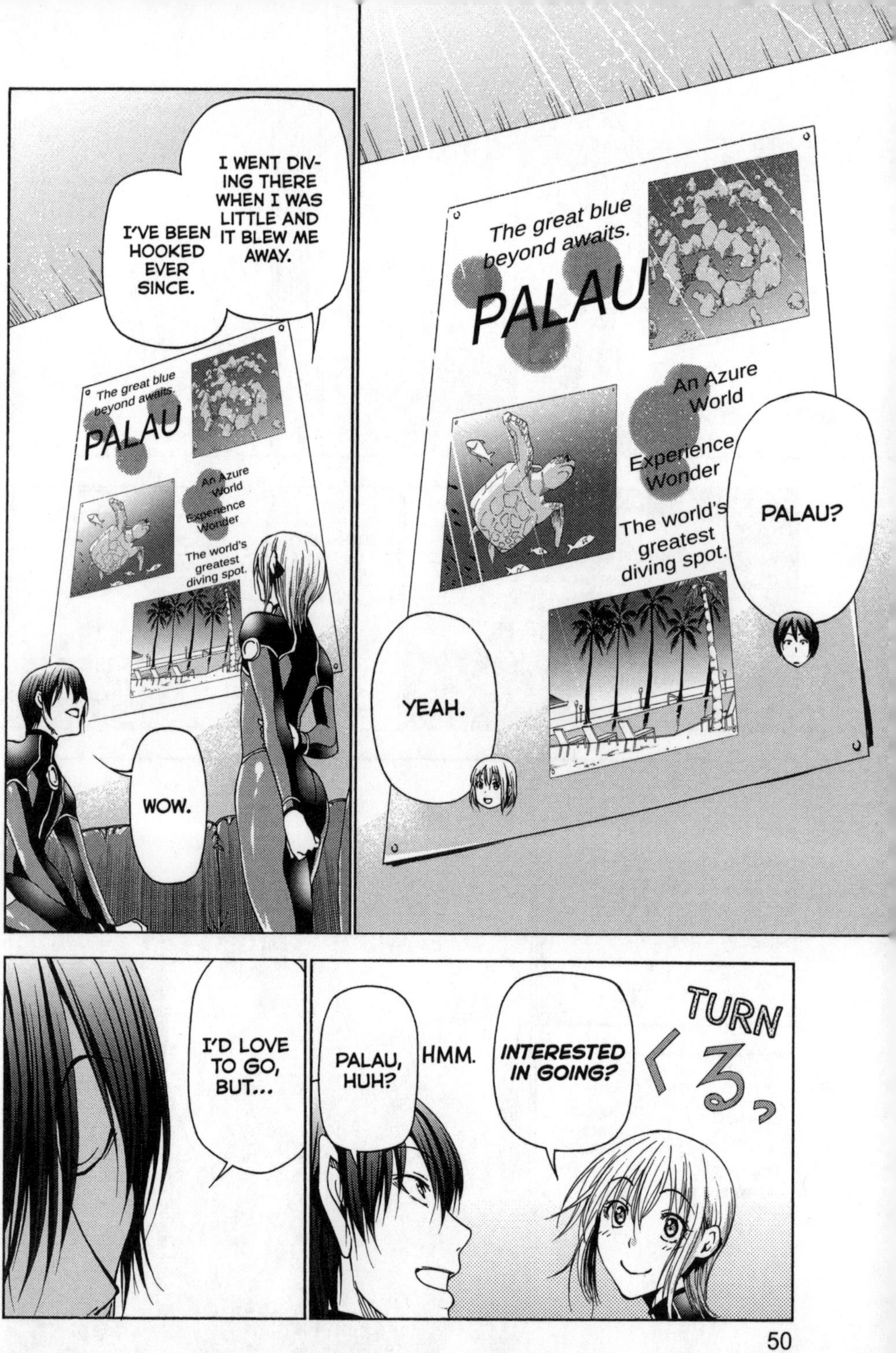
The great blue beyond awaits.
PALAU
An Azure World
Experience Wonder
The world's greatest diving spot.
PALAU?
YEAH.
I WENT DIVING THERE WHEN I WAS LITTLE AND IT BLEW ME AWAY.
I'VE BEEN HOOKED EVER SINCE.
The great blue beyond awaits.
PALAU
An Azure World
Experience Wonder
The world's greatest diving spot.
WOW.
TURN
INTERESTED IN GOING?
HMM.
PALAU, HUH?
I'D LOVE TO GO, BUT...

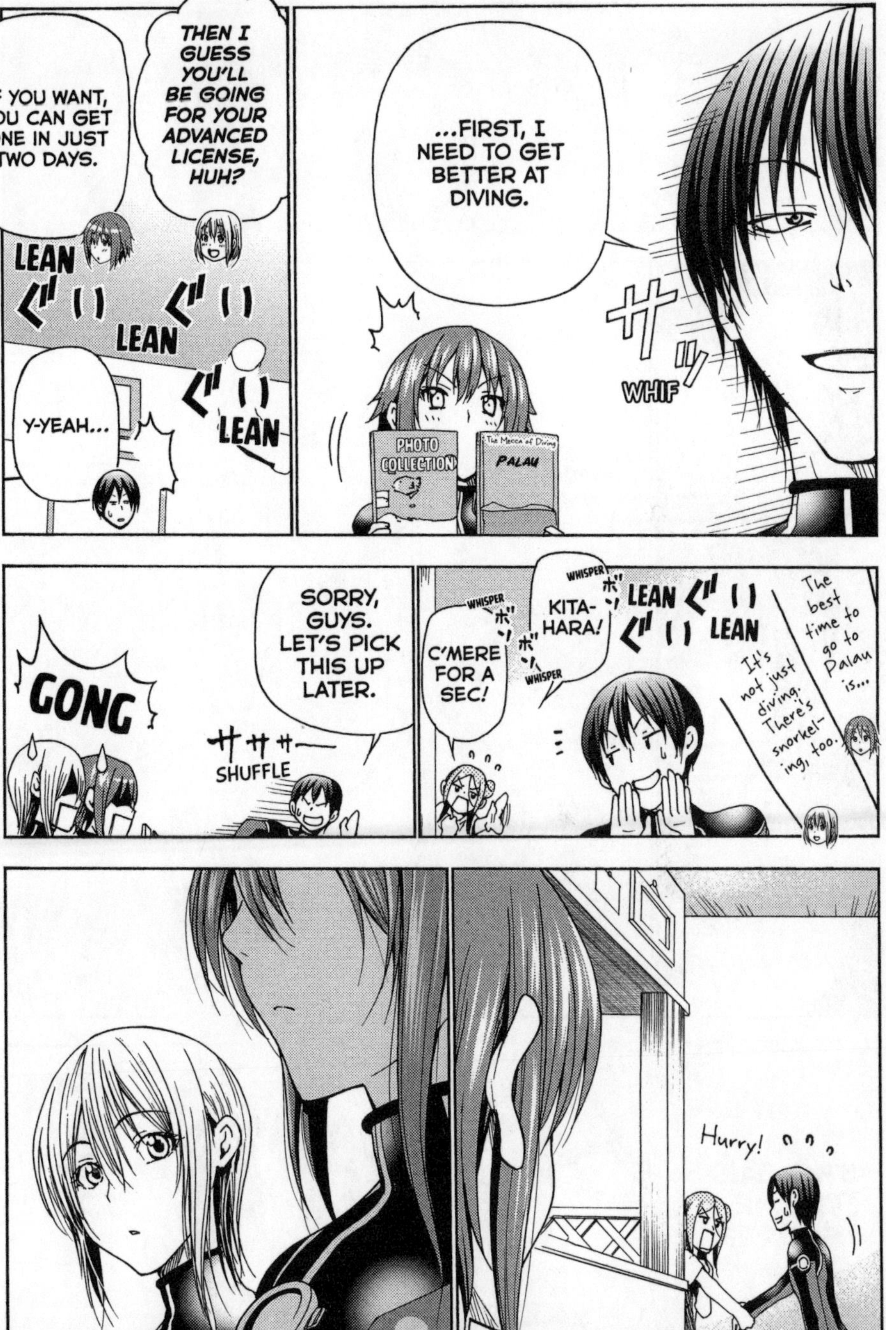
...FIRST, I NEED TO GET BETTER AT DIVING.
WHIF
PHOTO COLLECTION
The Mecca of Diving
PALAU
THEN I GUESS YOU'LL BE GOING FOR YOUR ADVANCED LICENSE, HUH?
IF YOU WANT, YOU CAN GET ONE IN JUST TWO DAYS.
LEAN
LEAN
LEAN
Y-YEAH...
The best time to go to Palau is...
It's not just diving. There's snorkel-ing, too.
LEAN
LEAN
WHISPER
KITA-HARA!
WHISPER
WHISPER
C'MERE FOR A SEC!
SORRY, GUYS. LET'S PICK THIS UP LATER.
SHUFFLE
GONG
Hurry!

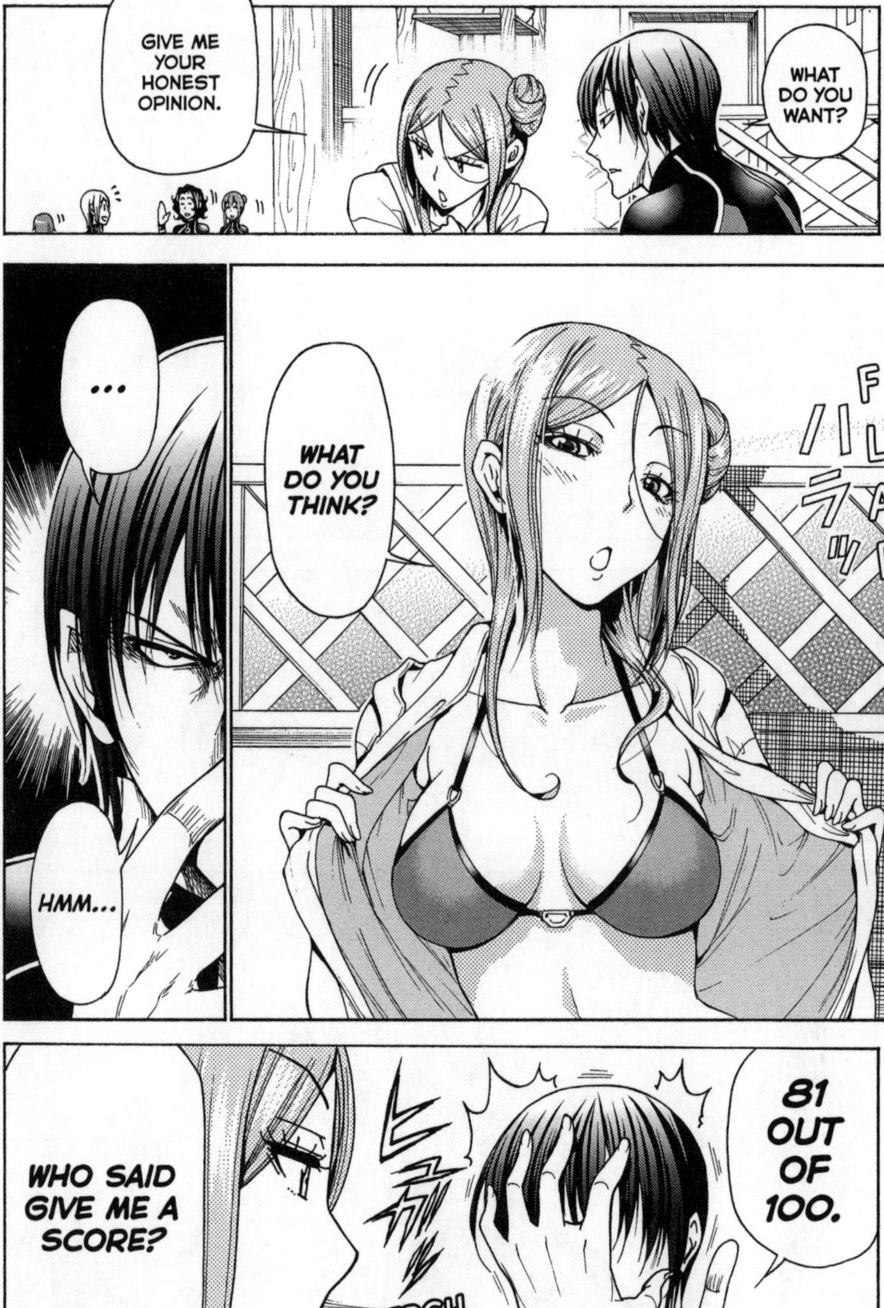

WHAT DO YOU WANT?
GIVE ME YOUR HONEST OPINION.
ハラッ
FLAP
WHAT DO YOU THINK?
...
HMM...
81 OUT OF 100.
FRGH
WHO SAID GIVE ME A SCORE?

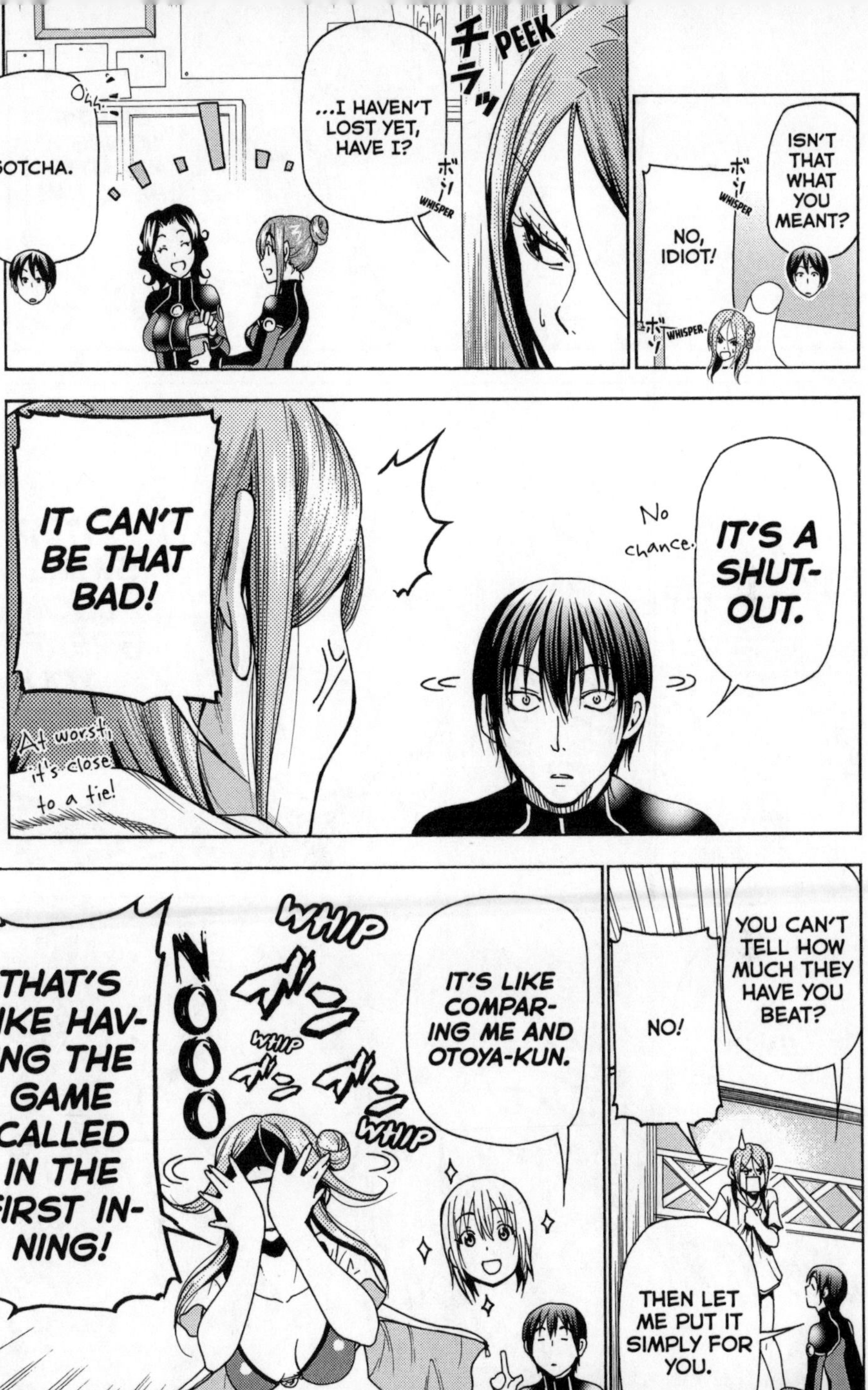
ISN'T THAT WHAT YOU MEANT?
ボソ WHISPER
NO, IDIOT!
ボソ WHISPER
チラッ PEEK
...I HAVEN'T LOST YET, HAVE I?
ボソ WHISPER
Ohh
GOTCHA.
IT'S A SHUT-OUT.
No chance.
IT CAN'T BE THAT BAD!
At worst, it's close to a tie!
YOU CAN'T TELL HOW MUCH THEY HAVE YOU BEAT?
NO!
THEN LET ME PUT IT SIMPLY FOR YOU.
IT'S LIKE COMPARING ME AND OTOYA-KUN.
WHIP
WHIP
WHIP
NOOOO
THAT'S LIKE HAVING THE GAME CALLED IN THE FIRST INNING!

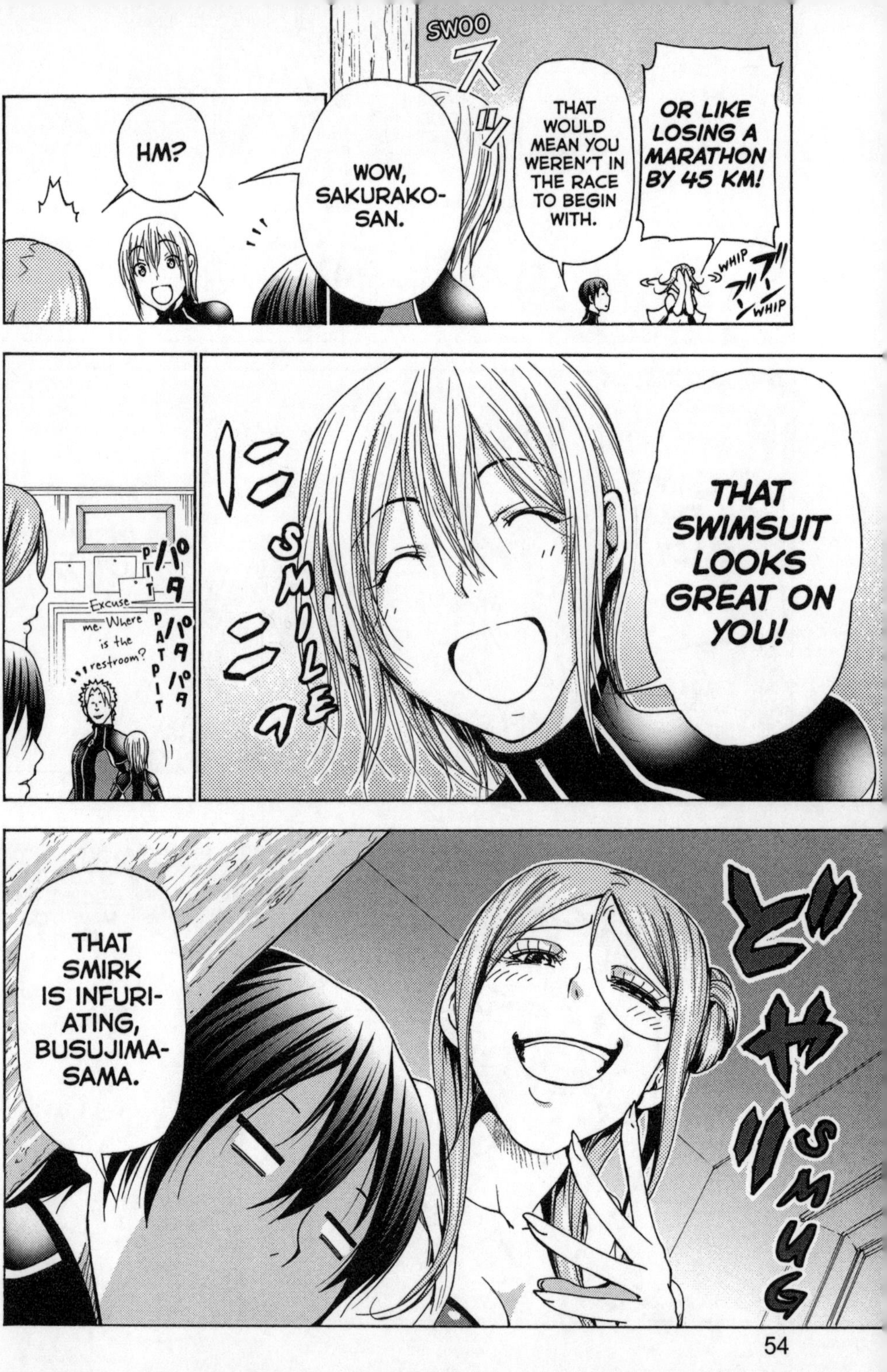
SWOO
OR LIKE LOSING A MARATHON BY 45 KM!
WHIP
WHIP
THAT WOULD MEAN YOU WEREN'T IN THE RACE TO BEGIN WITH.
WOW, SAKURAKO-SAN.
HM?
THAT SWIMSUIT LOOKS GREAT ON YOU!
SMILE
PIT
PAT
PIT
Excuse me. Where is the restroom?
SMUG
THAT SMIRK IS INFURIATING, BUSUJIMA-SAMA.

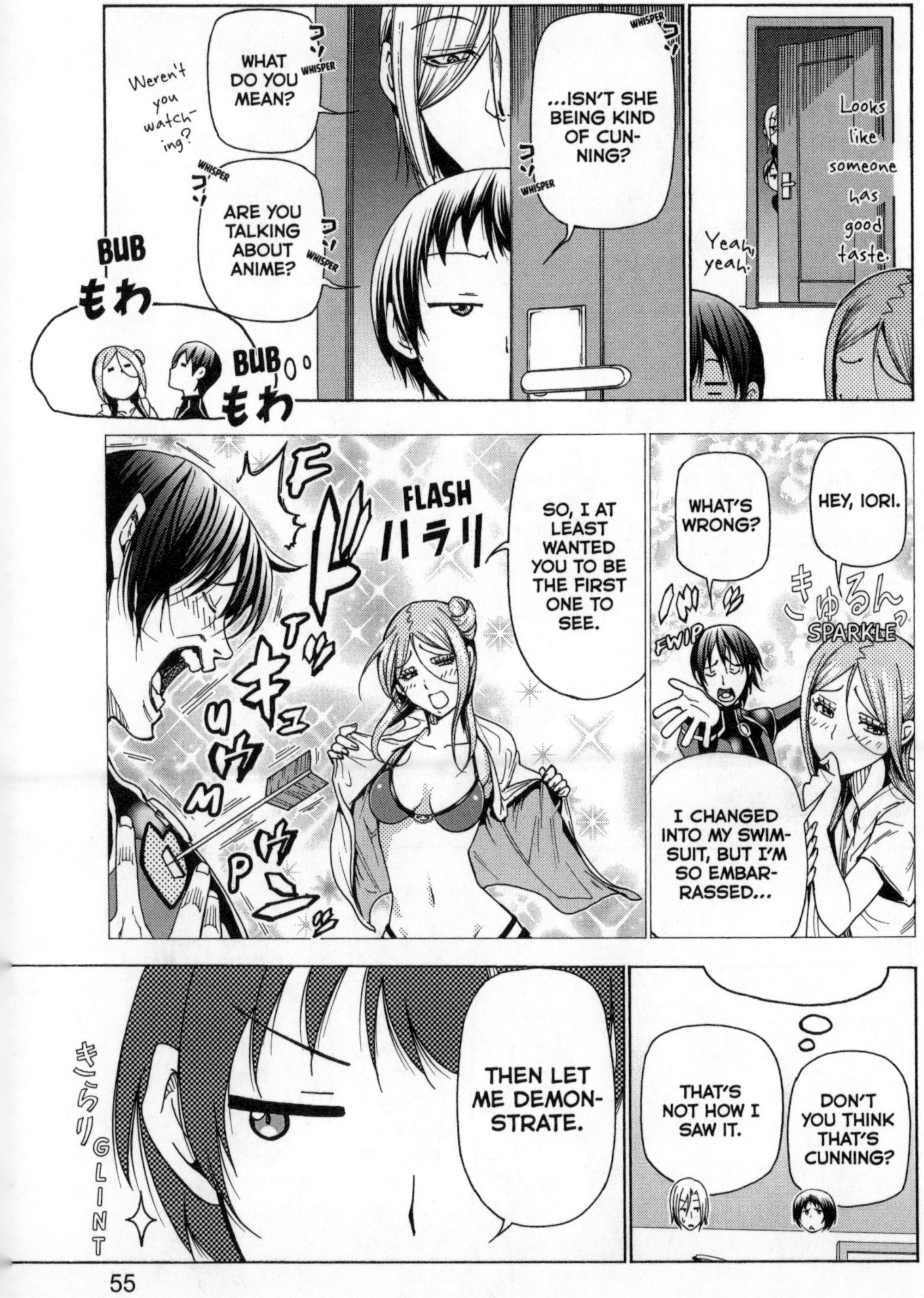
Looks like someone has good taste.
Yeah yeah.
WHISPER
...ISN'T SHE BEING KIND OF CUN-NING?
WHISPER
WHAT DO YOU MEAN?
WHISPER
Weren't you watch-ing?
WHISPER
ARE YOU TALKING ABOUT ANIME?
WHISPER
BUB もわ
BUB もわ
HEY, IORI.
きゅるんっ SPARKLE
WHAT'S WRONG?
FWIP
I CHANGED INTO MY SWIM-SUIT, BUT I'M SO EMBAR-RASSED...
SO, I AT LEAST WANTED YOU TO BE THE FIRST ONE TO SEE.
FLASH ハラリ
THUMP
DON'T YOU THINK THAT'S CUNNING?
THAT'S NOT HOW I SAW IT.
THEN LET ME DEMON-STRATE.
きらり GLINT

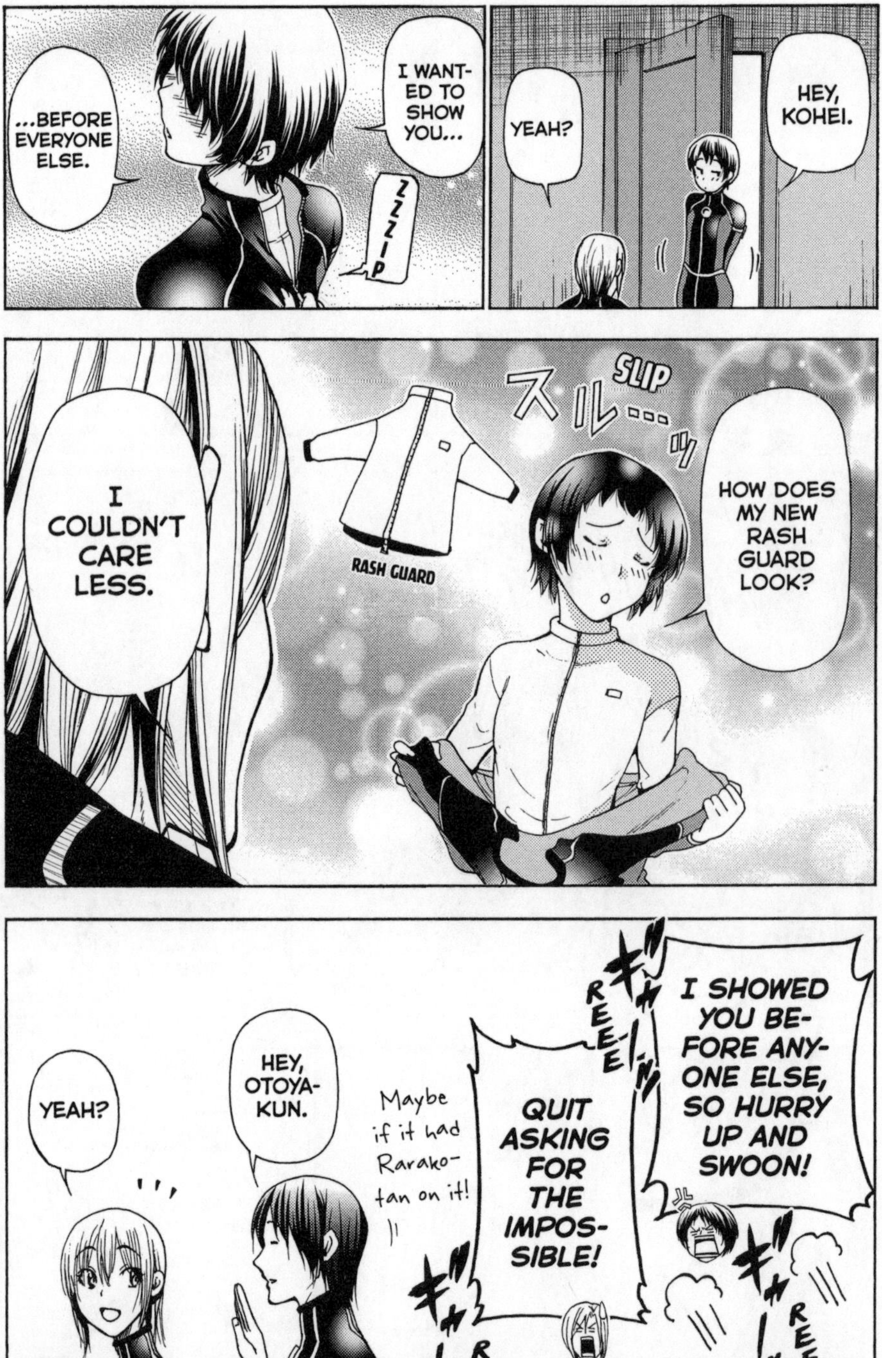

HEY, KOHEI.
YEAH?
I WANTED TO SHOW YOU...
ZZZIP
...BEFORE EVERYONE ELSE.
SLIP
HOW DOES MY NEW RASH GUARD LOOK?
RASH GUARD
I COULDN'T CARE LESS.
I SHOWED YOU BEFORE ANYONE ELSE, SO HURRY UP AND SWOON!
REEE
REEE
QUIT ASKING FOR THE IMPOSSIBLE!
REEE
Maybe if it had Rarako-tan on it!
HEY, OTOYA-KUN.
YEAH?

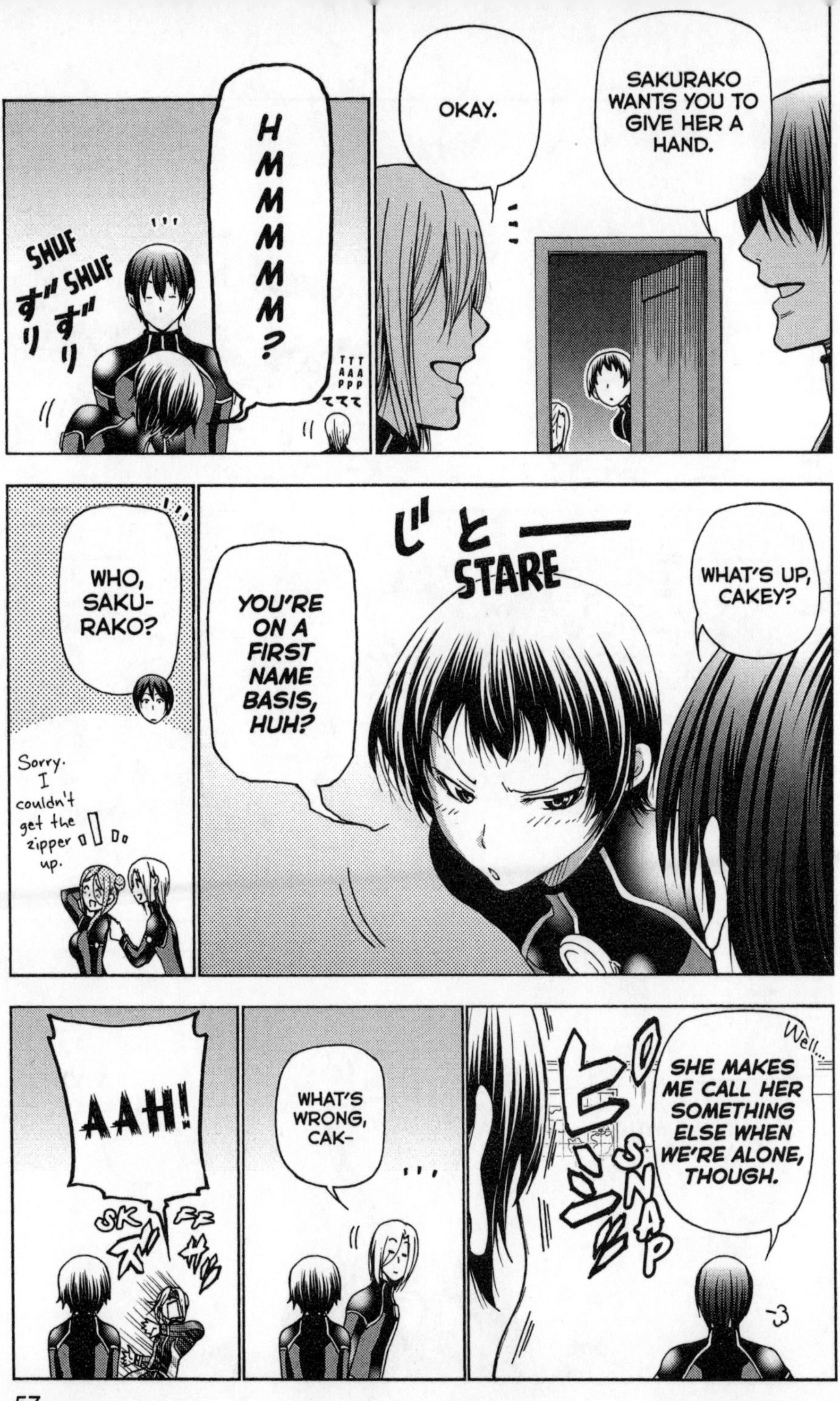
SAKURAKO WANTS YOU TO GIVE HER A HAND.
OKAY.
HMMMMMM?
SHUF すり SHUF すり
TAP TAP TAP てててて
WHAT'S UP, CAKEY?
じとー
STARE
YOU'RE ON A FIRST NAME BASIS, HUH?
WHO, SAKU-RAKO?
Sorry. I couldn't get the zipper up.
Well...
SHE MAKES ME CALL HER SOMETHING ELSE WHEN WE'RE ALONE, THOUGH.
SNAP
WHAT'S WRONG, CAK-
AAH!
SK
FF

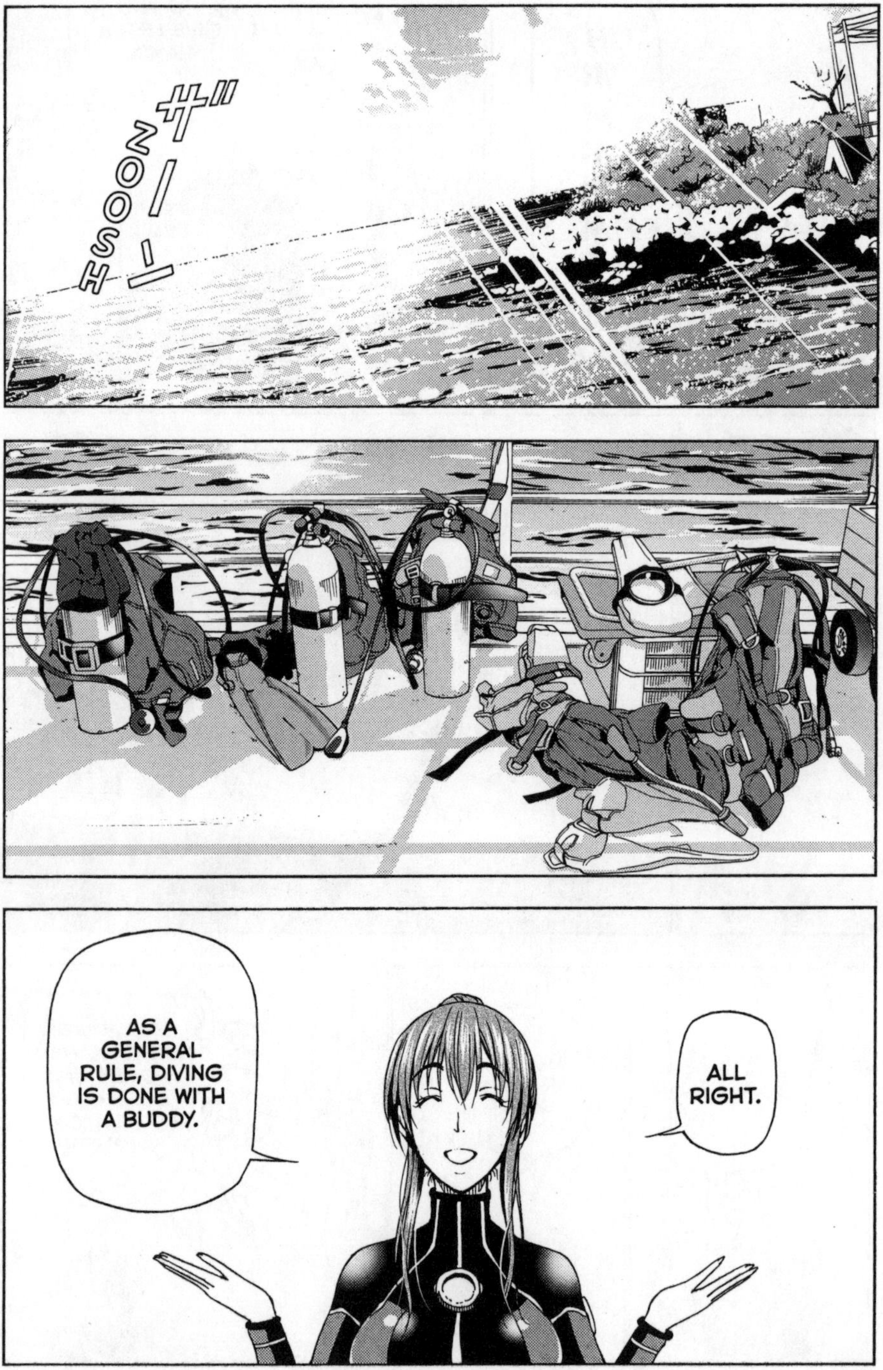
ザー
ZOOSH
ALL RIGHT.
AS A GENERAL RULE, DIVING IS DONE WITH A BUDDY.

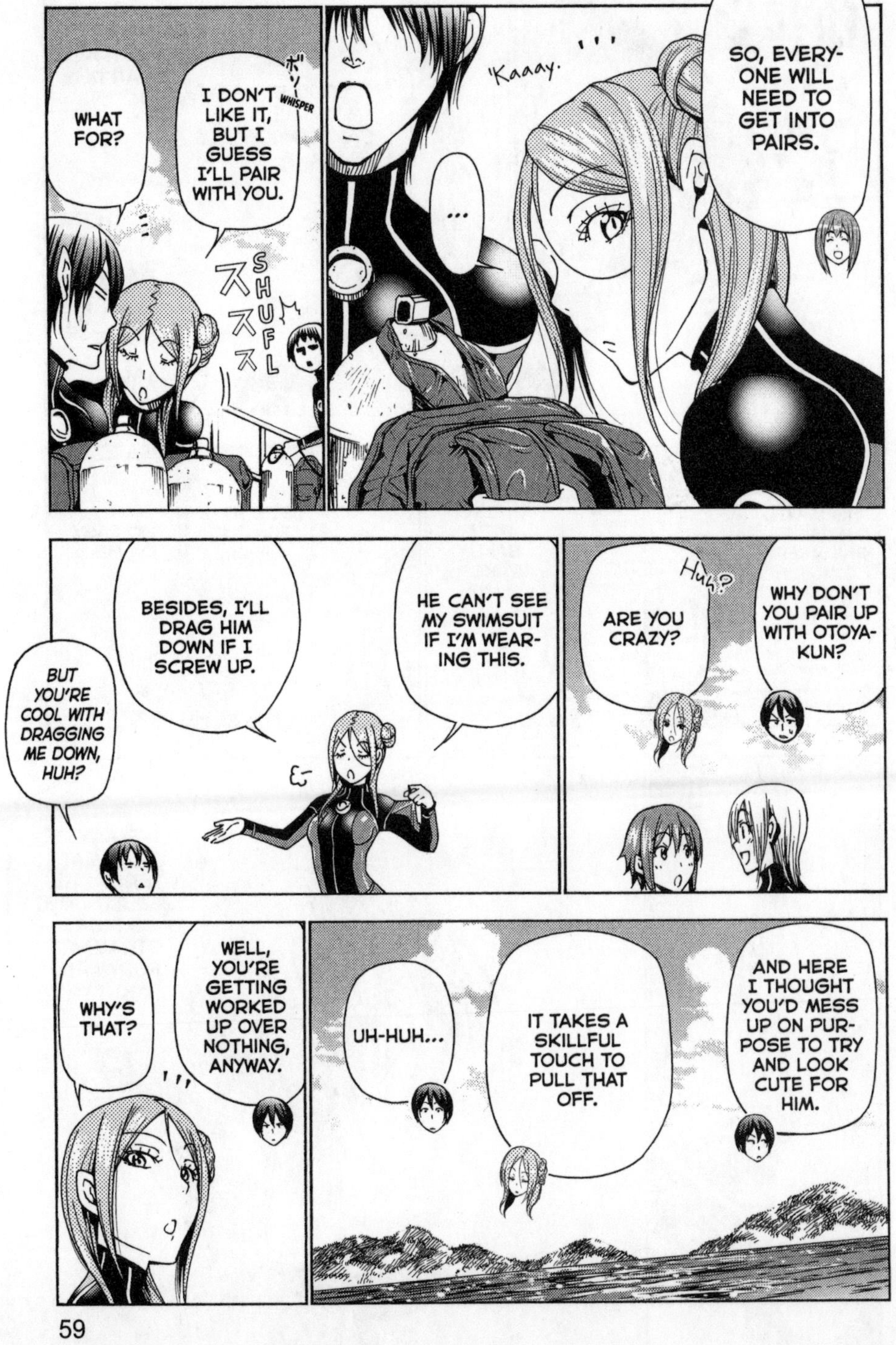
SO, EVERY-ONE WILL NEED TO GET INTO PAIRS.
'Kaaay.
...
ボソ WHISPER
I DON'T LIKE IT, BUT I GUESS I'LL PAIR WITH YOU.
WHAT FOR?
ススス SHUFL
WHY DON'T YOU PAIR UP WITH OTOYA-KUN?
Huh?
ARE YOU CRAZY?
HE CAN'T SEE MY SWIMSUIT IF I'M WEAR-ING THIS.
BESIDES, I'LL DRAG HIM DOWN IF I SCREW UP.
BUT YOU'RE COOL WITH DRAGGING ME DOWN, HUH?
AND HERE I THOUGHT YOU'D MESS UP ON PUR-POSE TO TRY AND LOOK CUTE FOR HIM.
IT TAKES A SKILLFUL TOUCH TO PULL THAT OFF.
UH-HUH...
WELL, YOU'RE GETTING WORKED UP OVER NOTHING, ANYWAY.
WHY'S THAT?

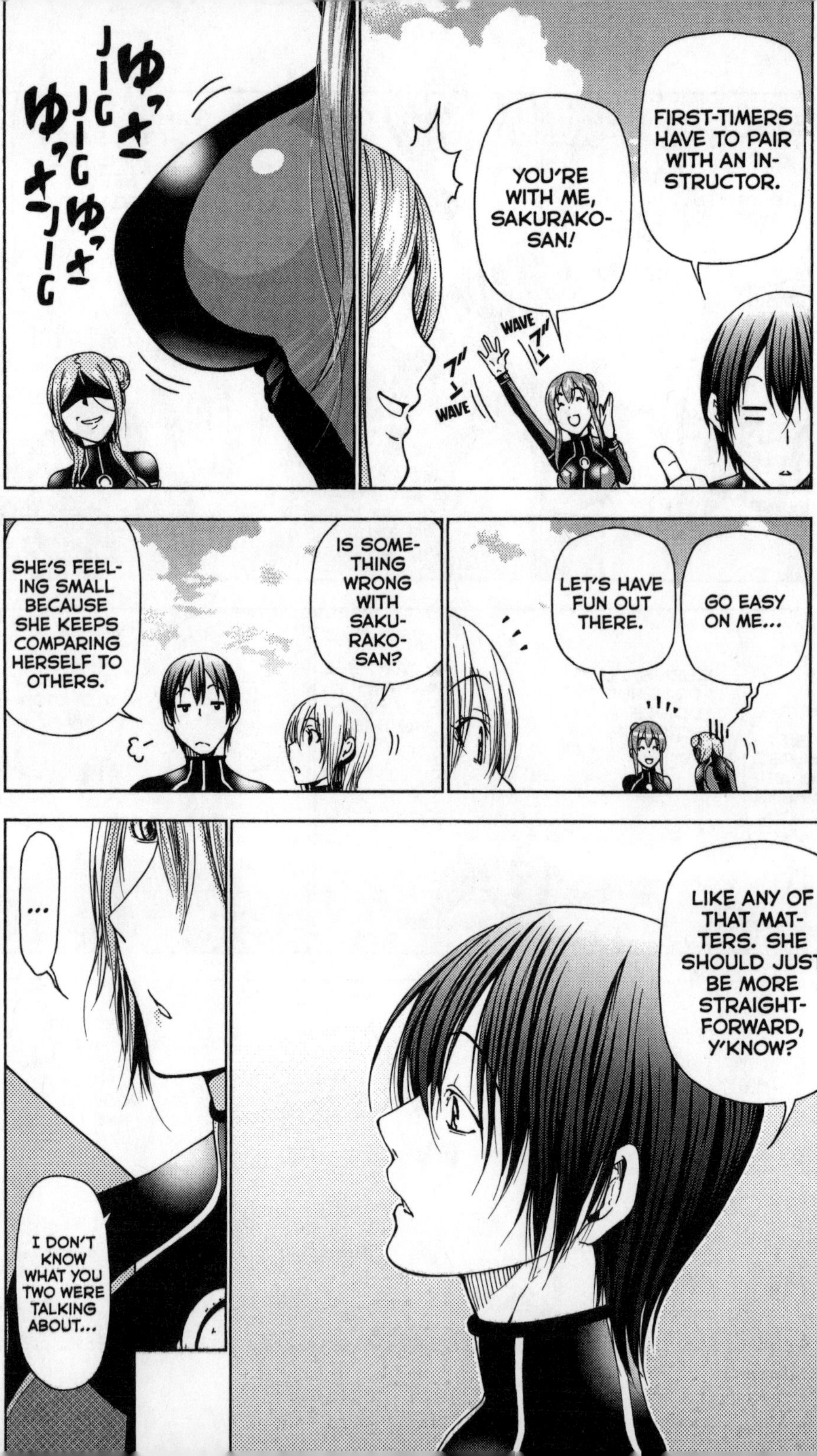
FIRST-TIMERS HAVE TO PAIR WITH AN IN-STRUCTOR.
YOU'RE WITH ME, SAKURAKO-SAN!
WAVE
WAVE
ゆっさ JIG
ゆっさ JIG ゆっさ JIG
GO EASY ON ME...
LET'S HAVE FUN OUT THERE.
IS SOME-THING WRONG WITH SAKU-RAKO-SAN?
SHE'S FEEL-ING SMALL BECAUSE SHE KEEPS COMPARING HERSELF TO OTHERS.
LIKE ANY OF THAT MAT-TERS. SHE SHOULD JUST BE MORE STRAIGHT-FORWARD, Y'KNOW?
...
I DON'T KNOW WHAT YOU TWO WERE TALKING ABOUT...

...I GET THE FEELING THAT YOU DON'T LIKE COMPARING YOURSELF TO OTHERS, KITAHARA-SAN.

BUT...

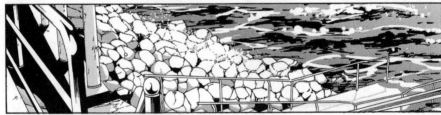

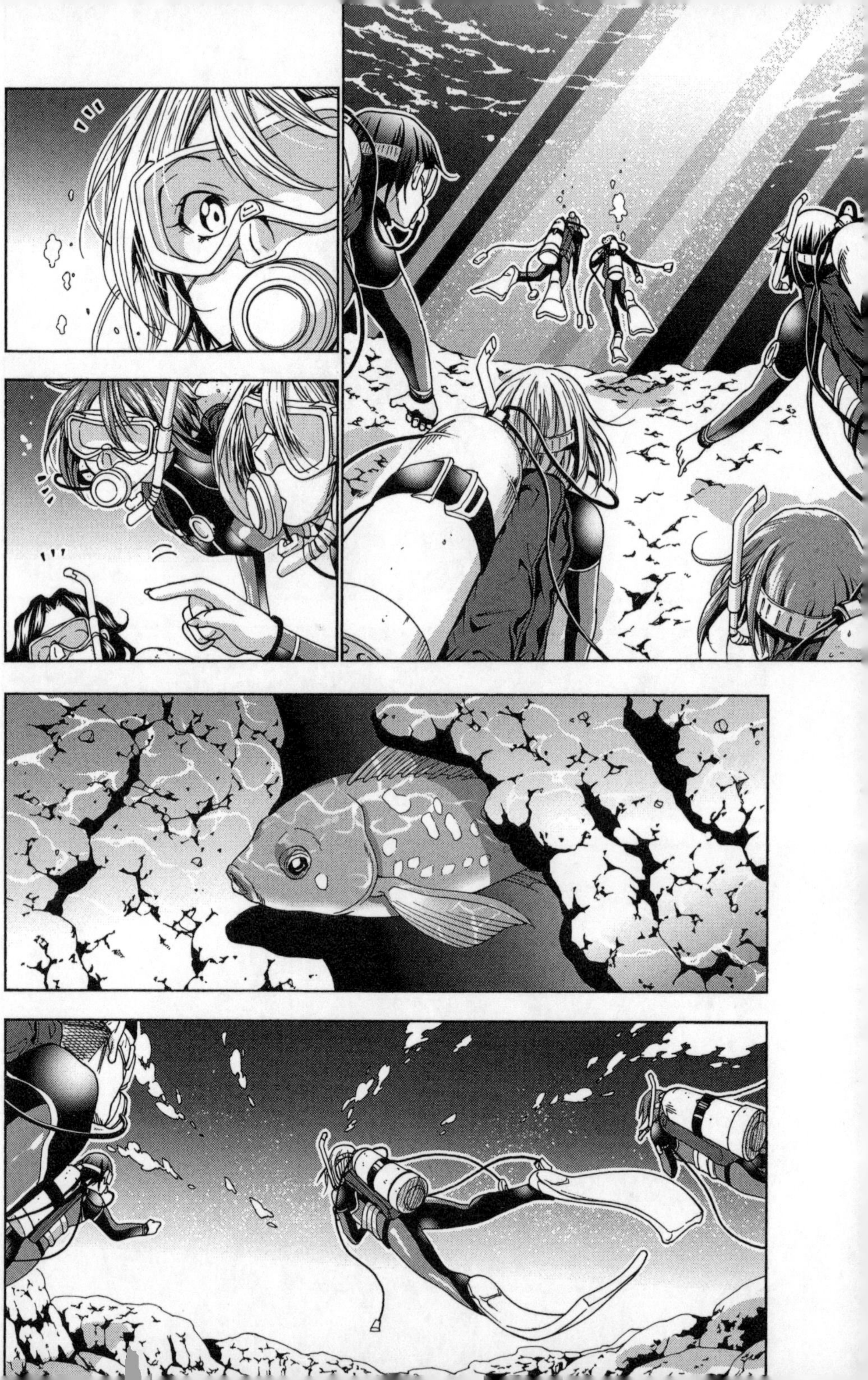

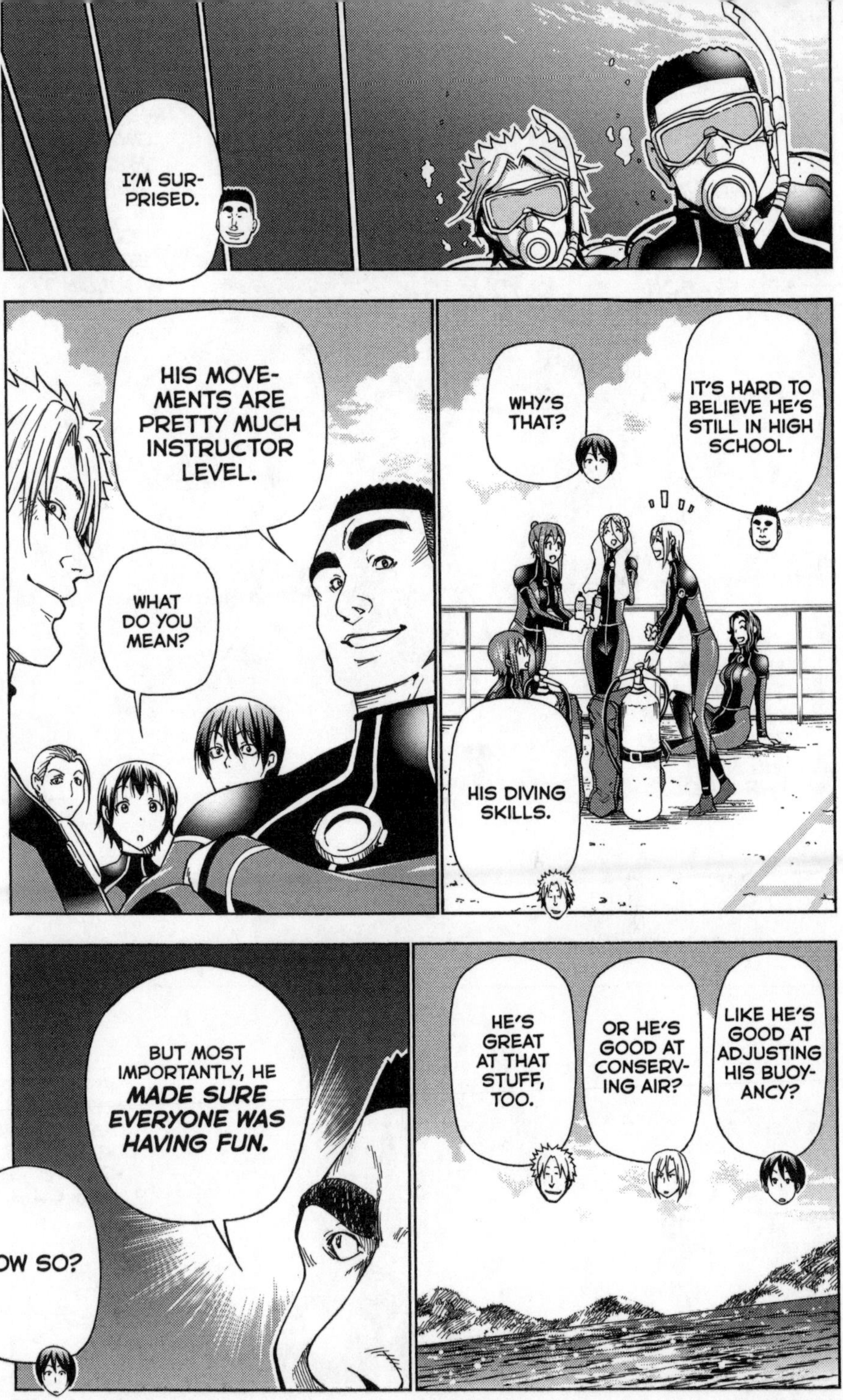
I'M SUR-PRISED.
IT'S HARD TO BELIEVE HE'S STILL IN HIGH SCHOOL.
WHY'S THAT?
HIS DIVING SKILLS.
HIS MOVE-MENTS ARE PRETTY MUCH INSTRUCTOR LEVEL.
WHAT DO YOU MEAN?
LIKE HE'S GOOD AT ADJUSTING HIS BUOY-ANCY?
OR HE'S GOOD AT CONSERV-ING AIR?
HE'S GREAT AT THAT STUFF, TOO.
BUT MOST IMPORTANTLY, HE *MADE SURE EVERYONE WAS HAVING FUN.*
HOW SO?

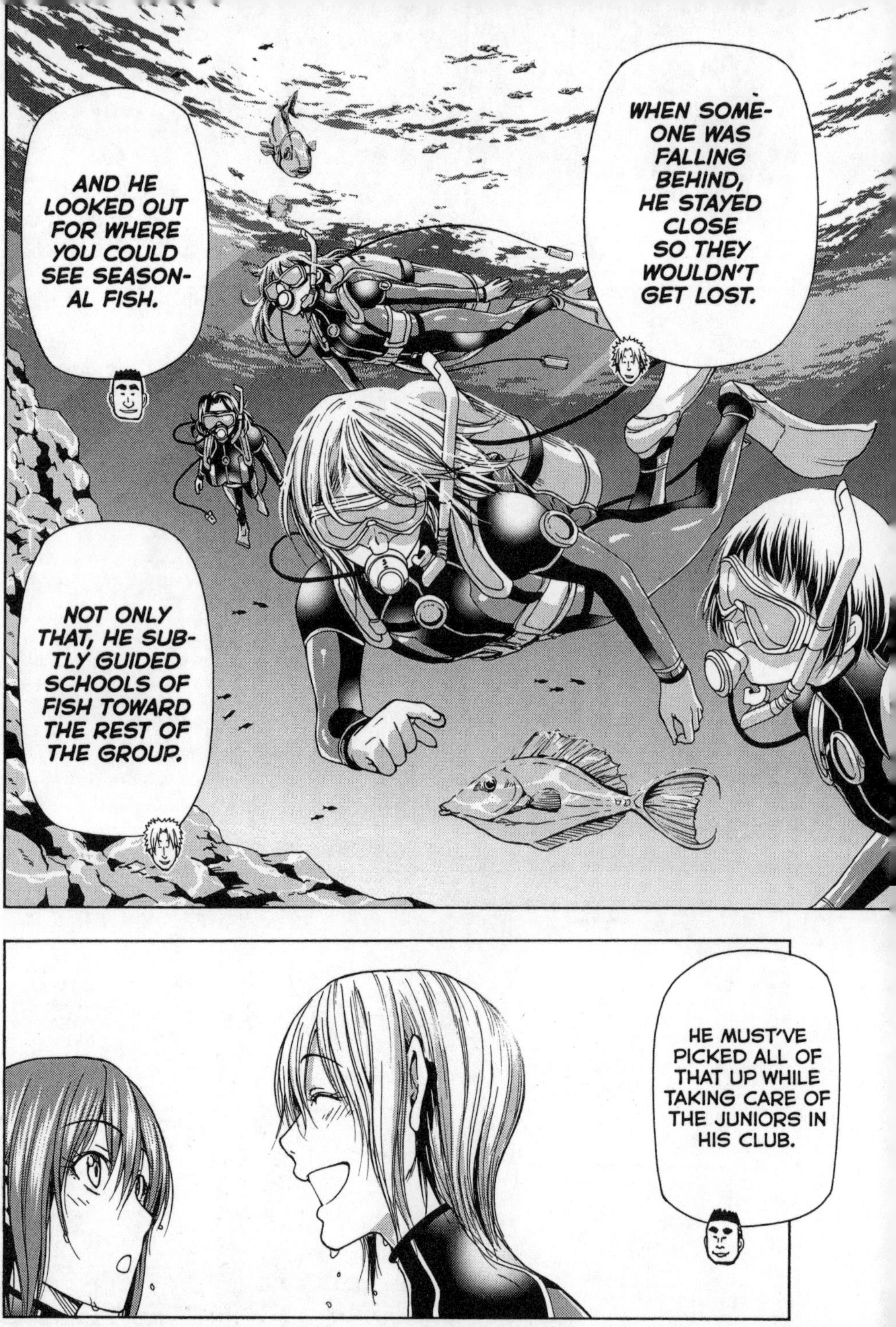
WHEN SOME-ONE WAS FALLING BEHIND, HE STAYED CLOSE SO THEY WOULDN'T GET LOST.
AND HE LOOKED OUT FOR WHERE YOU COULD SEE SEASON-AL FISH.
NOT ONLY THAT, HE SUB-TLY GUIDED SCHOOLS OF FISH TOWARD THE REST OF THE GROUP.
HE MUST'VE PICKED ALL OF THAT UP WHILE TAKING CARE OF THE JUNIORS IN HIS CLUB.

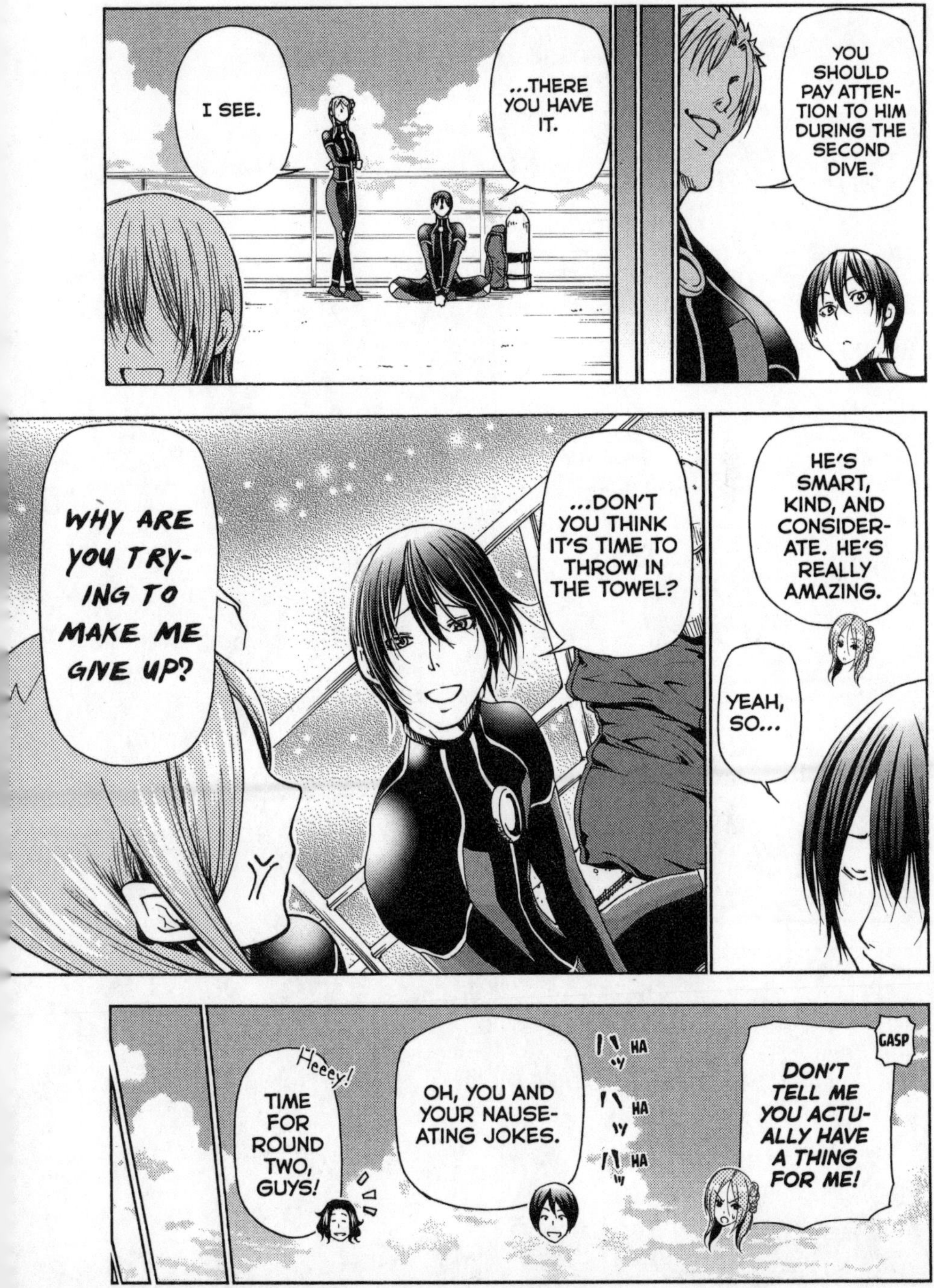
YOU SHOULD PAY ATTEN-TION TO HIM DURING THE SECOND DIVE.
...THERE YOU HAVE IT.
I SEE.
HE'S SMART, KIND, AND CONSIDER-ATE. HE'S REALLY AMAZING.
YEAH, SO...
...DON'T YOU THINK IT'S TIME TO THROW IN THE TOWEL?
WHY ARE YOU TRY-ING TO MAKE ME GIVE UP?
GASP
DON'T TELL ME YOU ACTU-ALLY HAVE A THING FOR ME!
HA HA HA
OH, YOU AND YOUR NAUSE-ATING JOKES.
Heeey!
TIME FOR ROUND TWO, GUYS!

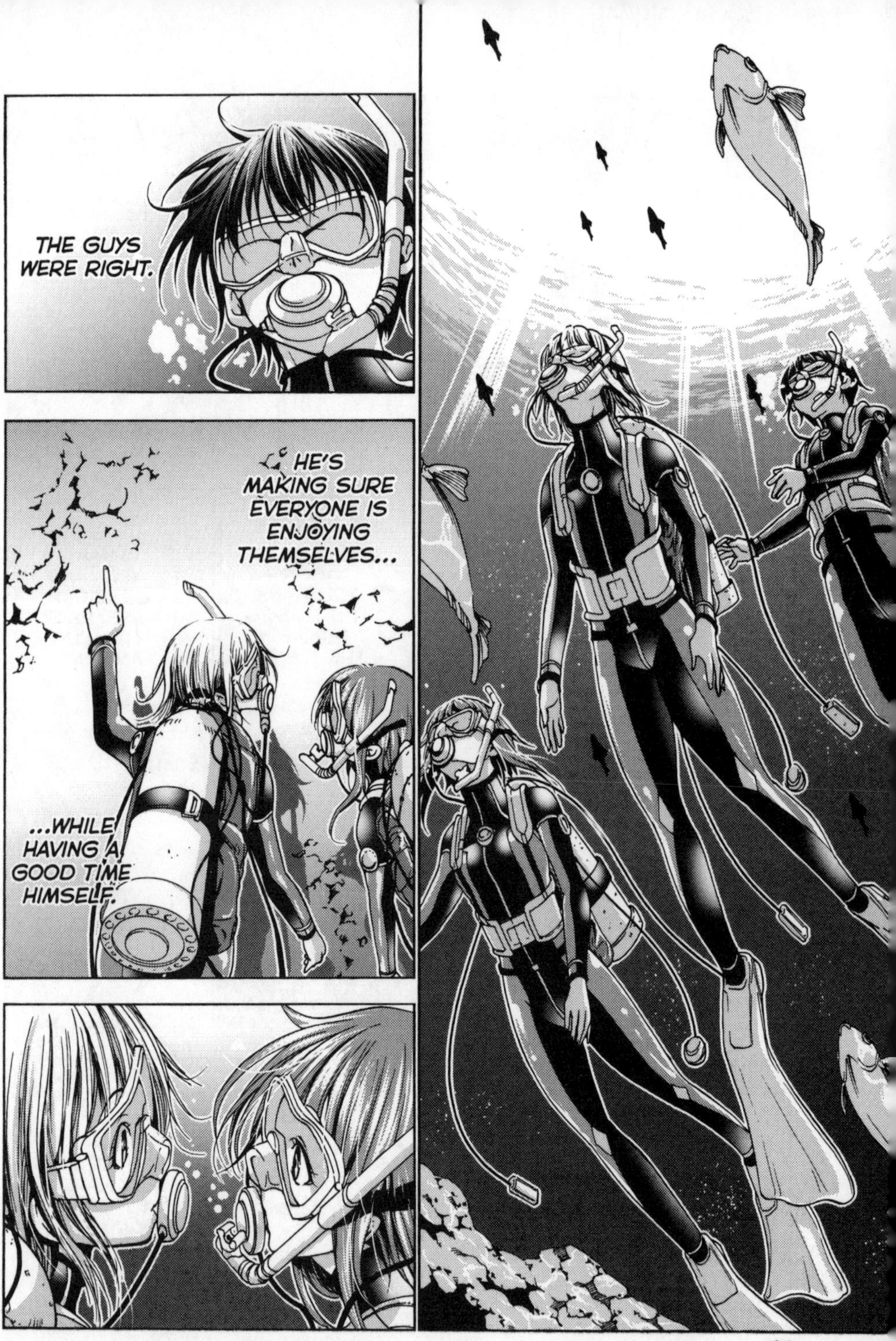
THE GUYS WERE RIGHT.
HE'S MAKING SURE EVERYONE IS ENJOYING THEMSELVES...
...WHILE HAVING A GOOD TIME HIMSELF.

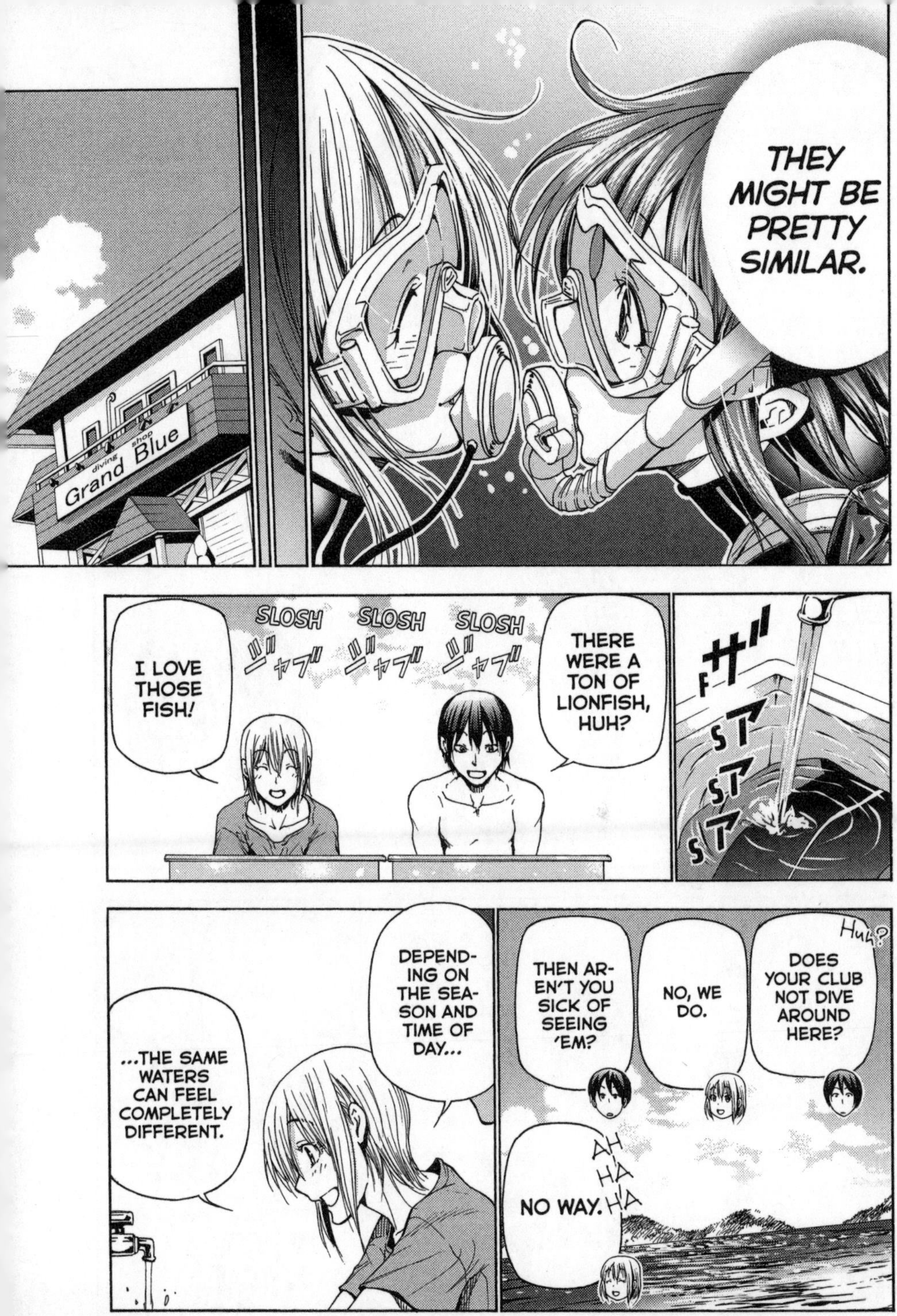
THEY MIGHT BE PRETTY SIMILAR.
diving shop
Grand Blue
FSSST
THERE WERE A TON OF LIONFISH, HUH?
SLOSH SLOSH SLOSH
I LOVE THOSE FISH!
Huh?
DOES YOUR CLUB NOT DIVE AROUND HERE?
NO, WE DO.
THEN AREN'T YOU SICK OF SEEING 'EM?
AH HA HA HA
NO WAY.
DEPENDING ON THE SEASON AND TIME OF DAY...
...THE SAME WATERS CAN FEEL COMPLETELY DIFFERENT.

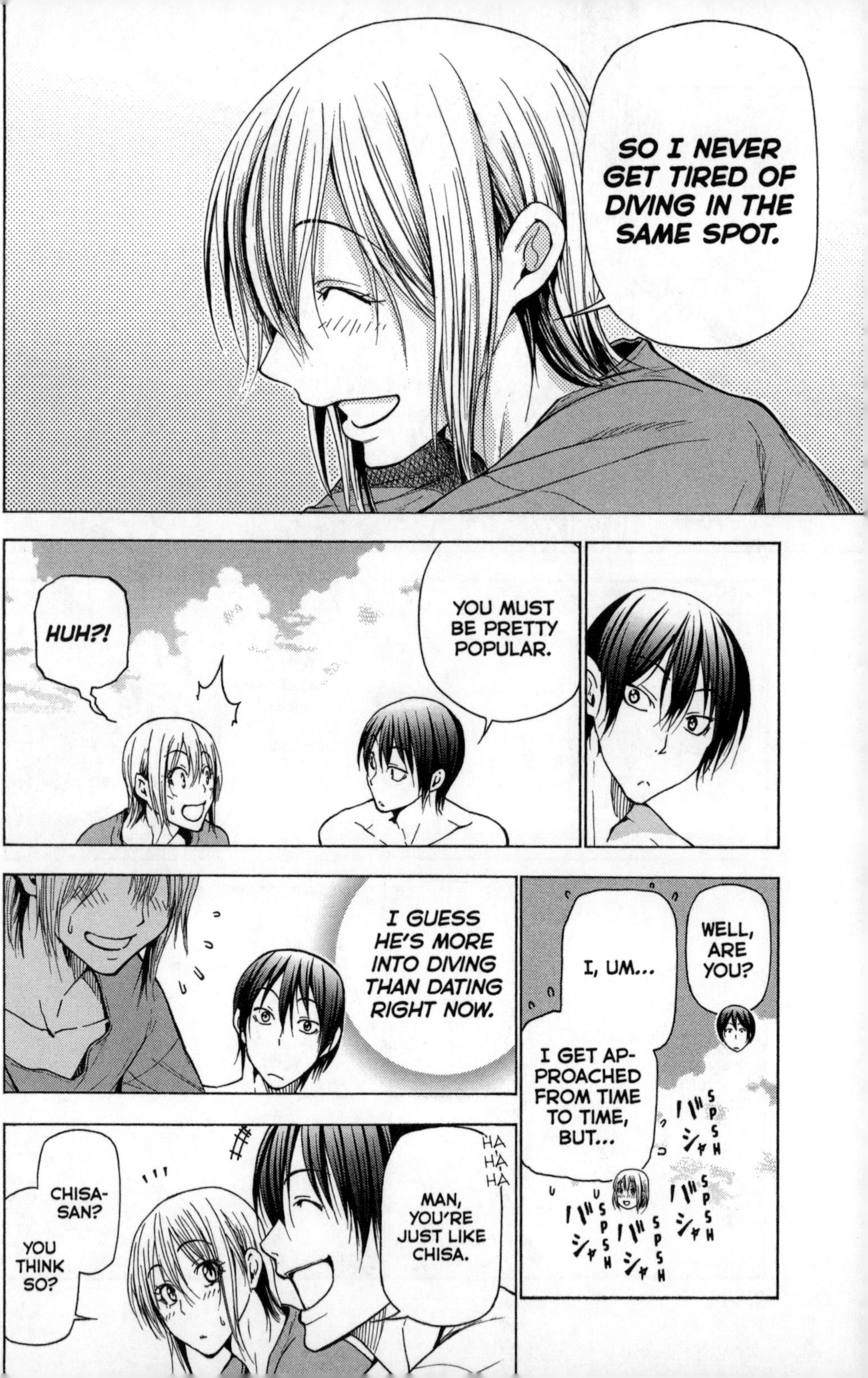

SO I NEVER GET TIRED OF DIVING IN THE SAME SPOT.
YOU MUST BE PRETTY POPULAR.
HUH?!
WELL, ARE YOU?
I, UM...
I GET AP-PROACHED FROM TIME TO TIME, BUT...
バシャ SPSH
バシャ SPSH
バシャ SPSH
バシャ SPSH
I GUESS HE'S MORE INTO DIVING THAN DATING RIGHT NOW.
HA HA HA
MAN, YOU'RE JUST LIKE CHISA.
CHISA-SAN?
YOU THINK SO?

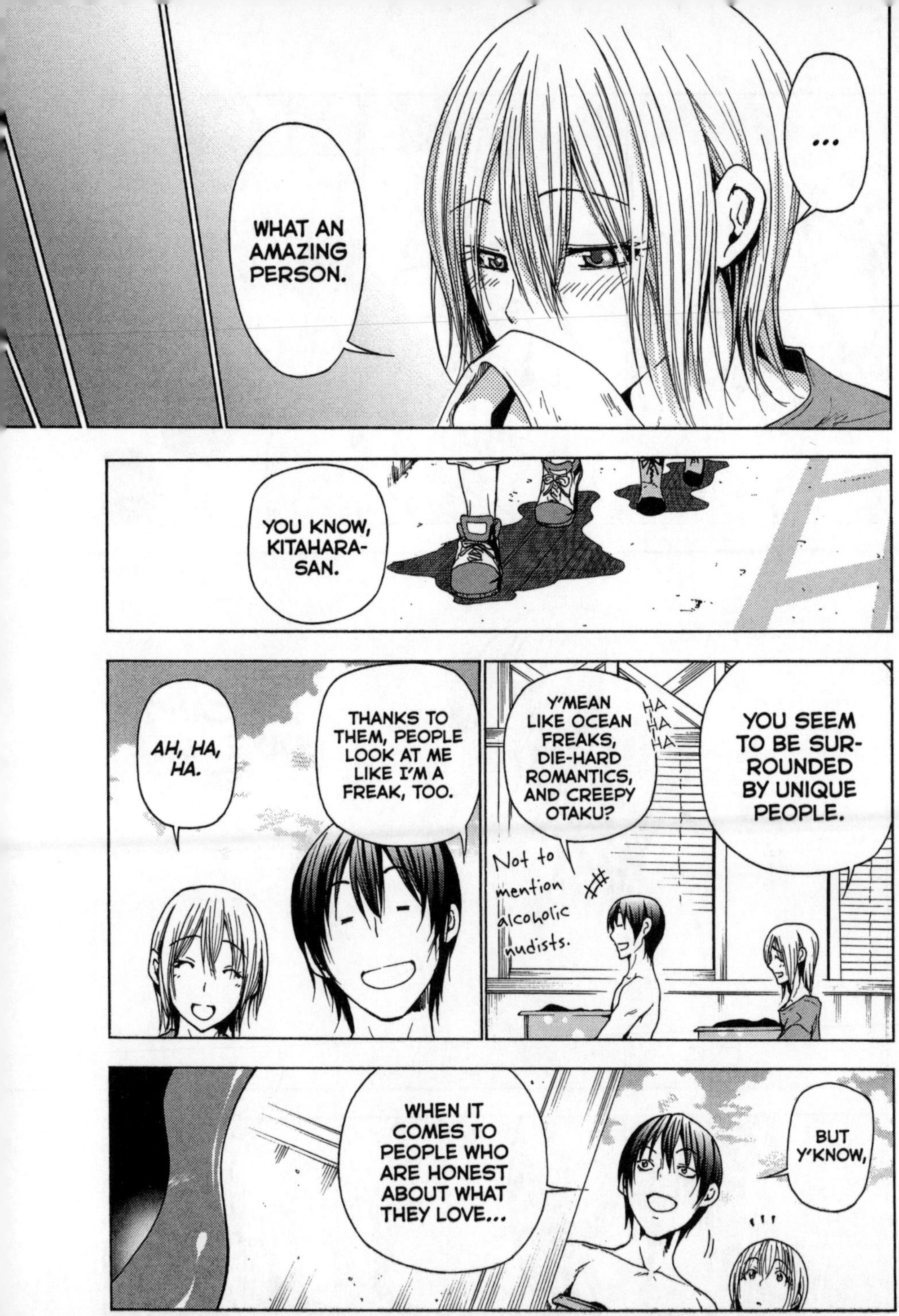
...
WHAT AN AMAZING PERSON.
YOU KNOW, KITAHARA-SAN.
YOU SEEM TO BE SURROUNDED BY UNIQUE PEOPLE.
Y'MEAN LIKE OCEAN FREAKS, DIE-HARD ROMANTICS, AND CREEPY OTAKU?
HA HA HA
Not to mention alcoholic nudists.
THANKS TO THEM, PEOPLE LOOK AT ME LIKE I'M A FREAK, TOO.
AH, HA, HA.
BUT Y'KNOW,
WHEN IT COMES TO PEOPLE WHO ARE HONEST ABOUT WHAT THEY LOVE...

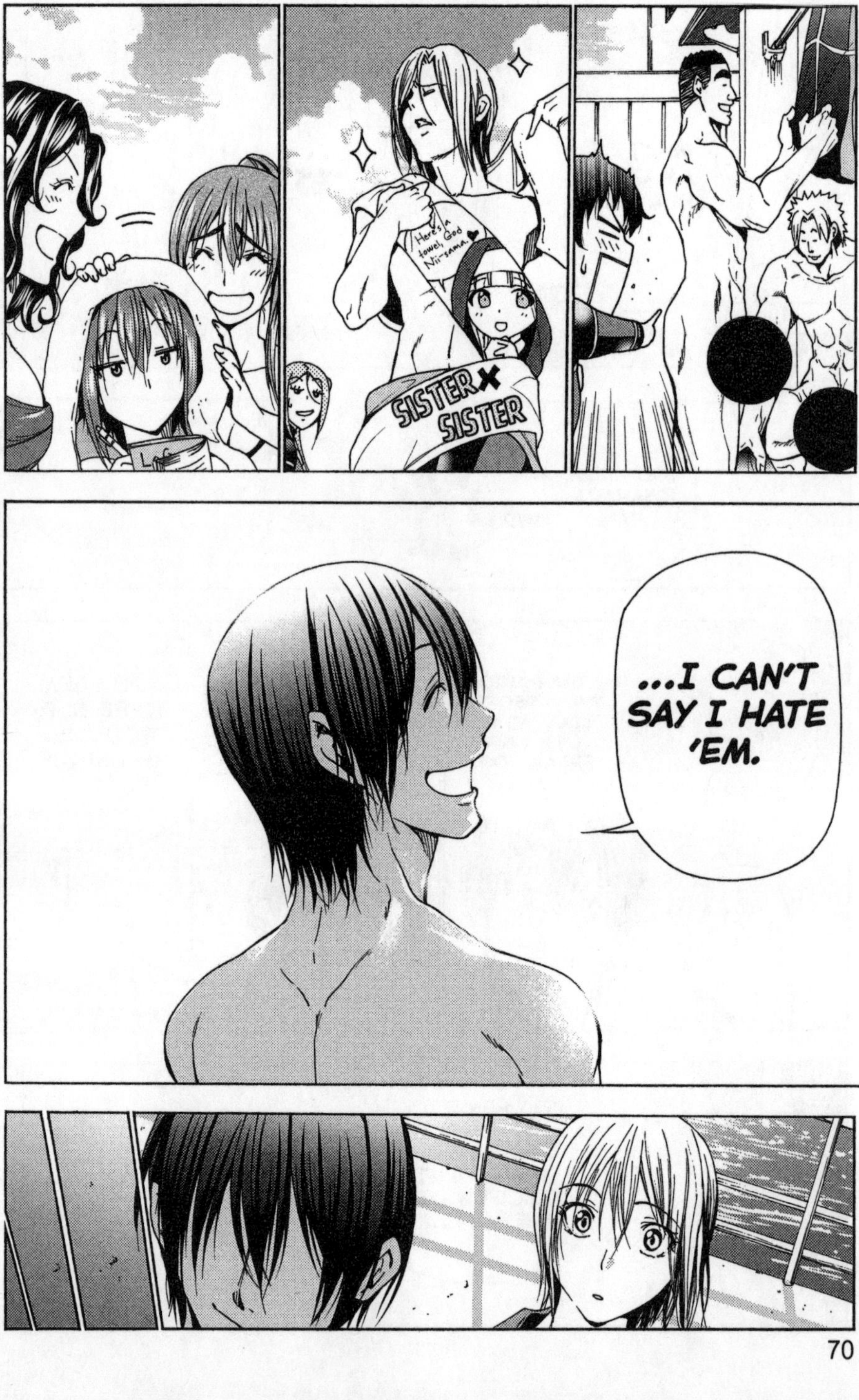
Here's a towel, God Nii-sama. ♥
SISTER × SISTER
...I CAN'T SAY I HATE 'EM.

AL-RIGHTY THEN.
GOOD WORK, EV-ERYONE!
WOOOO
NICE DIVE!

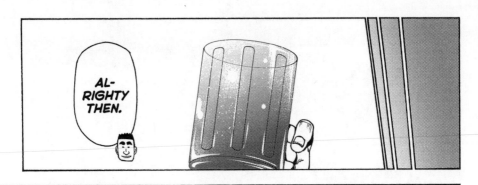

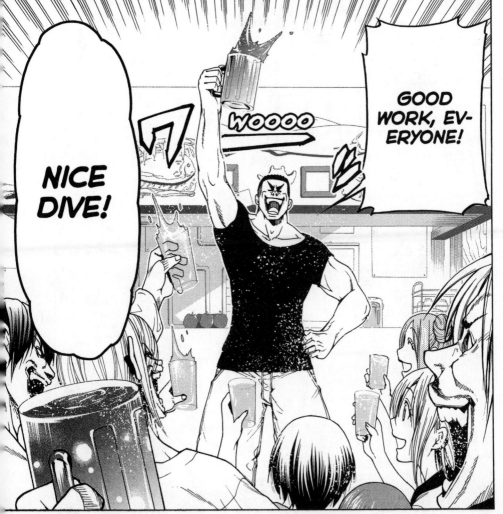

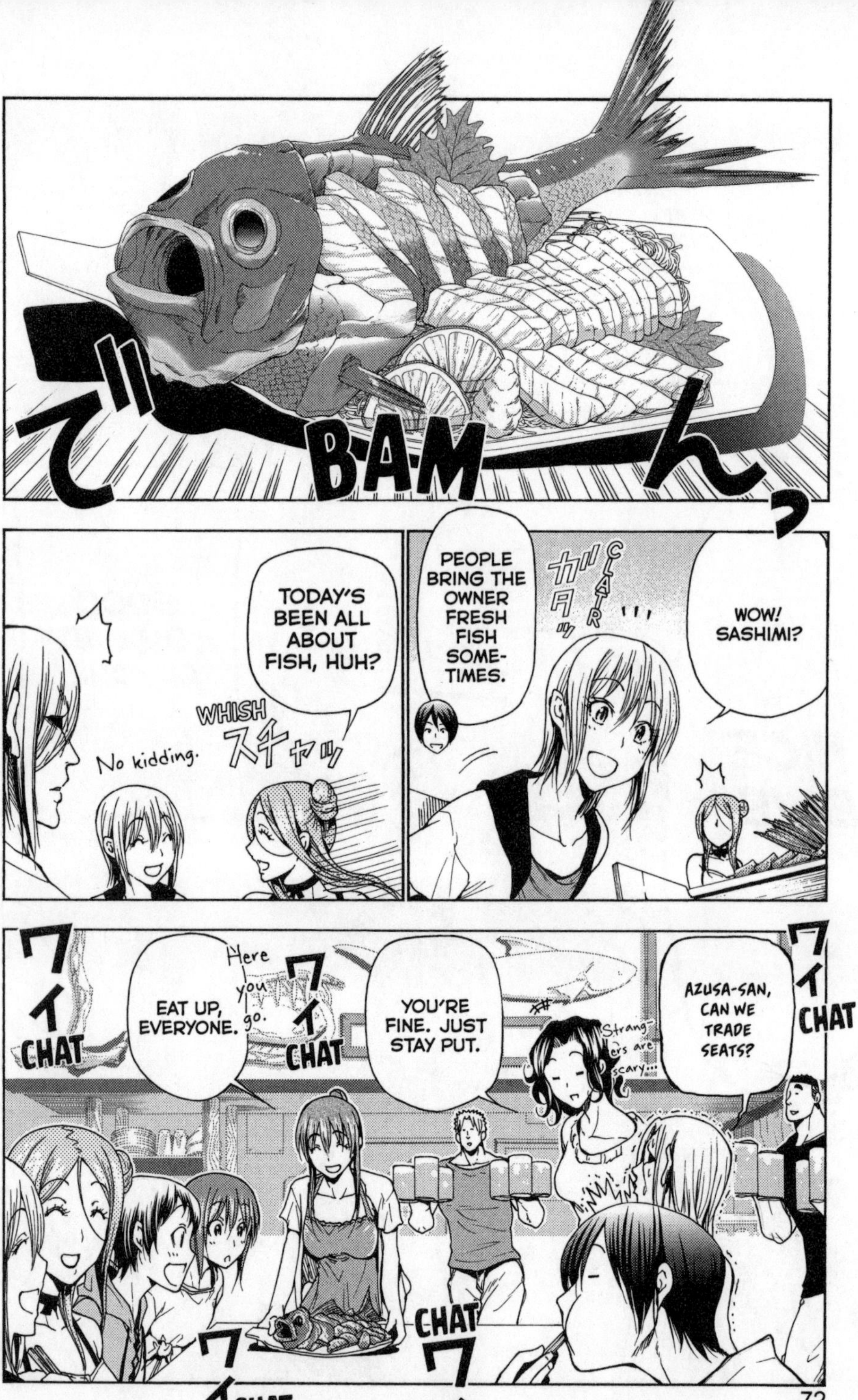
でん
BAM
WOW! SASHIMI?
カタッ
CLATR
PEOPLE BRING THE OWNER FRESH FISH SOMETIMES.
TODAY'S BEEN ALL ABOUT FISH, HUH?
スチャッ
WHISH
No kidding.
ワイ
CHAT
AZUSA-SAN, CAN WE TRADE SEATS?
Strang-ers are scary...
YOU'RE FINE. JUST STAY PUT.
ワイ
CHAT
Here you go.
EAT UP, EVERYONE.
ワイ
CHAT
CHAT
ワイ
ワイ
CHAT

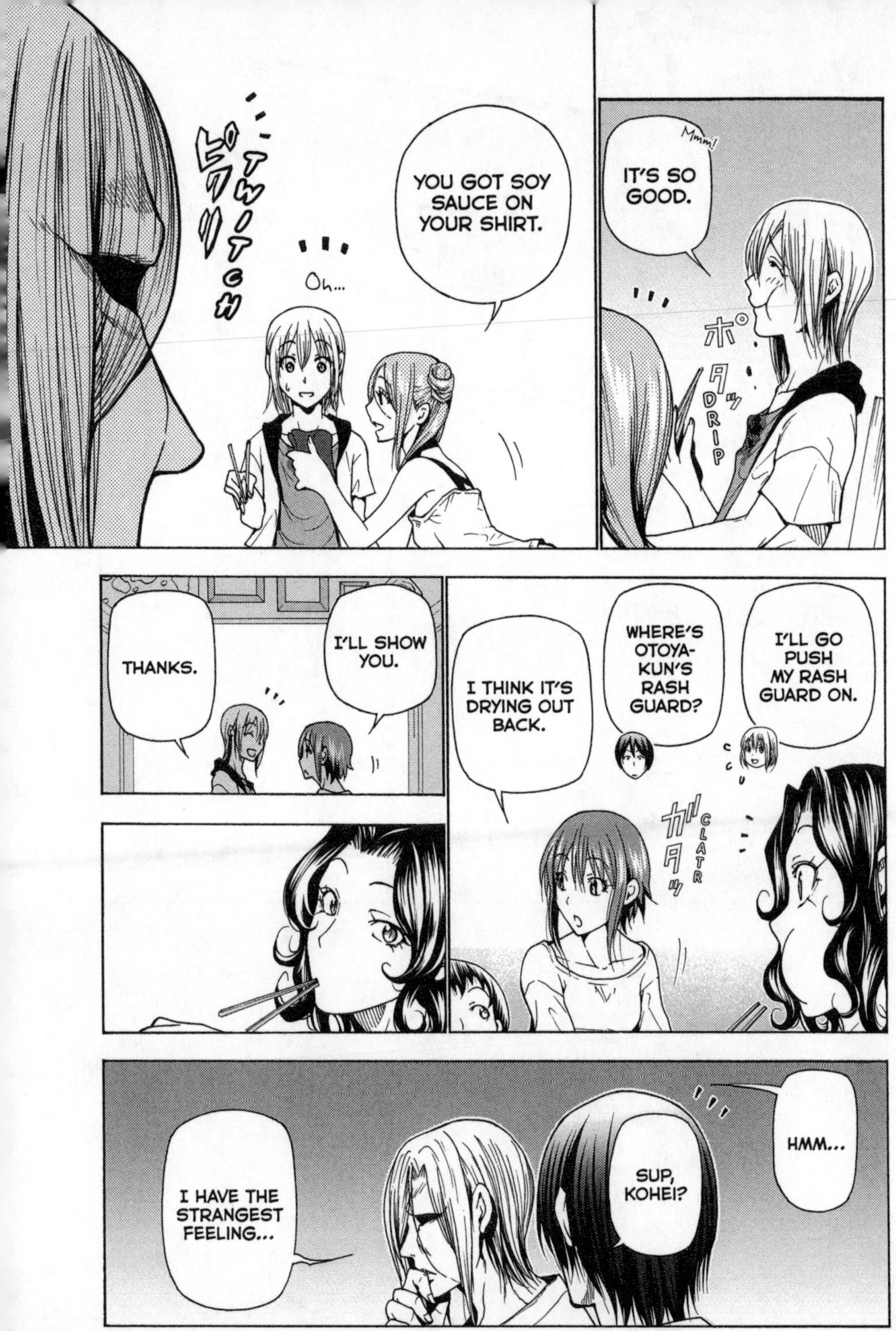
Mmm!
IT'S SO GOOD.
ポタッ
DRIP
YOU GOT SOY SAUCE ON YOUR SHIRT.
Oh...
TWITCH
I'LL GO PUSH MY RASH GUARD ON.
WHERE'S OTOYA-KUN'S RASH GUARD?
I THINK IT'S DRYING OUT BACK.
ガタッ
CLATR
I'LL SHOW YOU.
THANKS.
HMM...
SUP, KOHEI?
I HAVE THE STRANGEST FEELING...

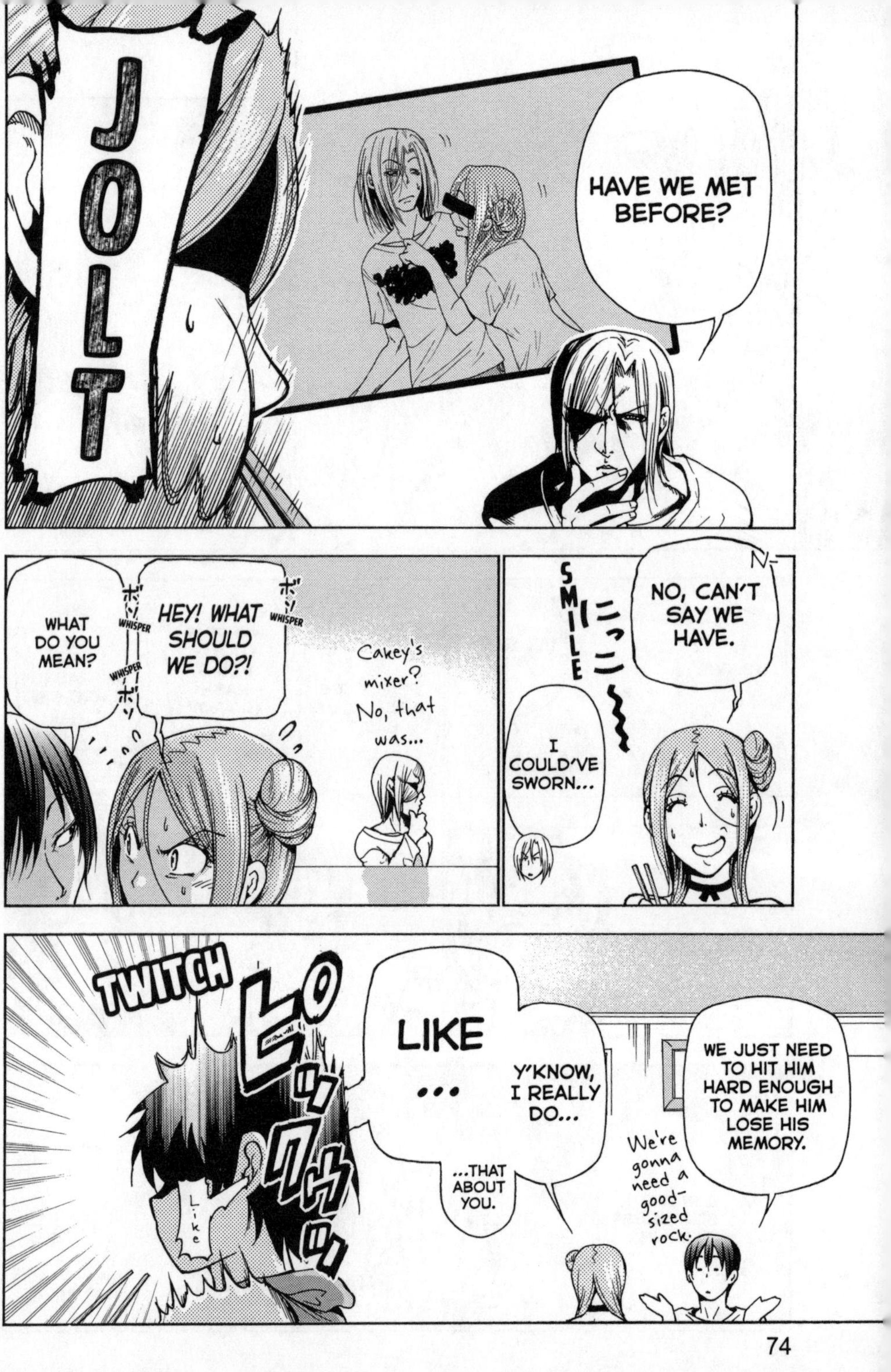
HAVE WE MET BEFORE?
JOLT
N–
NO, CAN'T SAY WE HAVE.
SMILE
にっこ〜
I COULD'VE SWORN...
Cakey's mixer? No, that was...
ボソ WHISPER
HEY! WHAT SHOULD WE DO?!
ボソ WHISPER
WHAT DO YOU MEAN?
WE JUST NEED TO HIT HIM HARD ENOUGH TO MAKE HIM LOSE HIS MEMORY.
We're gonna need a good-sized rock.
Y'KNOW, I REALLY DO...
...THAT ABOUT YOU.
LIKE ...
TWITCH
Like

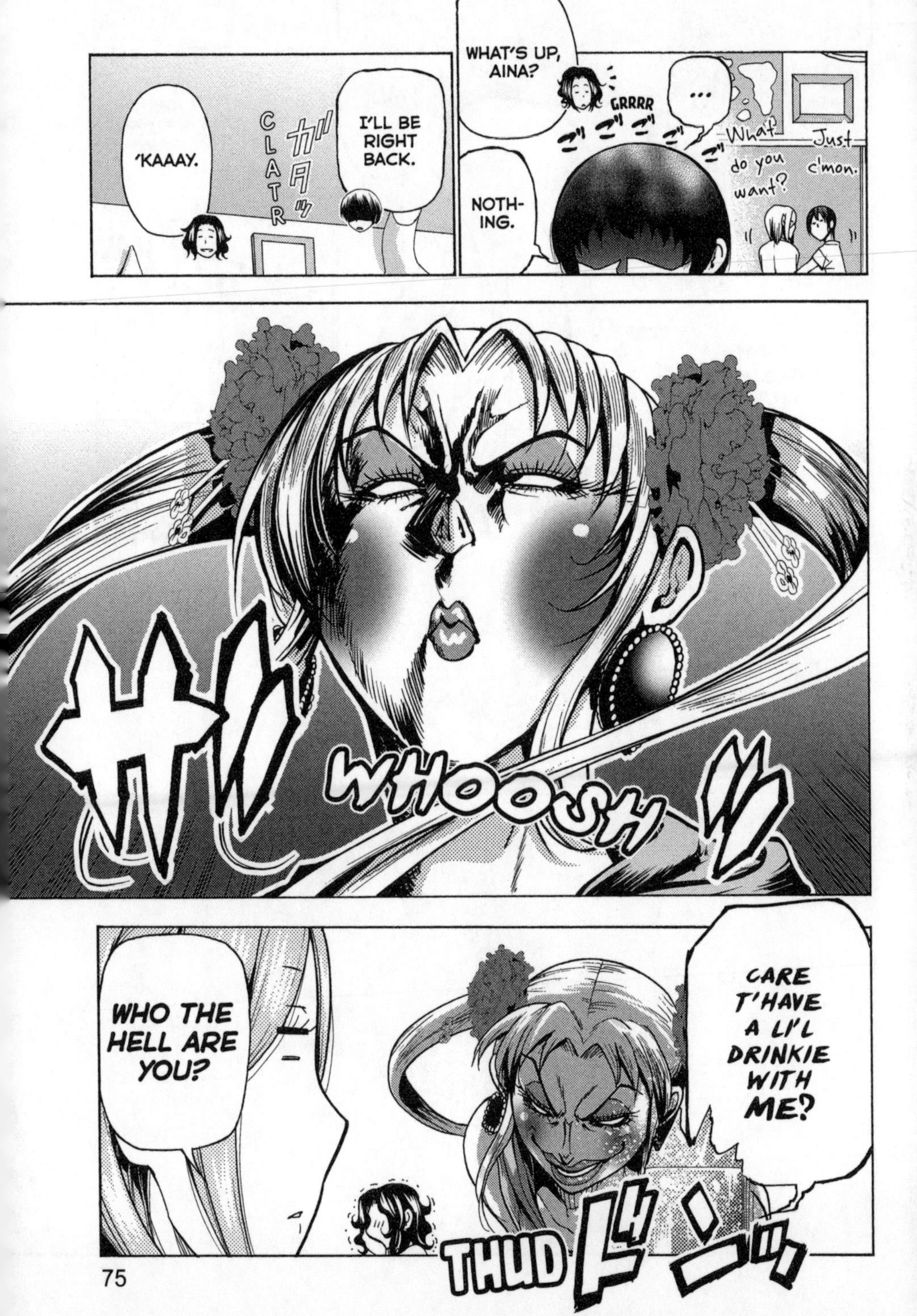
...
Just c'mon.
What do you want?
WHAT'S UP, AINA?
GRRRR
NOTHING.
I'LL BE RIGHT BACK.
CLATR
'KAAAY.
WHOOSH
CARE T'HAVE A LI'L DRINKIE WITH ME?
WHO THE HELL ARE YOU?
THUD

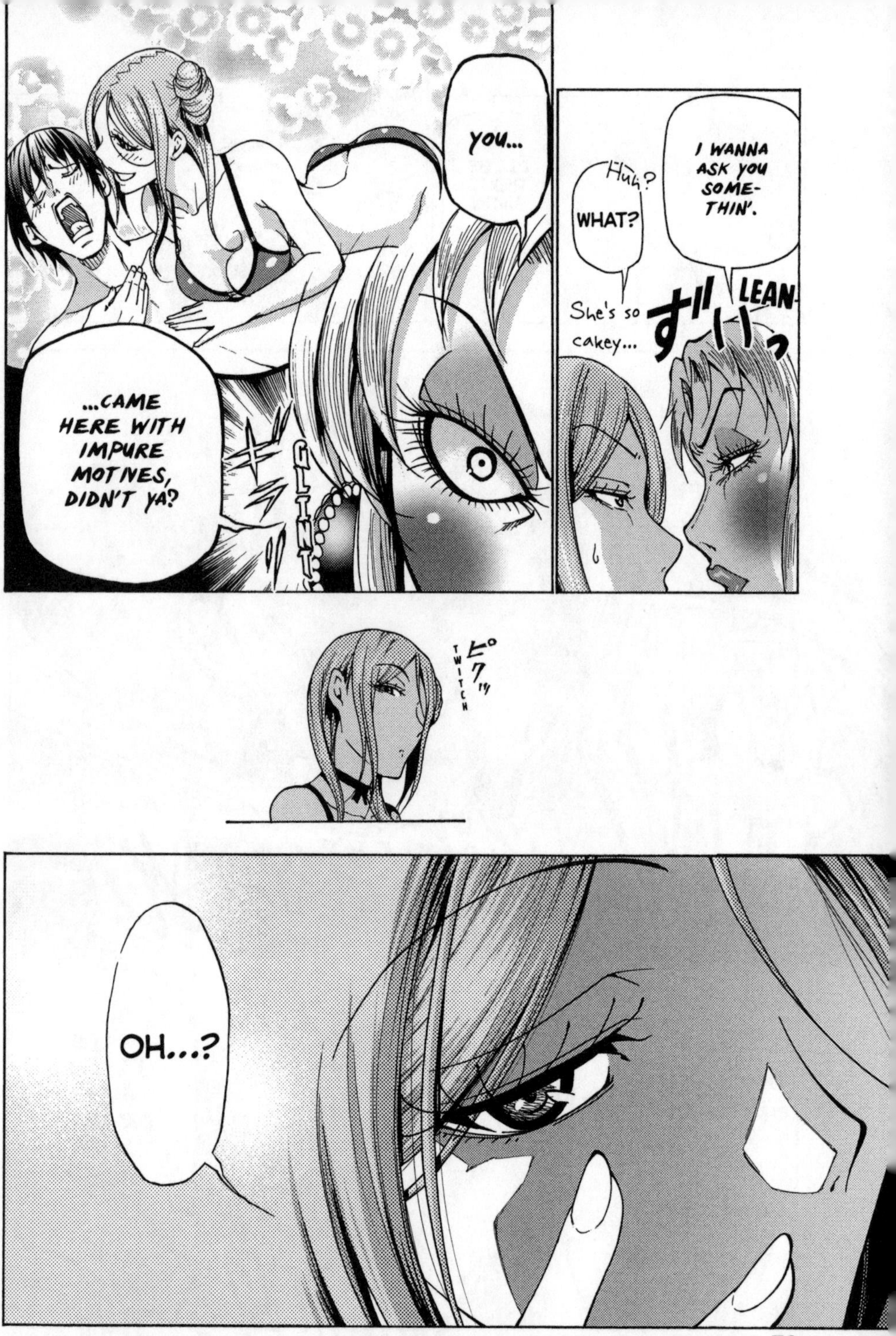
I WANNA ASK YOU SOME-THIN'.
LEAN-
Huh? WHAT?
She's so cakey...
YOU...
...CAME HERE WITH IMPURE MOTIVES, DIDN'T YA?
GLINT
TWITCH
OH...?

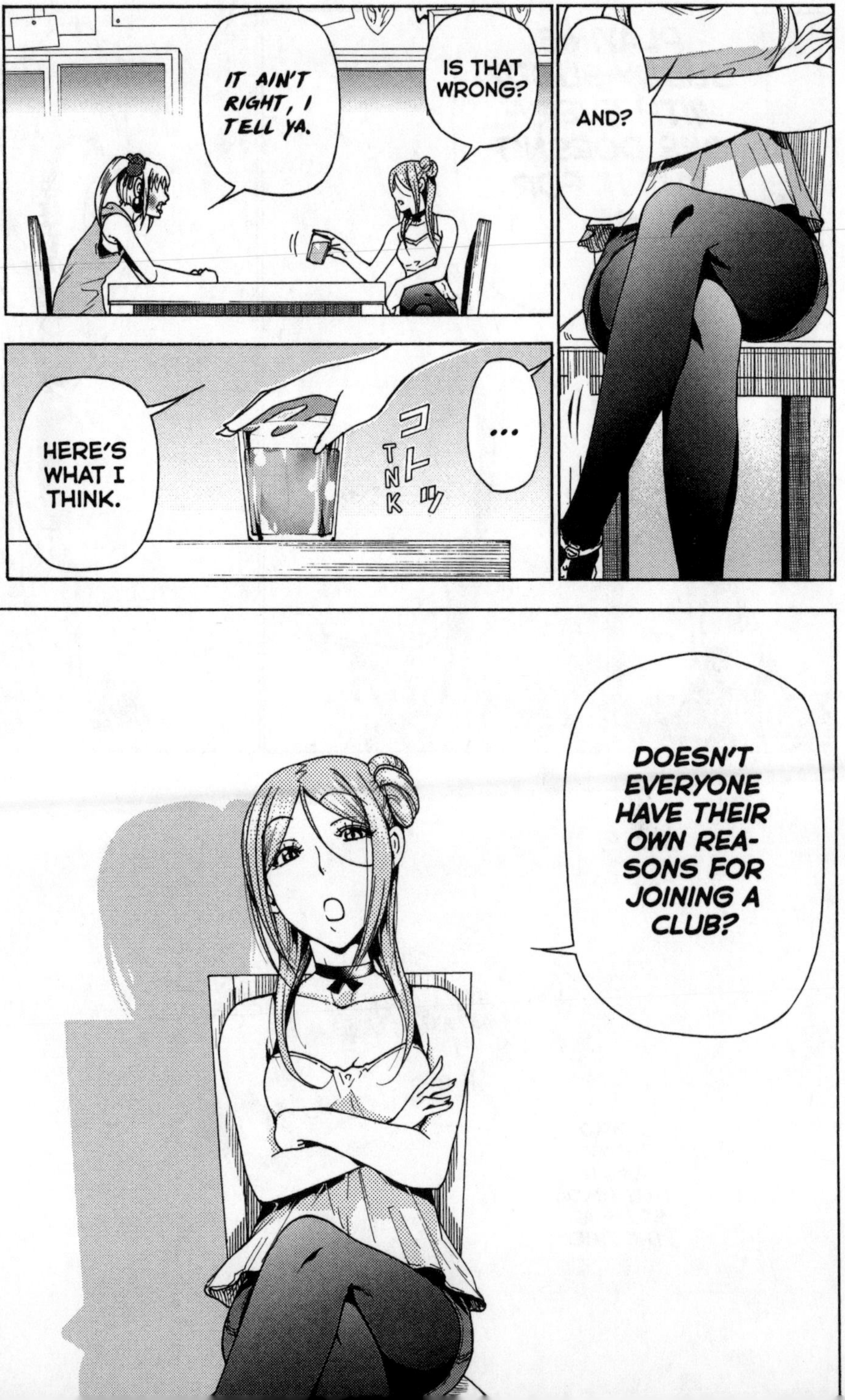
AND?
IS THAT WRONG?
IT AIN'T RIGHT, I TELL YA.
...
TNK
HERE'S WHAT I THINK.
DOESN'T EVERYONE HAVE THEIR OWN REA-SONS FOR JOINING A CLUB?

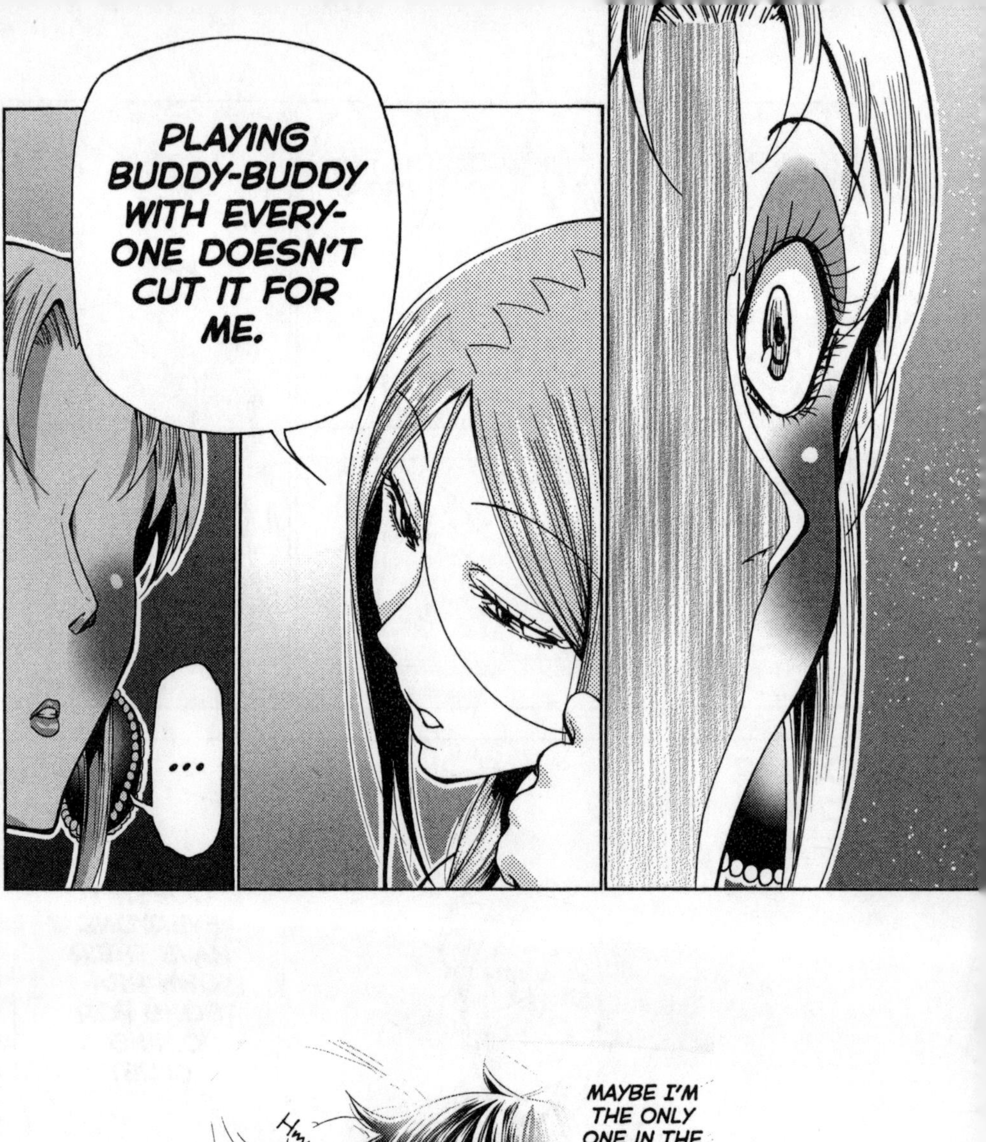
PLAYING BUDDY-BUDDY WITH EVERY-ONE DOESN'T CUT IT FOR ME.
...
MAYBE I'M THE ONLY ONE IN THE CLUB...
Hmm...
...WHO THINKS ABOUT THAT KINDA STUFF ALL THE TIME.

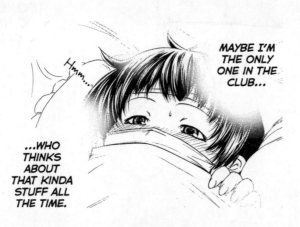

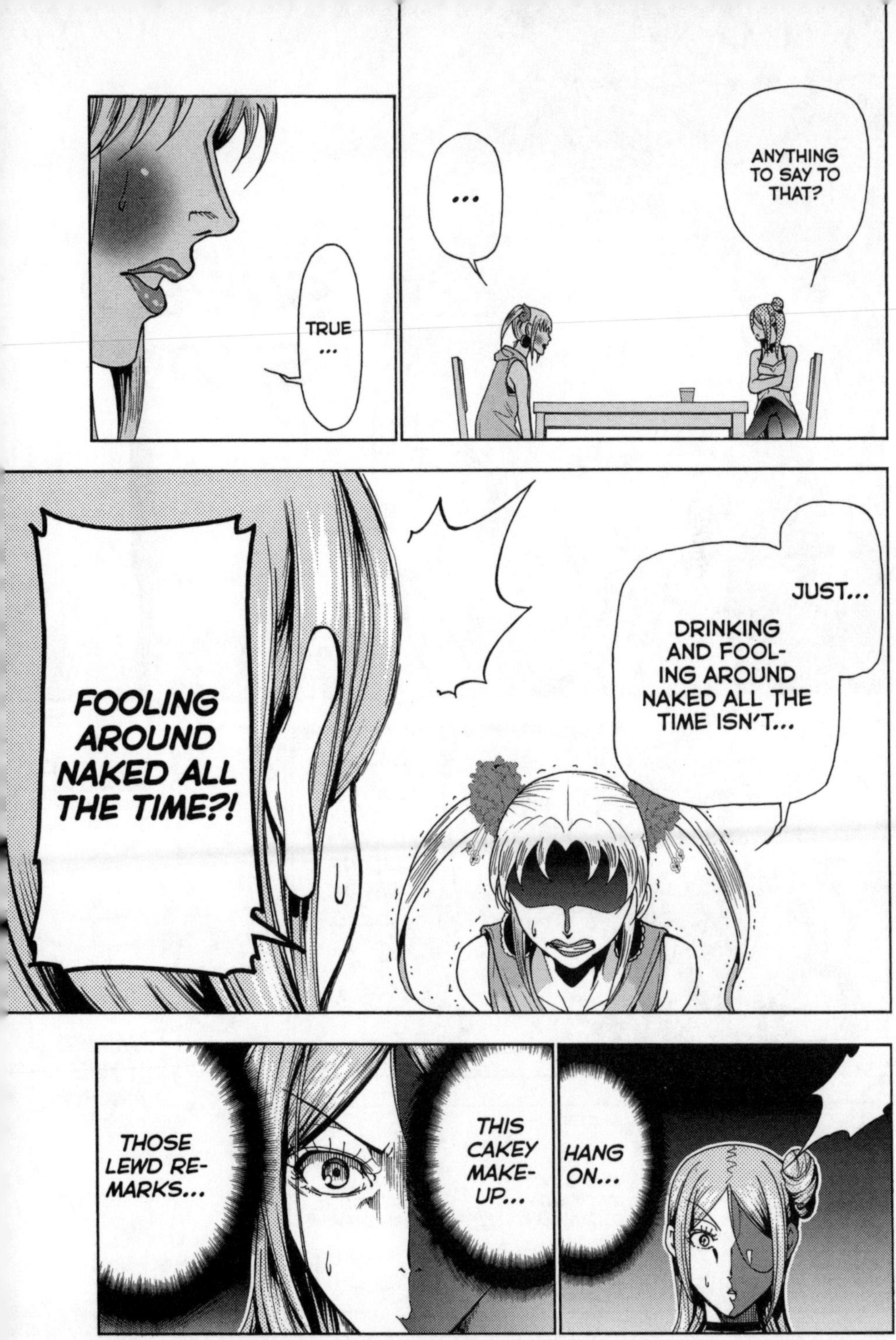
ANYTHING TO SAY TO THAT?
...
TRUE ...
JUST... DRINKING AND FOOLING AROUND NAKED ALL THE TIME ISN'T...
FOOLING AROUND NAKED ALL THE TIME?!
HANG ON...
THIS CAKEY MAKE-UP...
THOSE LEWD REMARKS...

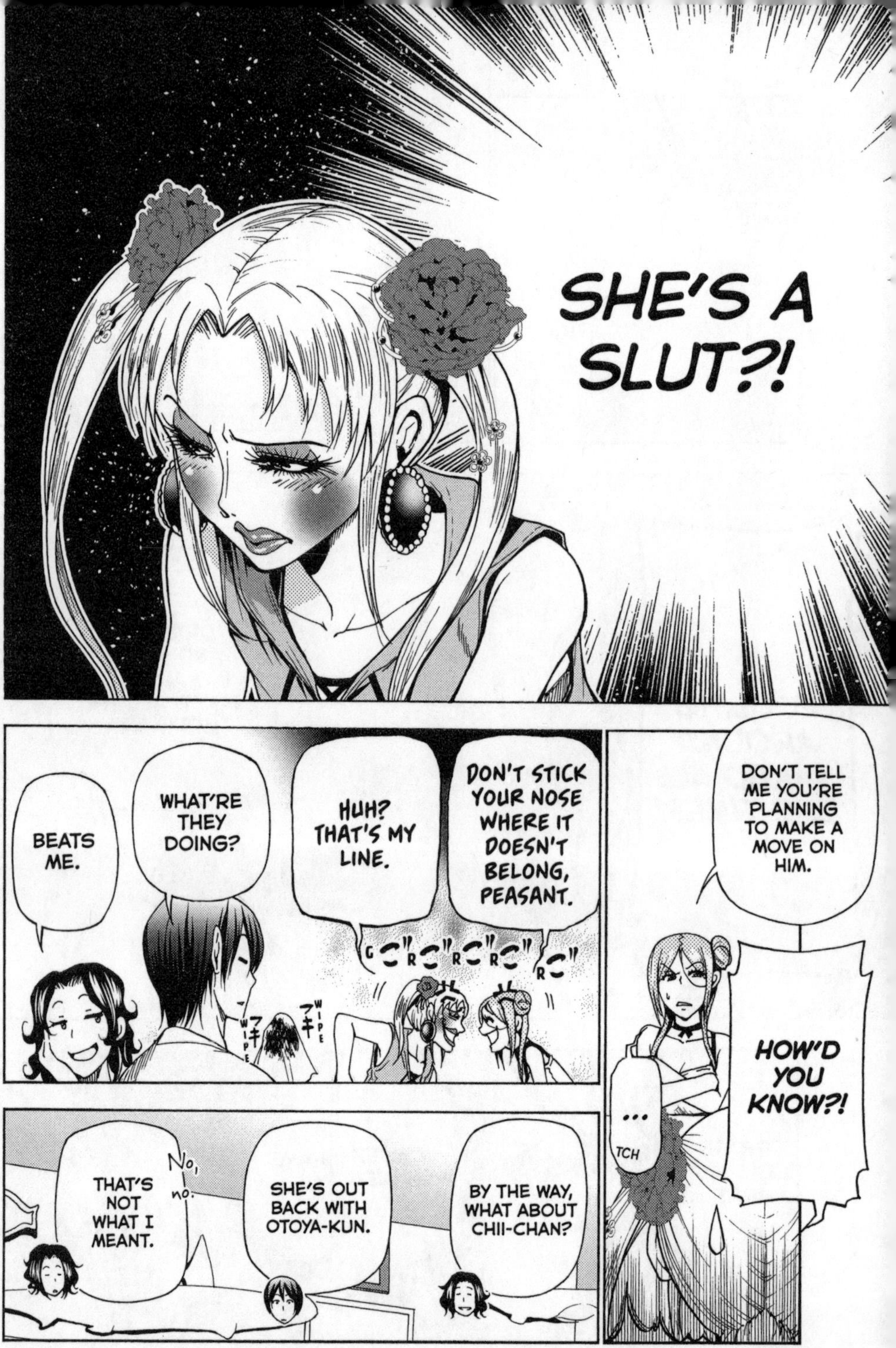
SHE'S A SLUT?!
DON'T TELL ME YOU'RE PLANNING TO MAKE A MOVE ON HIM.
HOW'D YOU KNOW?!
...
TCH
DON'T STICK YOUR NOSE WHERE IT DOESN'T BELONG, PEASANT.
HUH? THAT'S MY LINE.
GRRRRR
WHAT'RE THEY DOING?
BEATS ME.
WIPE
WIPE
BY THE WAY, WHAT ABOUT CHII-CHAN?
SHE'S OUT BACK WITH OTOYA-KUN.
No, no.
THAT'S NOT WHAT I MEANT.

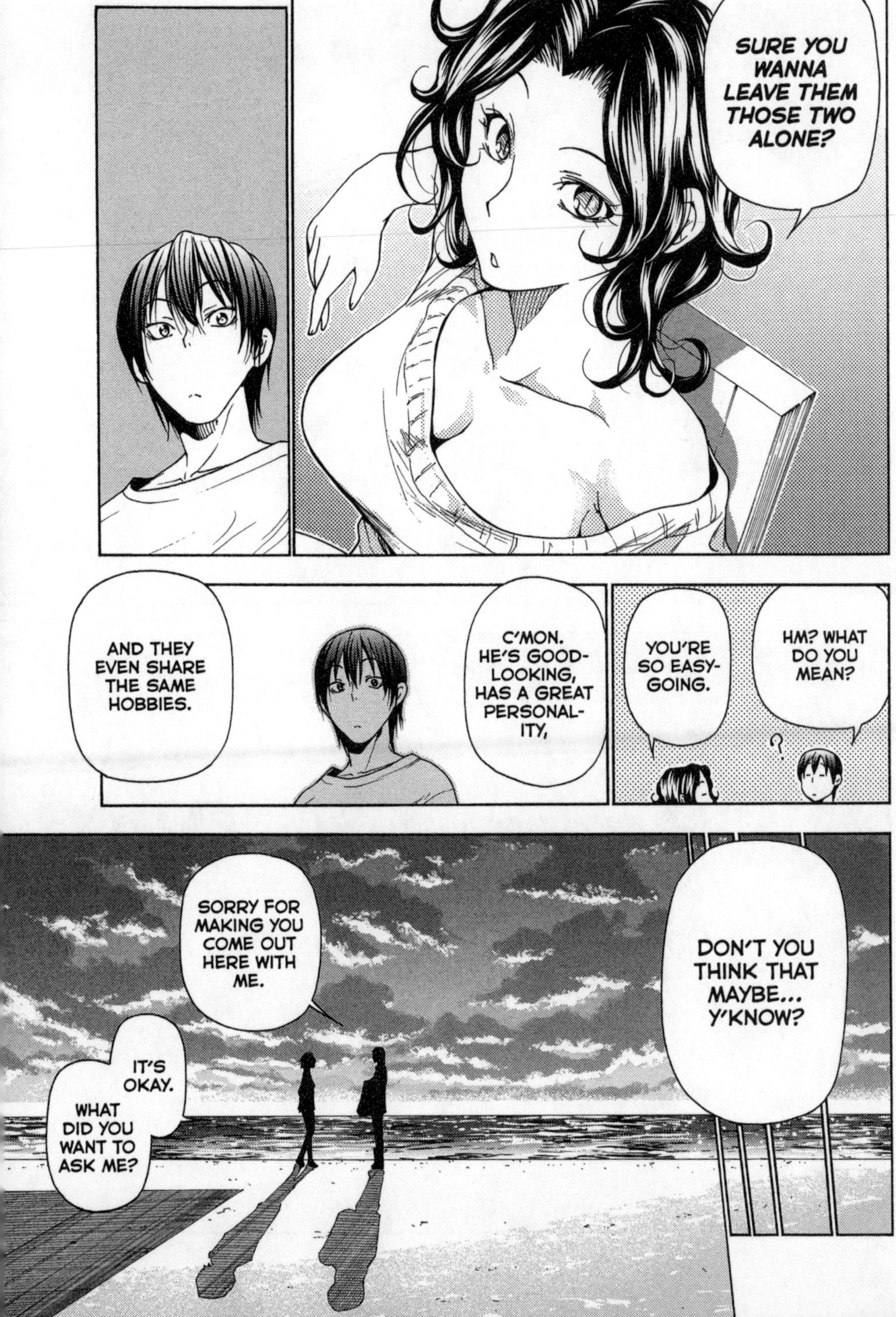
SURE YOU WANNA LEAVE THEM THOSE TWO ALONE?
HM? WHAT DO YOU MEAN?
YOU'RE SO EASY-GOING.
C'MON. HE'S GOOD-LOOKING, HAS A GREAT PERSONAL-ITY,
AND THEY EVEN SHARE THE SAME HOBBIES.
DON'T YOU THINK THAT MAYBE... Y'KNOW?
SORRY FOR MAKING YOU COME OUT HERE WITH ME.
IT'S OKAY.
WHAT DID YOU WANT TO ASK ME?

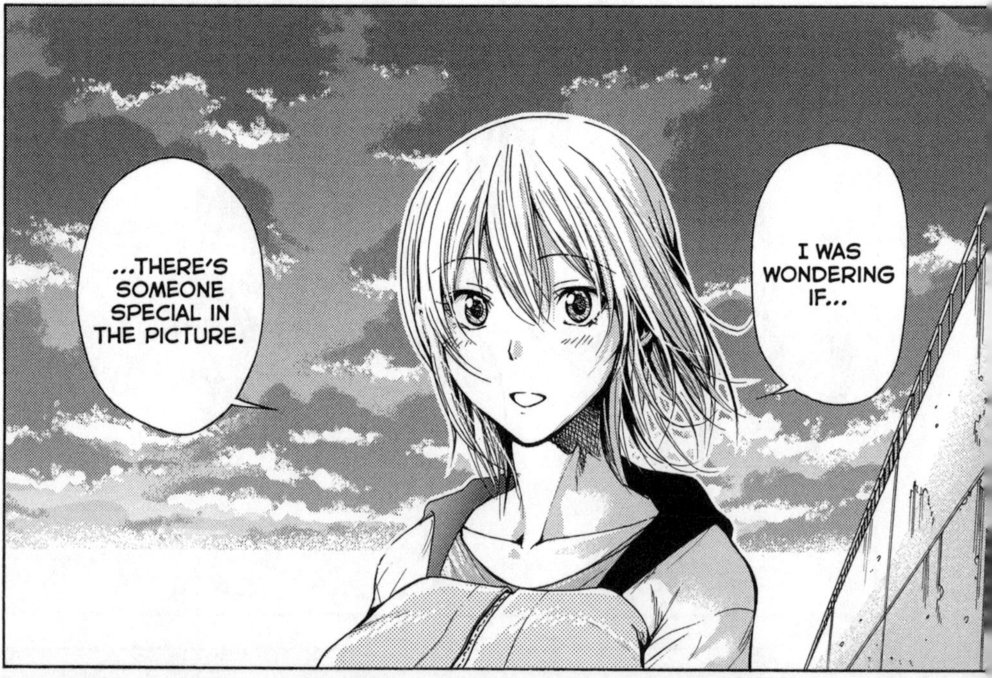
I WAS WONDERING IF...
...THERE'S SOMEONE SPECIAL IN THE PICTURE.
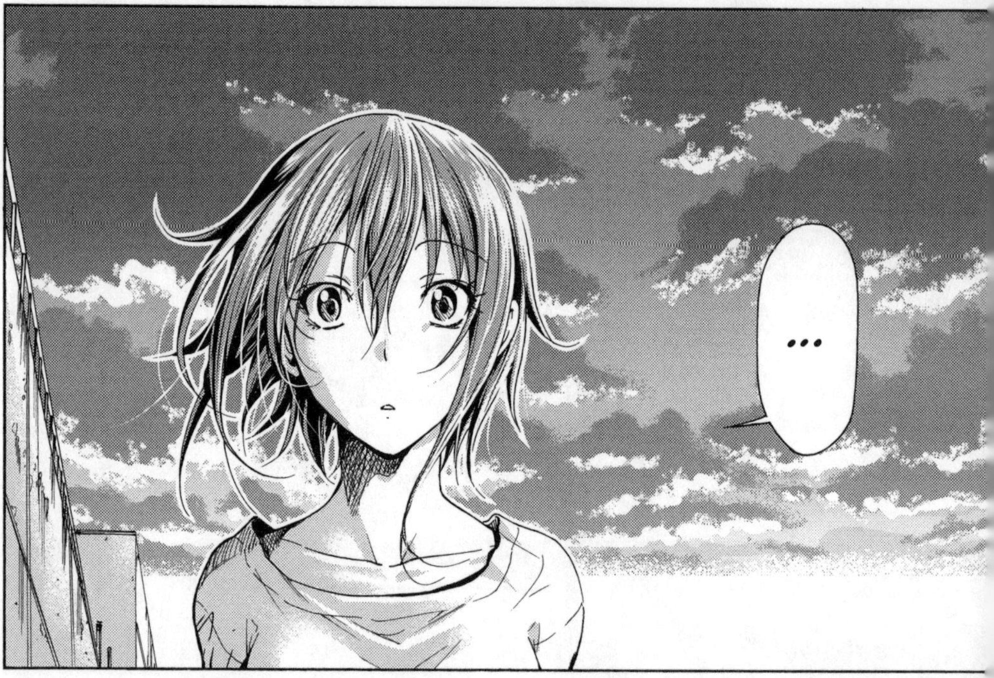
...

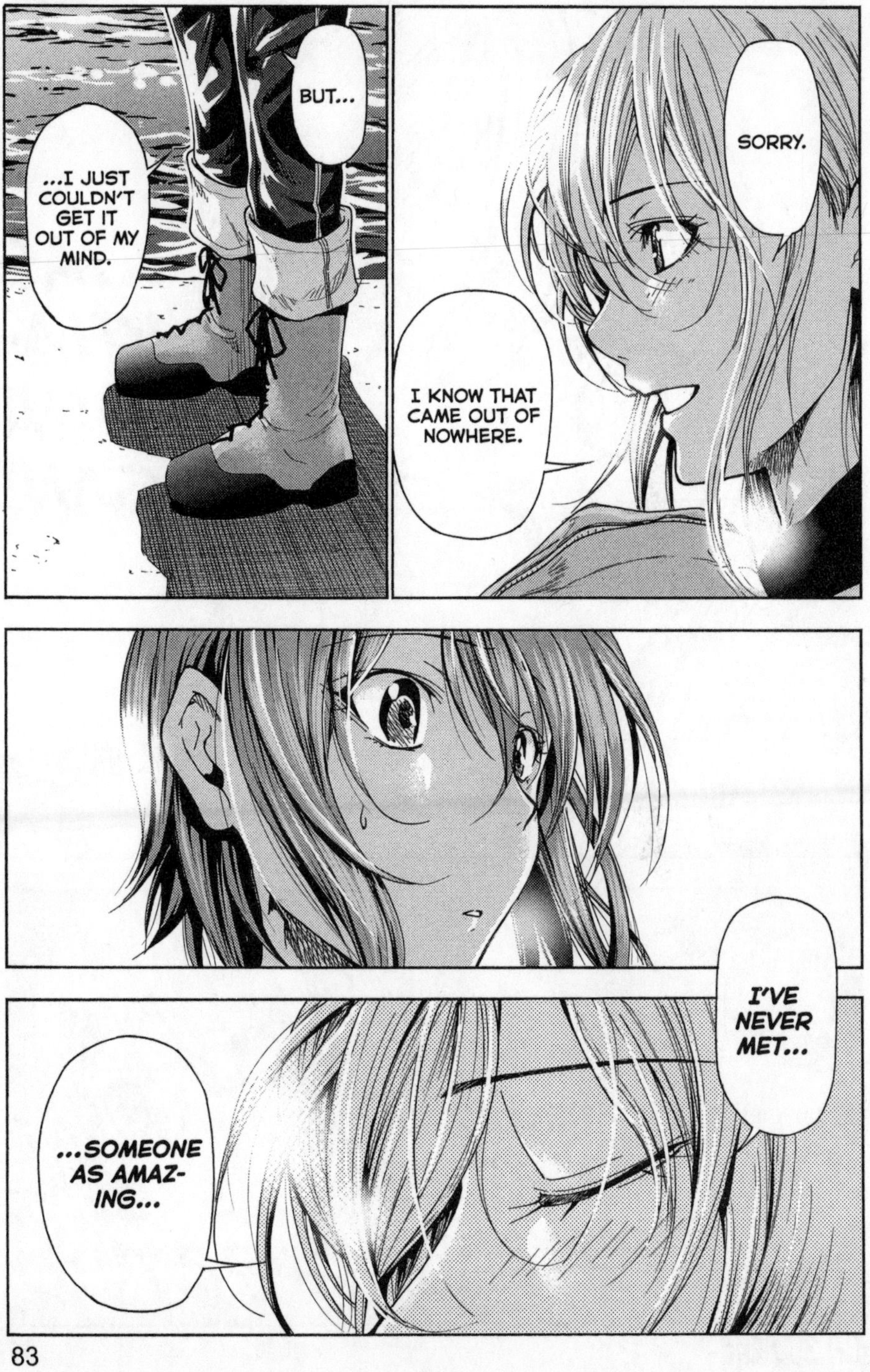
SORRY.
I KNOW THAT CAME OUT OF NOWHERE.
BUT...
...I JUST COULDN'T GET IT OUT OF MY MIND.
I'VE NEVER MET...
...SOMEONE AS AMAZ-ING...

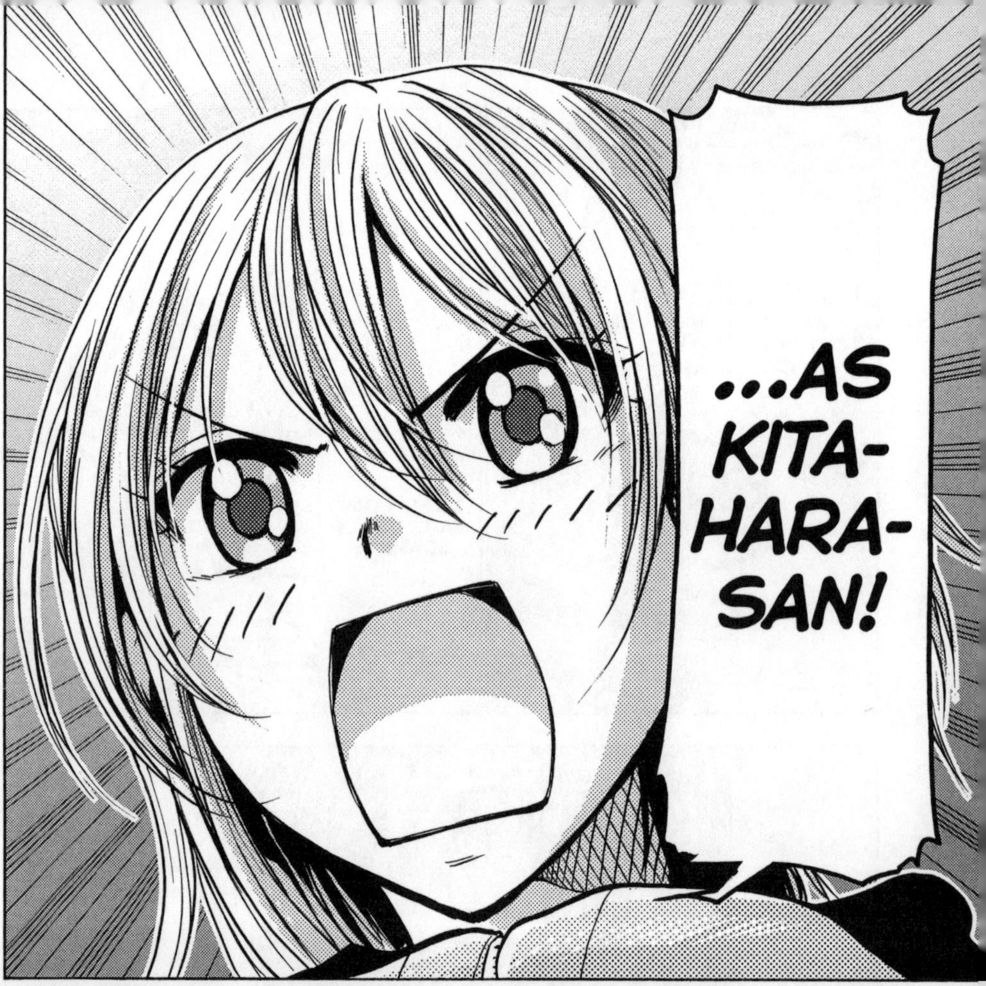
...AS KITA-HARA-SAN!

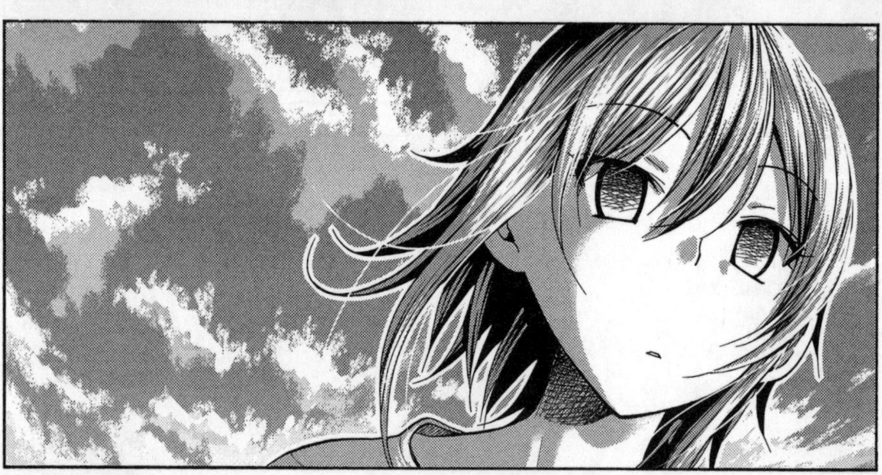

CH.35 / End

Thought he was confessing. Huh?

Shame? = Iori = Amazing?

Him?

The sunset's so bright...

And I finally made a diving friend, too.

Some-one, any-one...

Short-circuited

Grand Blue
Dreaming

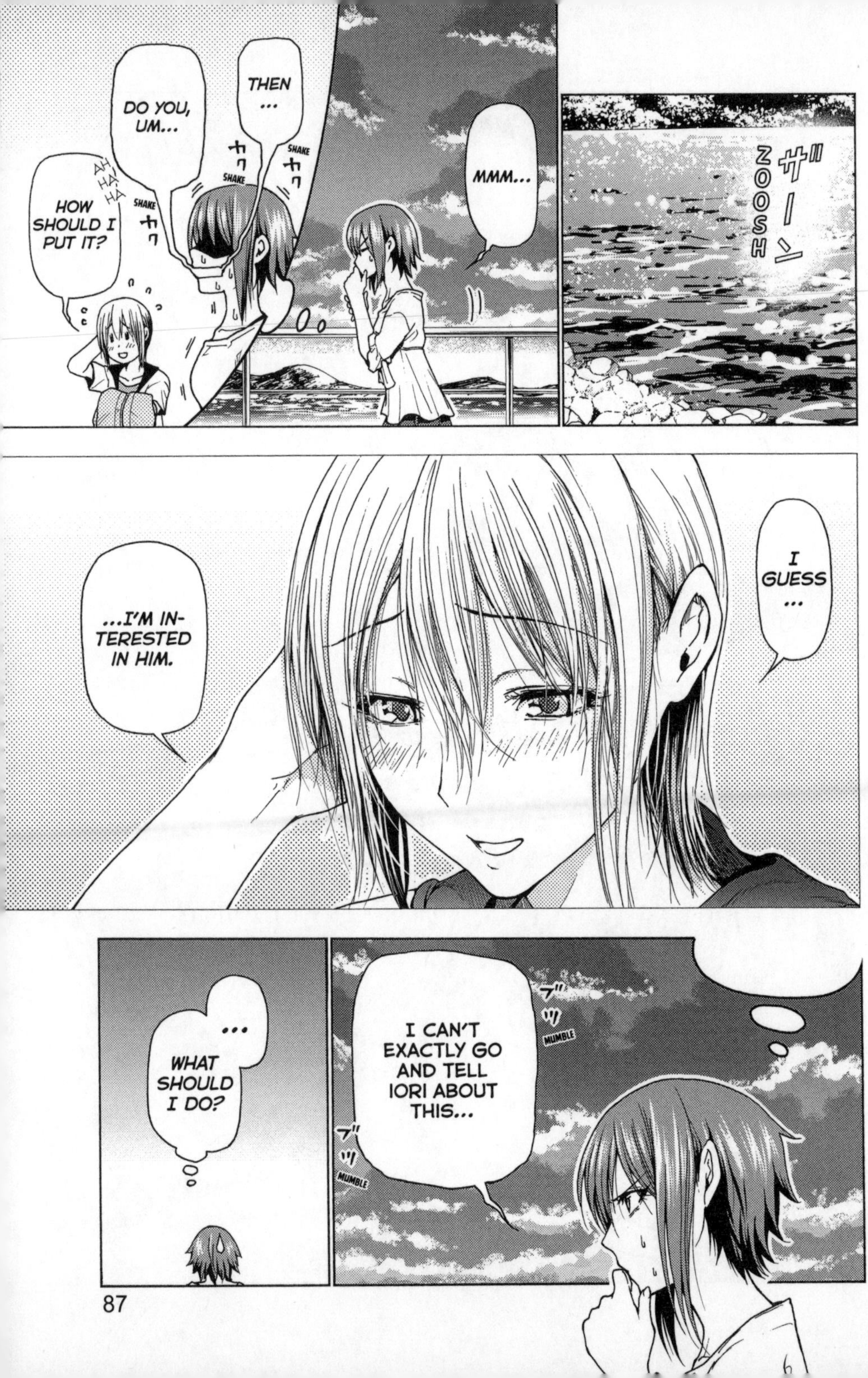
ZOOSH
MMM...
THEN ...
SHAKE
SHAKE
DO YOU, UM...
SHAKE
AH HA HA
HOW SHOULD I PUT IT?
I GUESS ...
...I'M INTERESTED IN HIM.
MUMBLE
I CAN'T EXACTLY GO AND TELL IORI ABOUT THIS...
MUMBLE
... WHAT SHOULD I DO?

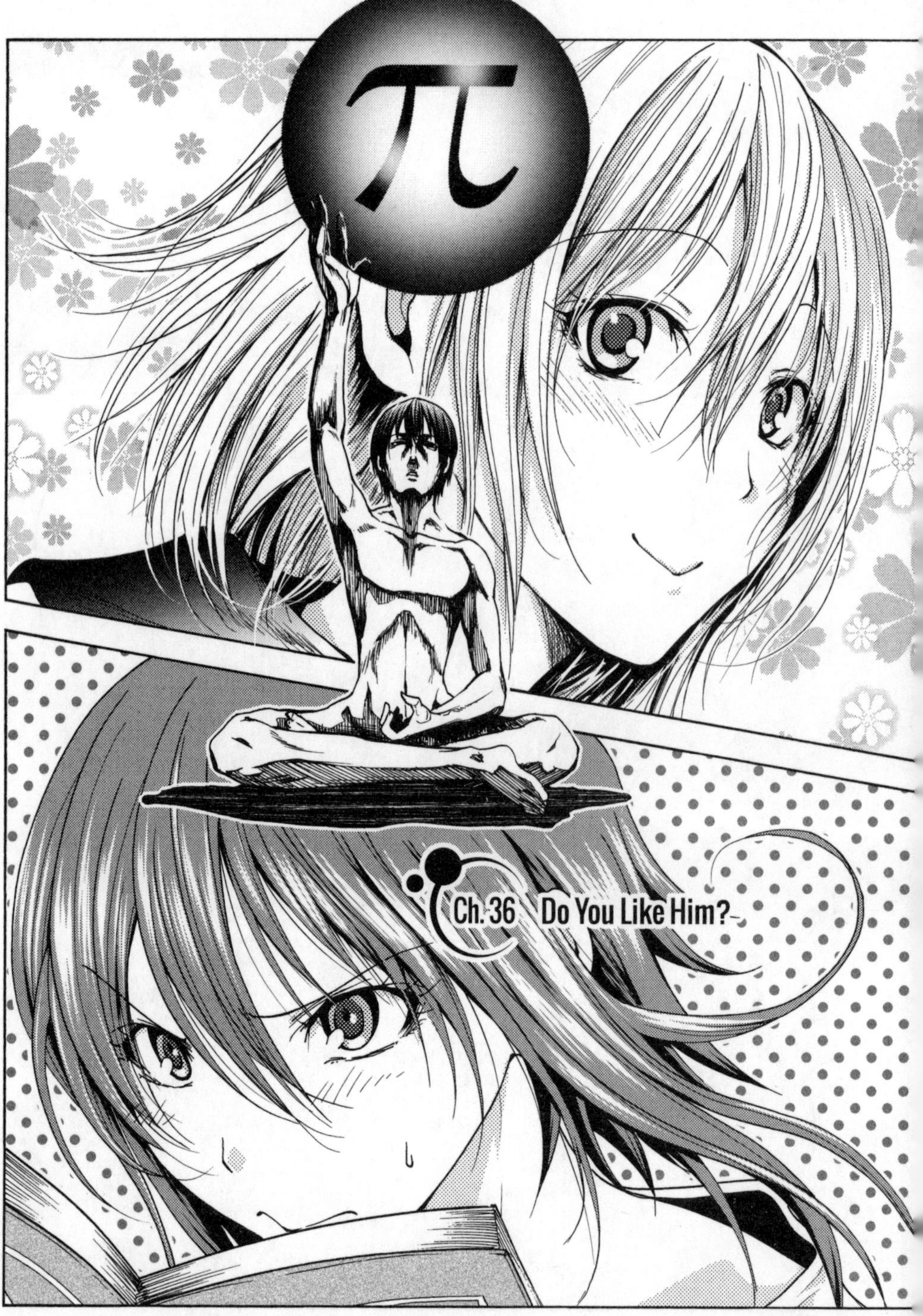
π
Ch. 36 Do You Like Him?

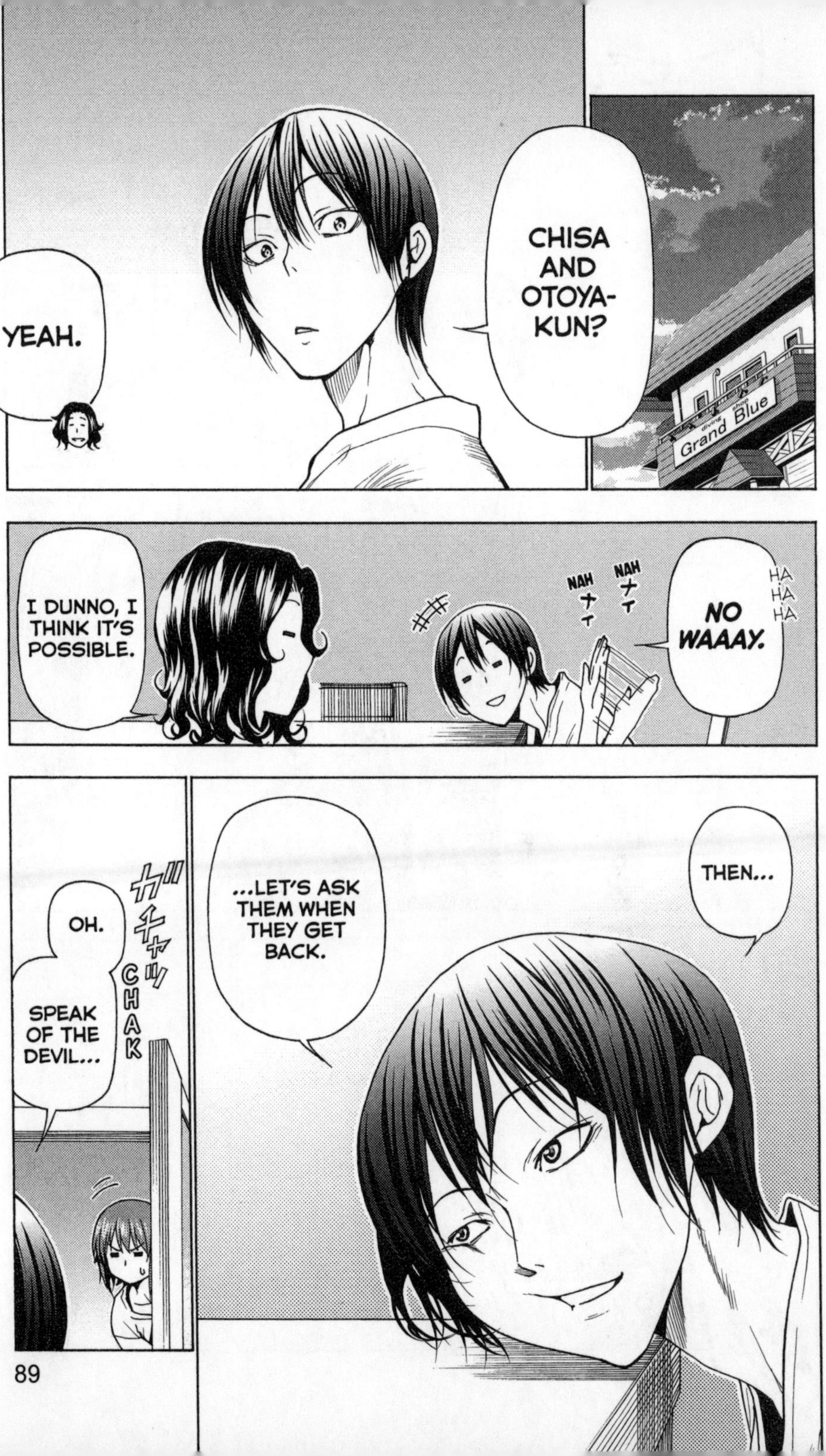
diving shop Grand Blue
CHISA AND OTOYA-KUN?
YEAH.
HA HA HA
NO WAAAY.
NAH ナイ NAH ナイ
I DUNNO, I THINK IT'S POSSIBLE.
THEN...
...LET'S ASK THEM WHEN THEY GET BACK.
ガチャッ CHAK
OH.
SPEAK OF THE DEVIL...

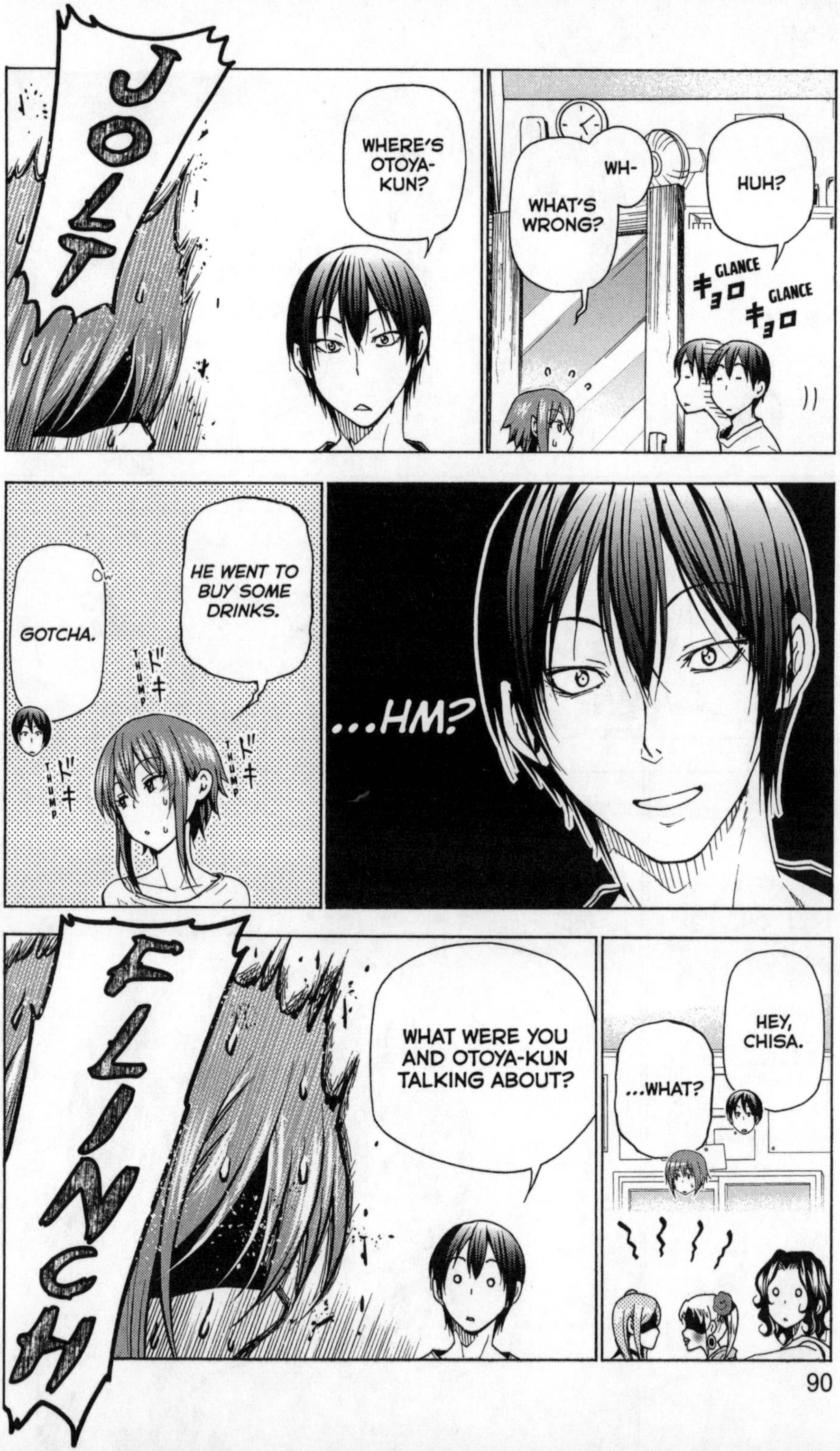
HUH?
GLANCE キョロ
GLANCE キョロ
WH- WHAT'S WRONG?
WHERE'S OTOYA-KUN?
JOLT
...HM?
HE WENT TO BUY SOME DRINKS.
THUMP ドキ
THUMP ドキ
Oh
GOTCHA.
HEY, CHISA.
...WHAT?
WHAT WERE YOU AND OTOYA-KUN TALKING ABOUT?
FLINCH

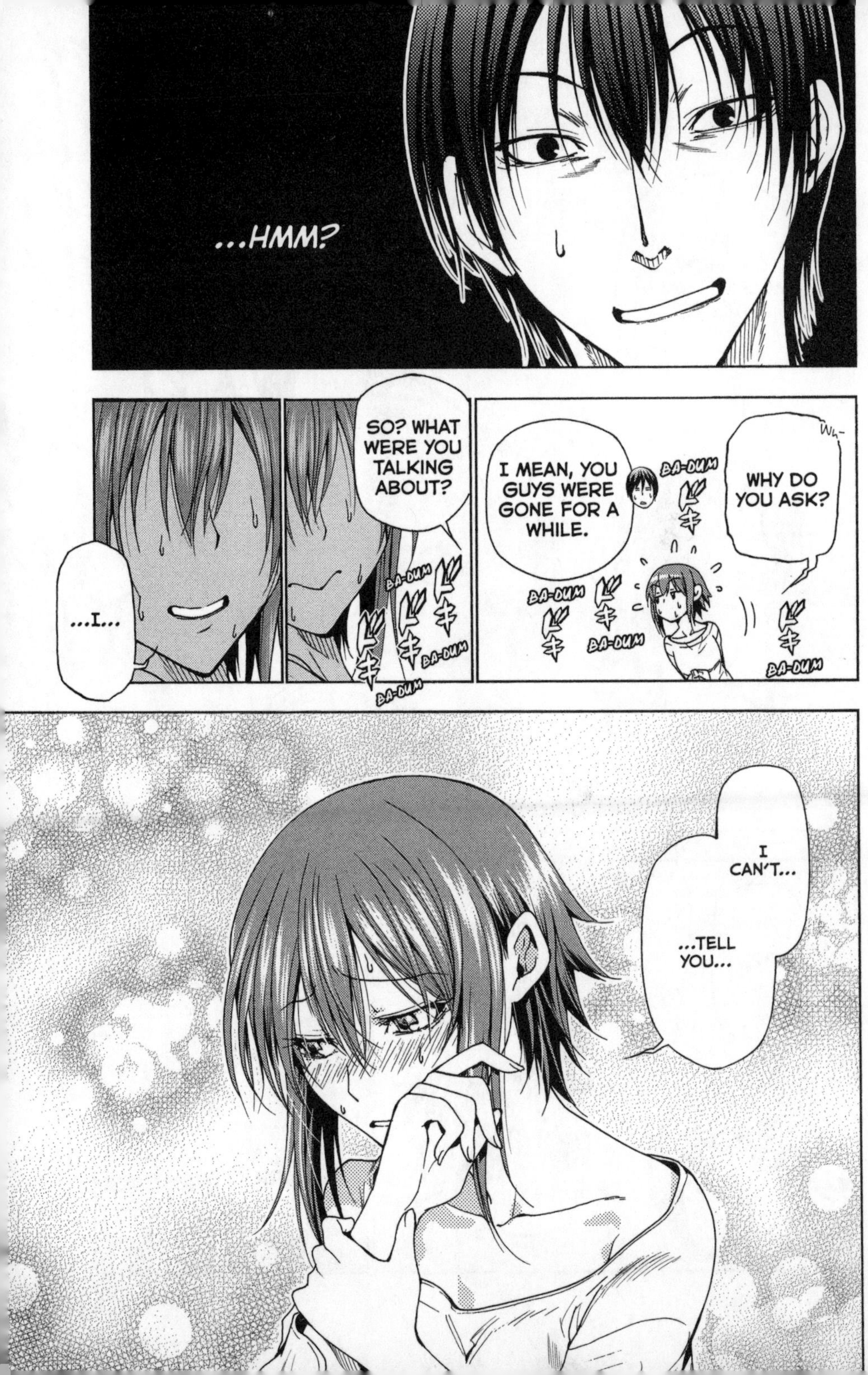
...HMM?
WHY DO YOU ASK?
BA-DUM
BA-DUM
I MEAN, YOU GUYS WERE GONE FOR A WHILE.
BA-DUM
BA-DUM
SO? WHAT WERE YOU TALKING ABOUT?
BA-DUM
BA-DUM
...I...
I CAN'T...
...TELL YOU...

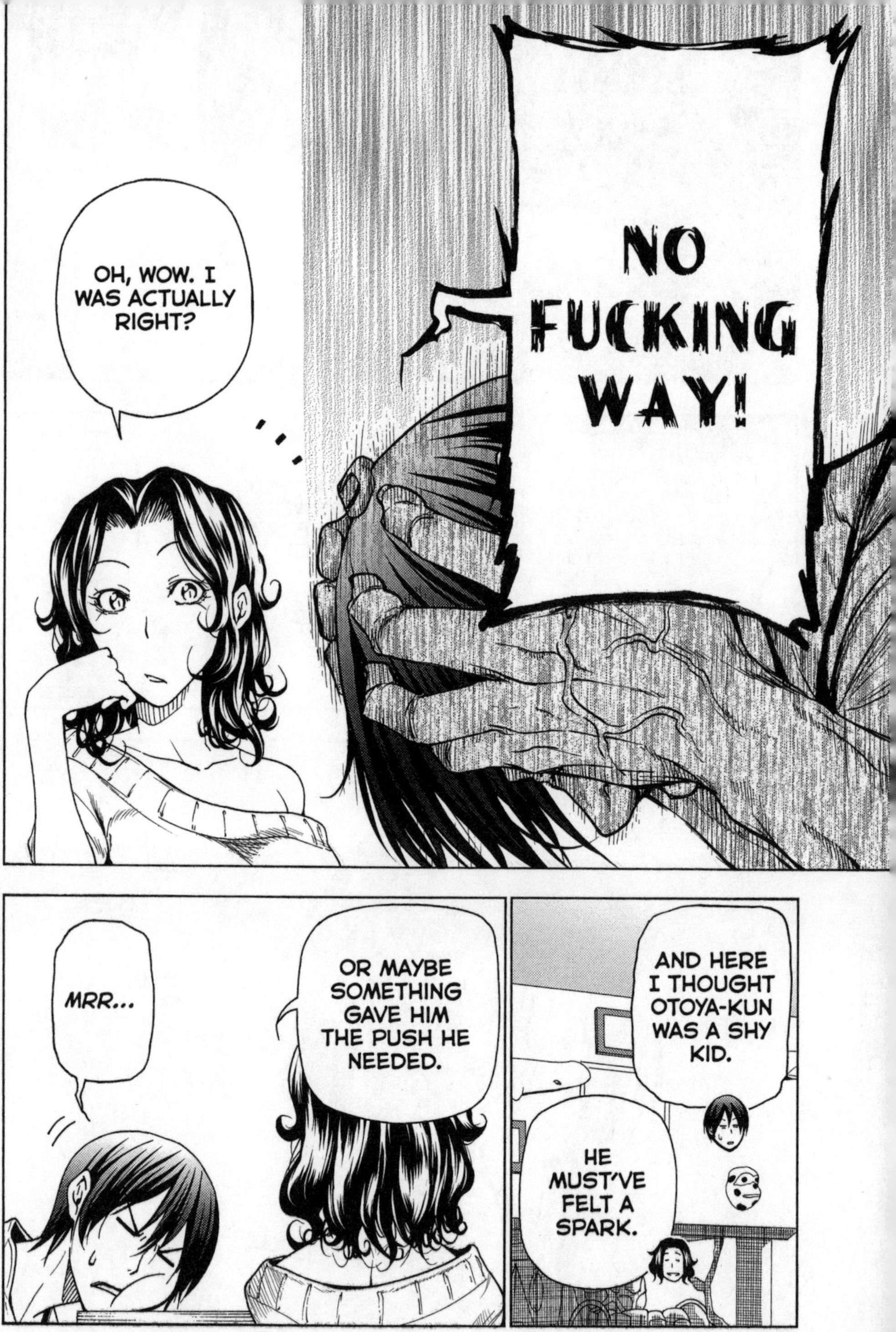
NO FUCKING WAY!
OH, WOW. I WAS ACTUALLY RIGHT?
...
AND HERE I THOUGHT OTOYA-KUN WAS A SHY KID.
HE MUST'VE FELT A SPARK.
OR MAYBE SOMETHING GAVE HIM THE PUSH HE NEEDED.
MRR...

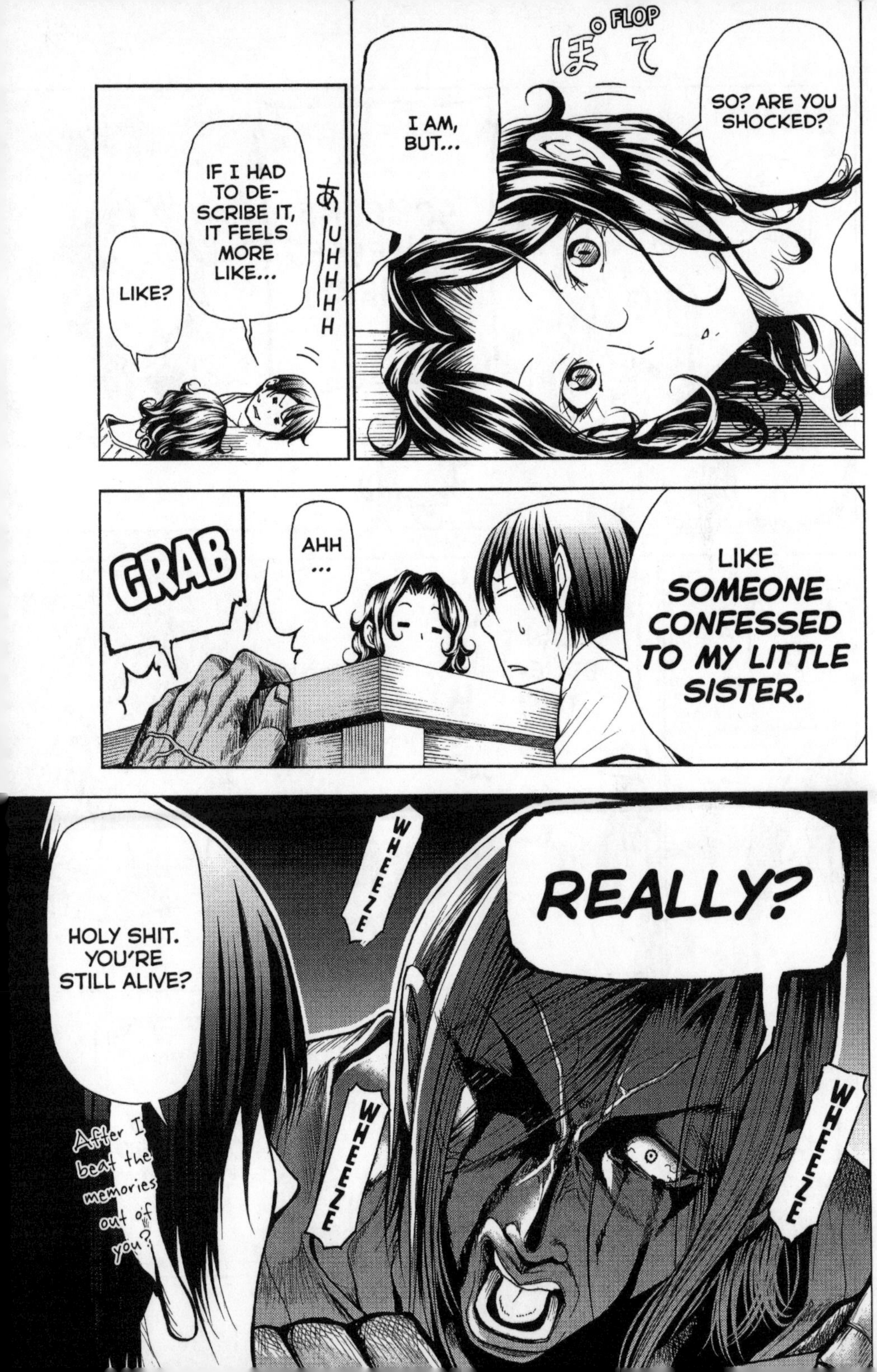
ぽて FLOP
SO? ARE YOU SHOCKED?
I AM, BUT...
IF I HAD TO DE-SCRIBE IT, IT FEELS MORE LIKE...
あ UHHHHHH
LIKE?
LIKE SOMEONE CONFESSED TO MY LITTLE SISTER.
AHH ...
GRAB
REALLY?
WHEEZE
HOLY SHIT. YOU'RE STILL ALIVE?
After I beat the memories out of you?
WHEEZE
WHEEZE

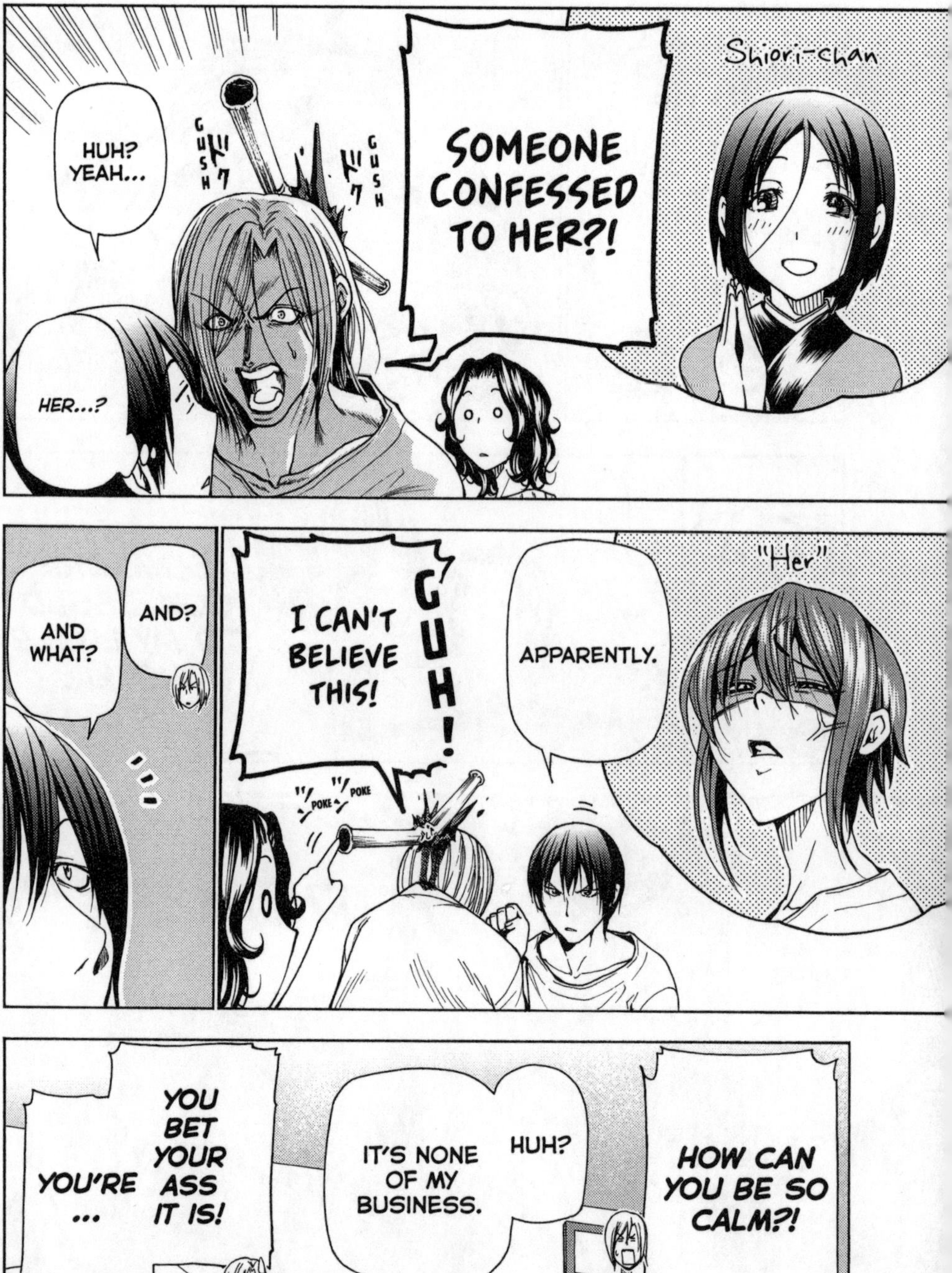
Shiori-chan
SOMEONE CONFESSED TO HER?!
GUSH
GUSH
HUH? YEAH...
HER...?
"Her"
APPARENTLY.
GUH!
I CAN'T BELIEVE THIS!
POKE POKE
AND?
AND WHAT?
...
HOW CAN YOU BE SO CALM?!
HUH?
IT'S NONE OF MY BUSINESS.
YOU BET YOUR ASS IT IS!
YOU'RE ...

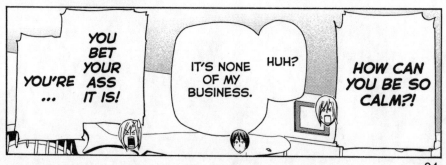

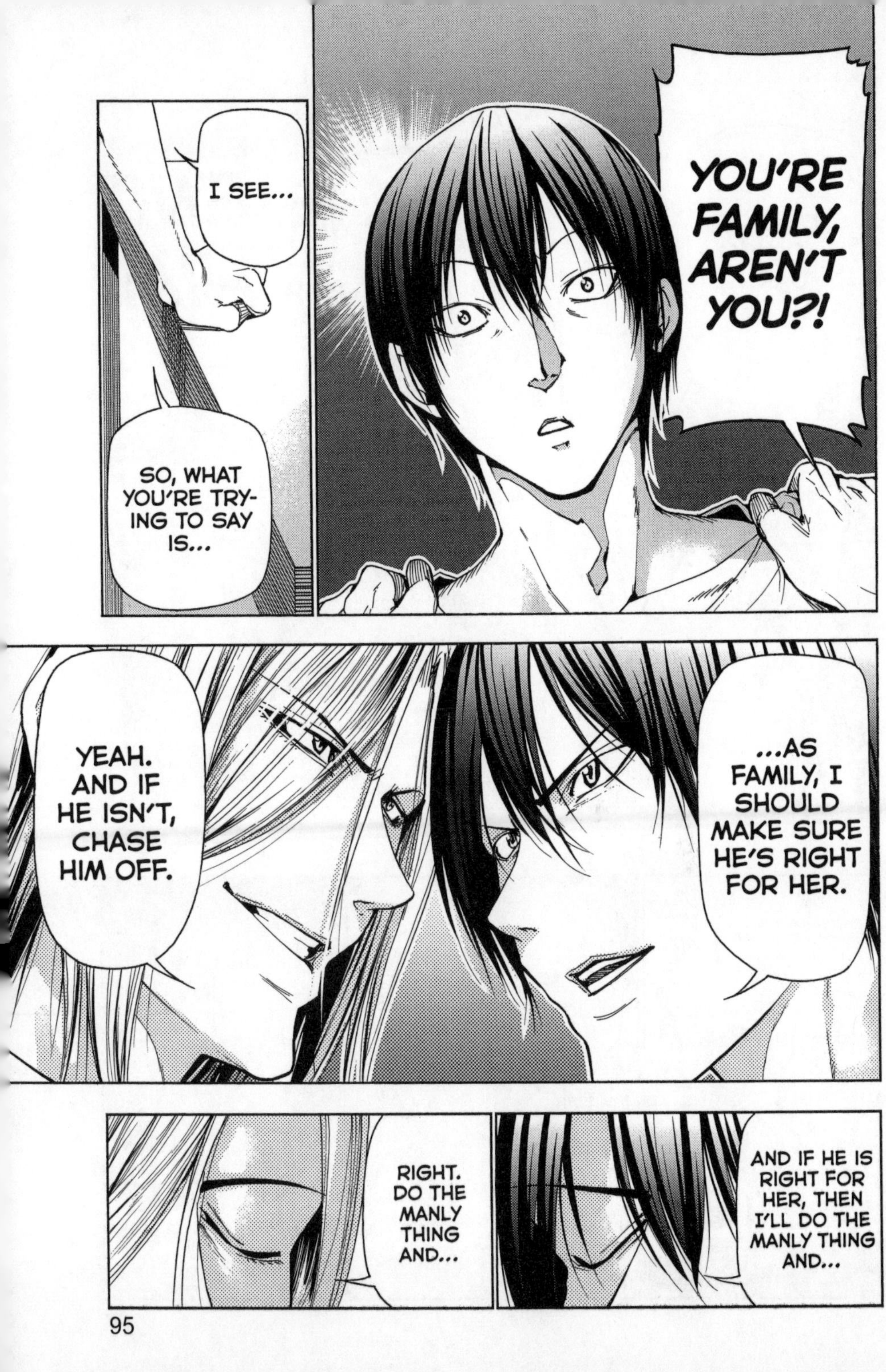
YOU'RE FAMILY, AREN'T YOU?!
I SEE...
SO, WHAT YOU'RE TRY-ING TO SAY IS...
...AS FAMILY, I SHOULD MAKE SURE HE'S RIGHT FOR HER.
YEAH. AND IF HE ISN'T, CHASE HIM OFF.
AND IF HE IS RIGHT FOR HER, THEN I'LL DO THE MANLY THING AND...
RIGHT. DO THE MANLY THING AND...

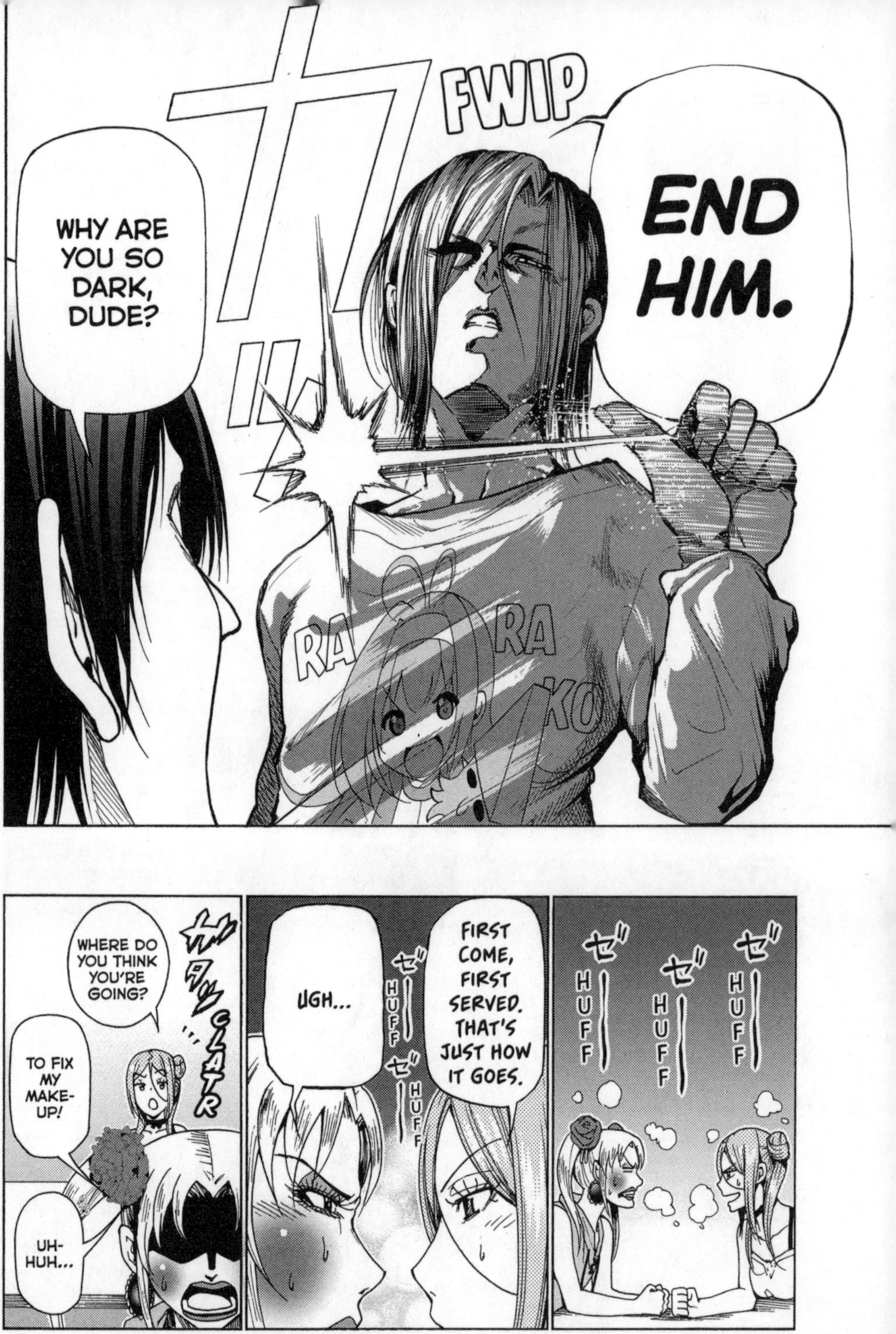
FWIP
END HIM.
WHY ARE YOU SO DARK, DUDE?
RA RA KO
HUFF
HUFF
HUFF
FIRST COME, FIRST SERVED. THAT'S JUST HOW IT GOES.
HUFF
HUFF
UGH...
CLATR
WHERE DO YOU THINK YOU'RE GOING?
TO FIX MY MAKE-UP!
UH-HUH...

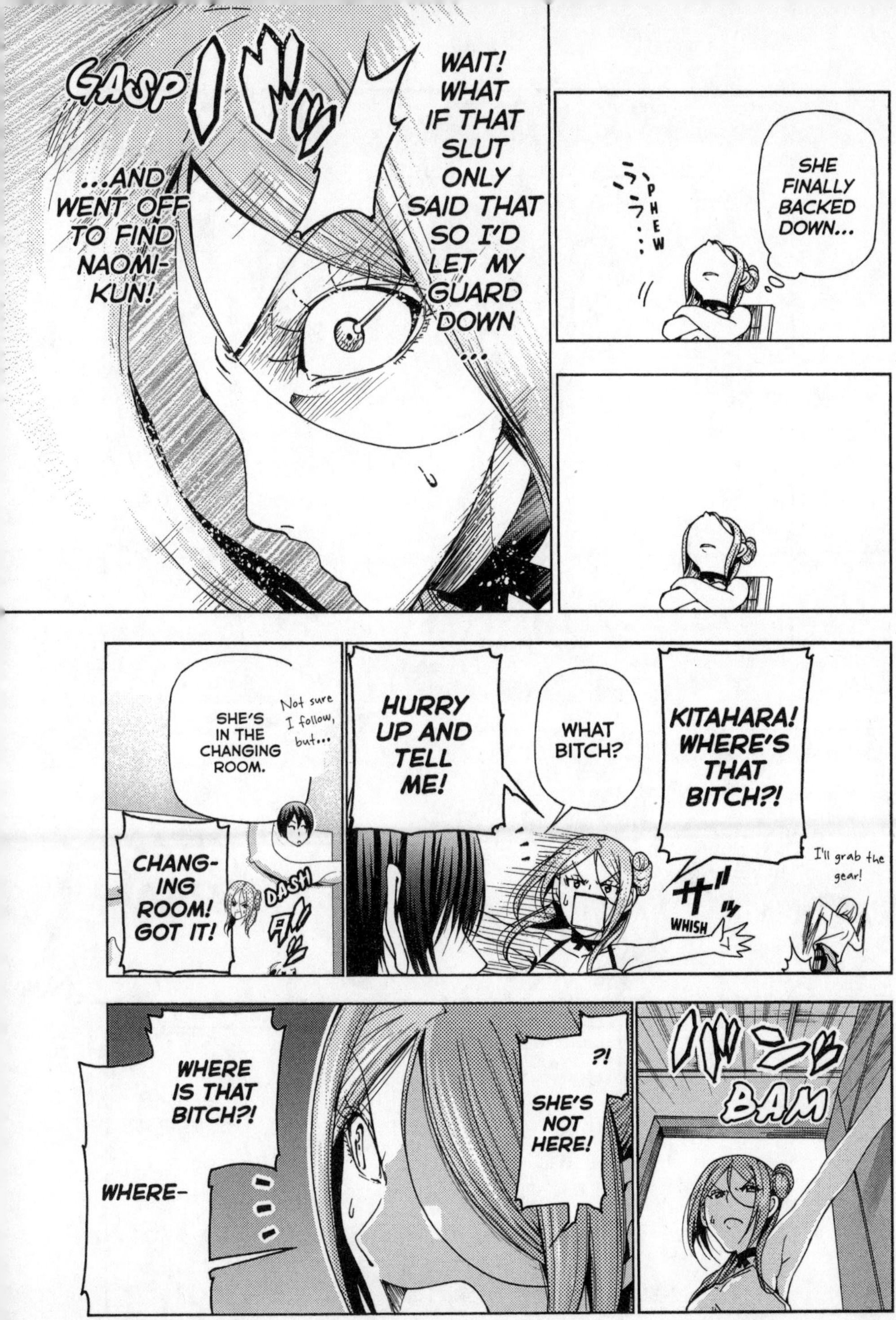
SHE FINALLY BACKED DOWN...
PHEW
GASP
WAIT! WHAT IF THAT SLUT ONLY SAID THAT SO I'D LET MY GUARD DOWN...
...AND WENT OFF TO FIND NAOMI-KUN!
KITAHARA! WHERE'S THAT BITCH?!
WHISH
I'll grab the gear!
WHAT BITCH?
HURRY UP AND TELL ME!
SHE'S IN THE CHANGING ROOM.
Not sure I follow, but...
CHANGING-ING ROOM! GOT IT!
DASH
BAM
?!
SHE'S NOT HERE!
WHERE IS THAT BITCH?!
WHERE-

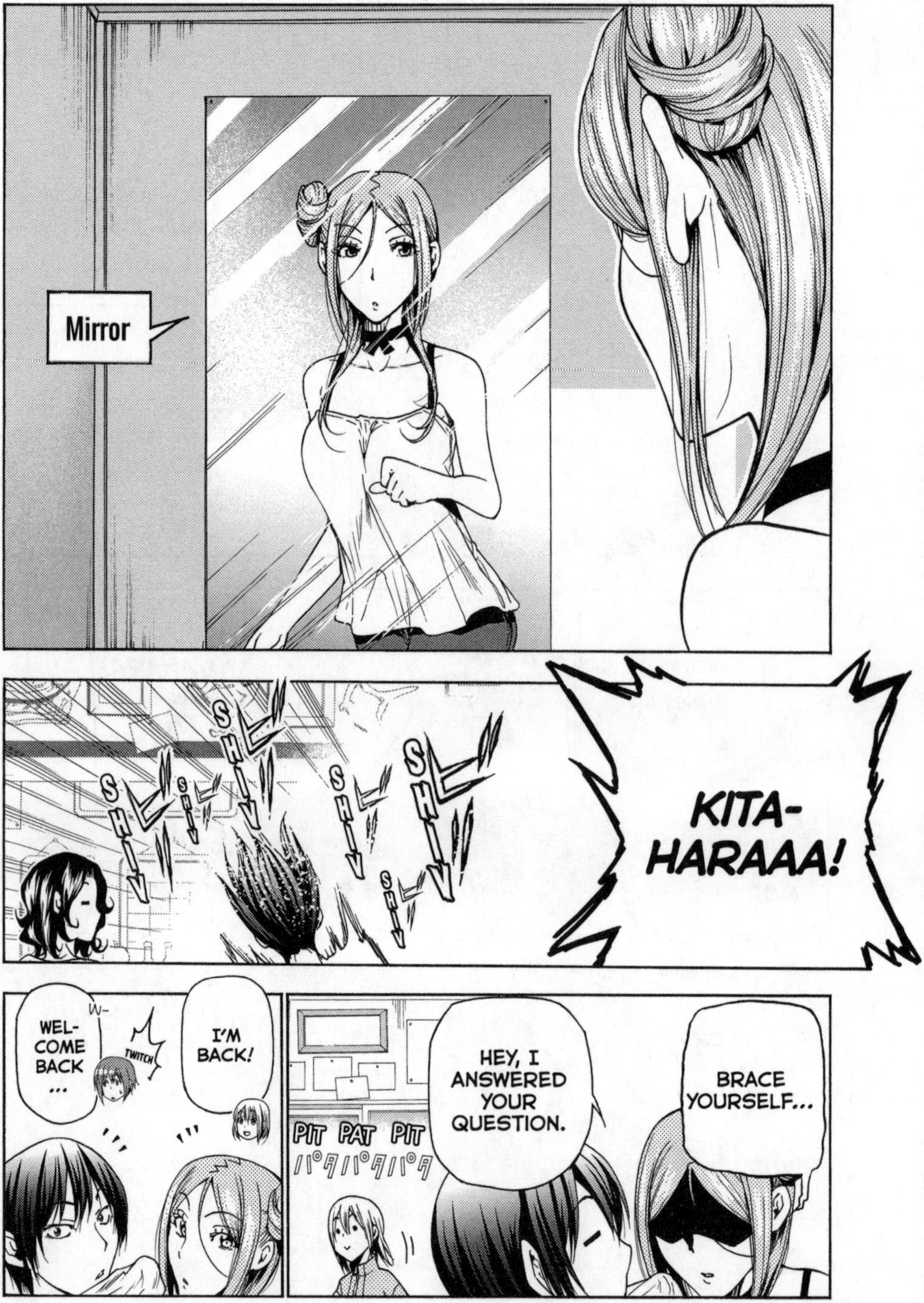
Mirror
KITA-HARAAA!
SHIV SHIV SHIV SHIV SHIV SHIV
BRACE YOURSELF...
HEY, I ANSWERED YOUR QUESTION.
PIT PAT PIT
パタパタパタ
I'M BACK!
TWITCH
W-
WEL-COME BACK ...

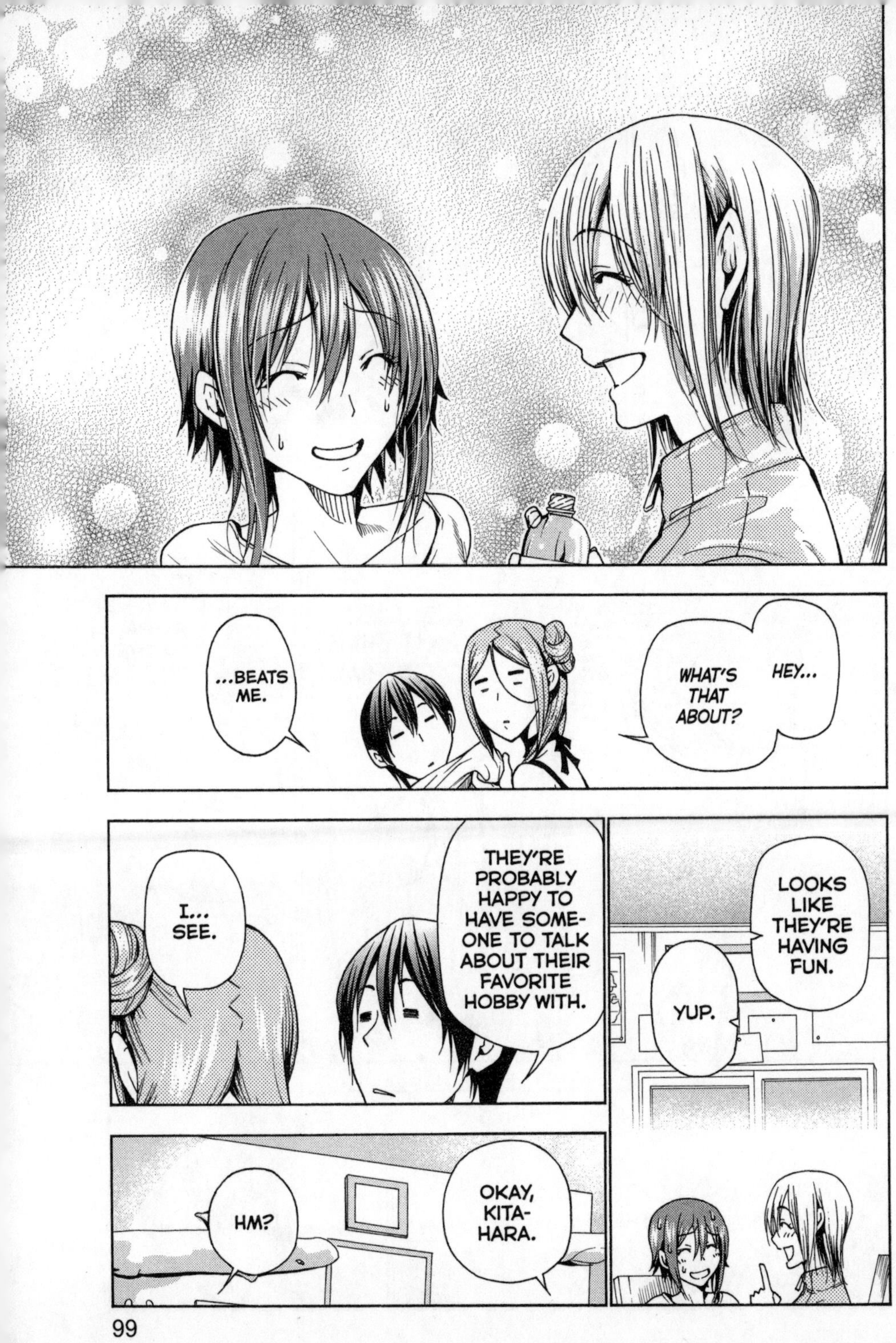
HEY...
WHAT'S THAT ABOUT?
...BEATS ME.
LOOKS LIKE THEY'RE HAVING FUN.
YUP.
THEY'RE PROBABLY HAPPY TO HAVE SOME-ONE TO TALK ABOUT THEIR FAVORITE HOBBY WITH.
I... SEE.
OKAY, KITA-HARA.
HM?

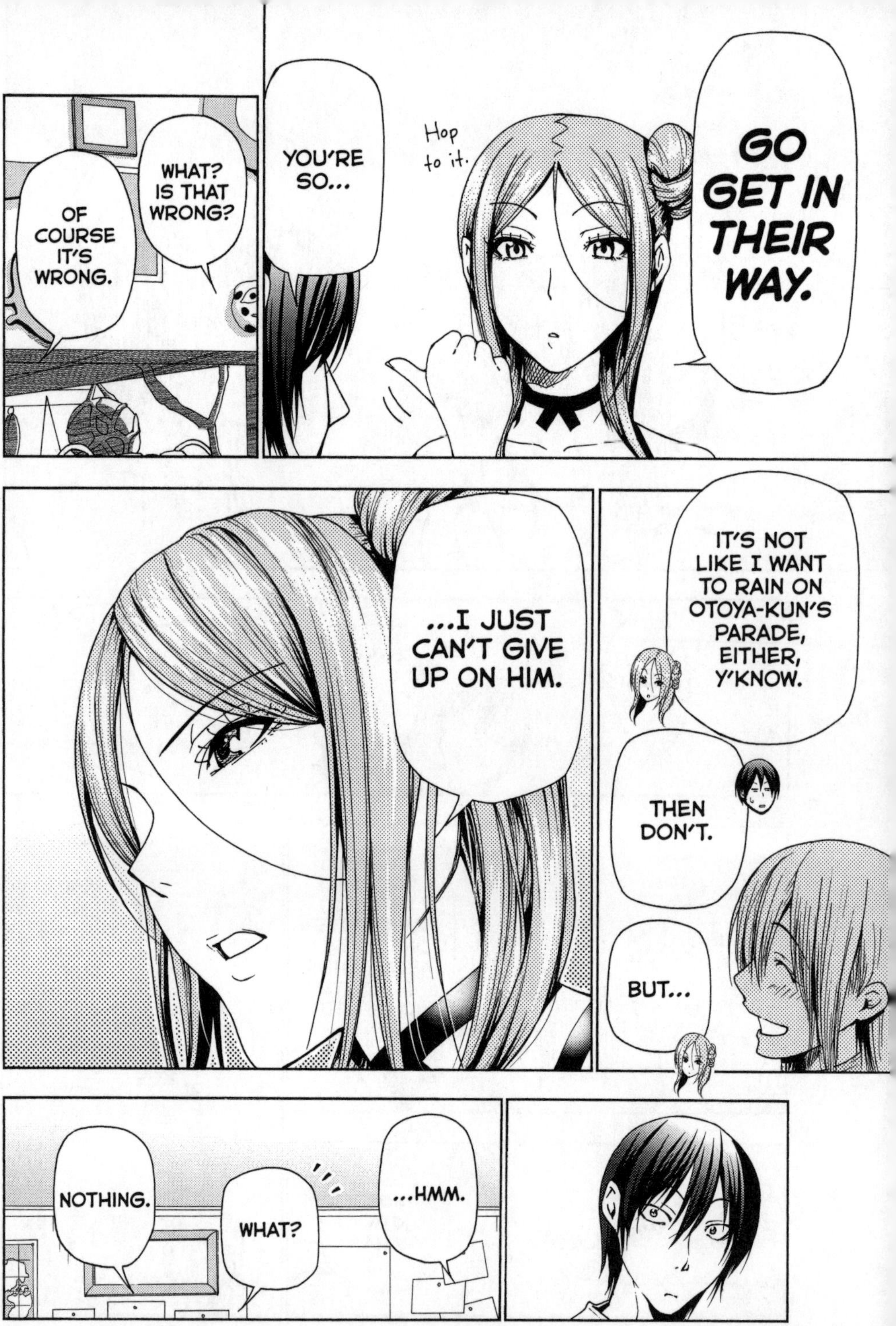
GO GET IN THEIR WAY.
Hop to it.
YOU'RE SO...
WHAT? IS THAT WRONG?
OF COURSE IT'S WRONG.
IT'S NOT LIKE I WANT TO RAIN ON OTOYA-KUN'S PARADE, EITHER, Y'KNOW.
THEN DON'T.
BUT...
...I JUST CAN'T GIVE UP ON HIM.
...HMM.
WHAT?
NOTHING.

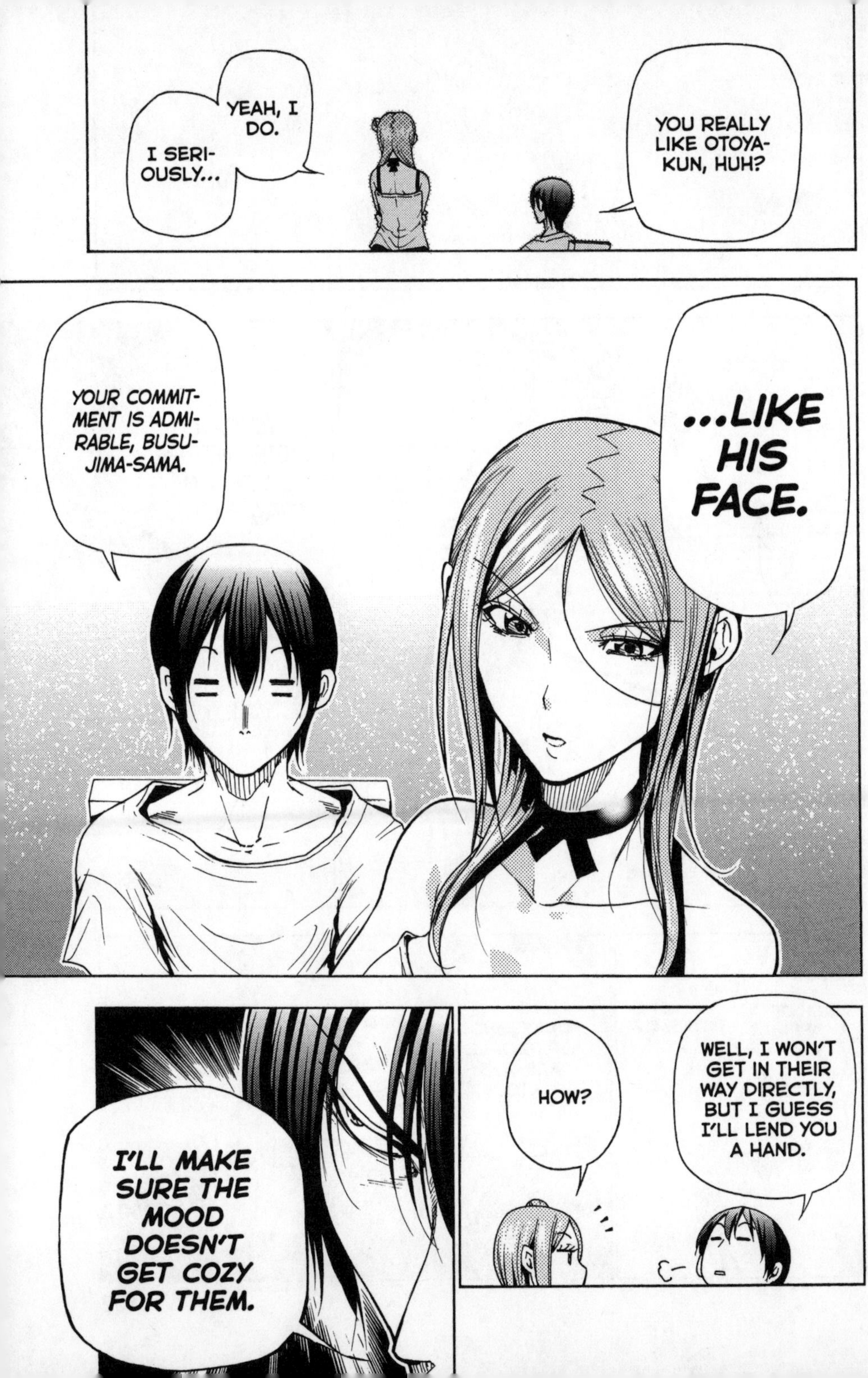
YOU REALLY LIKE OTOYA-KUN, HUH?
YEAH, I DO.
I SERI-OUSLY...
...LIKE HIS FACE.
YOUR COMMIT-MENT IS ADMI-RABLE, BUSU-JIMA-SAMA.
WELL, I WON'T GET IN THEIR WAY DIRECTLY, BUT I GUESS I'LL LEND YOU A HAND.
HOW?
I'LL MAKE SURE THE MOOD DOESN'T GET COZY FOR THEM.

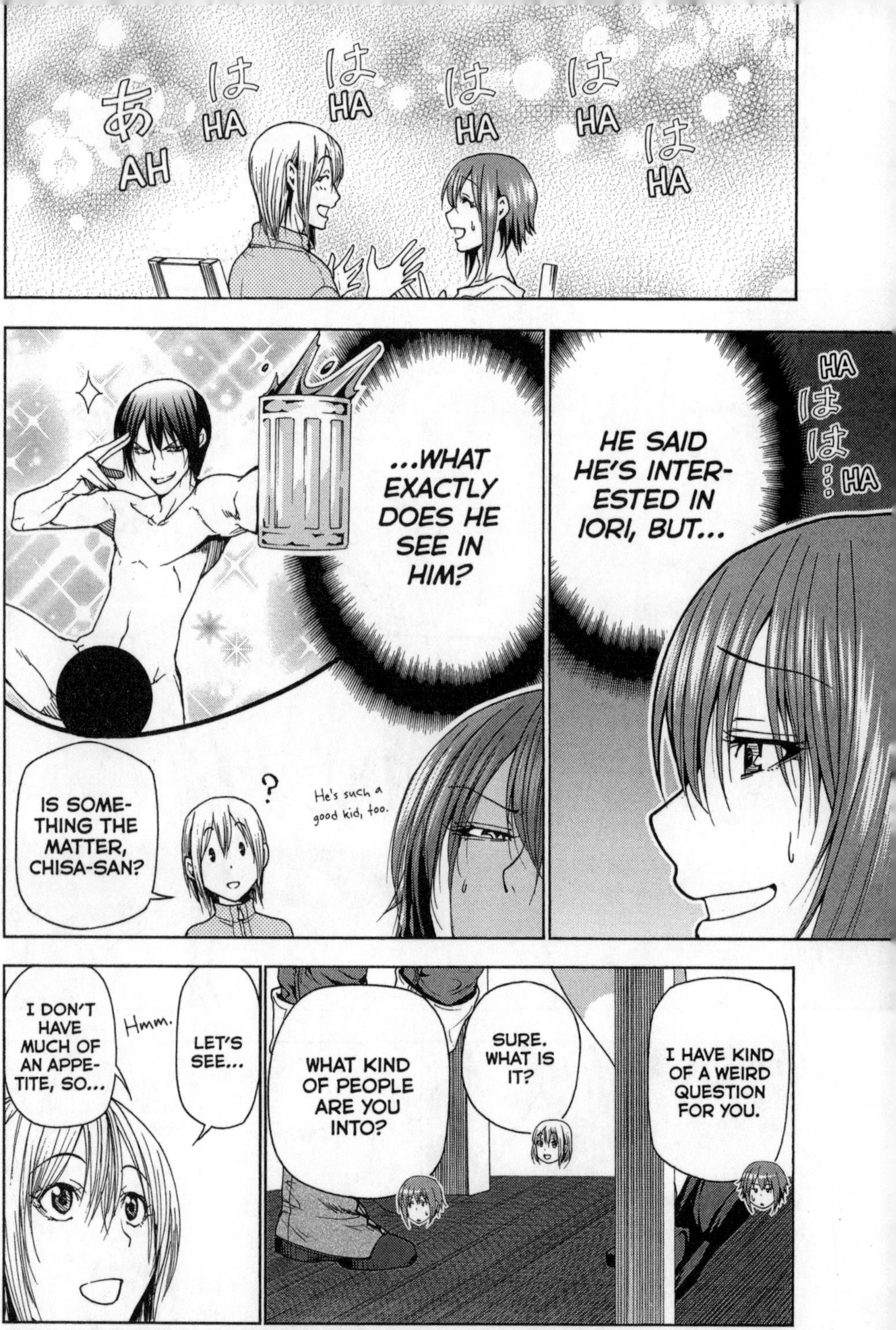
あ AH
は HA
は HA
は HA
は HA
は HA
HA はは... HA
HE SAID HE'S INTERESTED IN IORI, BUT...
...WHAT EXACTLY DOES HE SEE IN HIM?
He's such a good kid, too.
?
IS SOMETHING THE MATTER, CHISA-SAN?
I HAVE KIND OF A WEIRD QUESTION FOR YOU.
SURE. WHAT IS IT?
WHAT KIND OF PEOPLE ARE YOU INTO?
LET'S SEE...
Hmm.
I DON'T HAVE MUCH OF AN APPETITE, SO...

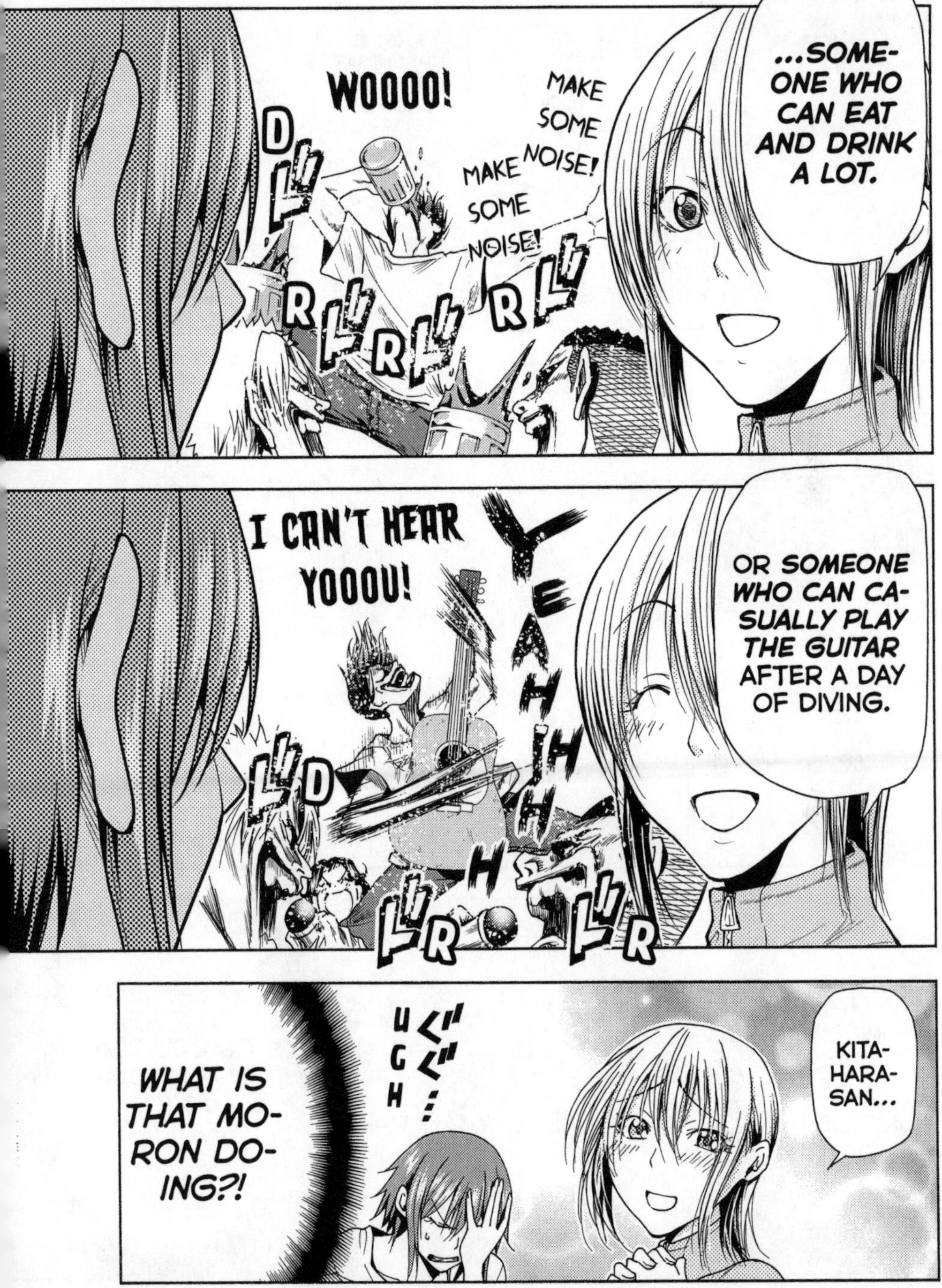
...SOME-ONE WHO CAN EAT AND DRINK A LOT.
MAKE SOME NOISE!
MAKE SOME NOISE!
WOOOO!
OR SOMEONE WHO CAN CA-SUALLY PLAY THE GUITAR AFTER A DAY OF DIVING.
YEAHHHHHH
I CAN'T HEAR YOOOU!
KITA-HARA-SAN...
UGH
WHAT IS THAT MO-RON DO-ING?!

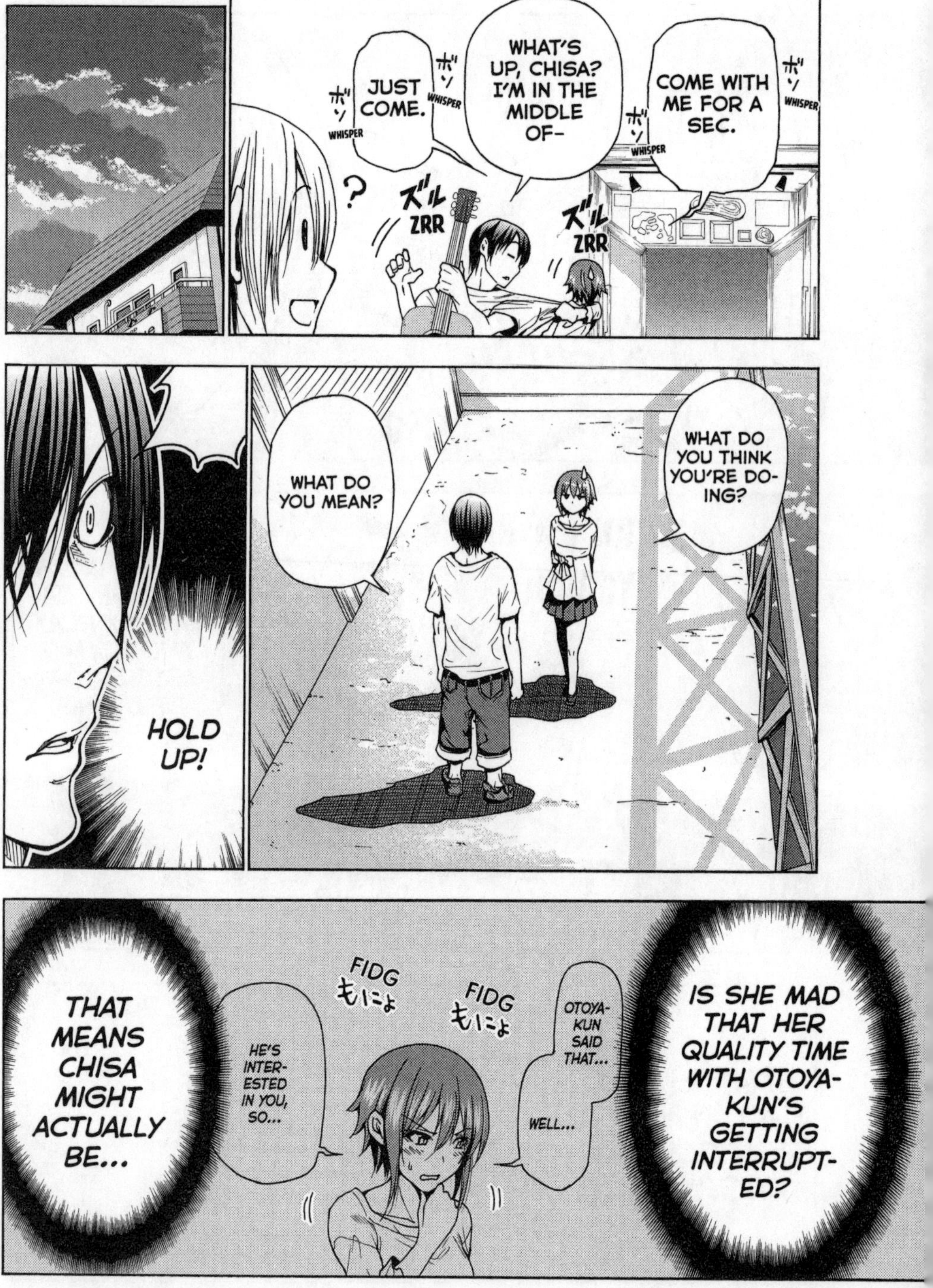
ボソ
WHISPER
COME WITH ME FOR A SEC.
ボソ
WHISPER
WHAT'S UP, CHISA? I'M IN THE MIDDLE OF-
ボソ
WHISPER
JUST COME.
ボソ
WHISPER
ズル
ZRR
ズル
ZRR
?
WHAT DO YOU THINK YOU'RE DOING?
WHAT DO YOU MEAN?
HOLD UP!
IS SHE MAD THAT HER QUALITY TIME WITH OTOYA-KUN'S GETTING INTERRUPTED?
OTOYA-KUN SAID THAT...
WELL...
FIDG
もにょ
FIDG
もにょ
HE'S INTERESTED IN YOU, SO...
THAT MEANS CHISA MIGHT ACTUALLY BE...

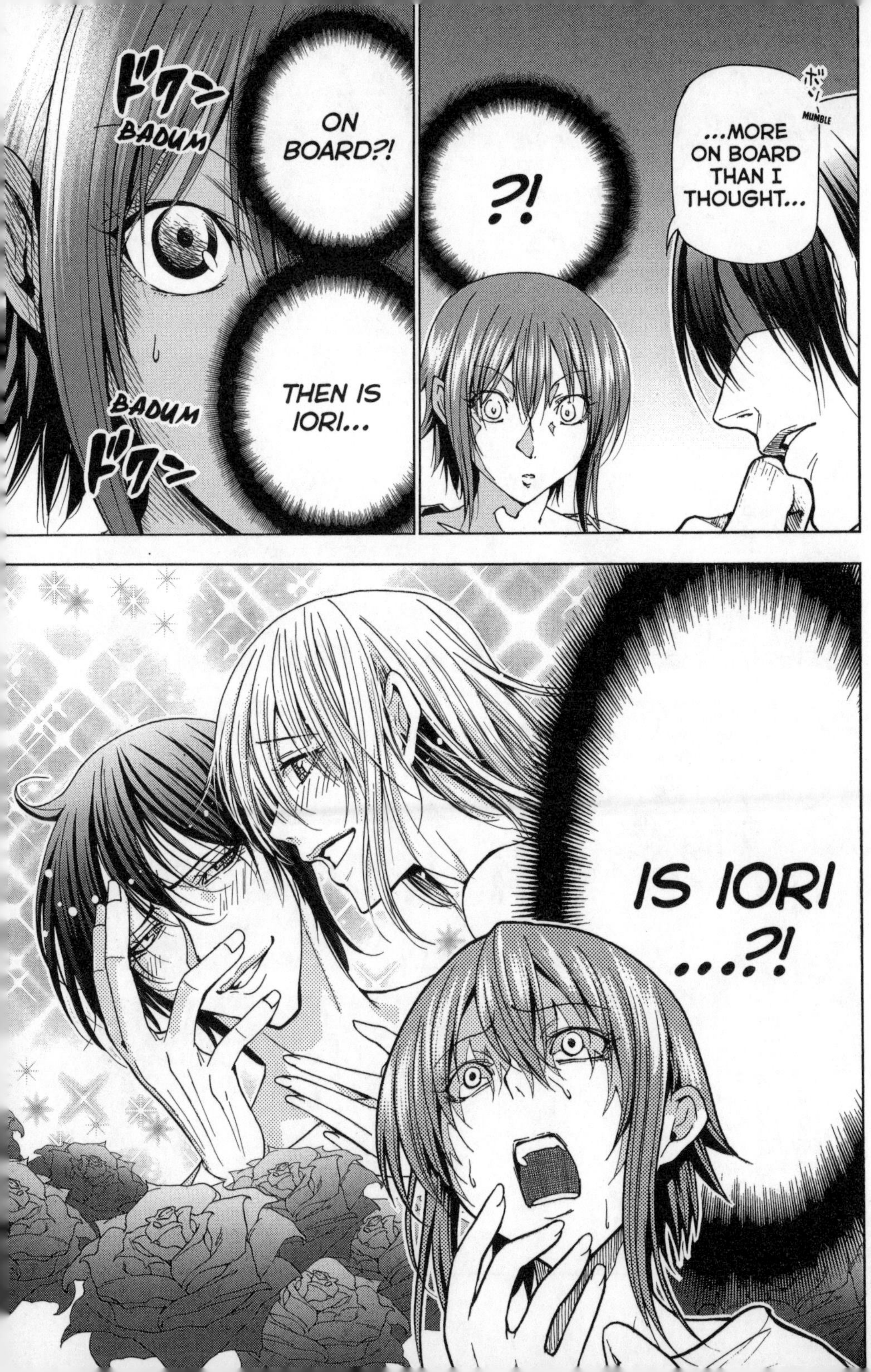
ボソ
MUMBLE
...MORE ON BOARD THAN I THOUGHT...
?!
ON BOARD?!
ドクン
BADUM
THEN IS IORI...
BADUM
ドクン
IS IORI ...?!

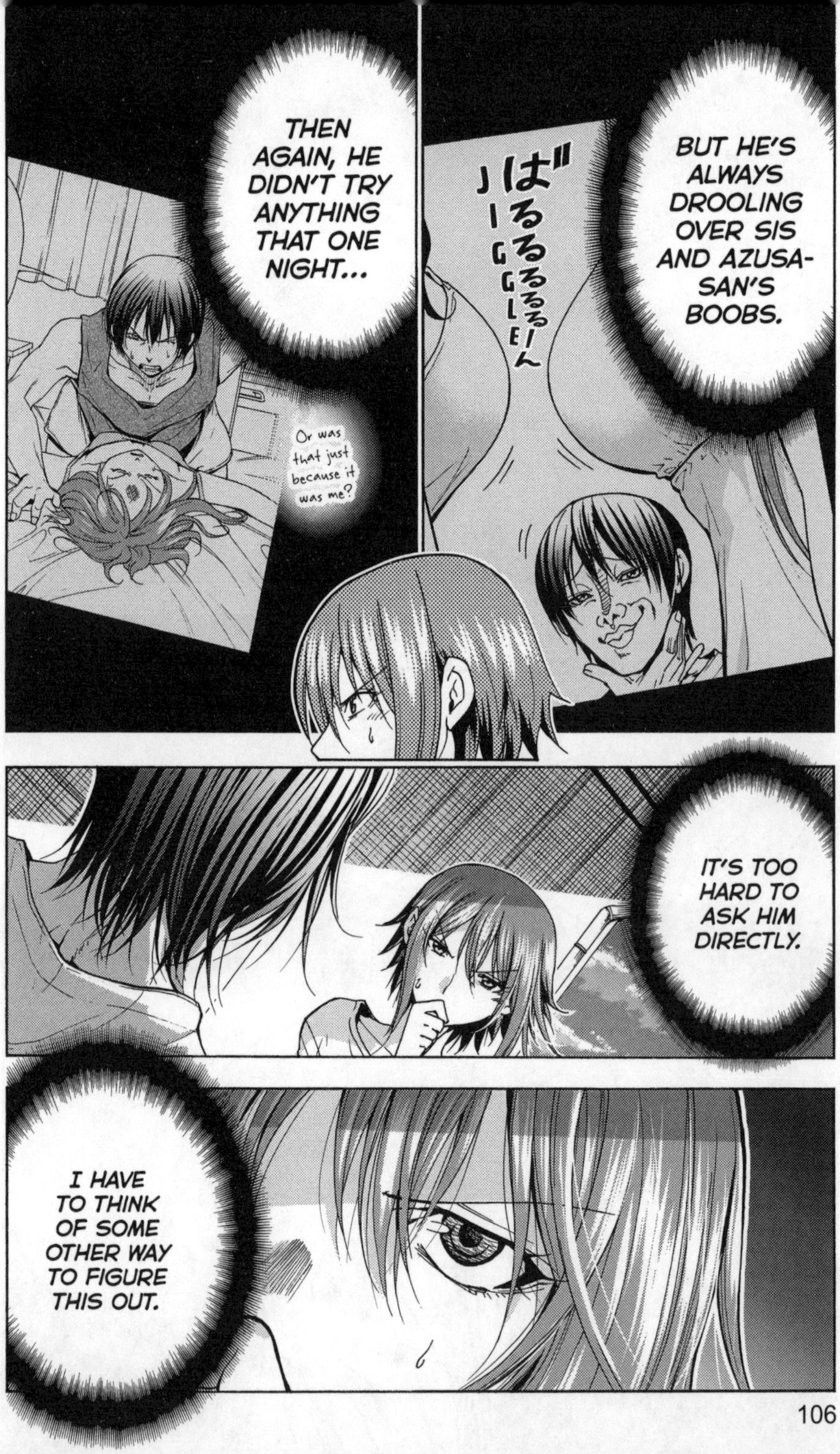
BUT HE'S ALWAYS DROOLING OVER SIS AND AZUSA-SAN'S BOOBS.
ばるるるるるん
JIGGLE
THEN AGAIN, HE DIDN'T TRY ANYTHING THAT ONE NIGHT...
Or was that just because it was me?
IT'S TOO HARD TO ASK HIM DIRECTLY.
I HAVE TO THINK OF SOME OTHER WAY TO FIGURE THIS OUT.

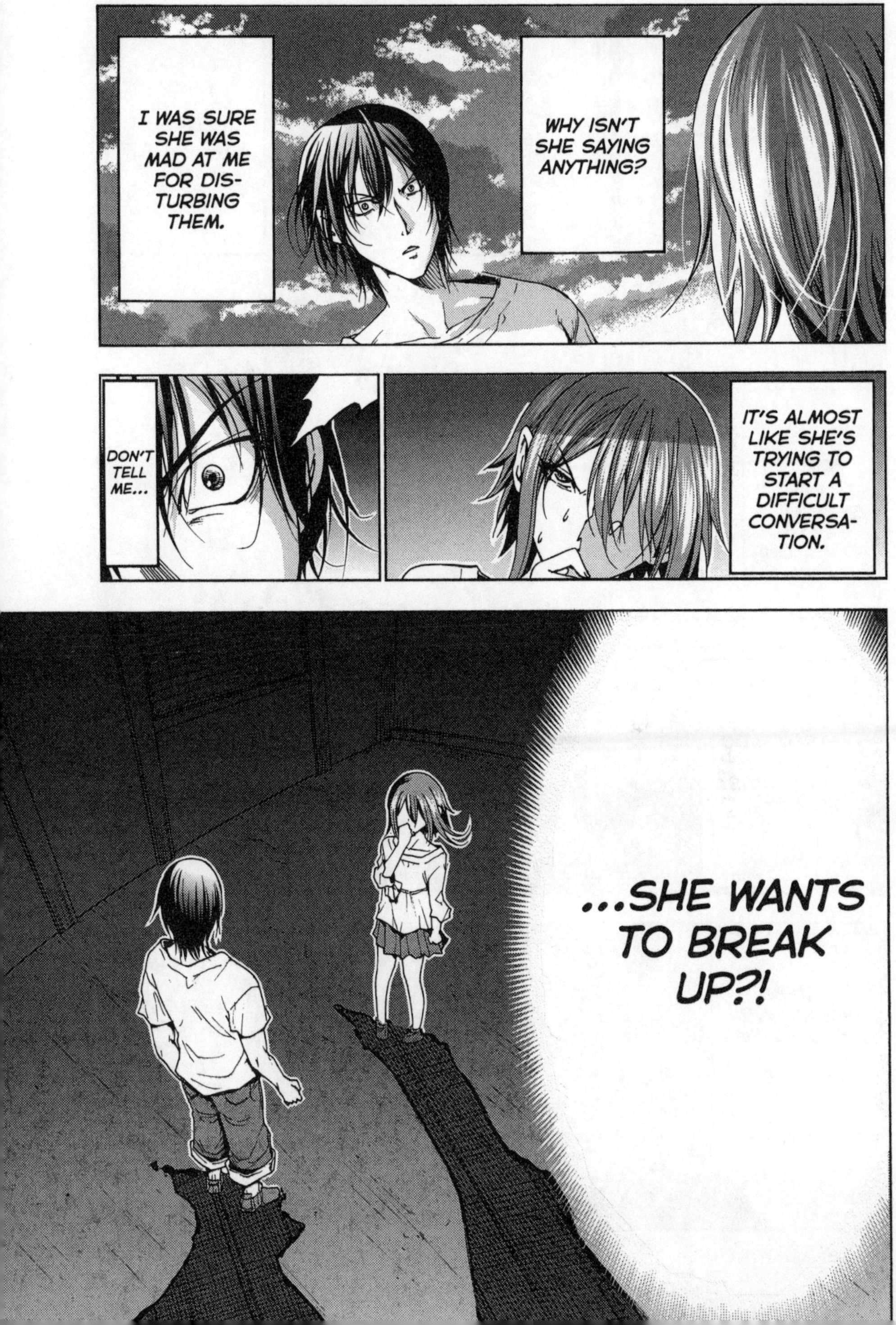
WHY ISN'T SHE SAYING ANYTHING?
I WAS SURE SHE WAS MAD AT ME FOR DIS-TURBING THEM.
IT'S ALMOST LIKE SHE'S TRYING TO START A DIFFICULT CONVERSA-TION.
DON'T TELL ME...
...SHE WANTS TO BREAK UP?!

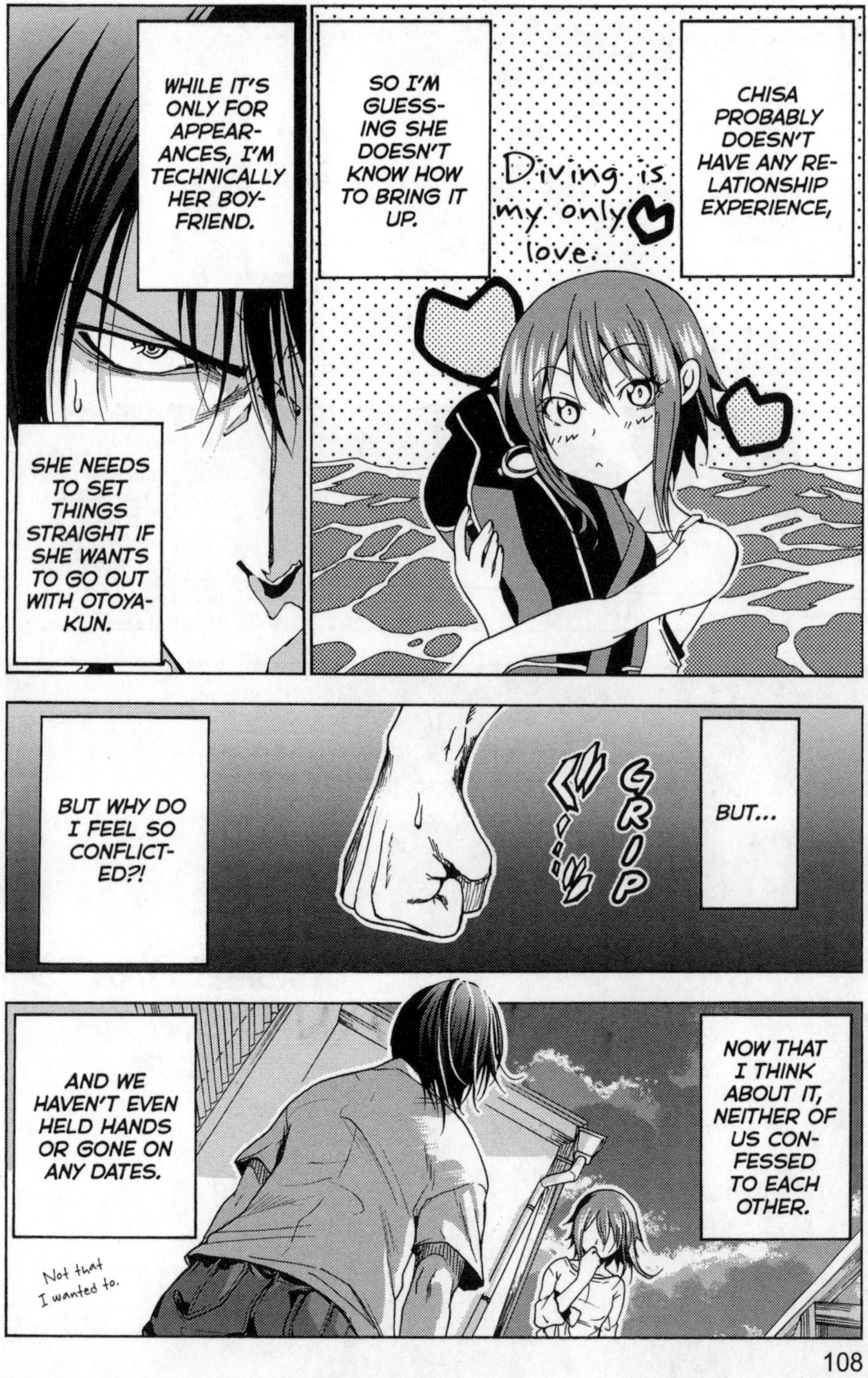
CHISA PROBABLY DOESN'T HAVE ANY RELATIONSHIP EXPERIENCE,
Diving is my only love.
SO I'M GUESSING SHE DOESN'T KNOW HOW TO BRING IT UP.
WHILE IT'S ONLY FOR APPEARANCES, I'M TECHNICALLY HER BOYFRIEND.
SHE NEEDS TO SET THINGS STRAIGHT IF SHE WANTS TO GO OUT WITH OTOYA-KUN.
BUT...
GRIP
BUT WHY DO I FEEL SO CONFLICTED?!
NOW THAT I THINK ABOUT IT, NEITHER OF US CONFESSED TO EACH OTHER.
AND WE HAVEN'T EVEN HELD HANDS OR GONE ON ANY DATES.
Not that I wanted to.

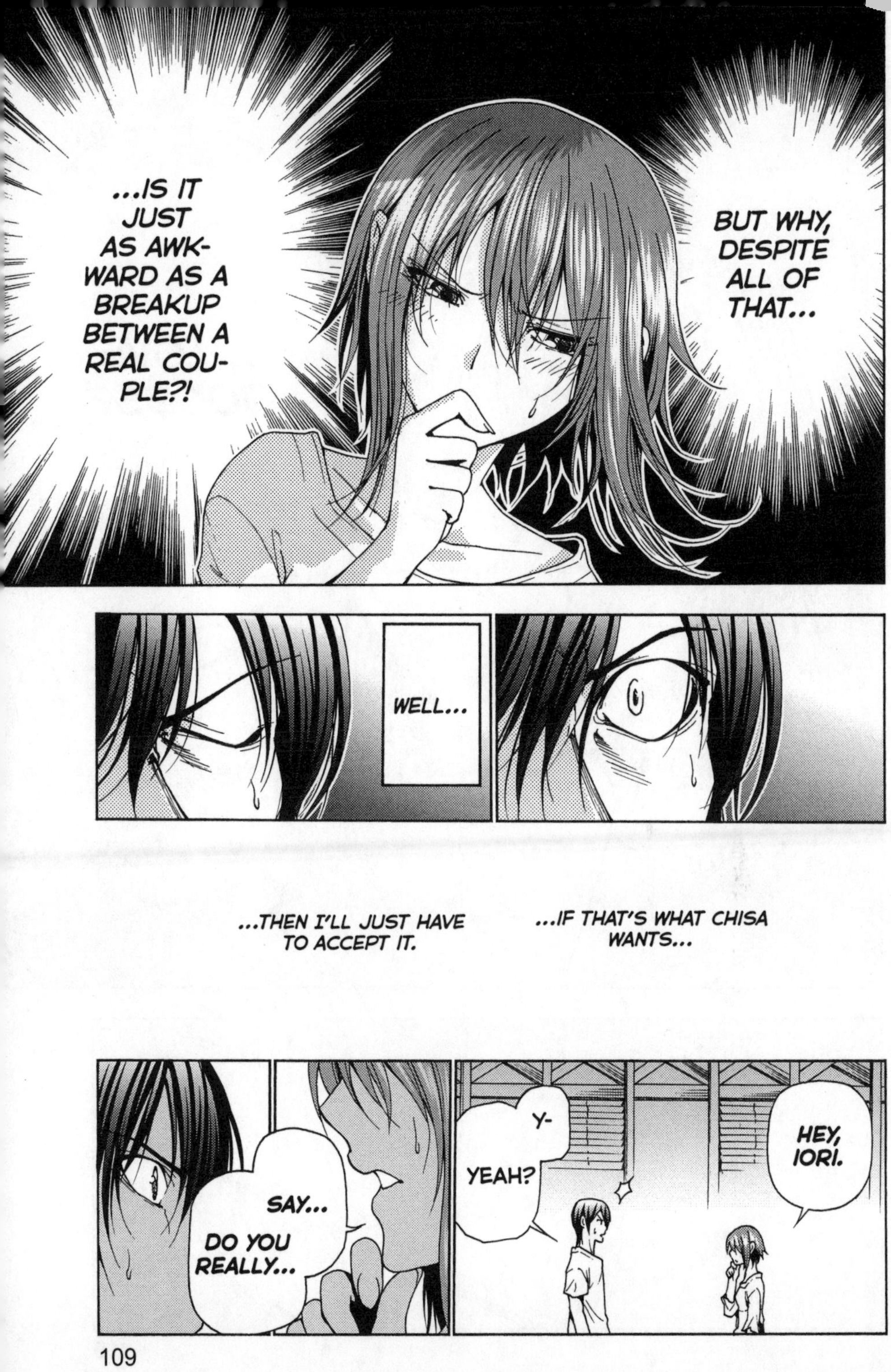
BUT WHY, DESPITE ALL OF THAT...
...IS IT JUST AS AWK-WARD AS A BREAKUP BETWEEN A REAL COU-PLE?!
WELL...
...IF THAT'S WHAT CHISA WANTS...
...THEN I'LL JUST HAVE TO ACCEPT IT.
HEY, IORI.
Y- YEAH?
SAY...
DO YOU REALLY...

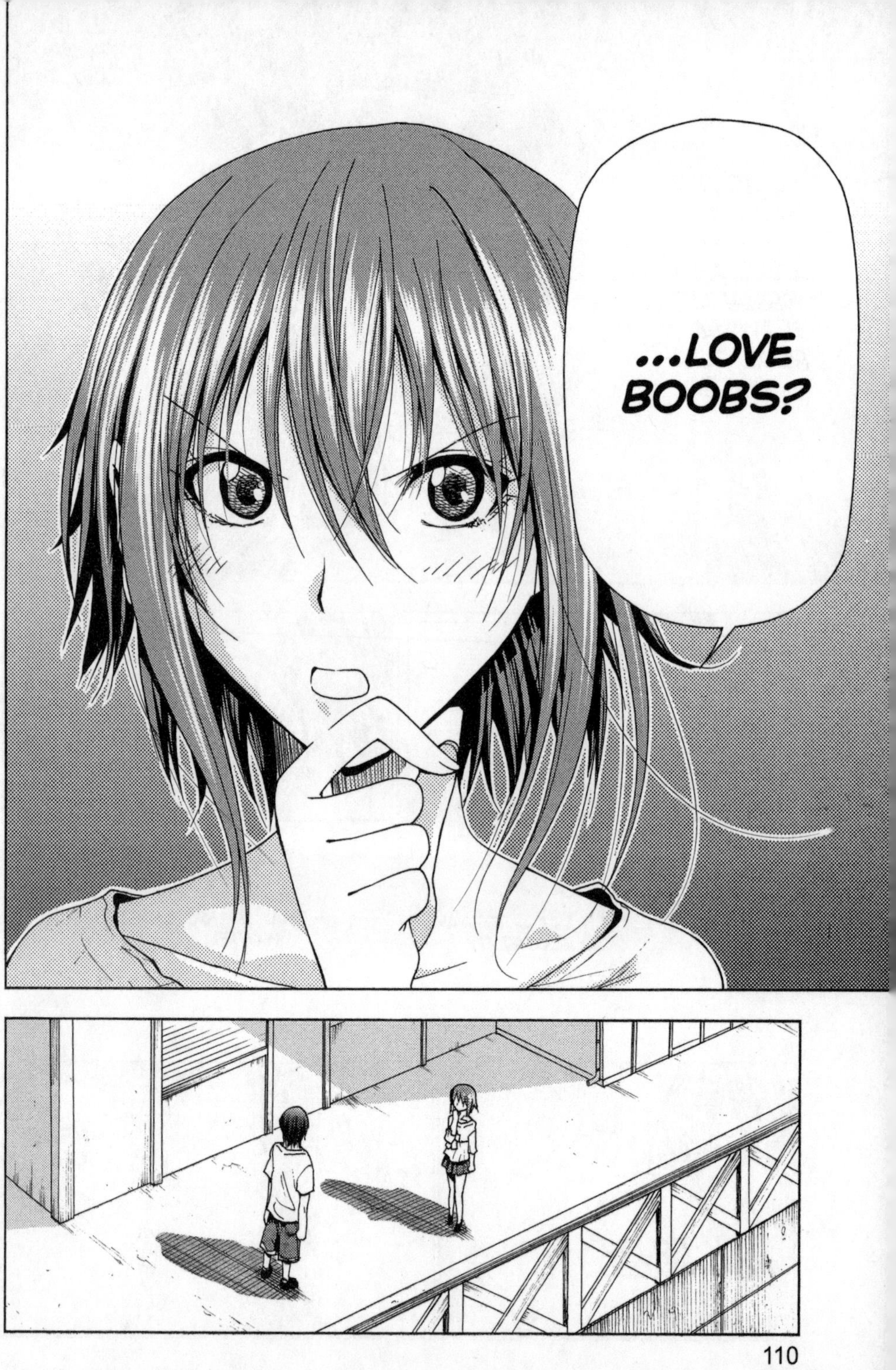
...LOVE BOOBS?

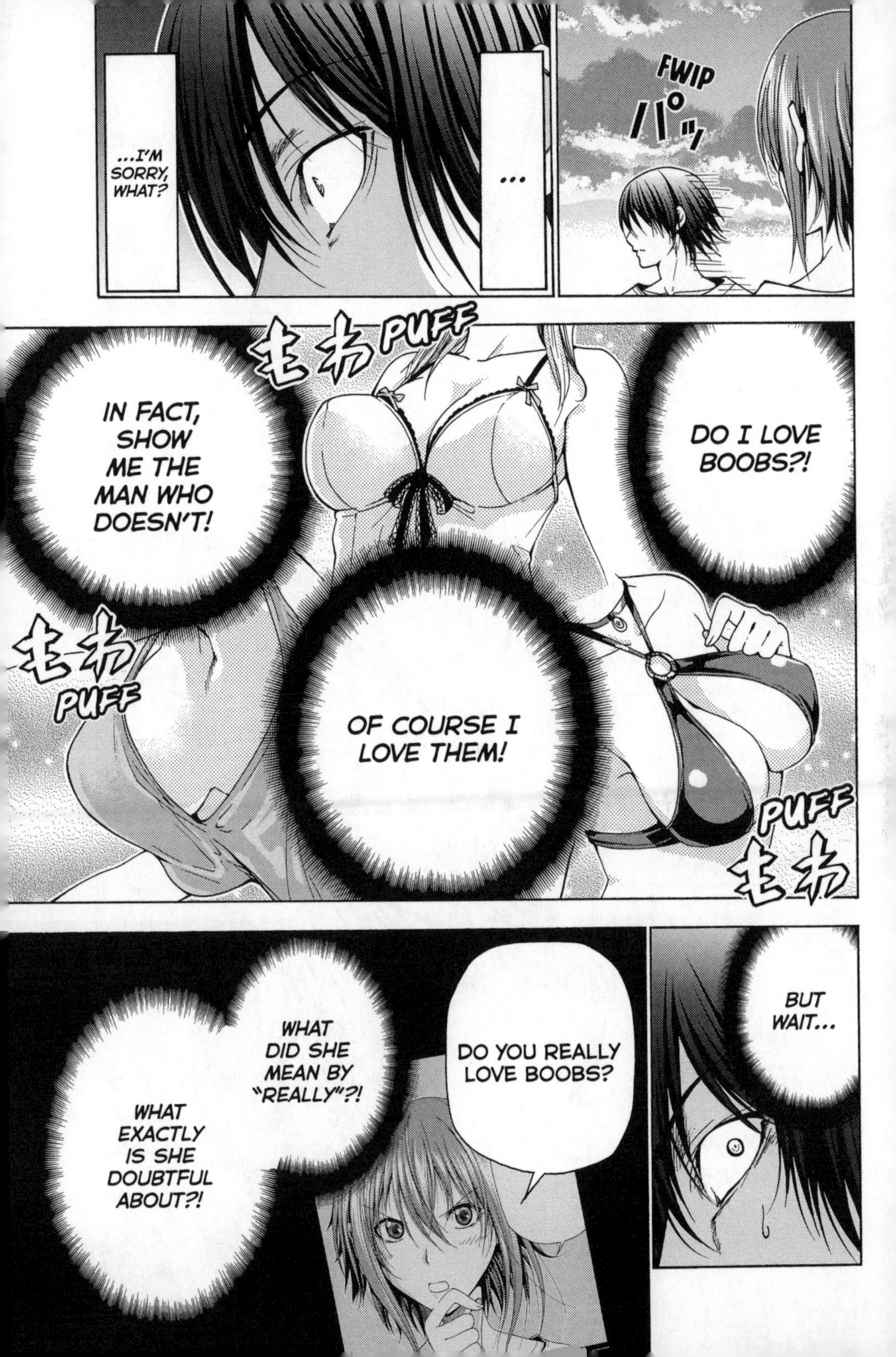
FWIP
パッ
...
...I'M SORRY, WHAT?
DO I LOVE BOOBS?!
もわ PUFF
IN FACT, SHOW ME THE MAN WHO DOESN'T!
OF COURSE I LOVE THEM!
PUFF もわ
もわ PUFF
BUT WAIT...
DO YOU REALLY LOVE BOOBS?
WHAT DID SHE MEAN BY "REALLY"?!
WHAT EXACTLY IS SHE DOUBTFUL ABOUT?!

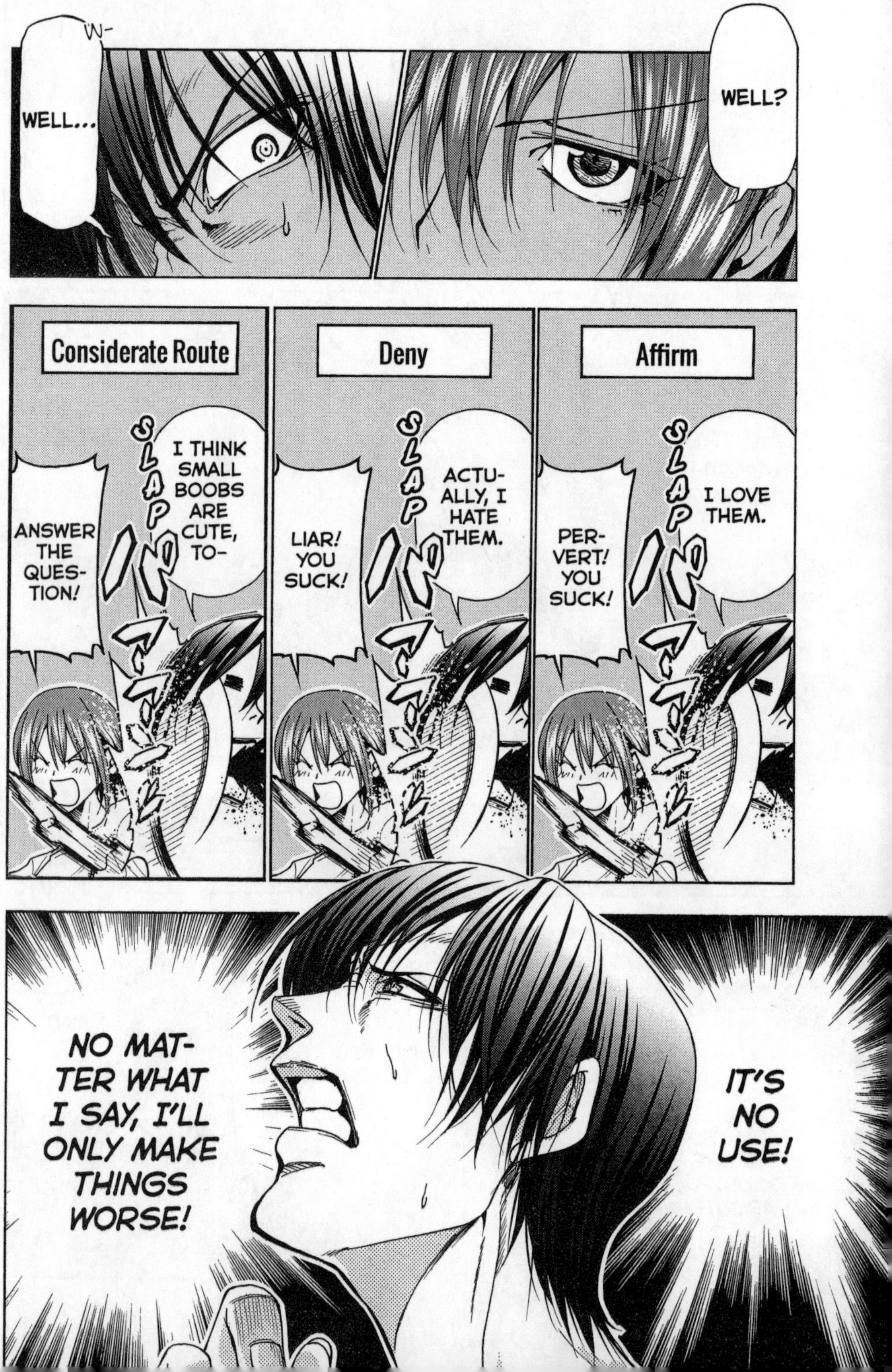
WELL?
W- WELL...
Affirm
I LOVE THEM.
SLAP
PERVERT! YOU SUCK!
Deny
ACTUALLY, I HATE THEM.
SLAP
LIAR! YOU SUCK!
Considerate Route
I THINK SMALL BOOBS ARE CUTE, TO-
SLAP
ANSWER THE QUESTION!
IT'S NO USE!
NO MATTER WHAT I SAY, I'LL ONLY MAKE THINGS WORSE!

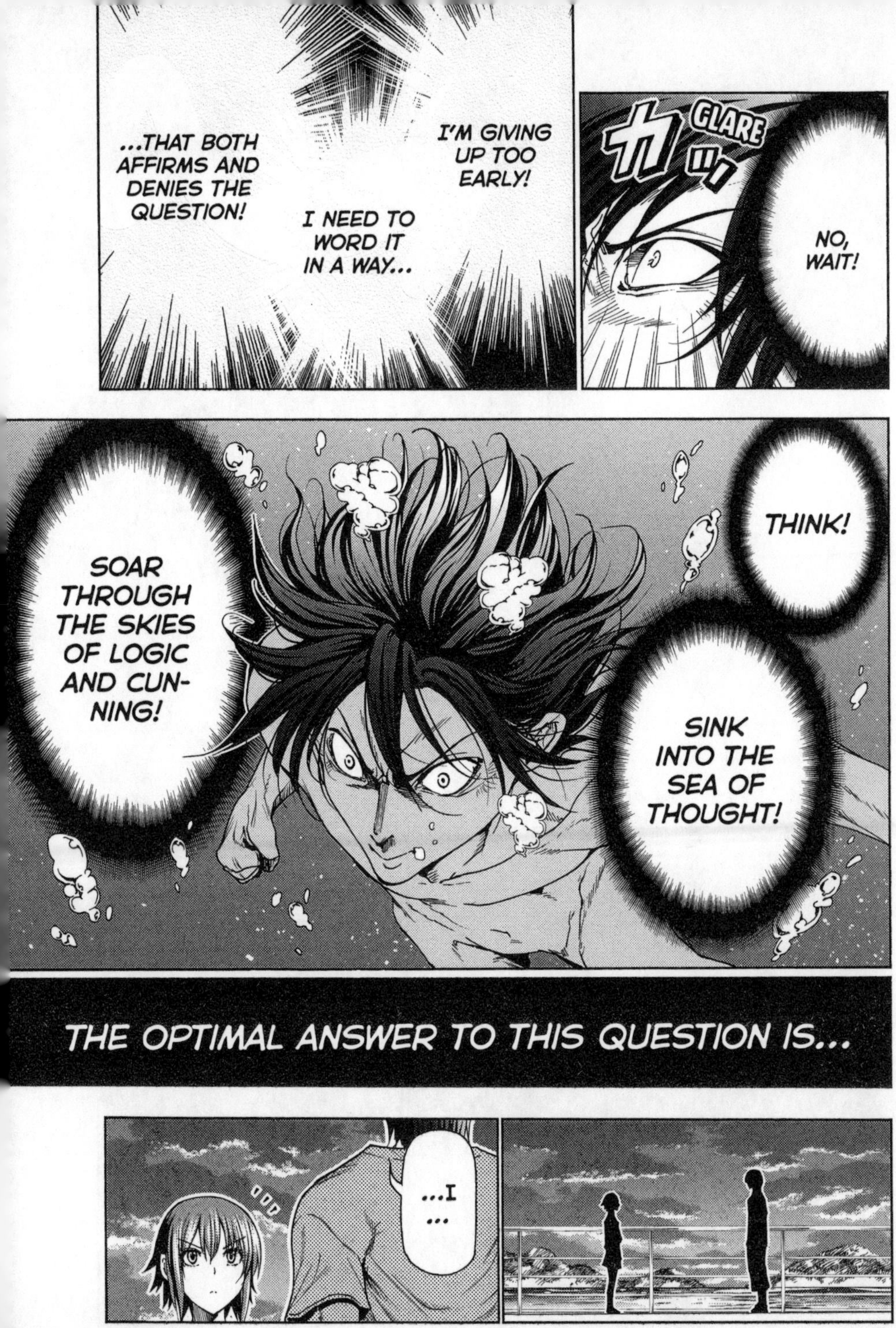
GLARE
カッ
NO, WAIT!
I'M GIVING UP TOO EARLY!
I NEED TO WORD IT IN A WAY...
...THAT BOTH AFFIRMS AND DENIES THE QUESTION!
THINK!
SINK INTO THE SEA OF THOUGHT!
SOAR THROUGH THE SKIES OF LOGIC AND CUN-NING!
THE OPTIMAL ANSWER TO THIS QUESTION IS...
...I ...

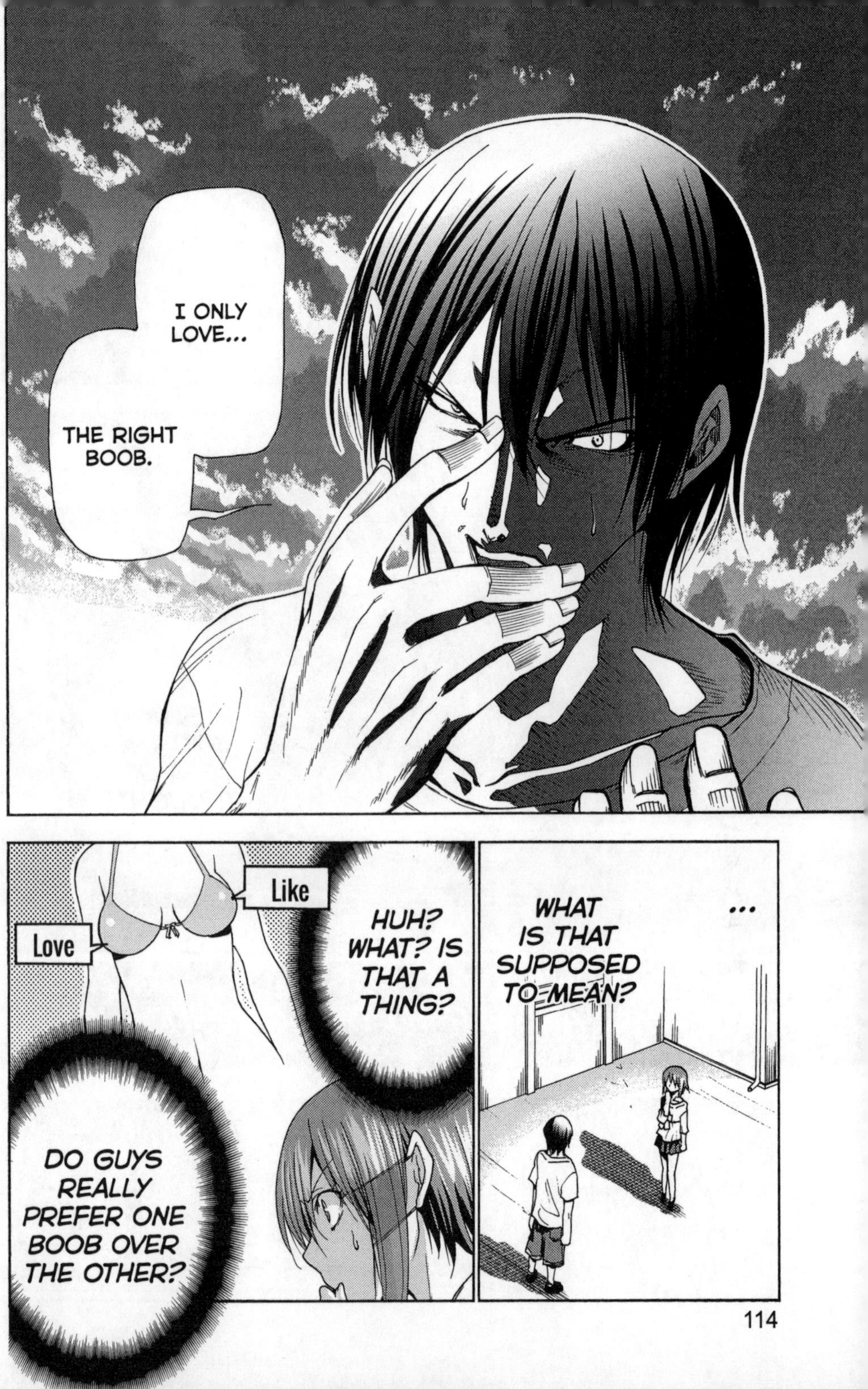
I ONLY LOVE...
THE RIGHT BOOB.
...
WHAT IS THAT SUPPOSED TO MEAN?
HUH? WHAT? IS THAT A THING?
Like
Love
DO GUYS REALLY PREFER ONE BOOB OVER THE OTHER?

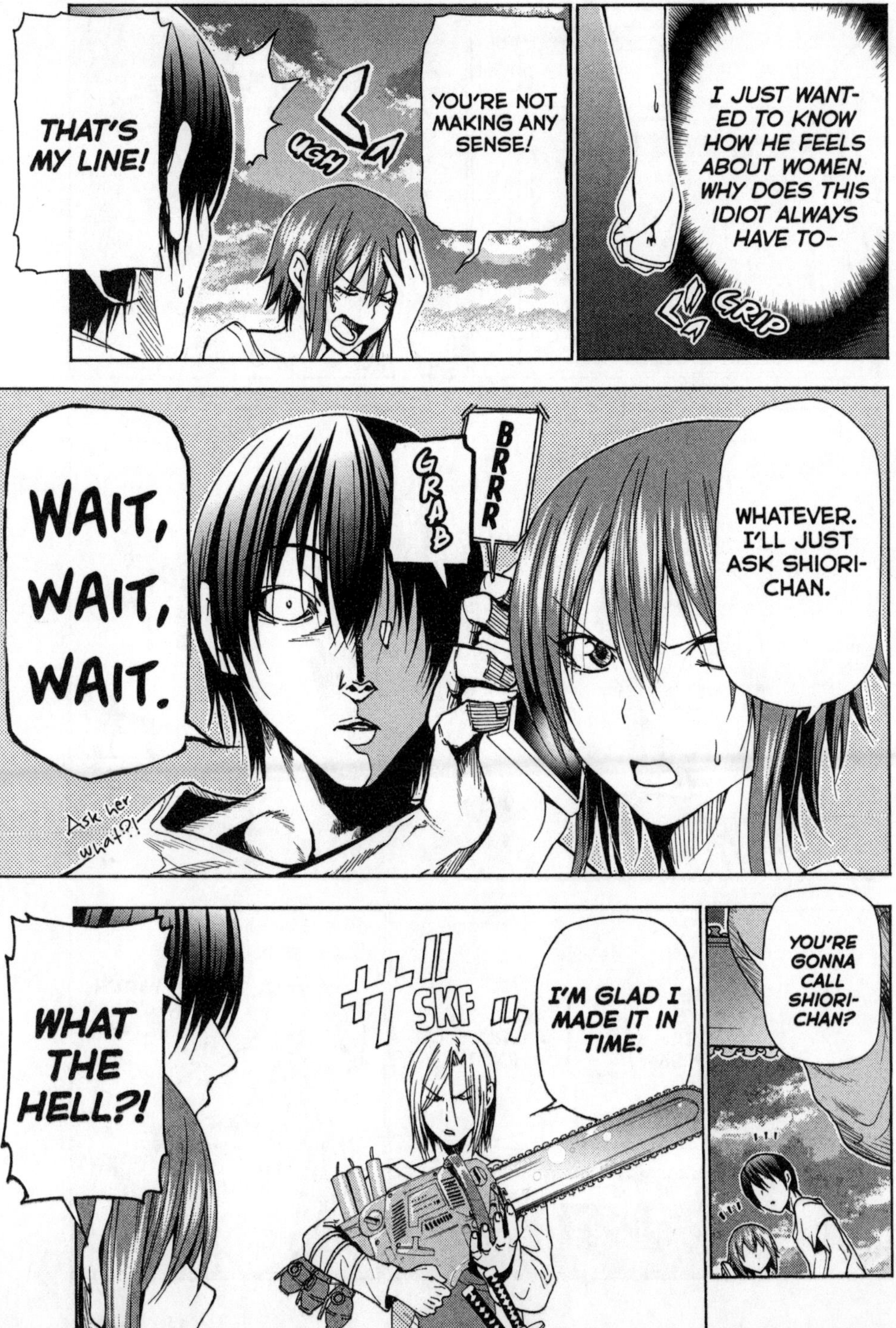
I JUST WANTED TO KNOW HOW HE FEELS ABOUT WOMEN. WHY DOES THIS IDIOT ALWAYS HAVE TO-
GRIP
YOU'RE NOT MAKING ANY SENSE!
UGH
THAT'S MY LINE!
WHATEVER. I'LL JUST ASK SHIORI-CHAN.
BRRR
GRAB
WAIT, WAIT, WAIT.
Ask her what?!
YOU'RE GONNA CALL SHIORI-CHAN?
I'M GLAD I MADE IT IN TIME.
SKF
WHAT THE HELL?!

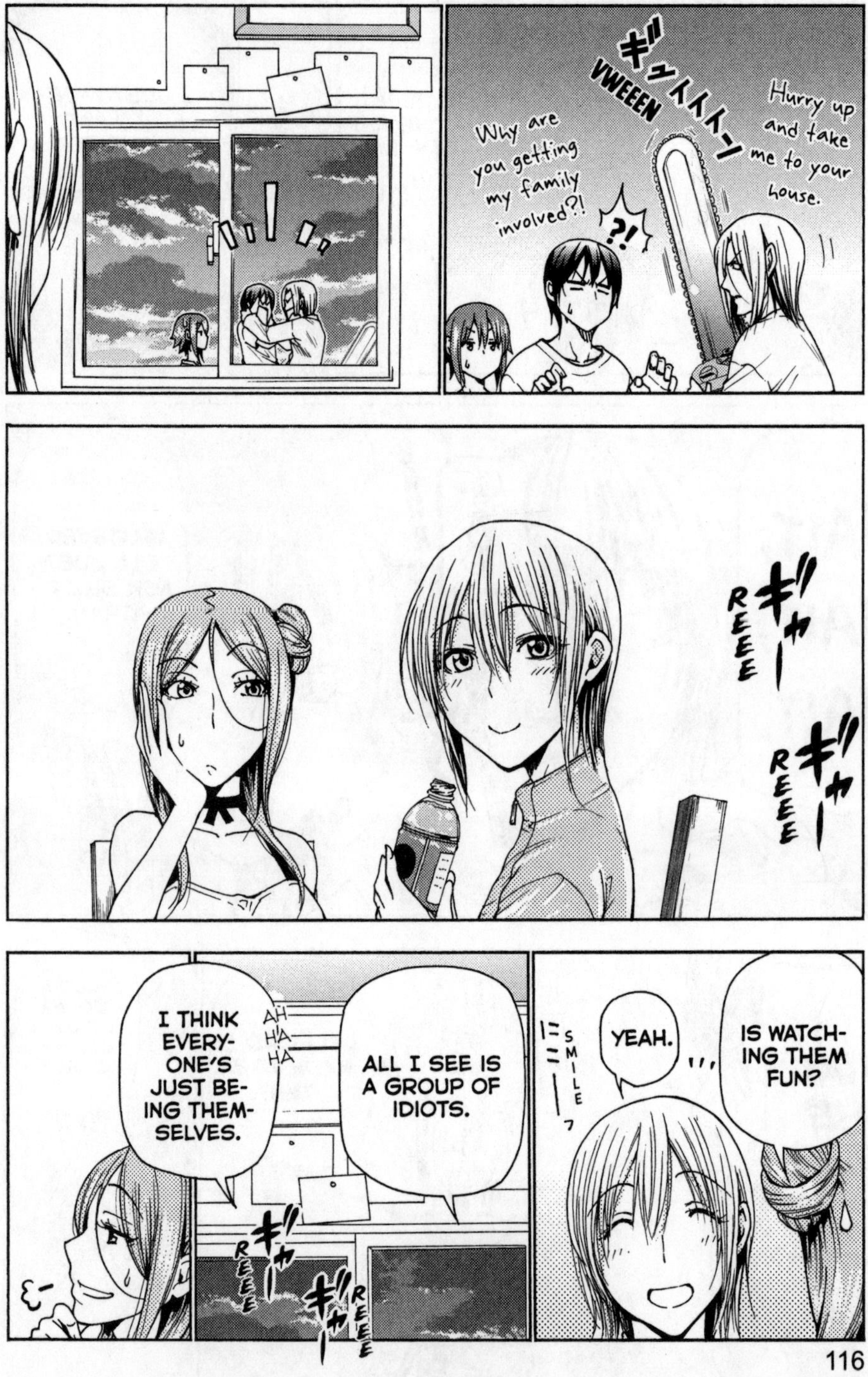
ギュイイーン
VWEEEN
Hurry up and take me to your house.
Why are you getting my family involved?!
?!
ギャー
REEE
ギャー
REEE
IS WATCHING THEM FUN?
YEAH.
ニコー
SMILE
ALL I SEE IS A GROUP OF IDIOTS.
ギャー
REEE
ギャー
REEE
AH HA HA
I THINK EVERYONE'S JUST BEING THEMSELVES.

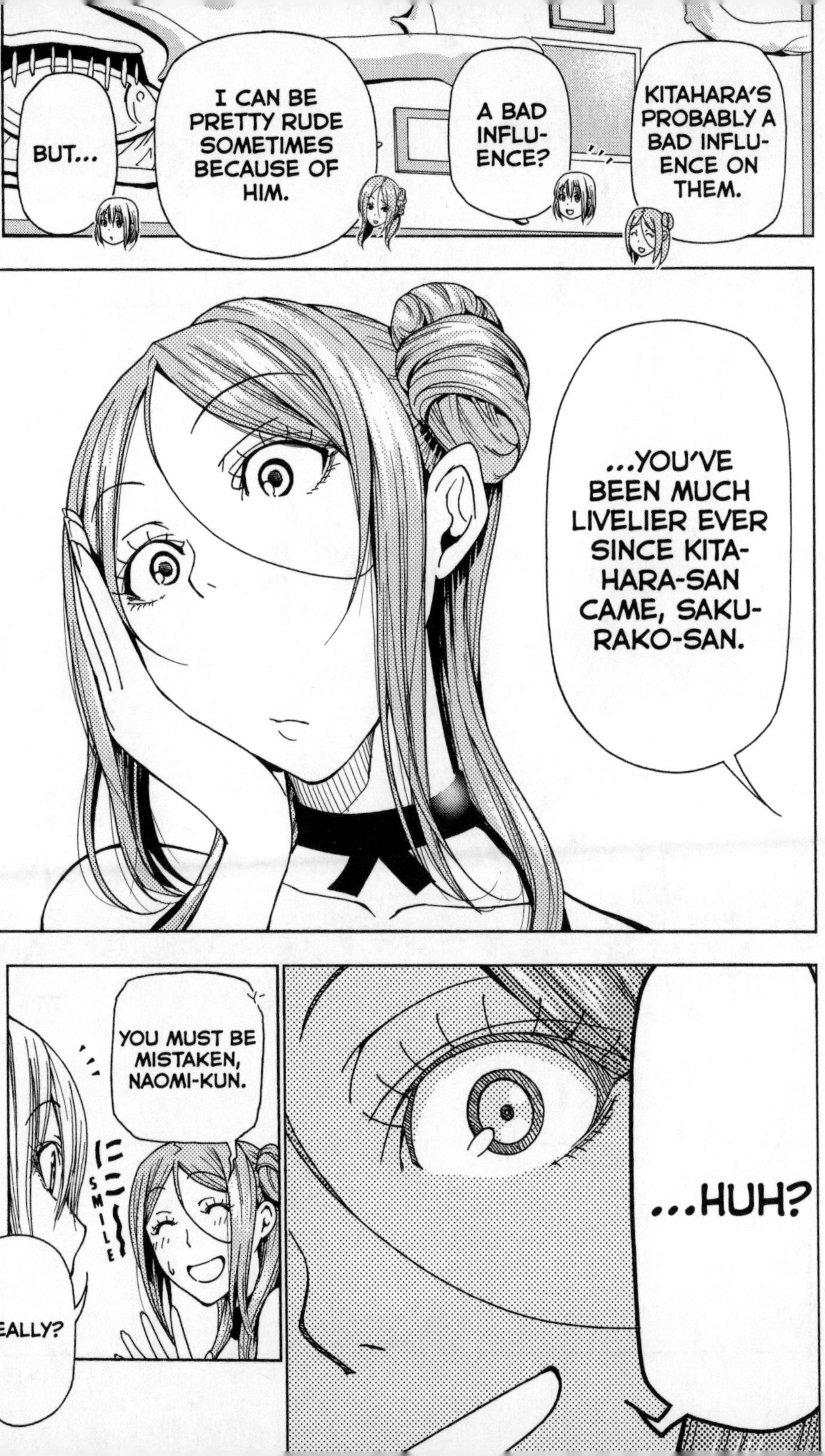
KITAHARA'S PROBABLY A BAD INFLUENCE ON THEM.
A BAD INFLUENCE?
I CAN BE PRETTY RUDE SOMETIMES BECAUSE OF HIM.
BUT...
...YOU'VE BEEN MUCH LIVELIER EVER SINCE KITAHARA-SAN CAME, SAKURAKO-SAN.
...HUH?
YOU MUST BE MISTAKEN, NAOMI-KUN.
SMILE
REALLY?

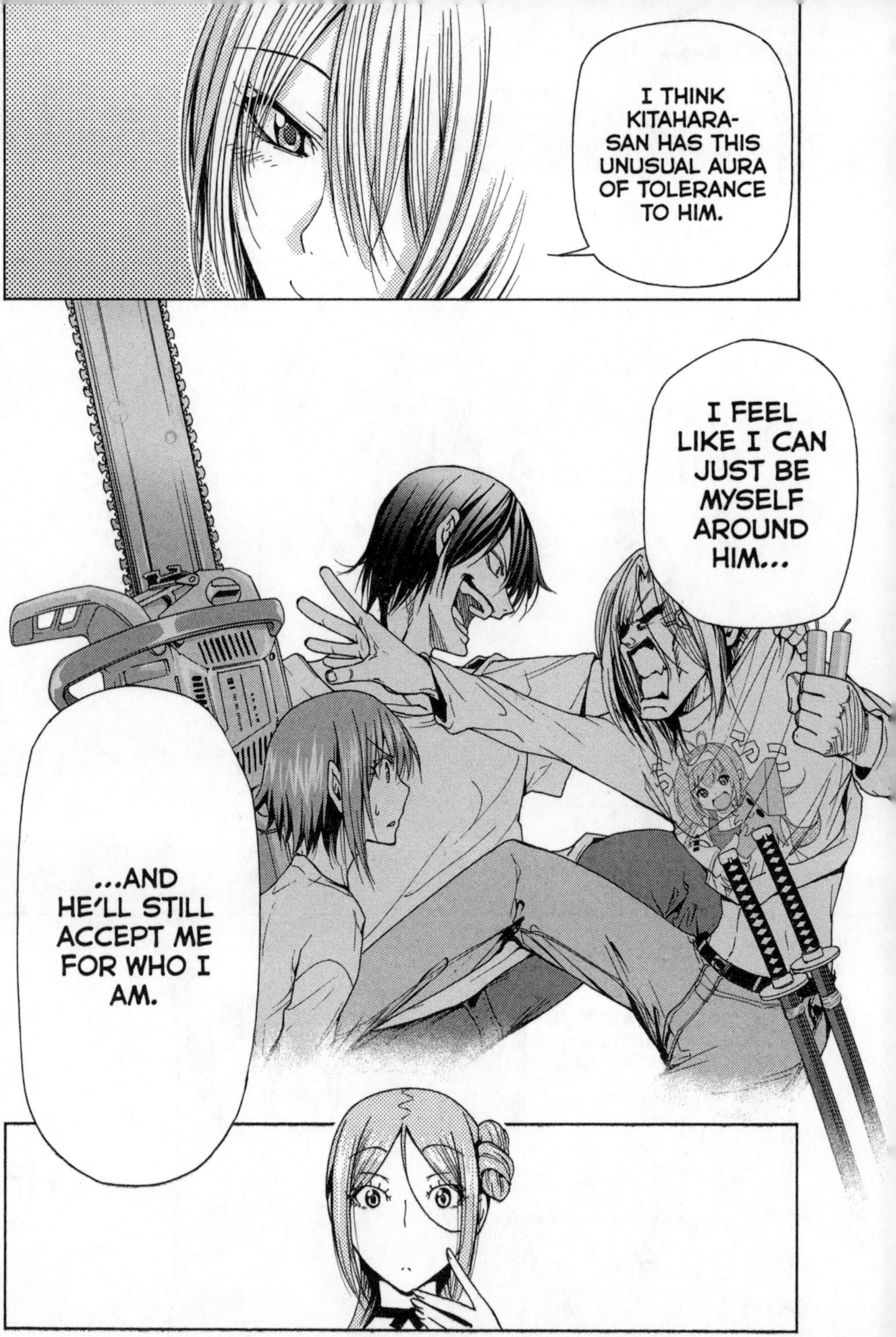
I THINK KITAHARA-SAN HAS THIS UNUSUAL AURA OF TOLERANCE TO HIM.
I FEEL LIKE I CAN JUST BE MYSELF AROUND HIM...
...AND HE'LL STILL ACCEPT ME FOR WHO I AM.

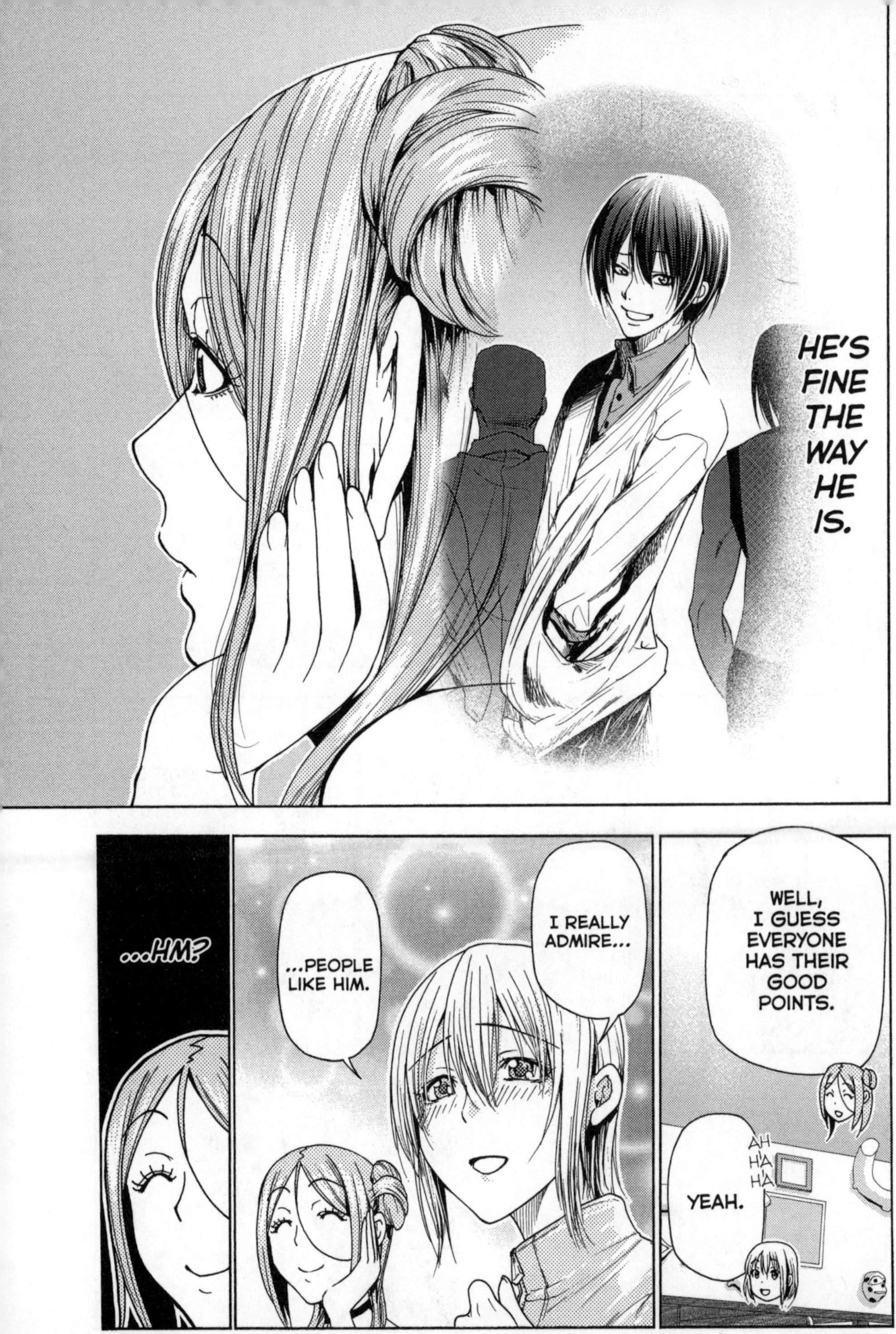
HE'S FINE THE WAY HE IS.
WELL, I GUESS EVERYONE HAS THEIR GOOD POINTS.
AH HA HA
YEAH.
I REALLY ADMIRE...
...PEOPLE LIKE HIM.
...HM?

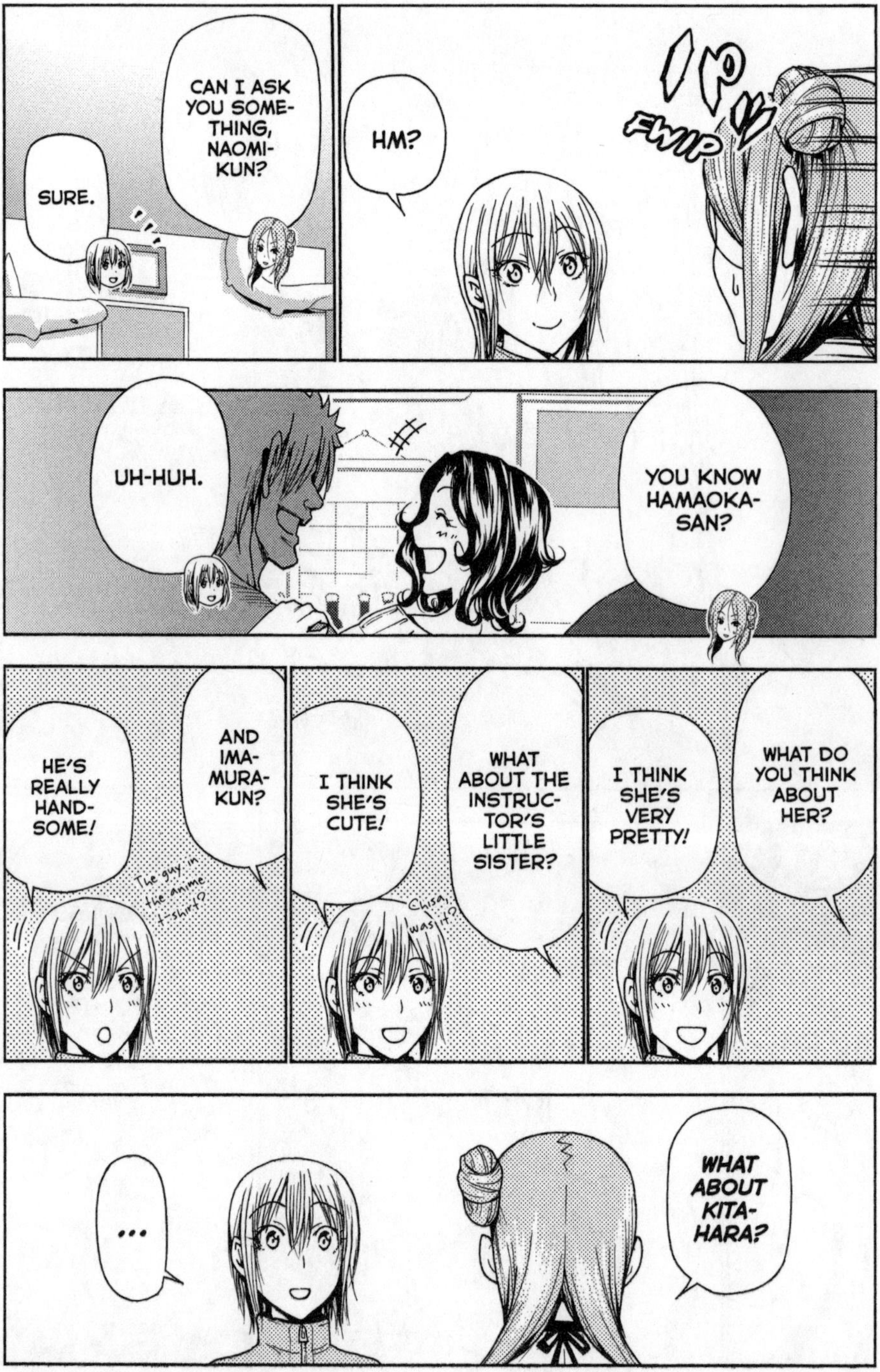
FWIP
HM?
CAN I ASK YOU SOMETHING, NAOMI-KUN?
SURE.
YOU KNOW HAMAOKA-SAN?
UH-HUH.
WHAT DO YOU THINK ABOUT HER?
I THINK SHE'S VERY PRETTY!
WHAT ABOUT THE INSTRUCTOR'S LITTLE SISTER?
Chisa, was it?
I THINK SHE'S CUTE!
AND IMAMURA-KUN?
The guy in the anime t-shirt?
HE'S REALLY HANDSOME!
WHAT ABOUT KITAHARA?
...

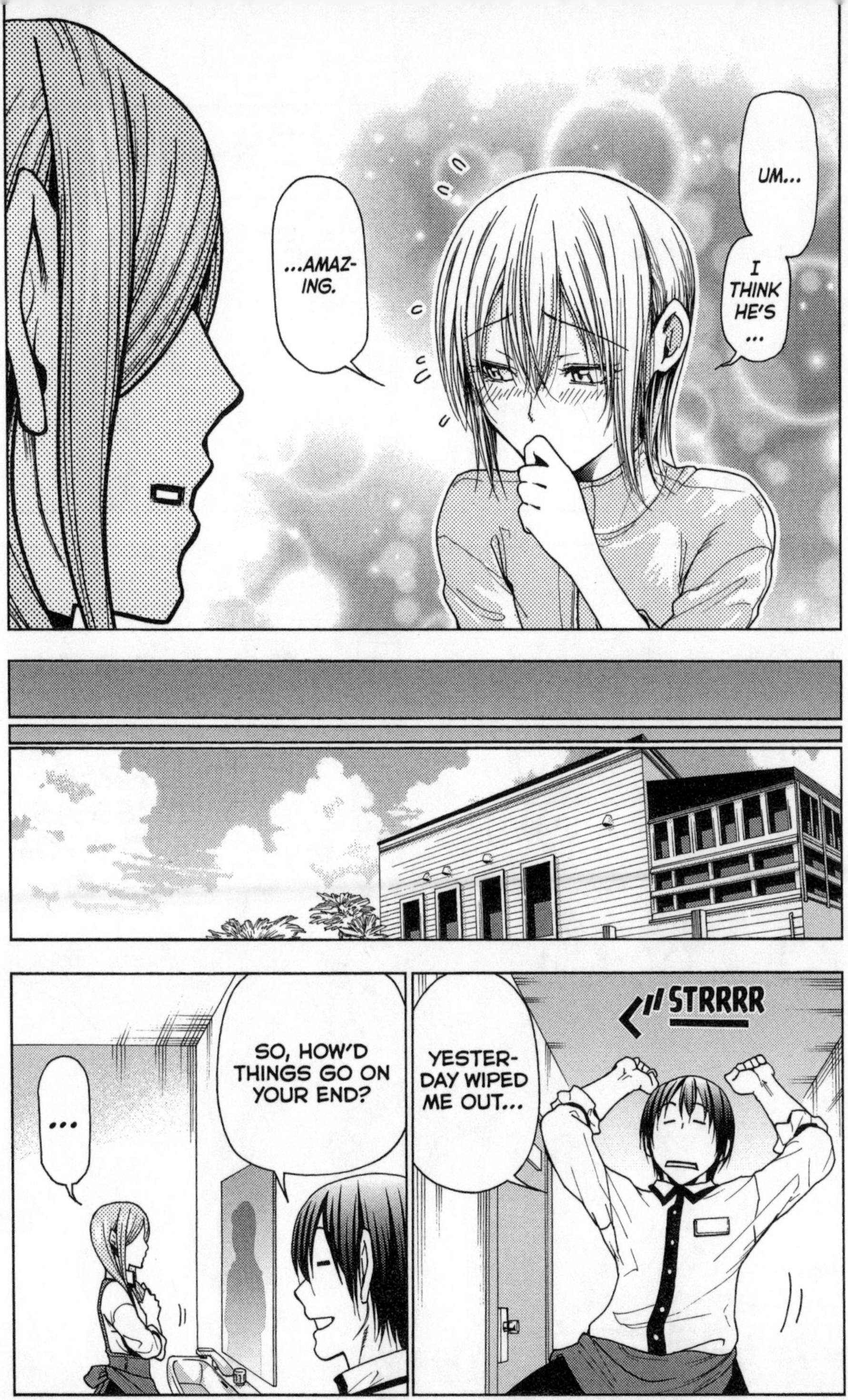
UM...
I THINK HE'S ...
...AMAZ-ING.
STRRRR
YESTER-DAY WIPED ME OUT...
SO, HOW'D THINGS GO ON YOUR END?
...

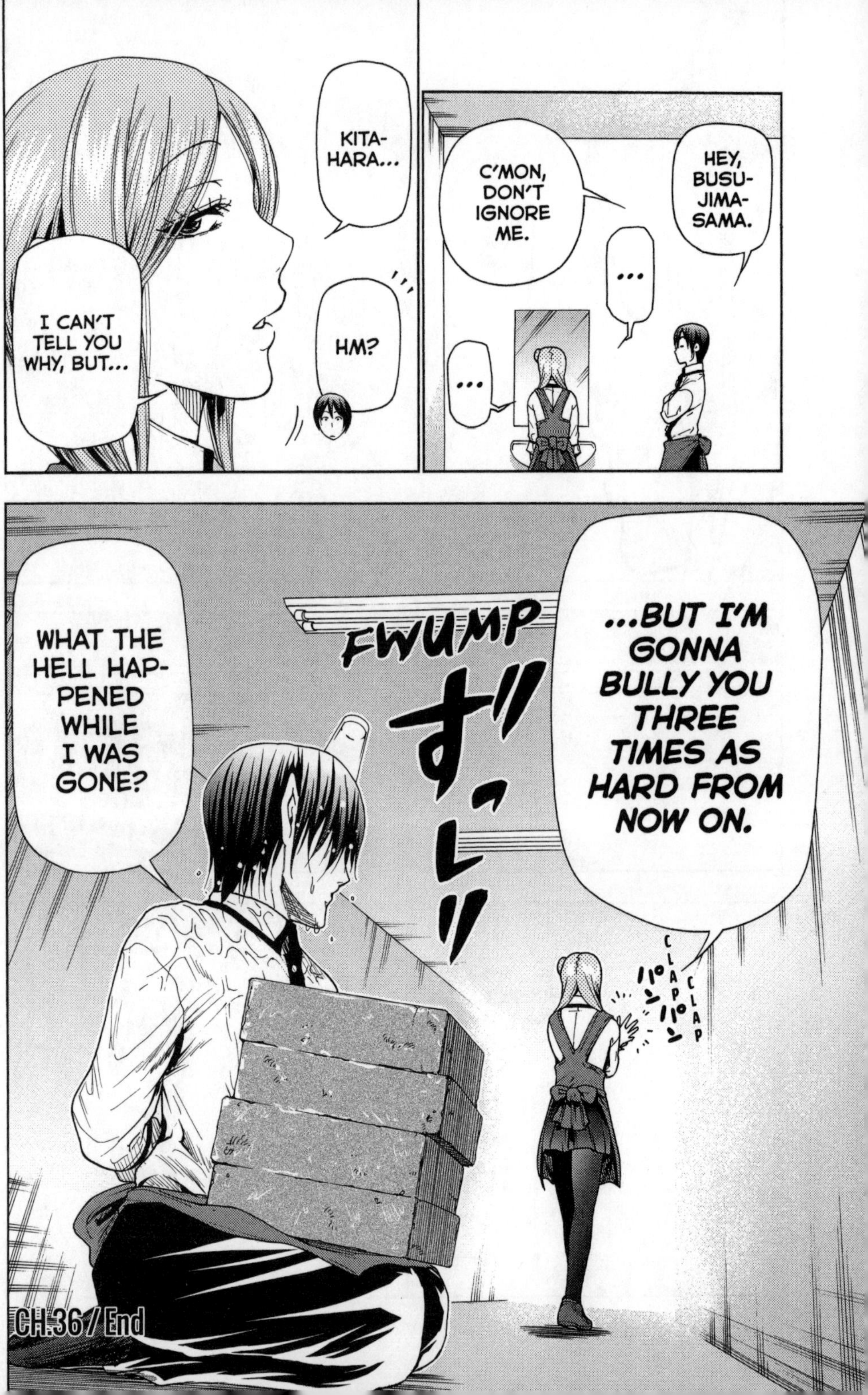

HEY, BUSU-JIMA-SAMA.
C'MON, DON'T IGNORE ME.
...
...
KITA-HARA...
HM?
I CAN'T TELL YOU WHY, BUT...
...BUT I'M GONNA BULLY YOU THREE TIMES AS HARD FROM NOW ON.
FWUMP
CLAP CLAP
WHAT THE HELL HAP-PENED WHILE I WAS GONE?
CH.36 / End

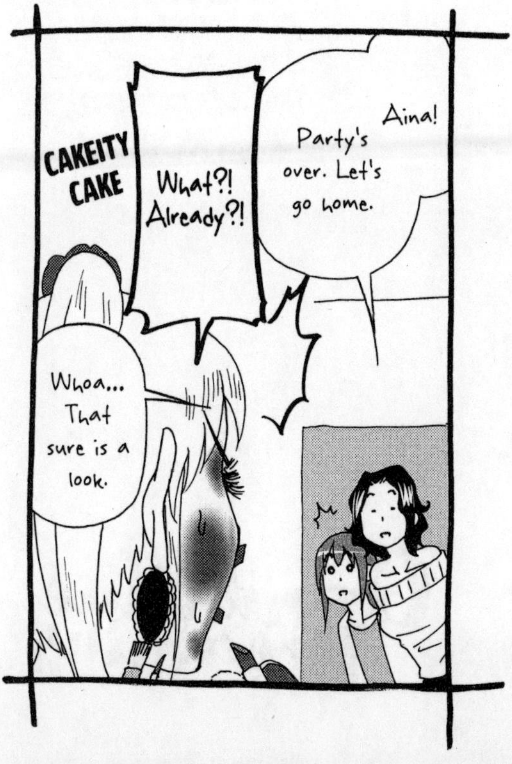
Aina!
Party's over. Let's go home.
What?! Already?!
CAKEITY CAKE
Whoa... That sure is a look.

Grand Blue Dreaming

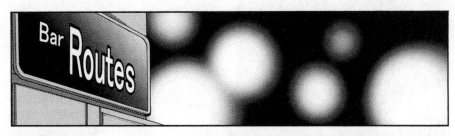

Bar Routes

YES...

I SEE. SO, YOU'RE WORRIED ABOUT *BULLYING*, ARE YOU?

SLIDE

I SEE, I SEE.

BUL-LYING, EH?

I'M NOT SURE WHAT TO DO ANY-MORE...

DON'T BE SO HARD ON YOUR-SELF.

HIT ME.

I DON'T KNOW THE DETAILS, BUT I DO HAVE ONE THING TO SAY.

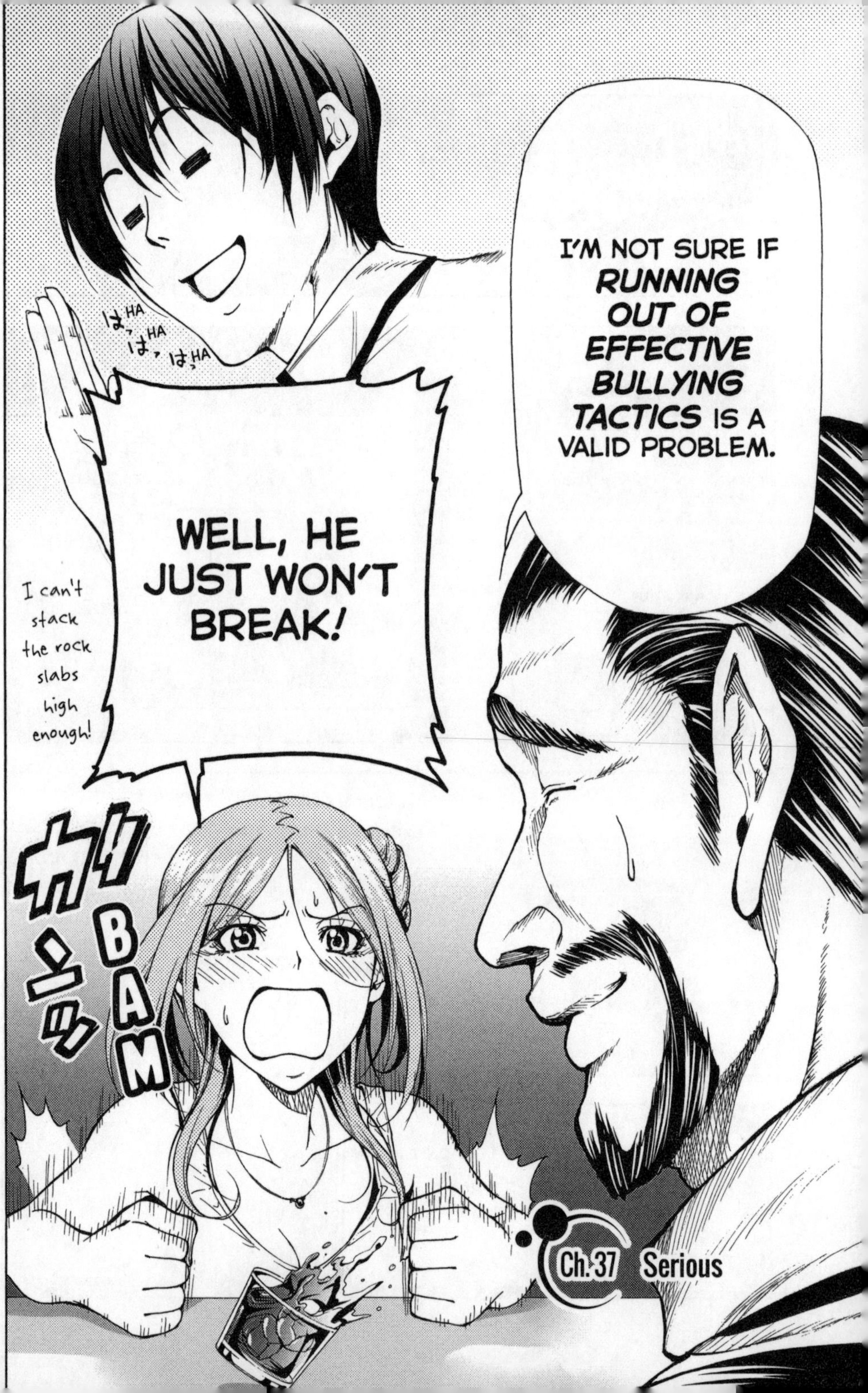
I'M NOT SURE IF RUNNING OUT OF EFFECTIVE BULLYING TACTICS IS A VALID PROBLEM.
は、HA は、HA は、HA
WELL, HE JUST WON'T BREAK!
I can't stack the rock slabs high enough!
ガタンッ BAM
Ch.37 Serious

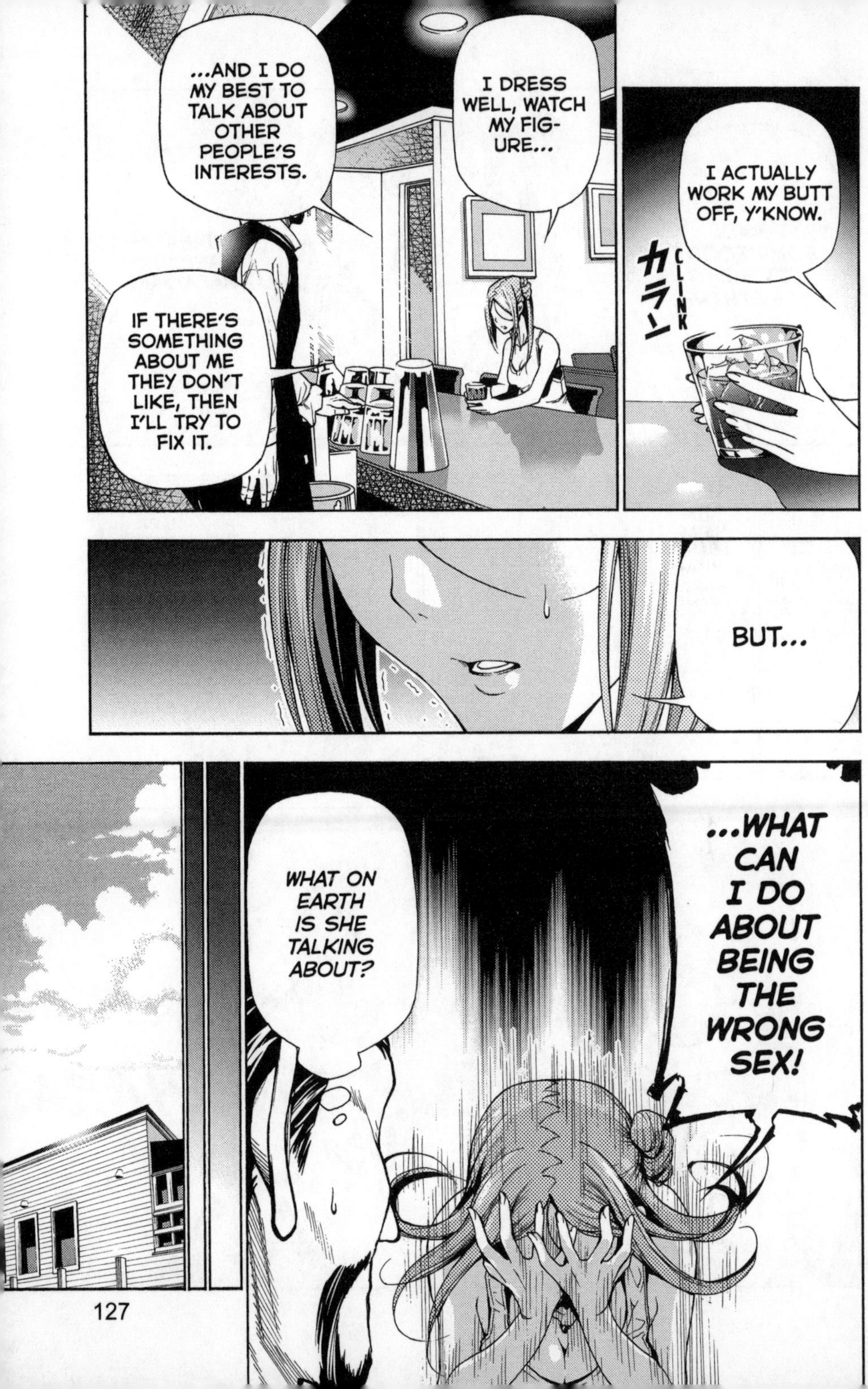
I ACTUALLY WORK MY BUTT OFF, Y'KNOW.
カラン
CLINK
I DRESS WELL, WATCH MY FIG-URE...
...AND I DO MY BEST TO TALK ABOUT OTHER PEOPLE'S INTERESTS.
IF THERE'S SOMETHING ABOUT ME THEY DON'T LIKE, THEN I'LL TRY TO FIX IT.
BUT...
...WHAT CAN I DO ABOUT BEING THE WRONG SEX!
WHAT ON EARTH IS SHE TALKING ABOUT?

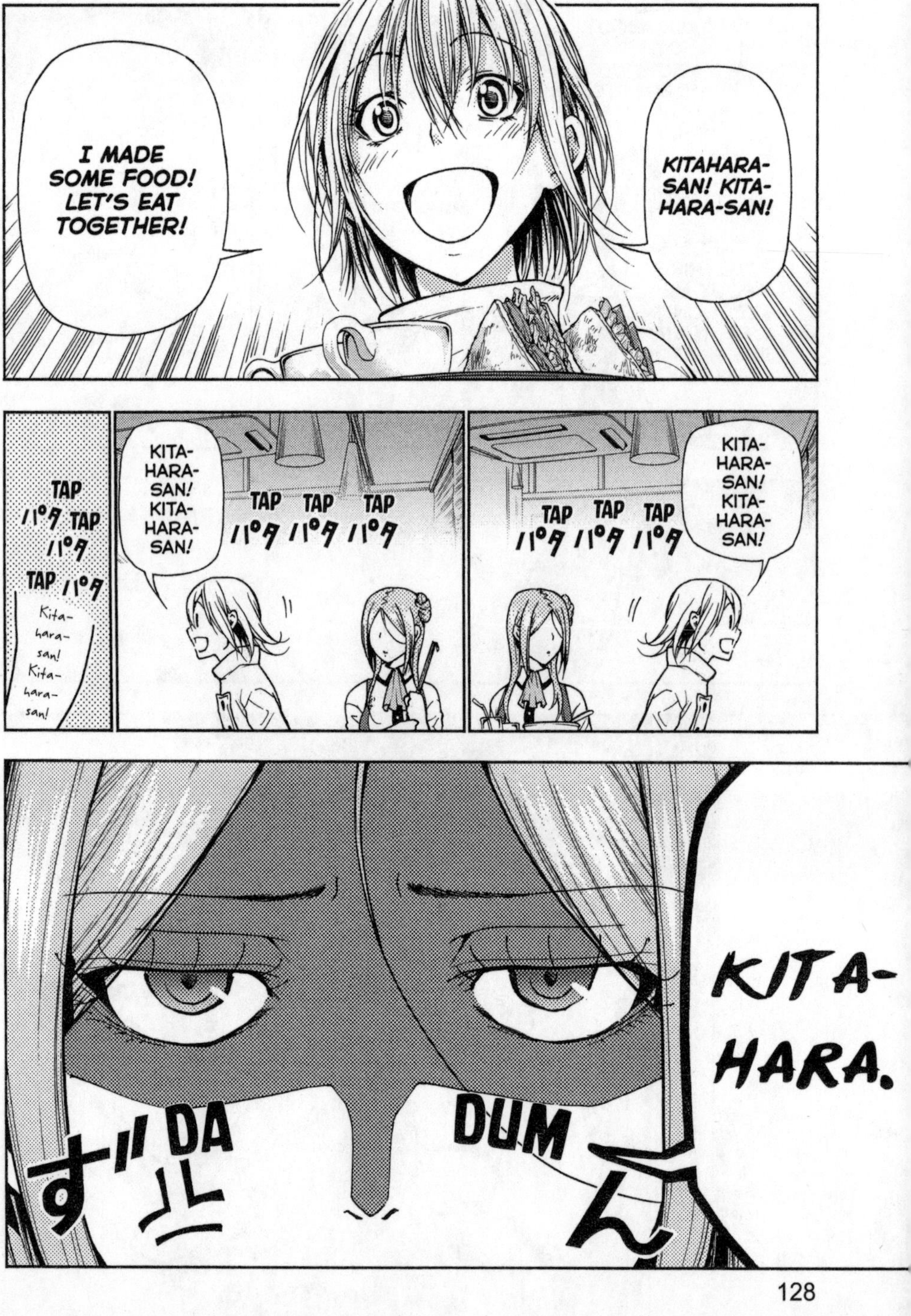
KITAHARA-SAN! KITA-HARA-SAN!
I MADE SOME FOOD! LET'S EAT TOGETHER!
KITA-HARA-SAN! KITA-HARA-SAN!
TAP パタ TAP パタ TAP パタ
KITA-HARA-SAN! KITA-HARA-SAN!
TAP パタ TAP パタ TAP パタ
TAP パタ TAP パタ TAP パタ
Kita-hara-san! Kita-hara-san!
KITA-HARA.
DUM
ん
DA
ずーん

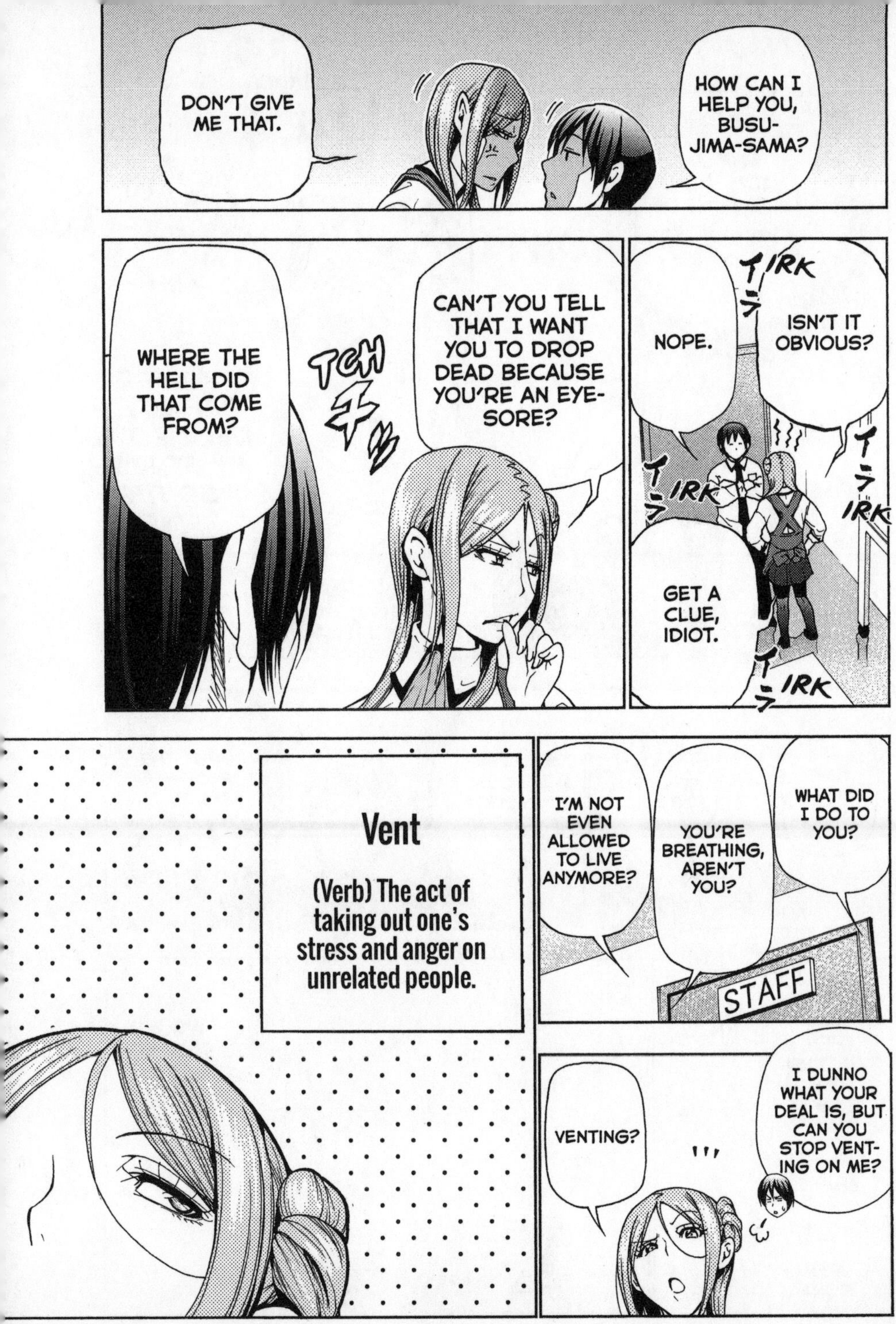
HOW CAN I HELP YOU, BUSU-JIMA-SAMA?
DON'T GIVE ME THAT.
IRK
ISN'T IT OBVIOUS?
IRK
NOPE.
IRK
GET A CLUE, IDIOT.
IRK
CAN'T YOU TELL THAT I WANT YOU TO DROP DEAD BECAUSE YOU'RE AN EYE-SORE?
TCH
WHERE THE HELL DID THAT COME FROM?
WHAT DID I DO TO YOU?
YOU'RE BREATHING, AREN'T YOU?
I'M NOT EVEN ALLOWED TO LIVE ANYMORE?
STAFF
I DUNNO WHAT YOUR DEAL IS, BUT CAN YOU STOP VENTING ON ME?
VENTING?
Vent
(Verb) The act of taking out one's stress and anger on unrelated people.

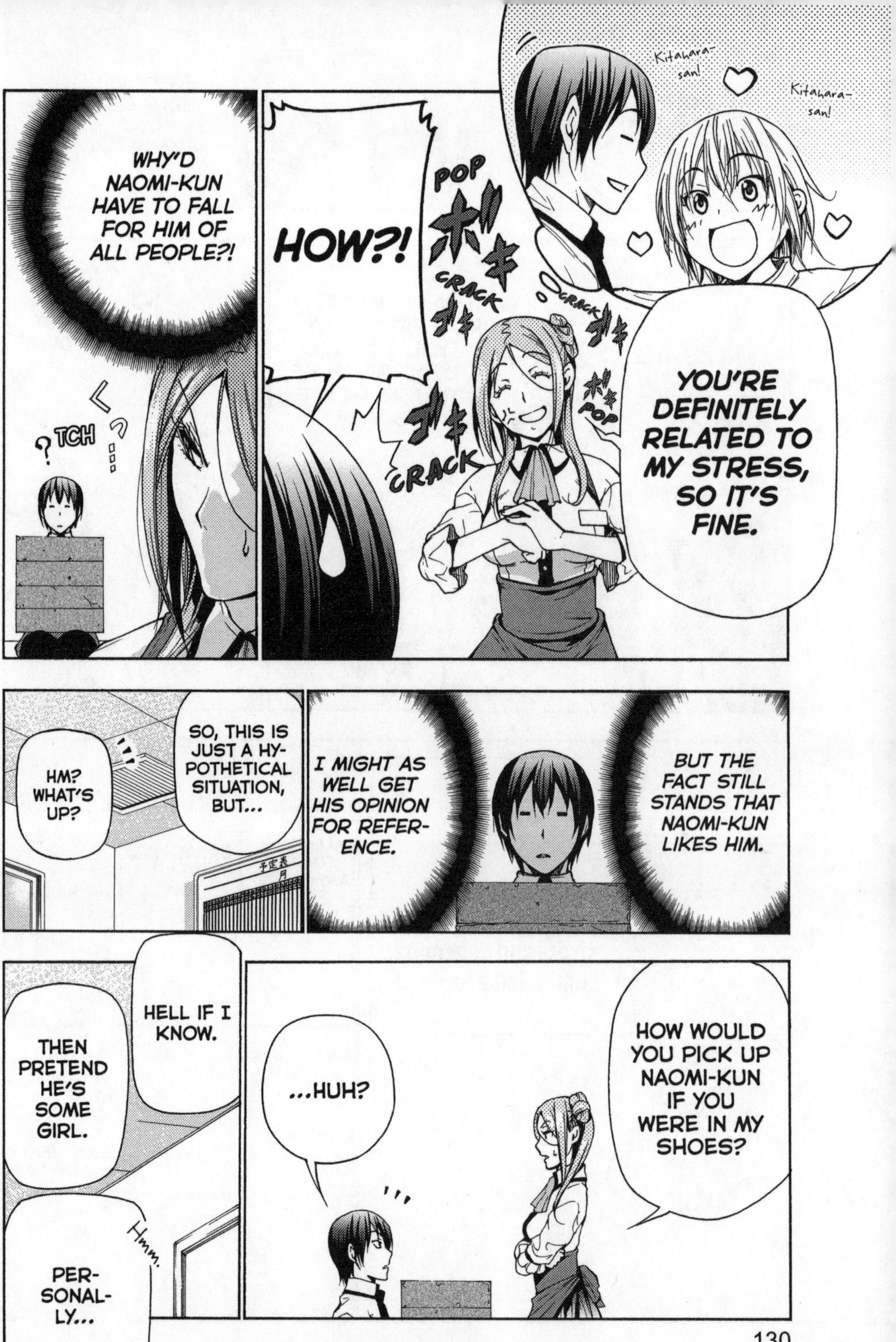
Kitahara-san!
Kitahara-san!
YOU'RE DEFINITELY RELATED TO MY STRESS, SO IT'S FINE.
POP
CRACK
CRACK
POP
CRACK
HOW?!
WHY'D NAOMI-KUN HAVE TO FALL FOR HIM OF ALL PEOPLE?!
TCH
BUT THE FACT STILL STANDS THAT NAOMI-KUN LIKES HIM.
I MIGHT AS WELL GET HIS OPINION FOR REFERENCE.
SO, THIS IS JUST A HYPOTHETICAL SITUATION, BUT...
HM? WHAT'S UP?
HOW WOULD YOU PICK UP NAOMI-KUN IF YOU WERE IN MY SHOES?
...HUH?
HELL IF I KNOW.
THEN PRETEND HE'S SOME GIRL.
Hmm.
PERSONALLY...

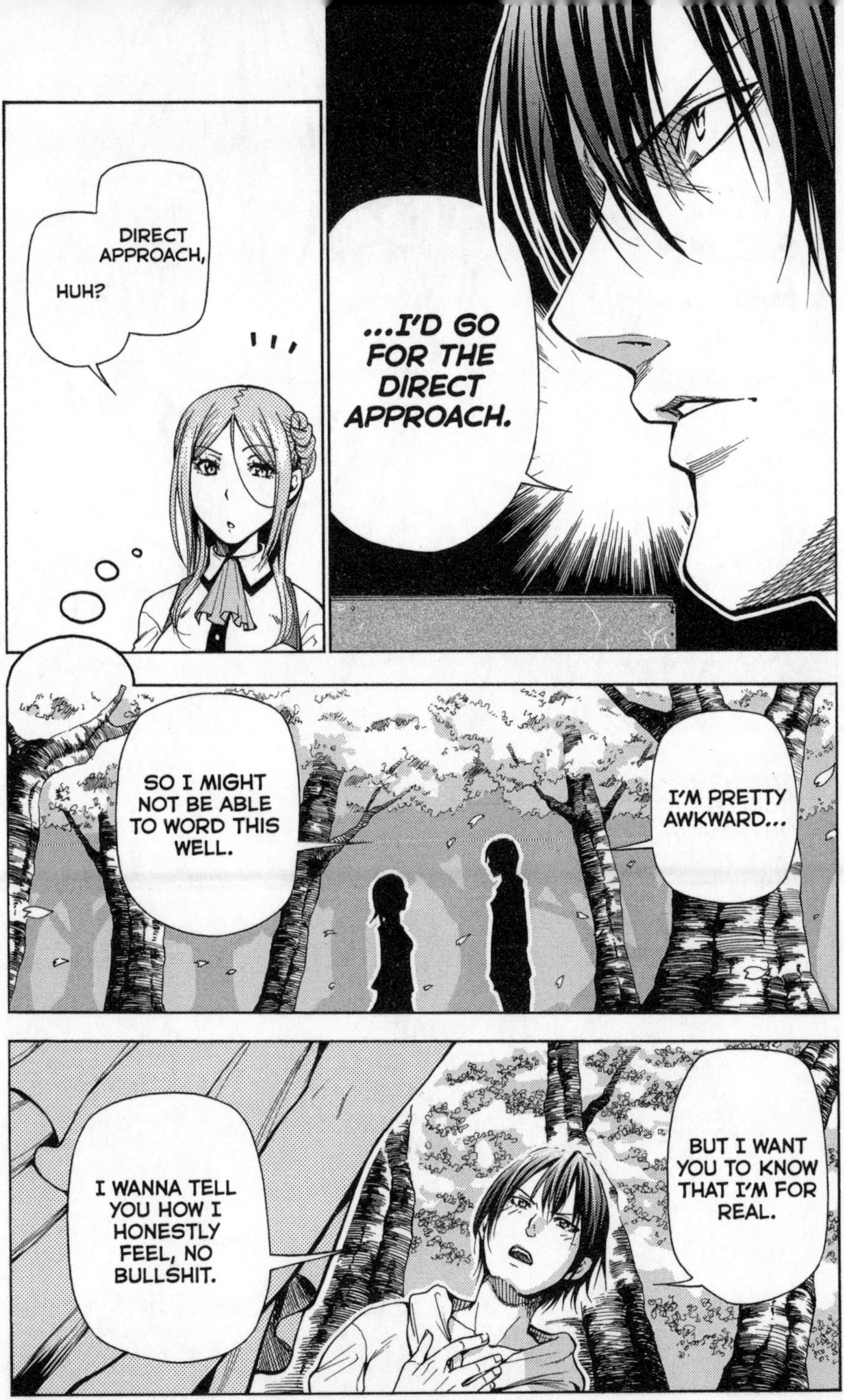
...I'D GO FOR THE DIRECT APPROACH.
DIRECT APPROACH, HUH?
I'M PRETTY AWKWARD...
SO I MIGHT NOT BE ABLE TO WORD THIS WELL.
BUT I WANT YOU TO KNOW THAT I'M FOR REAL.
I WANNA TELL YOU HOW I HONESTLY FEEL, NO BULLSHIT.

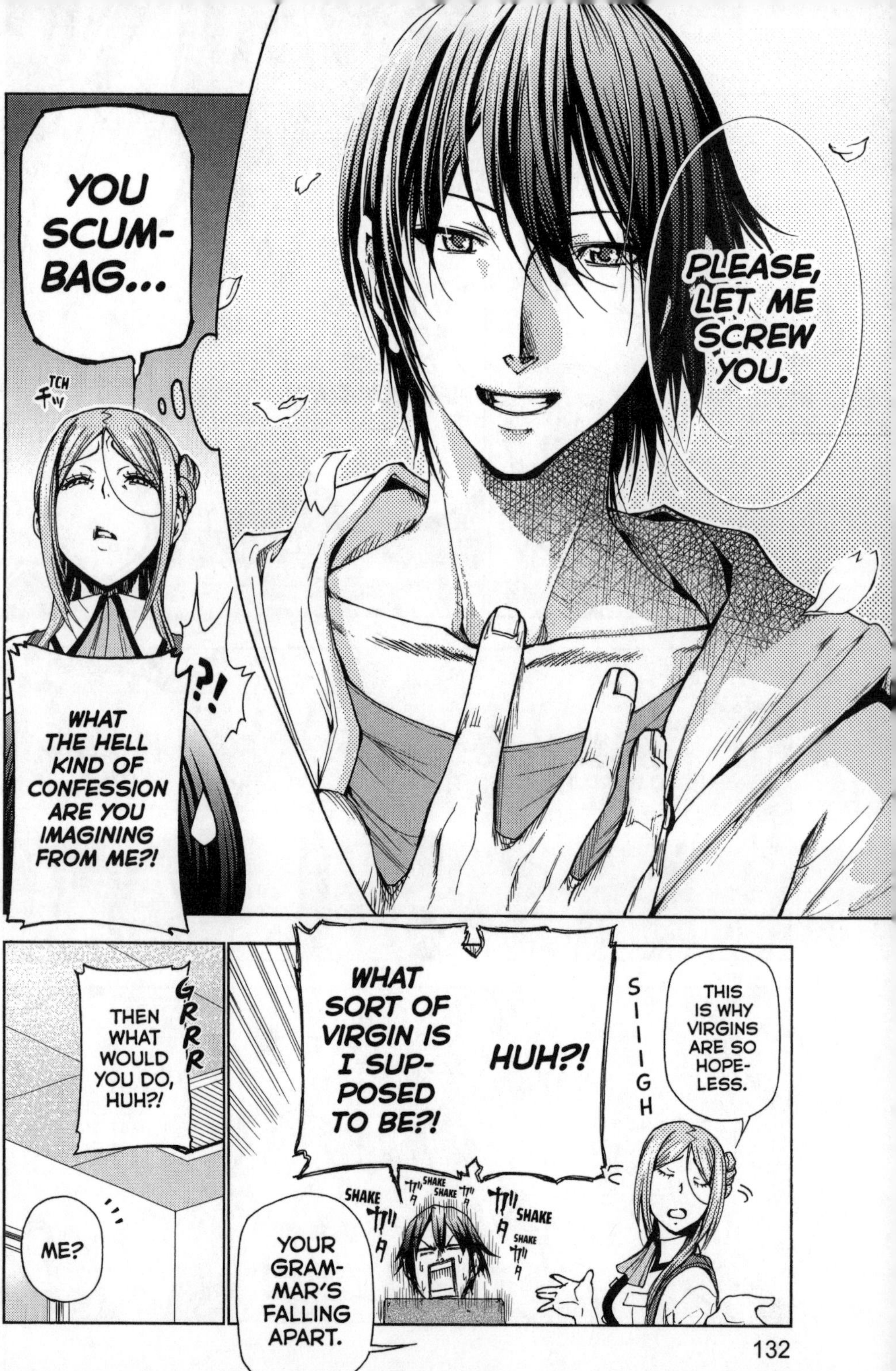
PLEASE, LET ME SCREW YOU.
YOU SCUM-BAG...
TCH チッ
?!
WHAT THE HELL KIND OF CONFESSION ARE YOU IMAGINING FROM ME?!
THIS IS WHY VIRGINS ARE SO HOPE-LESS.
SIIIIGH
HUH?!
WHAT SORT OF VIRGIN IS I SUP-POSED TO BE?!
SHAKE SHAKE SHAKE SHAKE SHAKE
YOUR GRAM-MAR'S FALLING APART.
GRRR
THEN WHAT WOULD YOU DO, HUH?!
ME?

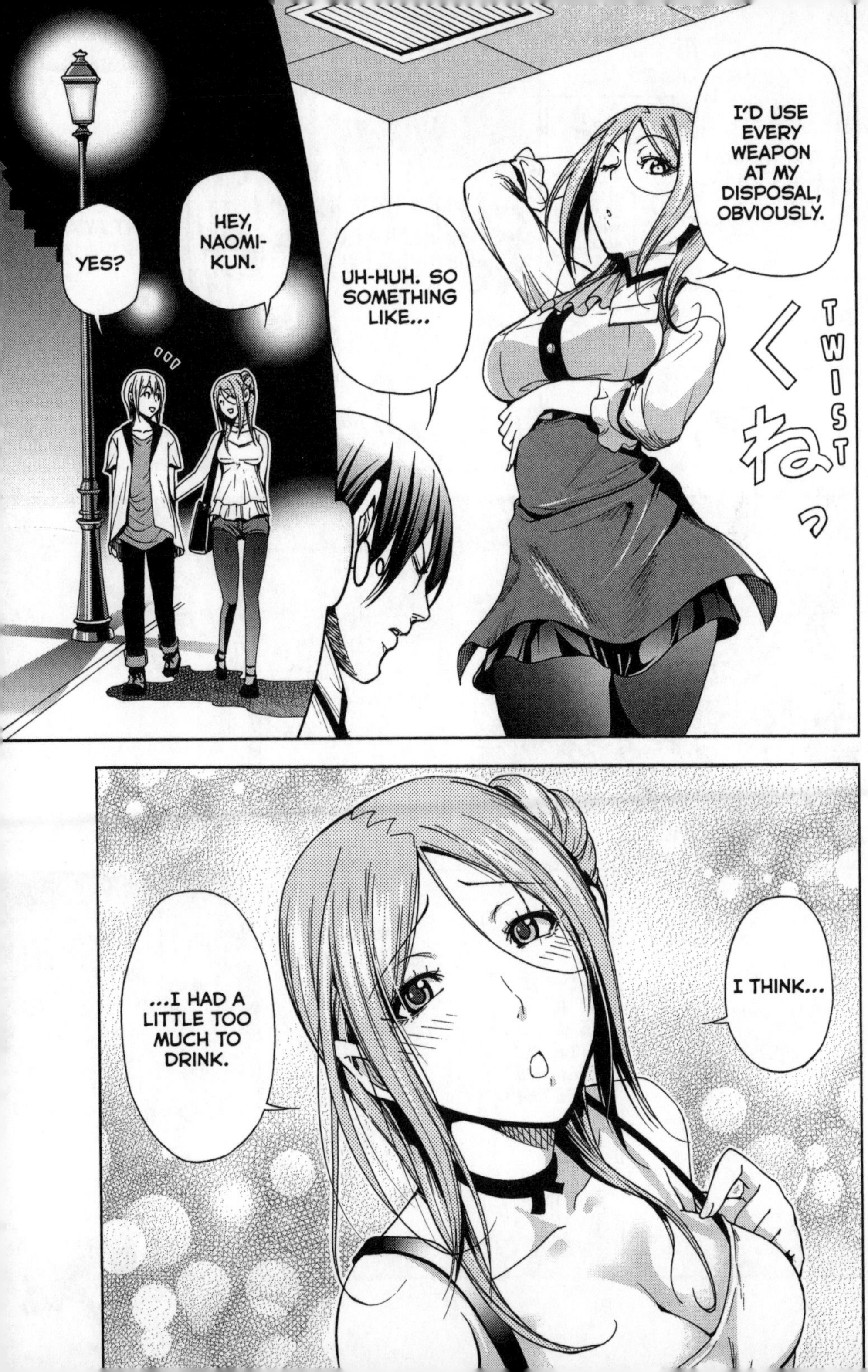
I'D USE EVERY WEAPON AT MY DISPOSAL, OBVIOUSLY.
UH-HUH. SO SOMETHING LIKE...
TWIST
HEY, NAOMI-KUN.
YES?
I THINK...
...I HAD A LITTLE TOO MUCH TO DRINK.

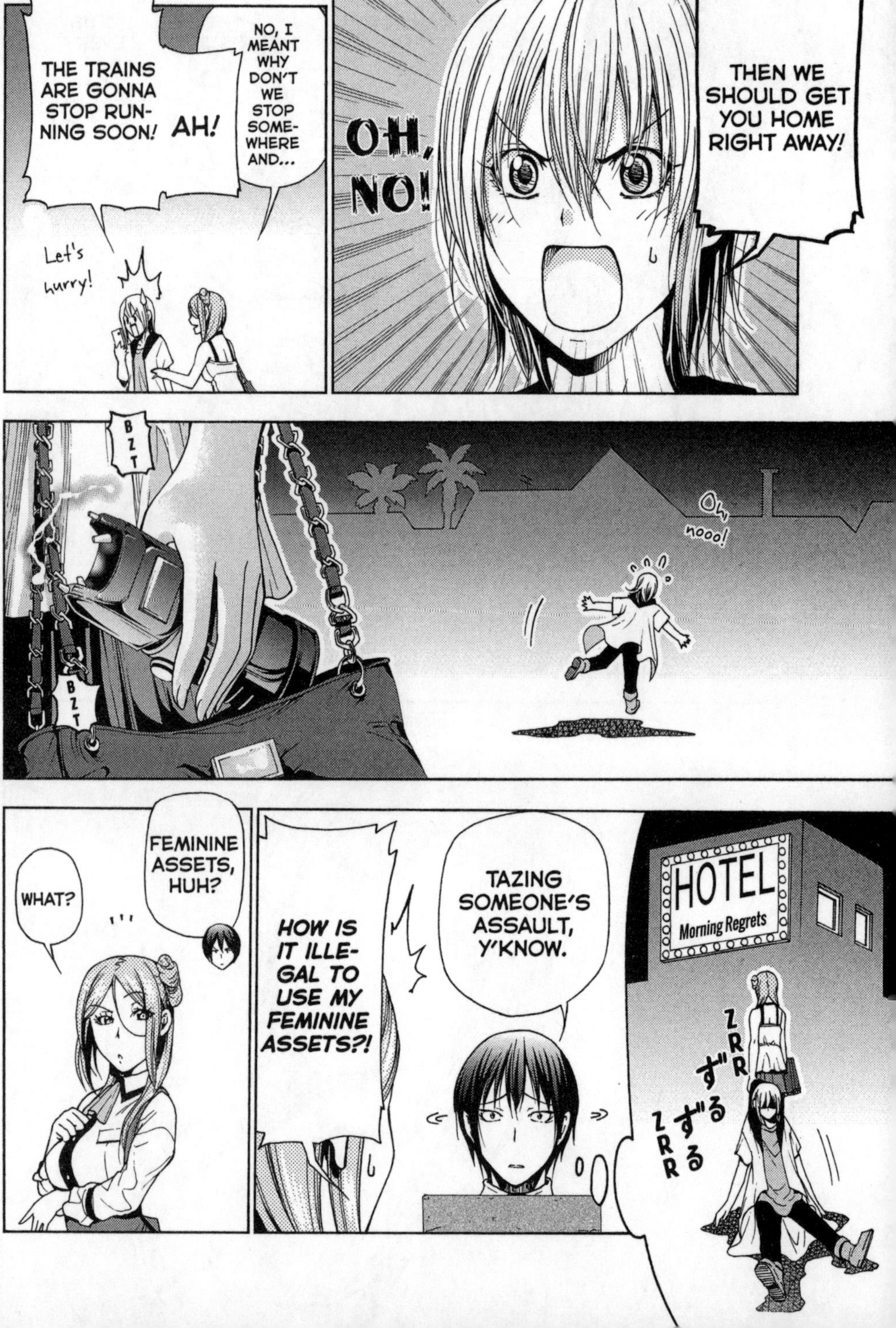
THEN WE SHOULD GET YOU HOME RIGHT AWAY!
OH, NO!
NO, I MEANT WHY DON'T WE STOP SOMEWHERE AND...
AH!
THE TRAINS ARE GONNA STOP RUNNING SOON!
Let's hurry!
Ow nooo!
BZT
BZT
HOTEL
Morning Regrets
ZRR
ずる
ずる
ZRR
TAZING SOMEONE'S ASSAULT, Y'KNOW.
HOW IS IT ILLEGAL TO USE MY FEMININE ASSETS?!
FEMININE ASSETS, HUH?
WHAT?
...

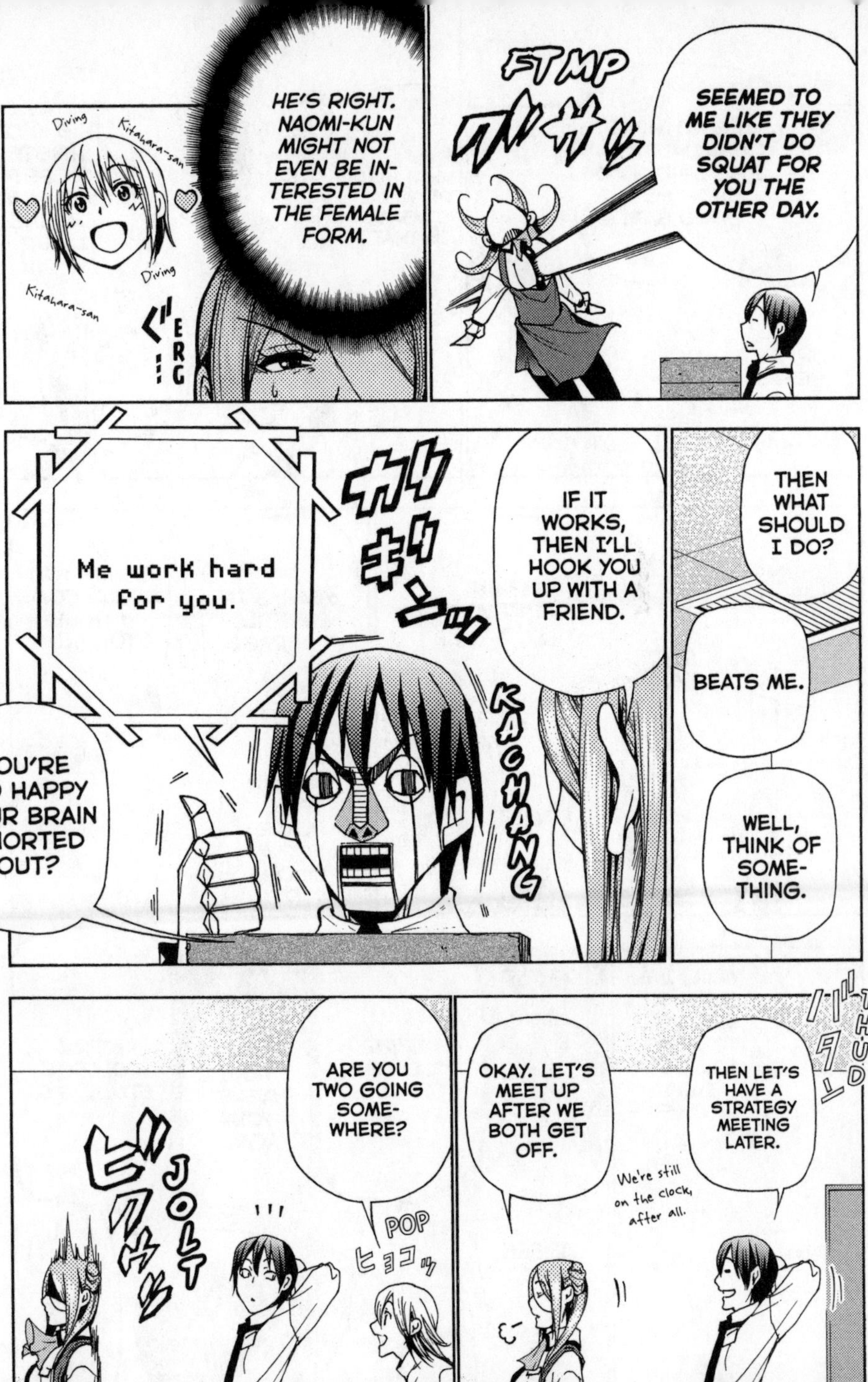
FTMP
SEEMED TO ME LIKE THEY DIDN'T DO SQUAT FOR YOU THE OTHER DAY.
HE'S RIGHT. NAOMI-KUN MIGHT NOT EVEN BE INTERESTED IN THE FEMALE FORM.
Diving
Kitahara-san
Diving
Kitahara-san
ERG
THEN WHAT SHOULD I DO?
BEATS ME.
WELL, THINK OF SOMETHING.
IF IT WORKS, THEN I'LL HOOK YOU UP WITH A FRIEND.
KACHANG
Me work hard for you.
YOU'RE SO HAPPY YOUR BRAIN SHORTED OUT?
THUD
THEN LET'S HAVE A STRATEGY MEETING LATER.
We're still on the clock, after all.
OKAY. LET'S MEET UP AFTER WE BOTH GET OFF.
ARE YOU TWO GOING SOMEWHERE?
POP
ヒョコッ
JOLT

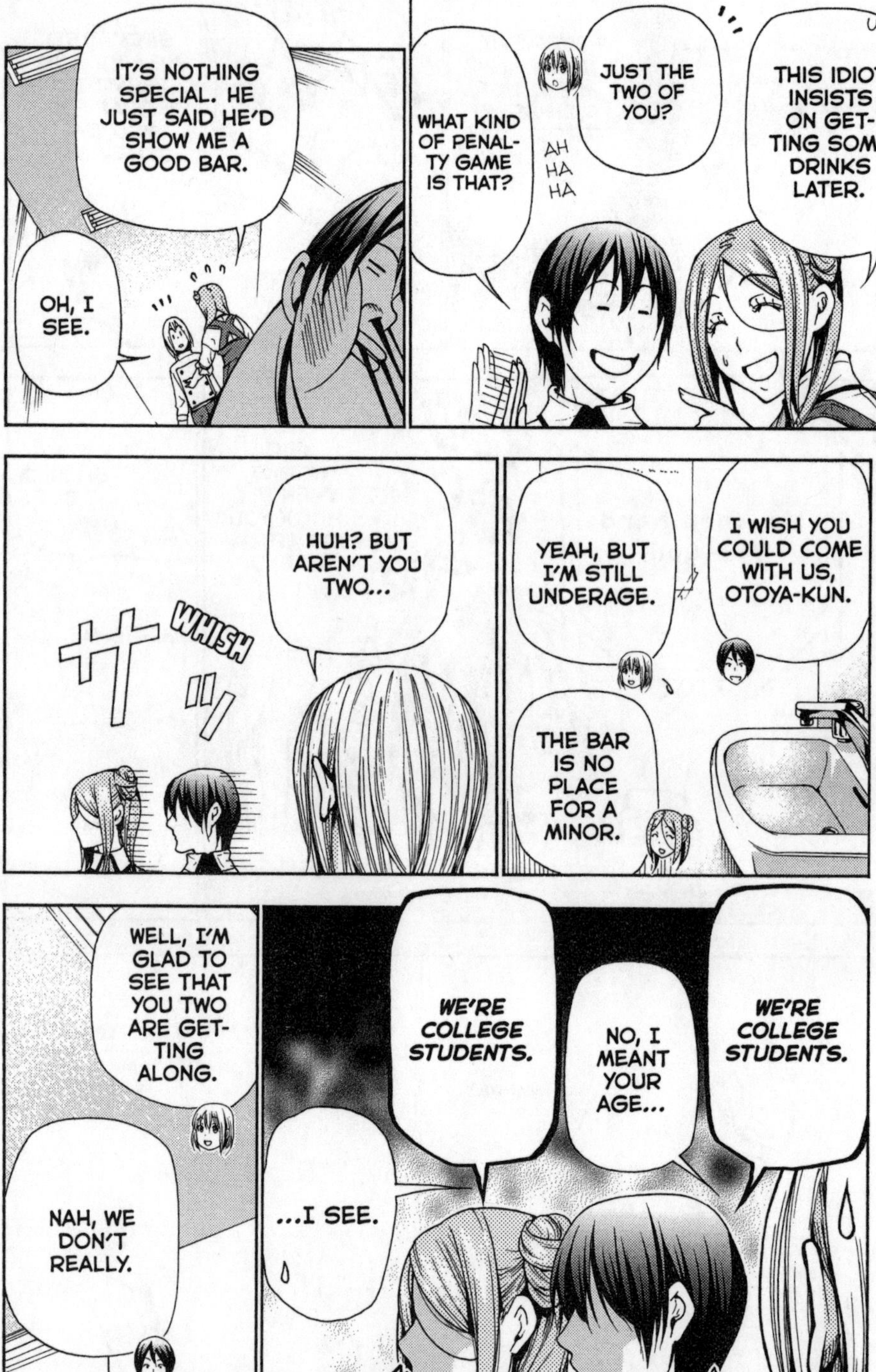
Umm...
THIS IDIOT INSISTS ON GETTING SOME DRINKS LATER.
JUST THE TWO OF YOU?
AH HA HA
WHAT KIND OF PENALTY GAME IS THAT?
IT'S NOTHING SPECIAL. HE JUST SAID HE'D SHOW ME A GOOD BAR.
OH, I SEE.
I WISH YOU COULD COME WITH US, OTOYA-KUN.
YEAH, BUT I'M STILL UNDERAGE.
THE BAR IS NO PLACE FOR A MINOR.
HUH? BUT AREN'T YOU TWO...
WHISH
WE'RE COLLEGE STUDENTS.
NO, I MEANT YOUR AGE...
WE'RE COLLEGE STUDENTS.
...I SEE.
G R R R R R
WELL, I'M GLAD TO SEE THAT YOU TWO ARE GETTING ALONG.
NAH, WE DON'T REALLY.

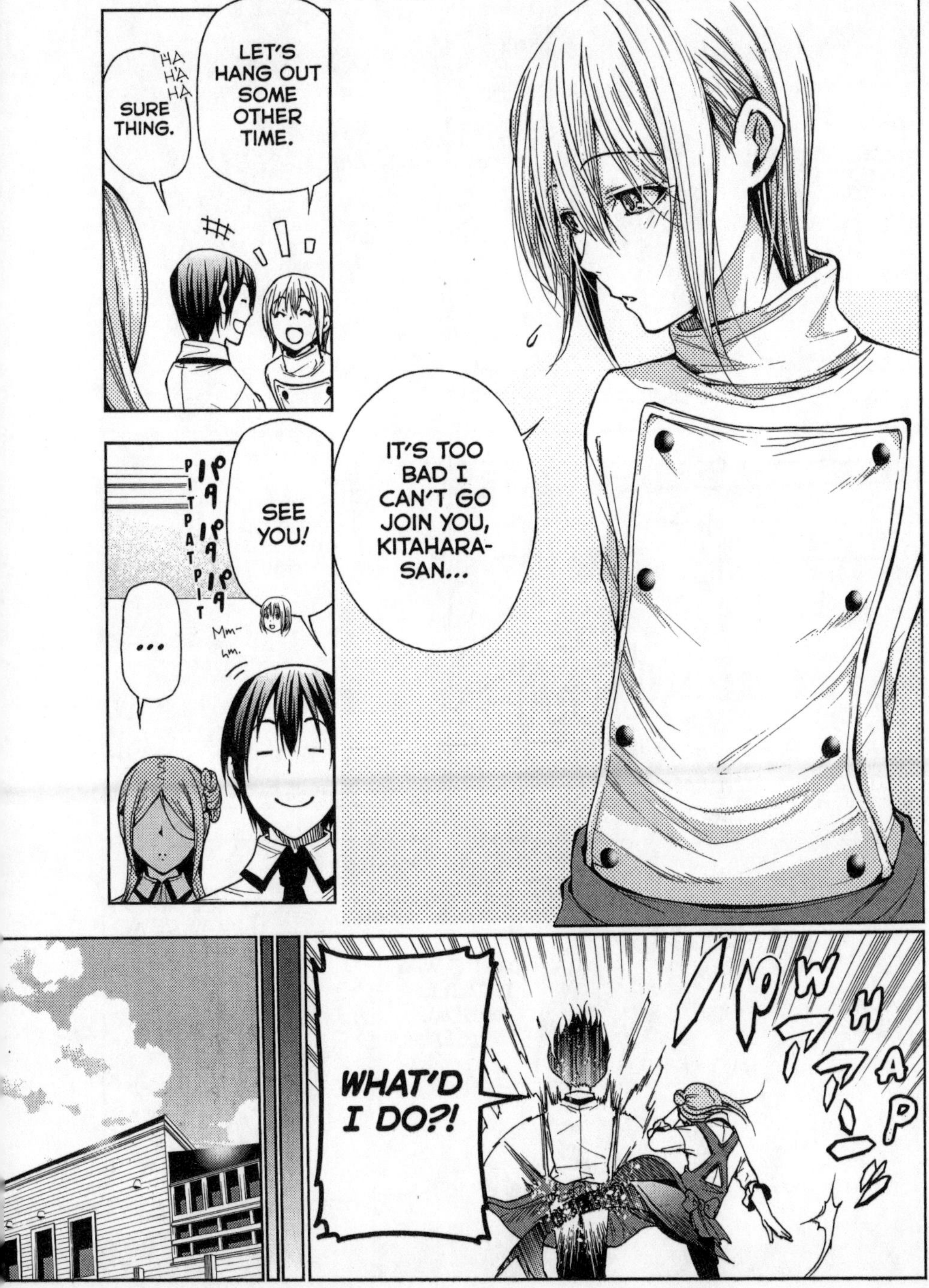
IT'S TOO BAD I CAN'T GO JOIN YOU, KITAHARA-SAN...
LET'S HANG OUT SOME OTHER TIME.
HA HA HA
SURE THING.
SEE YOU!
PIT PAT PIT
Mm-hm.
...
WHAP
WHAT'D I DO?!

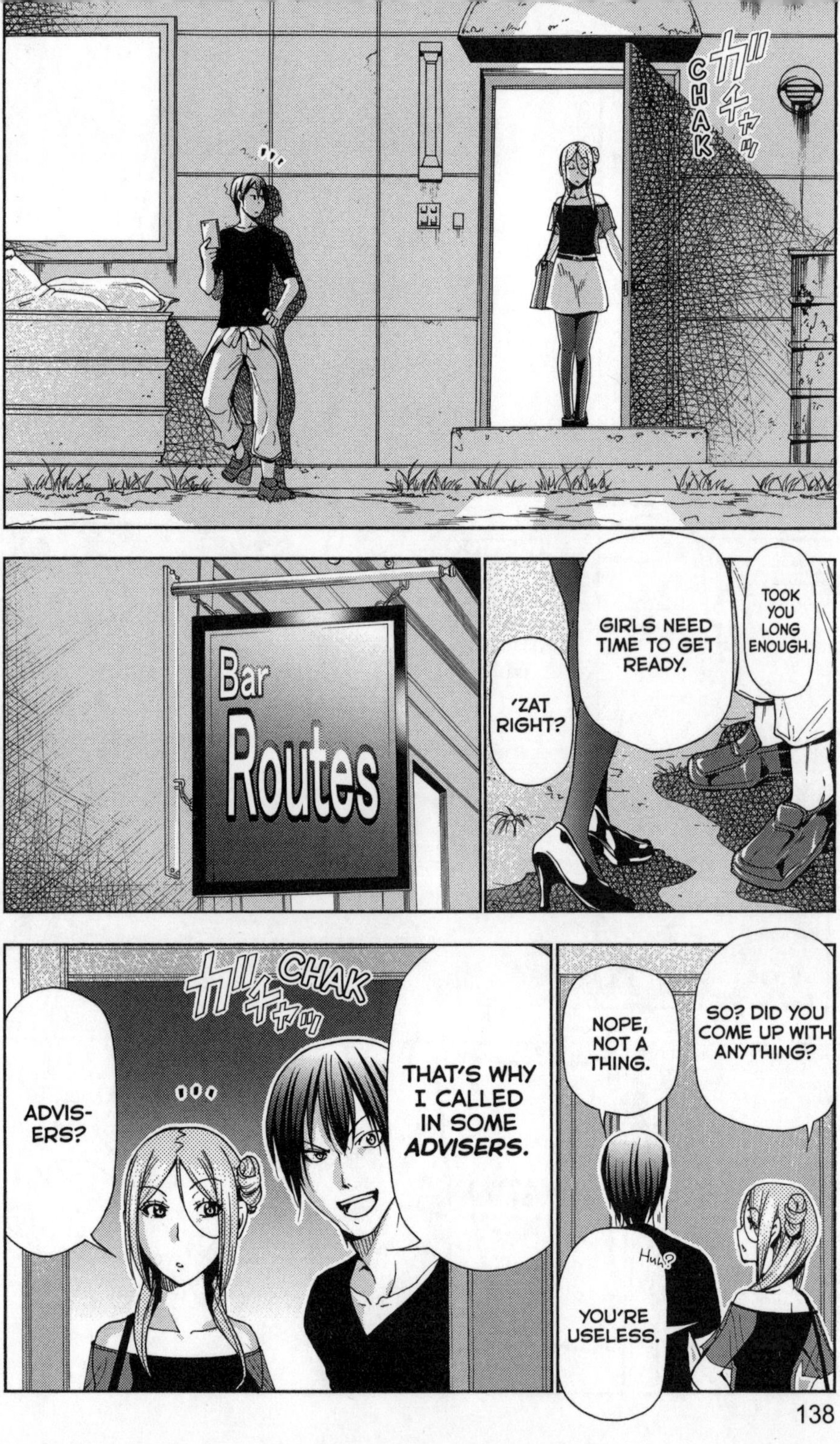
ガチャッ
CHAK
...
TOOK YOU LONG ENOUGH.
GIRLS NEED TIME TO GET READY.
'ZAT RIGHT?
Bar
Routes
SO? DID YOU COME UP WITH ANYTHING?
NOPE, NOT A THING.
Huh?
YOU'RE USELESS.
ガチャッ
CHAK
THAT'S WHY I CALLED IN SOME ADVISERS.
...
ADVIS-
ERS?

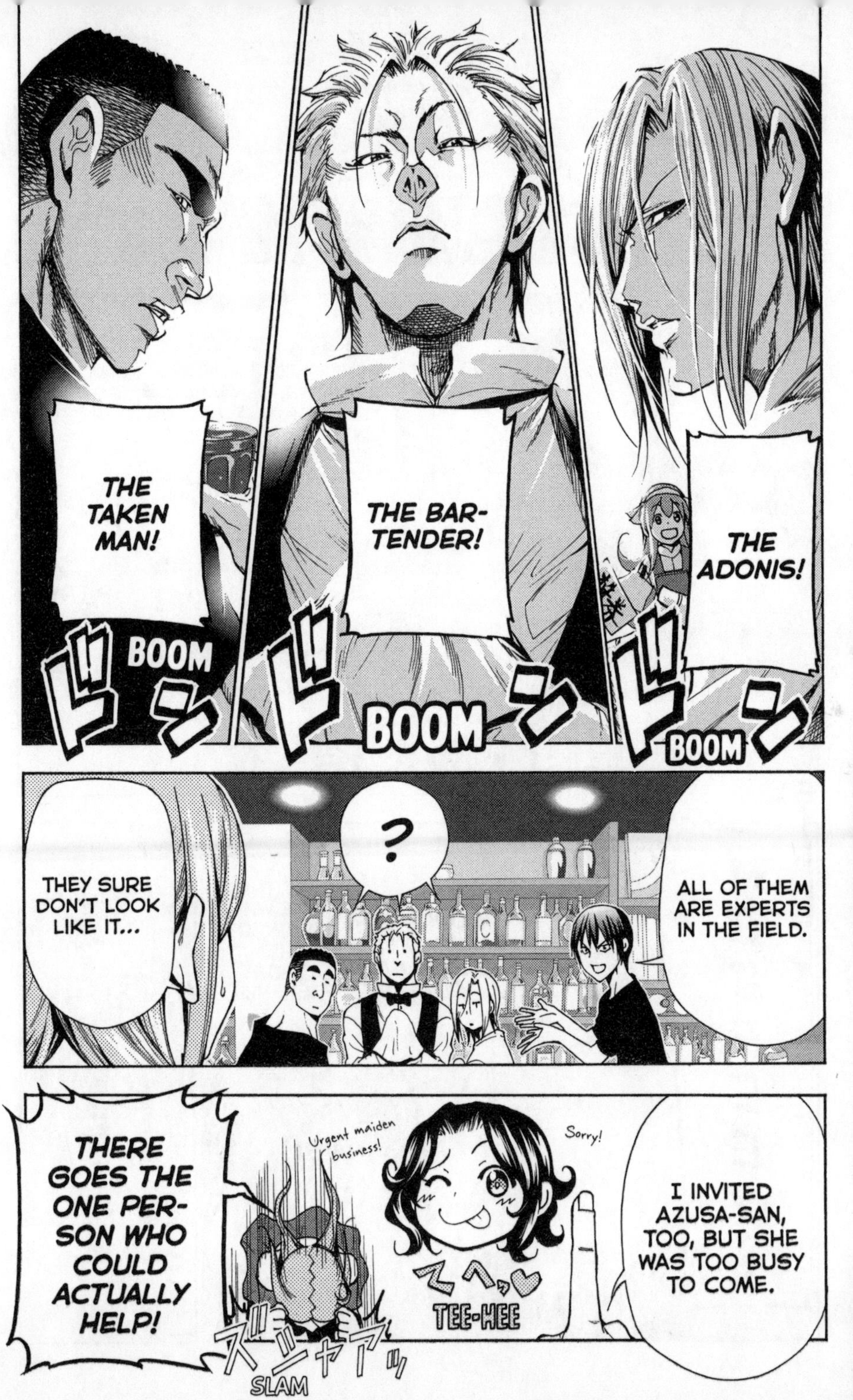
THE ADONIS!
BOOM
THE BAR-TENDER!
BOOM
THE TAKEN MAN!
BOOM
ALL OF THEM ARE EXPERTS IN THE FIELD.
?
THEY SURE DON'T LOOK LIKE IT...
I INVITED AZUSA-SAN, TOO, BUT SHE WAS TOO BUSY TO COME.
Sorry!
TEE-HEE
Urgent maiden business!
SLAM
THERE GOES THE ONE PERSON WHO COULD ACTUALLY HELP!

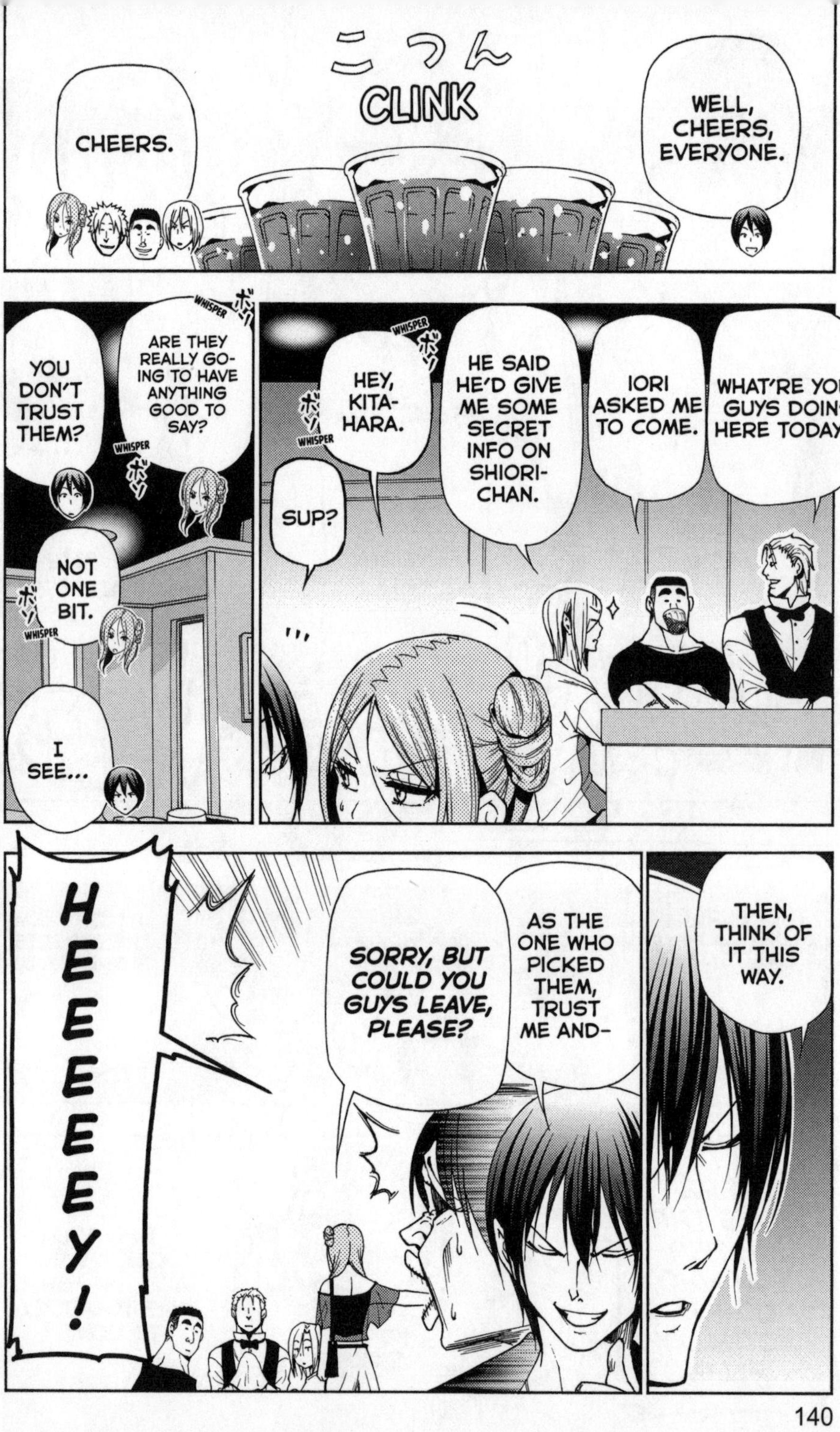
WELL, CHEERS, EVERYONE.
こつん
CLINK
CHEERS.
WHAT'RE YOU GUYS DOIN' HERE TODAY?
IORI ASKED ME TO COME.
HE SAID HE'D GIVE ME SOME SECRET INFO ON SHIORI-CHAN.
ボソ WHISPER
HEY, KITA-HARA.
ボソ WHISPER
SUP?
ボソ WHISPER
ARE THEY REALLY GO-ING TO HAVE ANYTHING GOOD TO SAY?
ボソ WHISPER
YOU DON'T TRUST THEM?
ボソ WHISPER
NOT ONE BIT.
I SEE...
THEN, THINK OF IT THIS WAY.
AS THE ONE WHO PICKED THEM, TRUST ME AND-
SORRY, BUT COULD YOU GUYS LEAVE, PLEASE?
HEEEEEY!

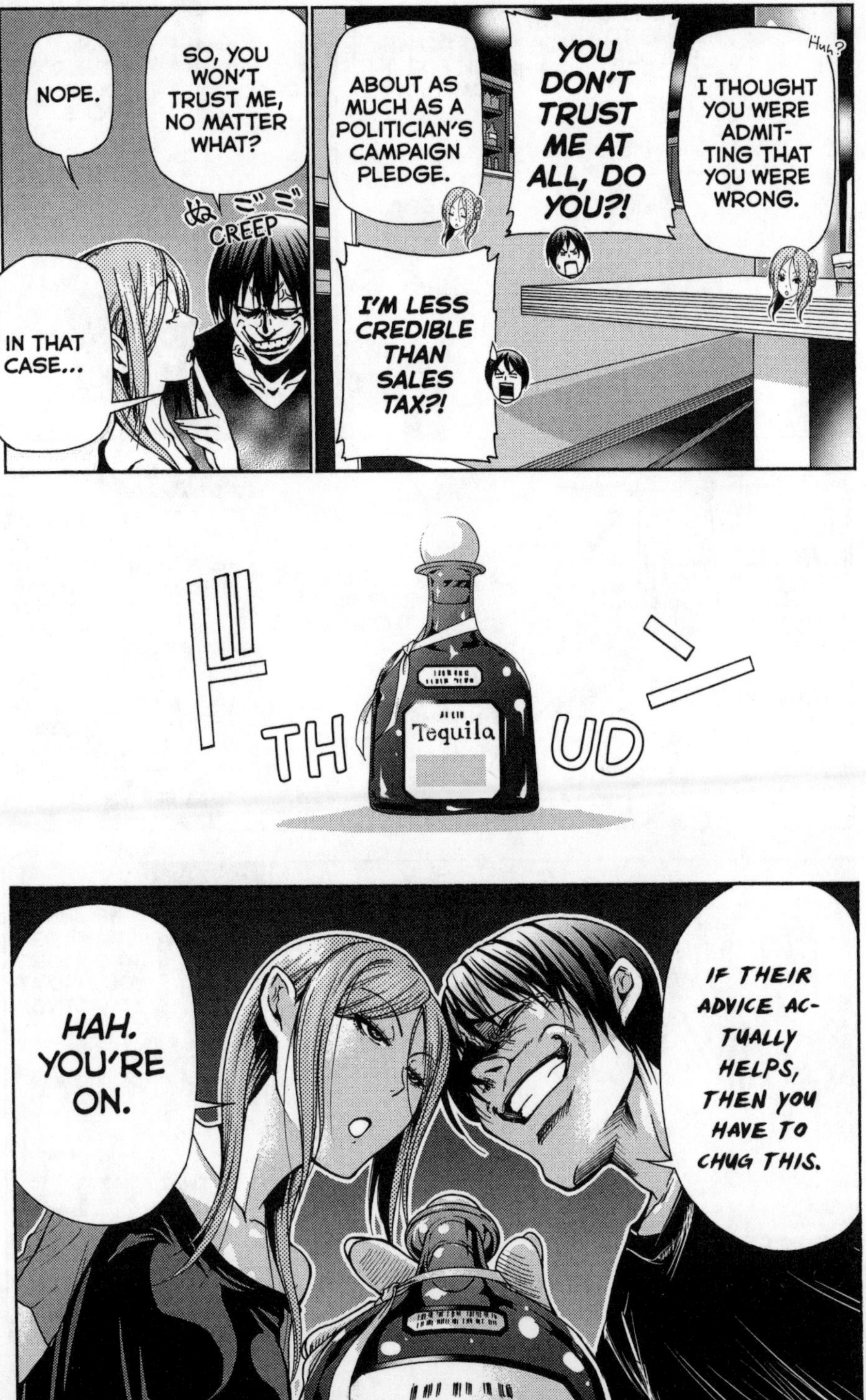
Huh?
I THOUGHT YOU WERE ADMITTING THAT YOU WERE WRONG.
YOU DON'T TRUST ME AT ALL, DO YOU?!
ABOUT AS MUCH AS A POLITICIAN'S CAMPAIGN PLEDGE.
I'M LESS CREDIBLE THAN SALES TAX?!
SO, YOU WON'T TRUST ME, NO MATTER WHAT?
NOPE.
CREEP
IN THAT CASE...
THUD
Tequila
IF THEIR ADVICE ACTUALLY HELPS, THEN YOU HAVE TO CHUG THIS.
HAH. YOU'RE ON.

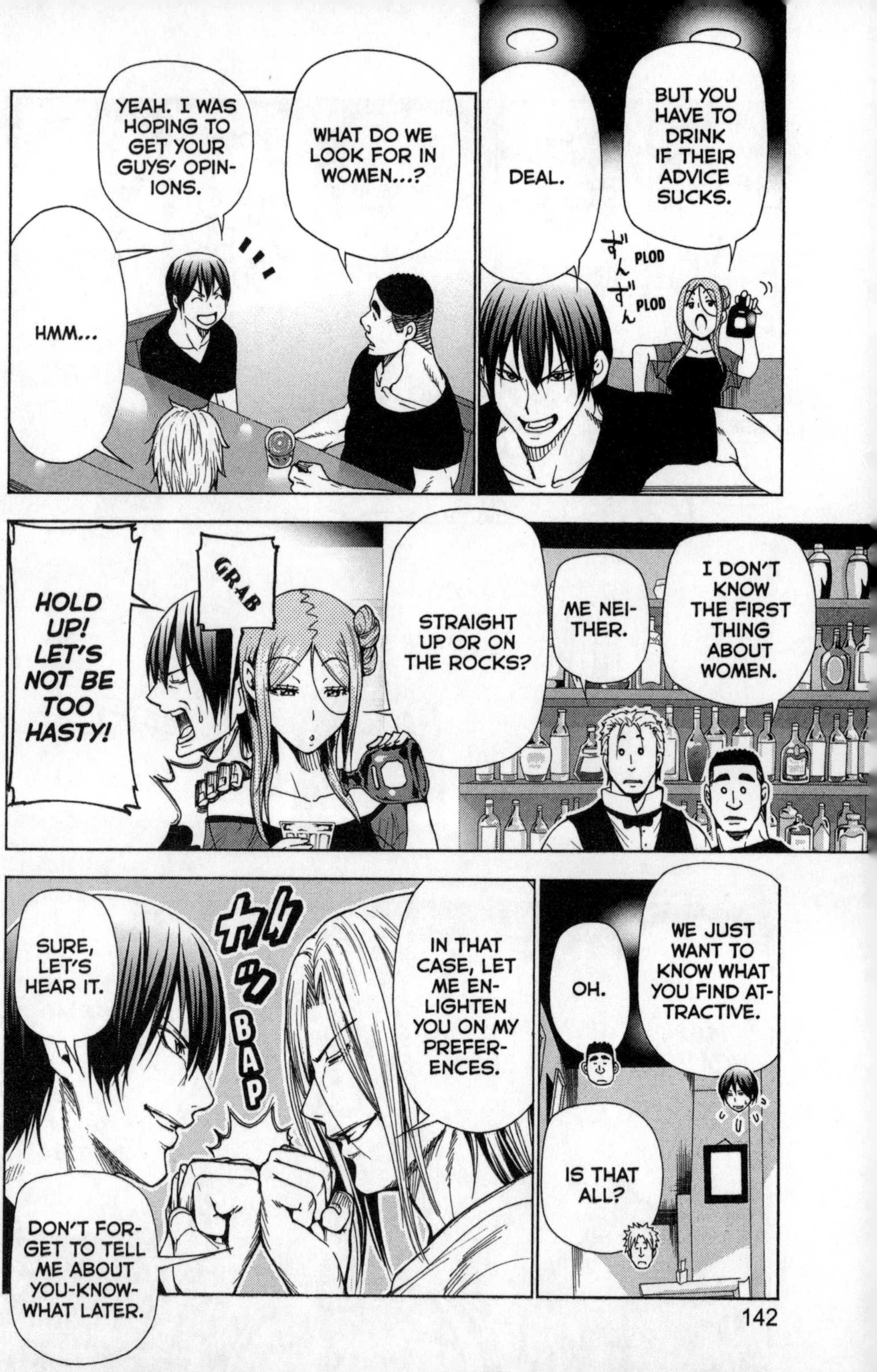

BUT YOU HAVE TO DRINK IF THEIR ADVICE SUCKS.
DEAL.
ずんずん PLOD PLOD
WHAT DO WE LOOK FOR IN WOMEN...?
YEAH. I WAS HOPING TO GET YOUR GUYS' OPINIONS.
HMM...
I DON'T KNOW THE FIRST THING ABOUT WOMEN.
ME NEITHER.
STRAIGHT UP OR ON THE ROCKS?
GRAB
HOLD UP! LET'S NOT BE TOO HASTY!
WE JUST WANT TO KNOW WHAT YOU FIND ATTRACTIVE.
OH.
IS THAT ALL?
IN THAT CASE, LET ME ENLIGHTEN YOU ON MY PREFERENCES.
カタッ BAP
SURE, LET'S HEAR IT.
DON'T FORGET TO TELL ME ABOUT YOU-KNOW-WHAT LATER.

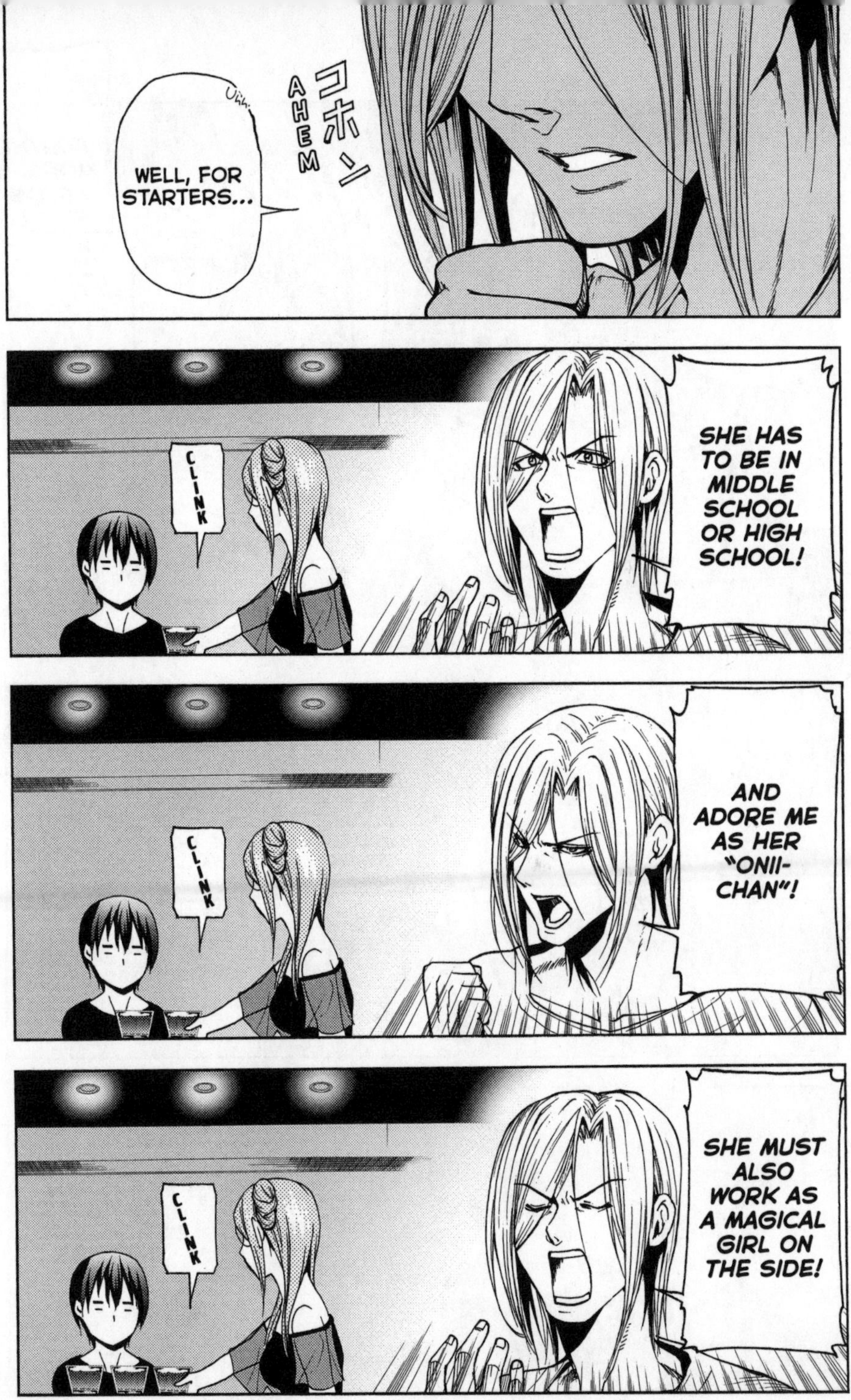
コホン
AHEM
Uhh.
WELL, FOR STARTERS...
SHE HAS TO BE IN MIDDLE SCHOOL OR HIGH SCHOOL!
CLINK
AND ADORE ME AS HER "ONII-CHAN"!
CLINK
SHE MUST ALSO WORK AS A MAGICAL GIRL ON THE SIDE!
CLINK

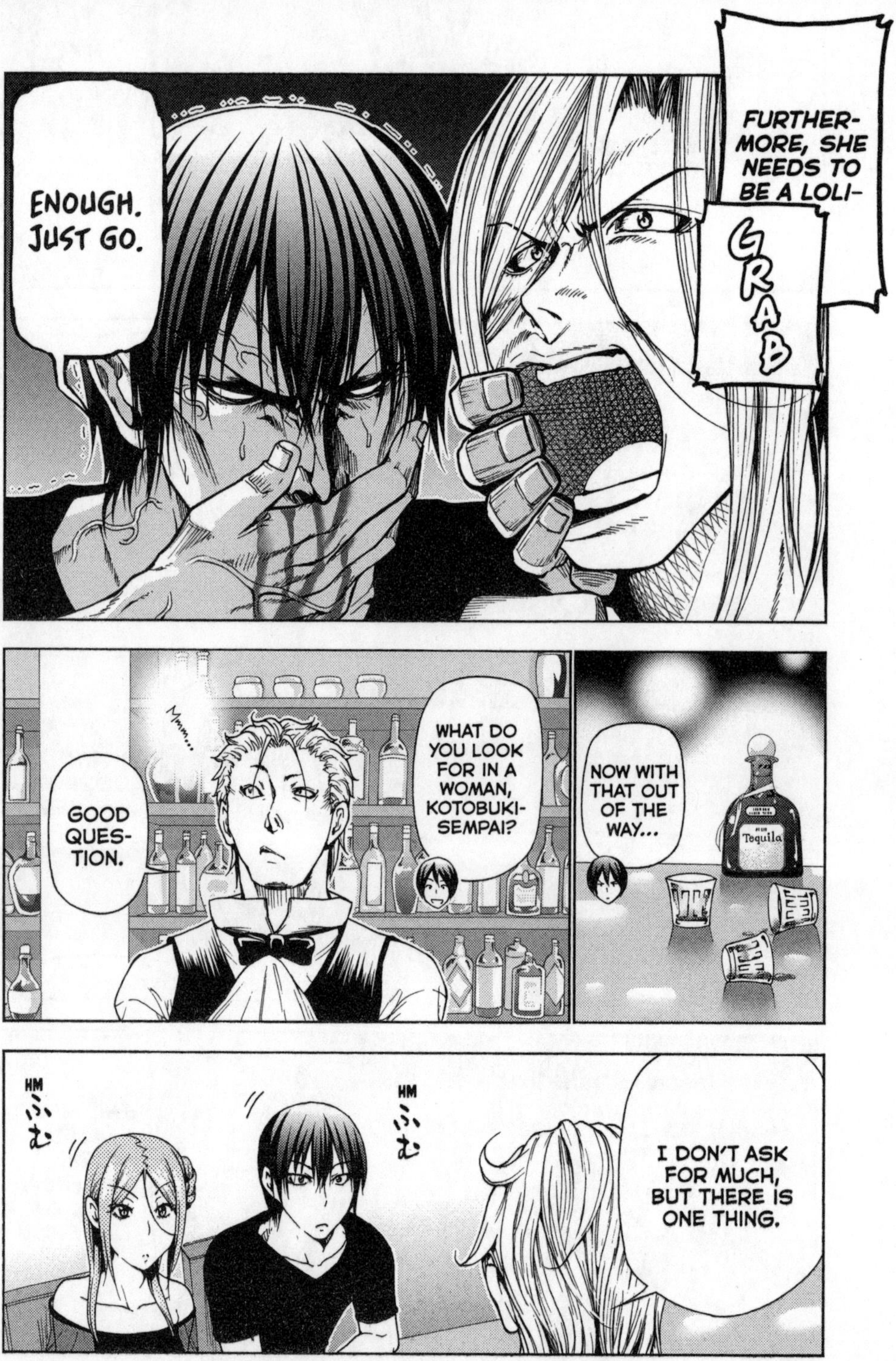
FURTHER-MORE, SHE NEEDS TO BE A LOLI-
GRAB
ENOUGH. JUST GO.
NOW WITH THAT OUT OF THE WAY...
Tequila
WHAT DO YOU LOOK FOR IN A WOMAN, KOTOBUKI-SEMPAI?
Mmm...
GOOD QUES-TION.
I DON'T ASK FOR MUCH, BUT THERE IS ONE THING.
HM ふむ
HM ふむ

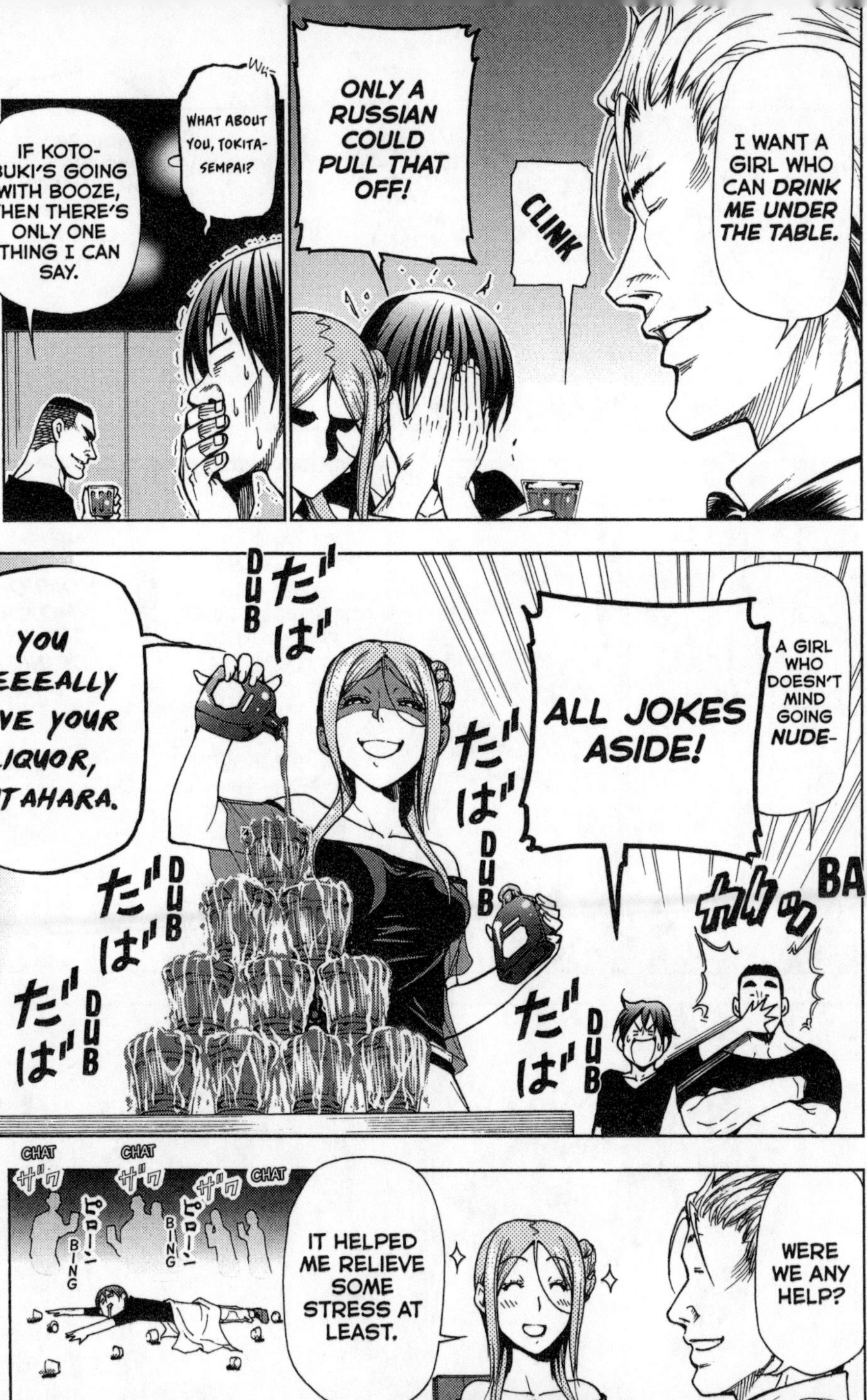
I WANT A GIRL WHO CAN DRINK ME UNDER THE TABLE.
CLINK
ONLY A RUSSIAN COULD PULL THAT OFF!
WU-
WHAT ABOUT YOU, TOKITA-SEMPAI?
IF KOTOBUKI'S GOING WITH BOOZE, THEN THERE'S ONLY ONE THING I CAN SAY.
A GIRL WHO DOESN'T MIND GOING NUDE-
ALL JOKES ASIDE!
BAP
だば DUB
だば DUB
だば DUB
だば DUB
だば DUB
YOU REEEALLY LOVE YOUR LIQUOR, KITAHARA.
WERE WE ANY HELP?
IT HELPED ME RELIEVE SOME STRESS AT LEAST.
ザワ CHAT
ザワ CHAT
ザワ CHAT
BING
BING

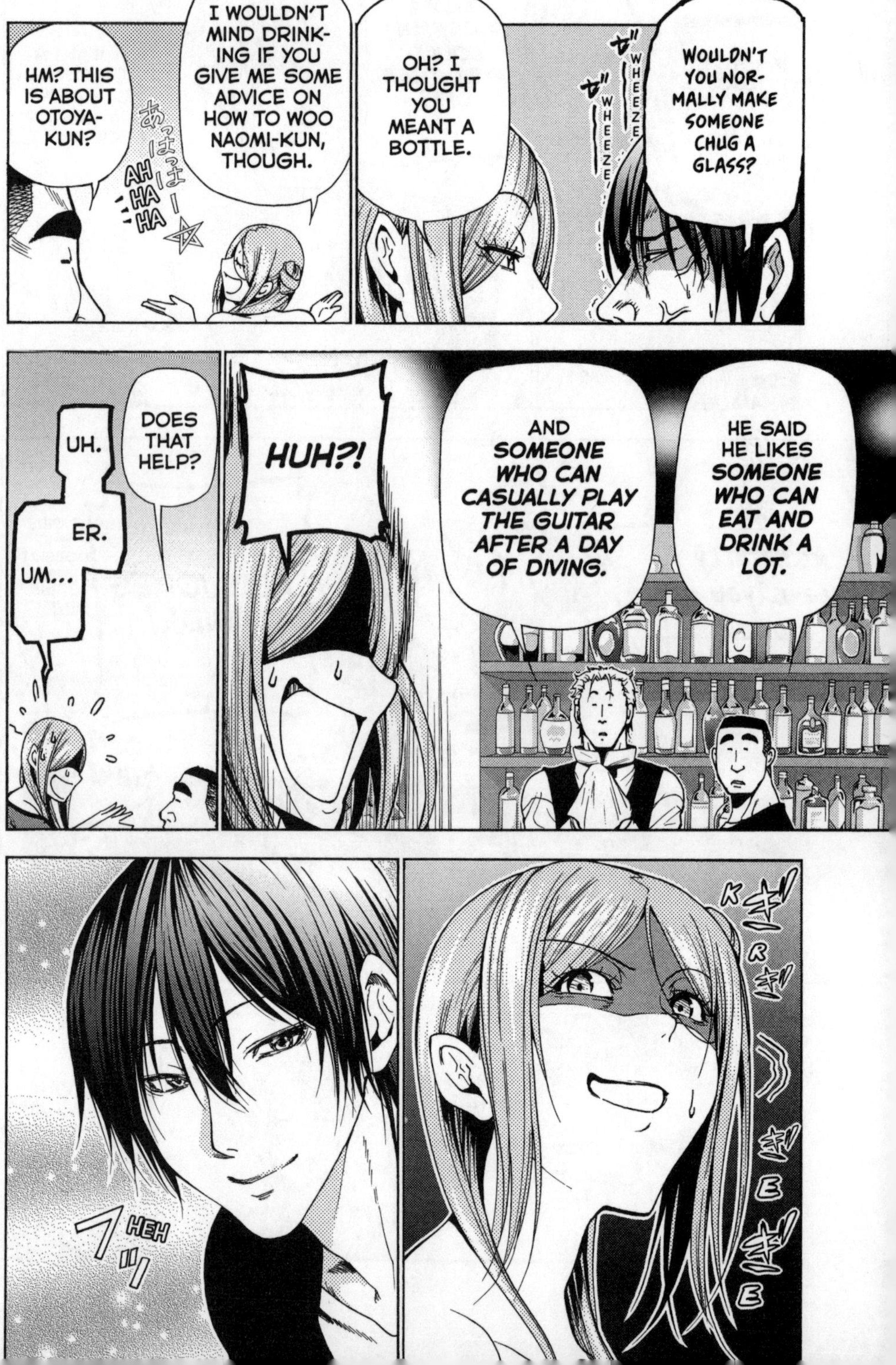

WOULDN'T YOU NORMALLY MAKE SOMEONE CHUG A GLASS?
WHEEZE WHEEZE
OH? I THOUGHT YOU MEANT A BOTTLE.
I WOULDN'T MIND DRINKING IF YOU GIVE ME SOME ADVICE ON HOW TO WOO NAOMI-KUN, THOUGH.
AH HA HA
HM? THIS IS ABOUT OTOYA-KUN?
HE SAID HE LIKES SOMEONE WHO CAN EAT AND DRINK A LOT.
AND SOMEONE WHO CAN CASUALLY PLAY THE GUITAR AFTER A DAY OF DIVING.
HUH?!
DOES THAT HELP?
UH.
ER.
UM...
KREEE
HEH

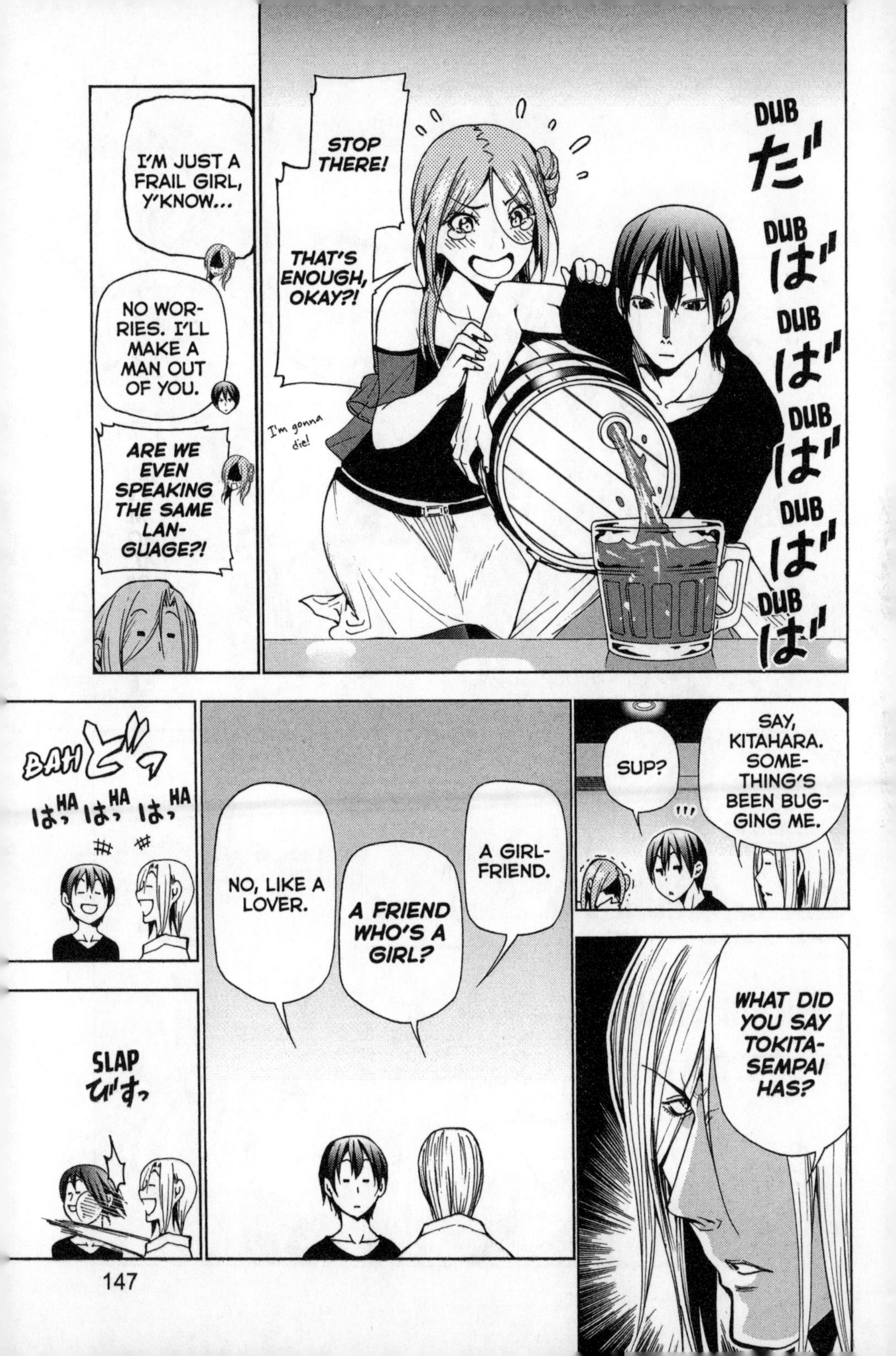

DUB だ DUB ば DUB ば DUB ば DUB ば DUB ば
STOP THERE!
THAT'S ENOUGH, OKAY?!
I'm gonna die!
I'M JUST A FRAIL GIRL, Y'KNOW...
NO WORRIES. I'LL MAKE A MAN OUT OF YOU.
ARE WE EVEN SPEAKING THE SAME LANGUAGE?!
SAY, KITAHARA. SOMETHING'S BEEN BUGGING ME.
SUP?
WHAT DID YOU SAY TOKITA-SEMPAI HAS?
A GIRLFRIEND.
A FRIEND WHO'S A GIRL?
NO, LIKE A LOVER.
BAH どっ
HA はっ HA はっ HA はっ
SLAP びすっ

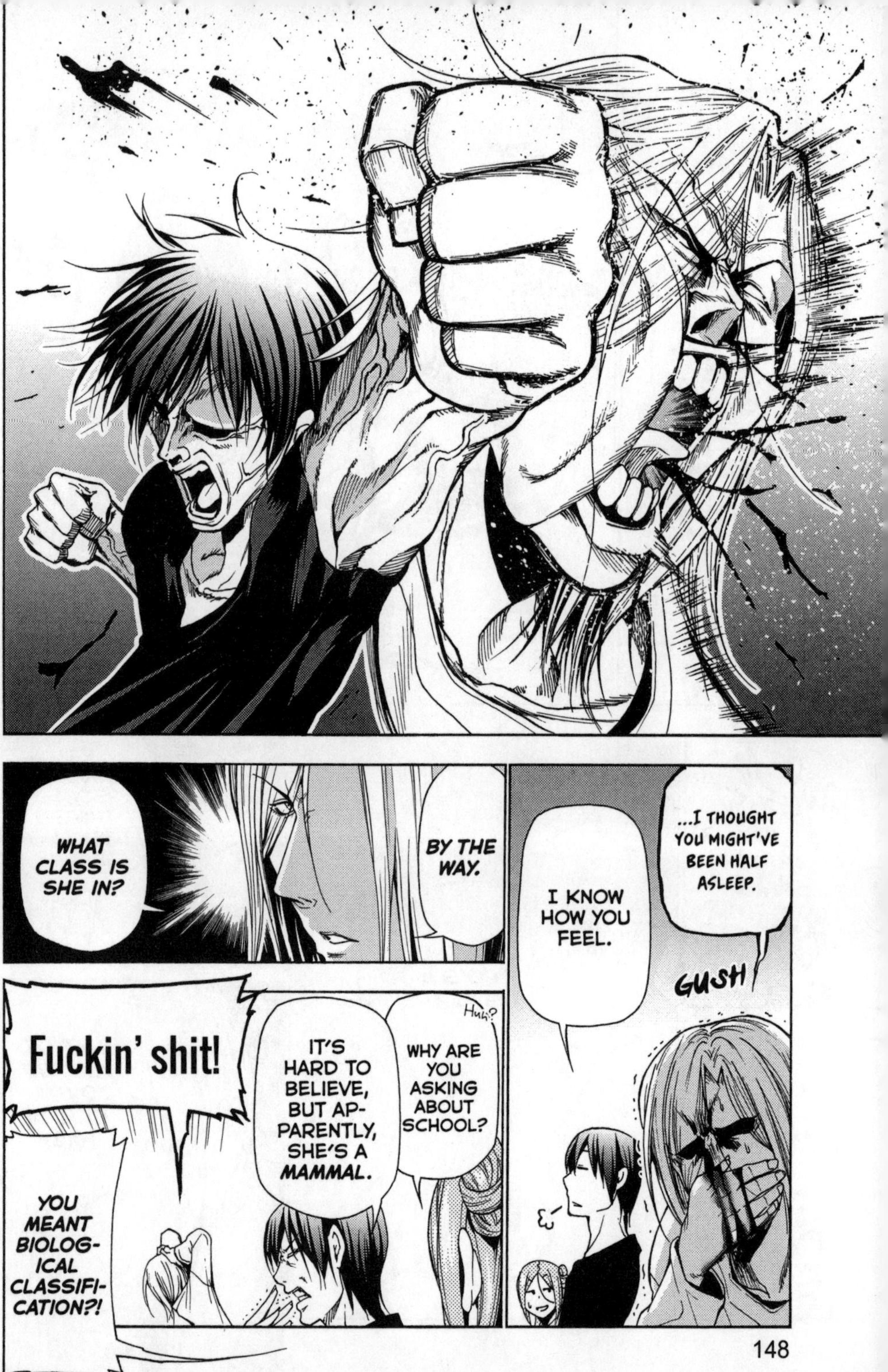
...I THOUGHT YOU MIGHT'VE BEEN HALF ASLEEP.
I KNOW HOW YOU FEEL.
GUSH
BY THE WAY.
WHAT CLASS IS SHE IN?
Huh?
WHY ARE YOU ASKING ABOUT SCHOOL?
IT'S HARD TO BELIEVE, BUT APPARENTLY, SHE'S A MAMMAL.
Fuckin' shit!
YOU MEANT BIOLOGICAL CLASSIFICATION?!

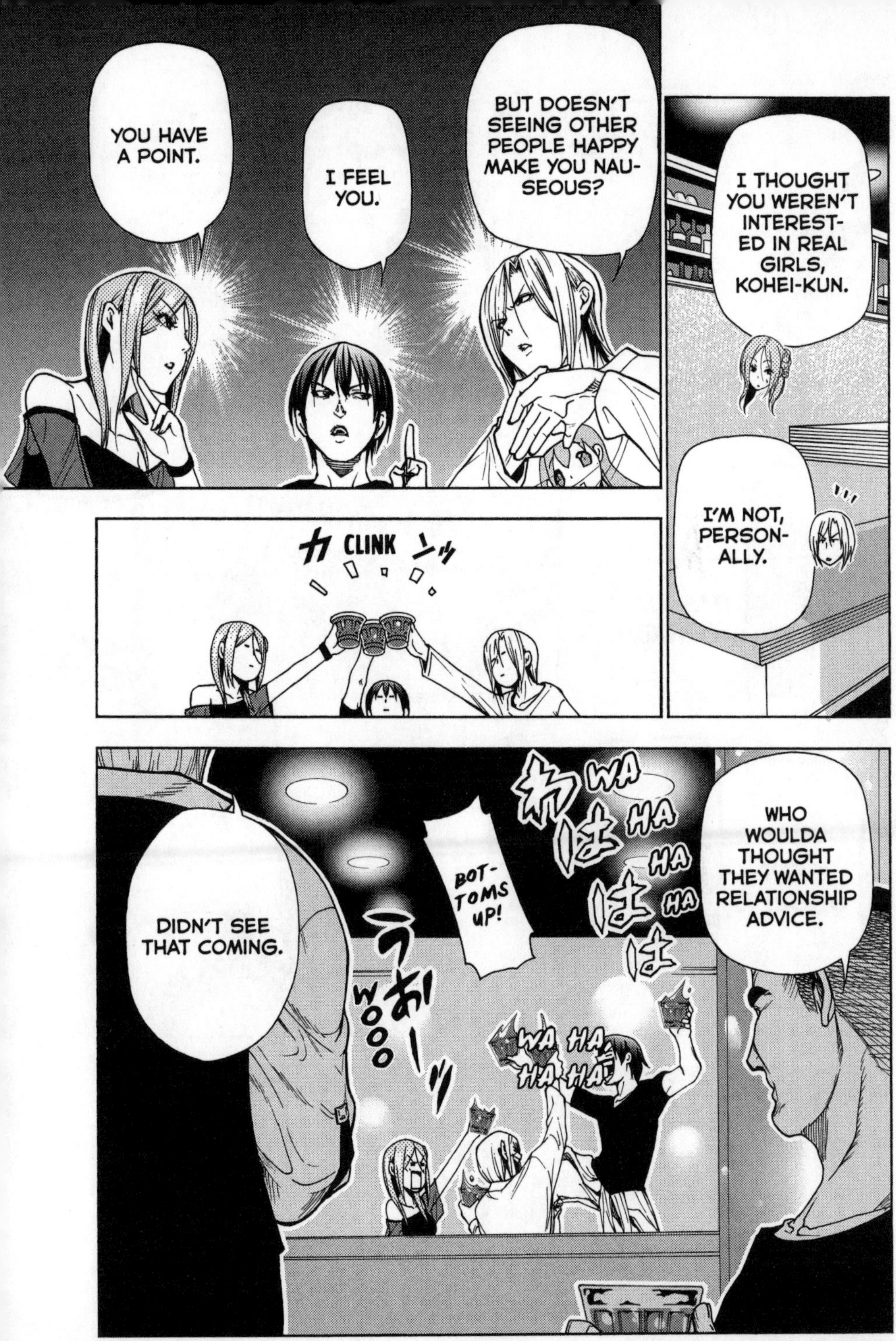
I THOUGHT YOU WEREN'T INTEREST-ED IN REAL GIRLS, KOHEI-KUN.
I'M NOT, PERSON-ALLY.
BUT DOESN'T SEEING OTHER PEOPLE HAPPY MAKE YOU NAU-SEOUS?
I FEEL YOU.
YOU HAVE A POINT.
カンッ
CLINK
WHO WOULDA THOUGHT THEY WANTED RELATIONSHIP ADVICE.
わはははは
WA HA HA HA
BOT-TOMS UP!
うあーッ
WOOO
WA HA HA HA
DIDN'T SEE THAT COMING.

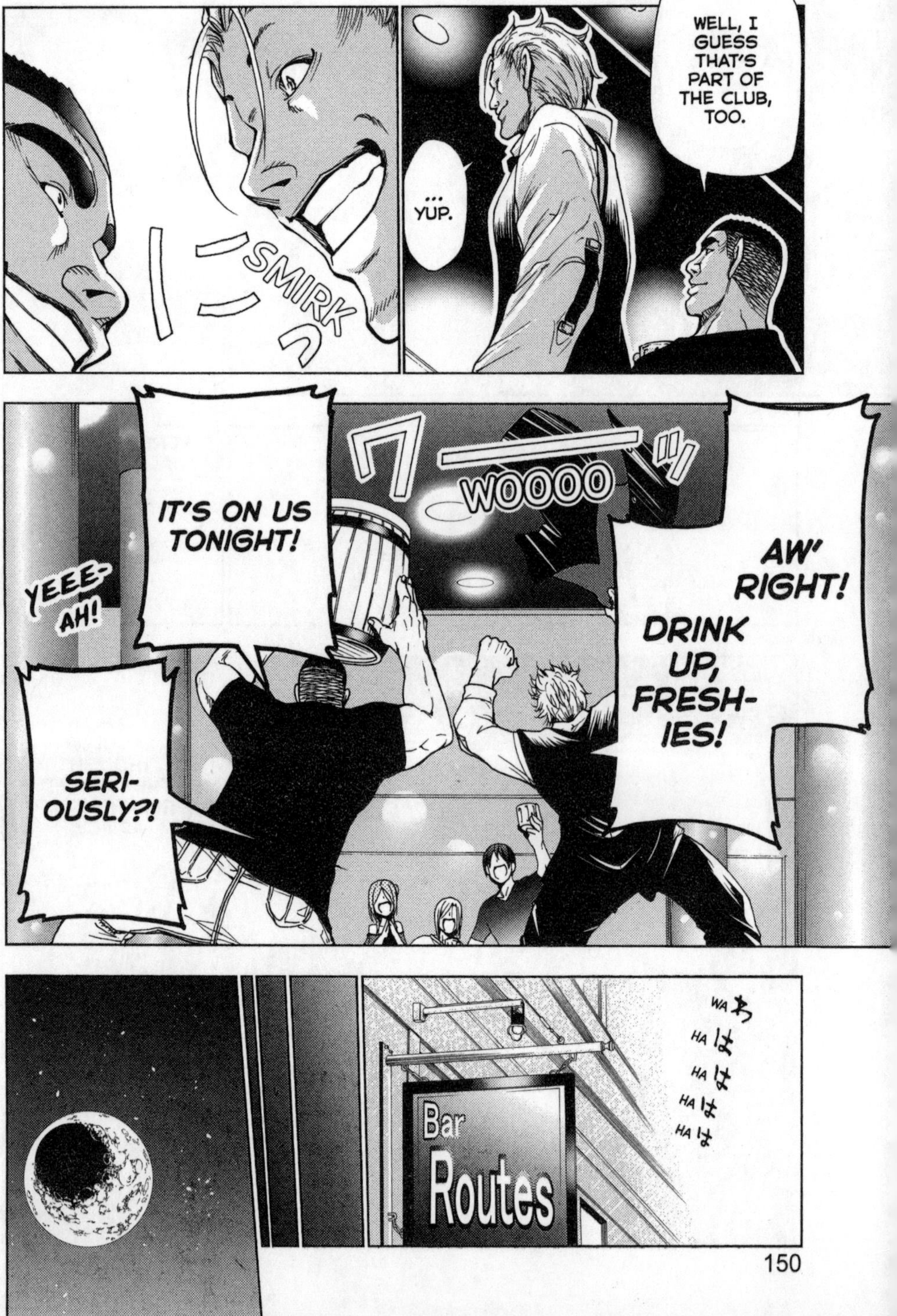
WELL, I GUESS THAT'S PART OF THE CLUB, TOO.
... YUP.
SMIRK
AW' RIGHT! DRINK UP, FRESH-IES!
WOOOO
IT'S ON US TONIGHT!
YEEE-AH!
SERI-OUSLY?!
WA わ HA は HA は HA は HA は
Bar Routes

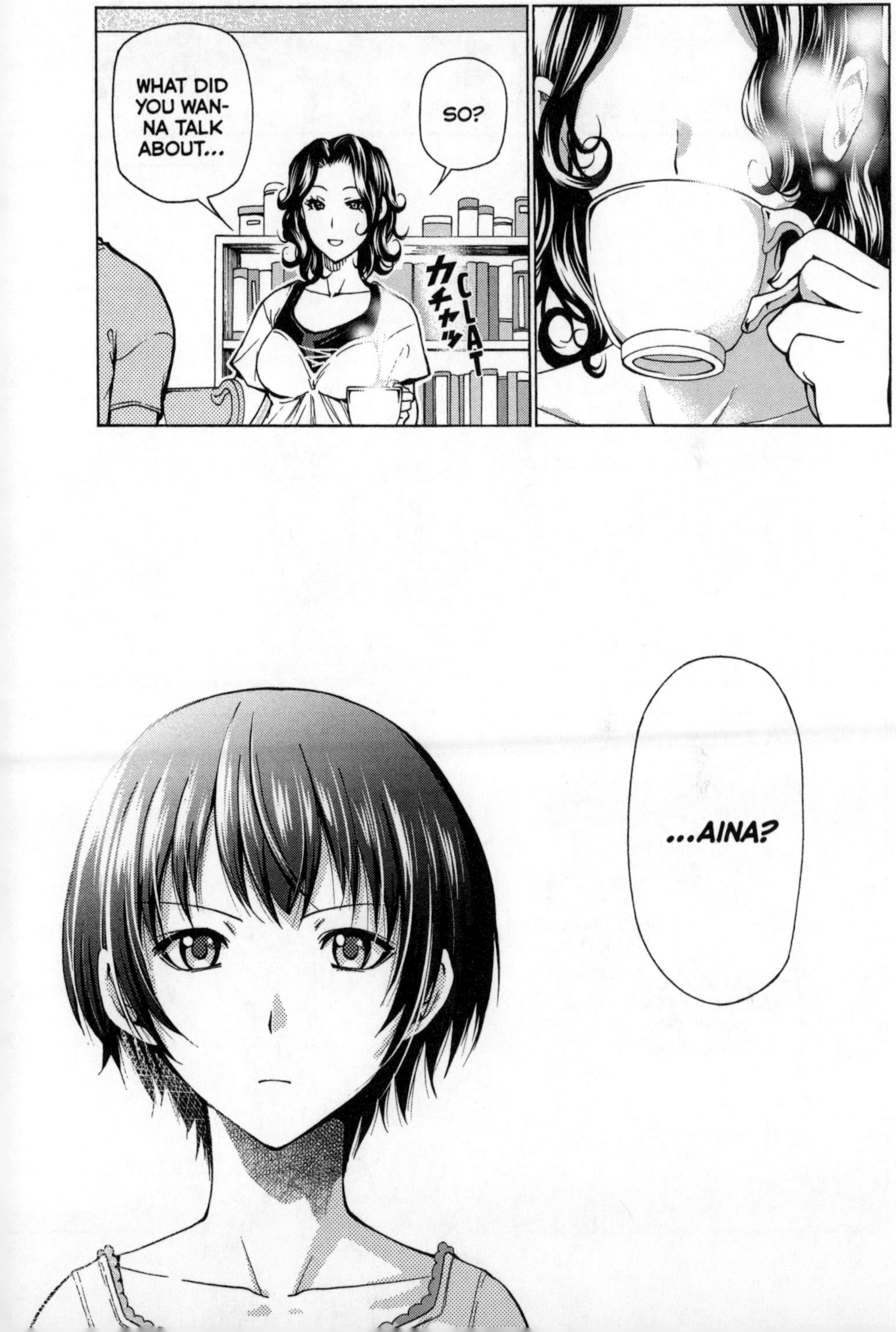
SO?
WHAT DID YOU WAN-NA TALK ABOUT...
カチャッ
CLAT
...AINA?

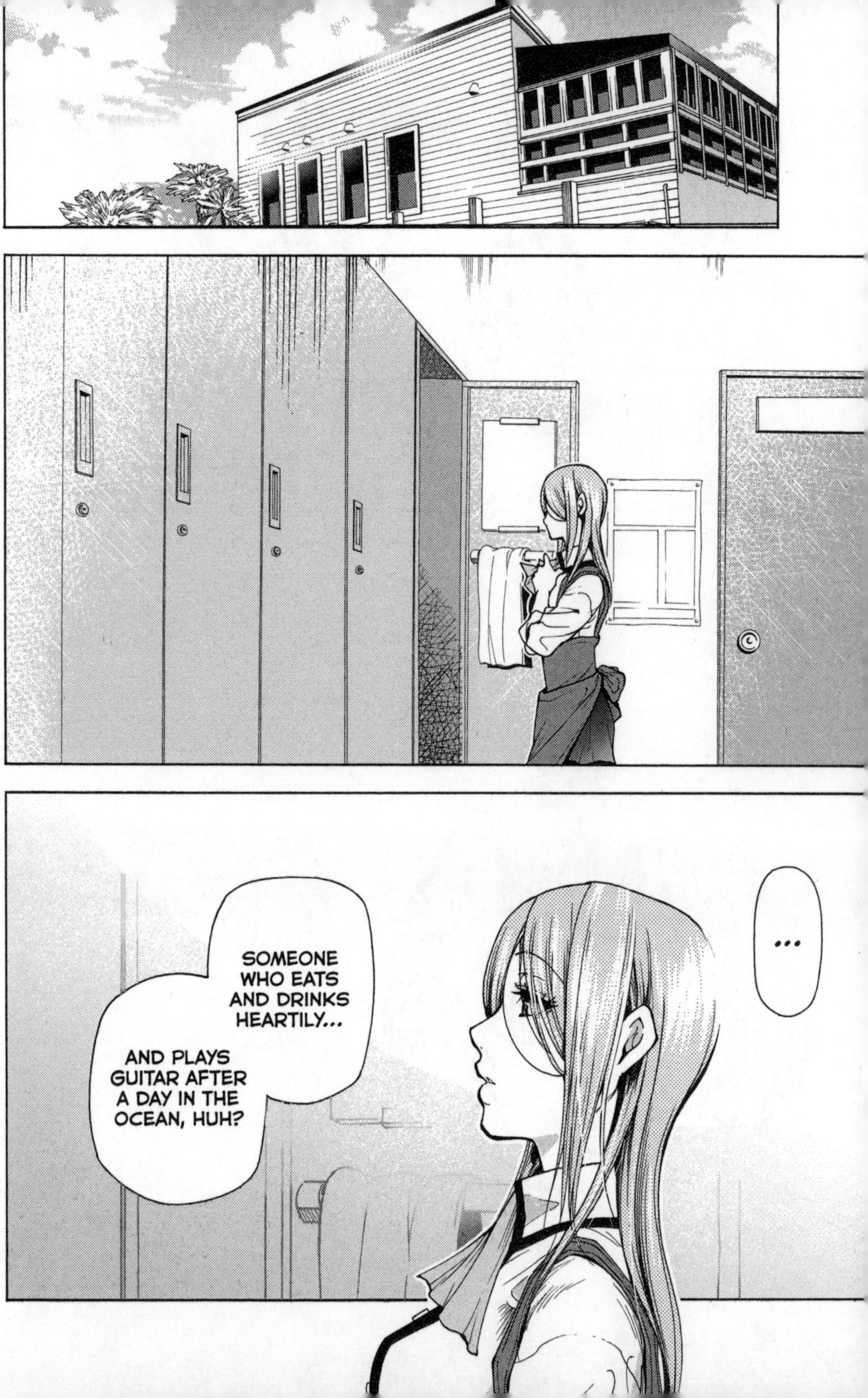
...
SOMEONE WHO EATS AND DRINKS HEARTILY...
AND PLAYS GUITAR AFTER A DAY IN THE OCEAN, HUH?

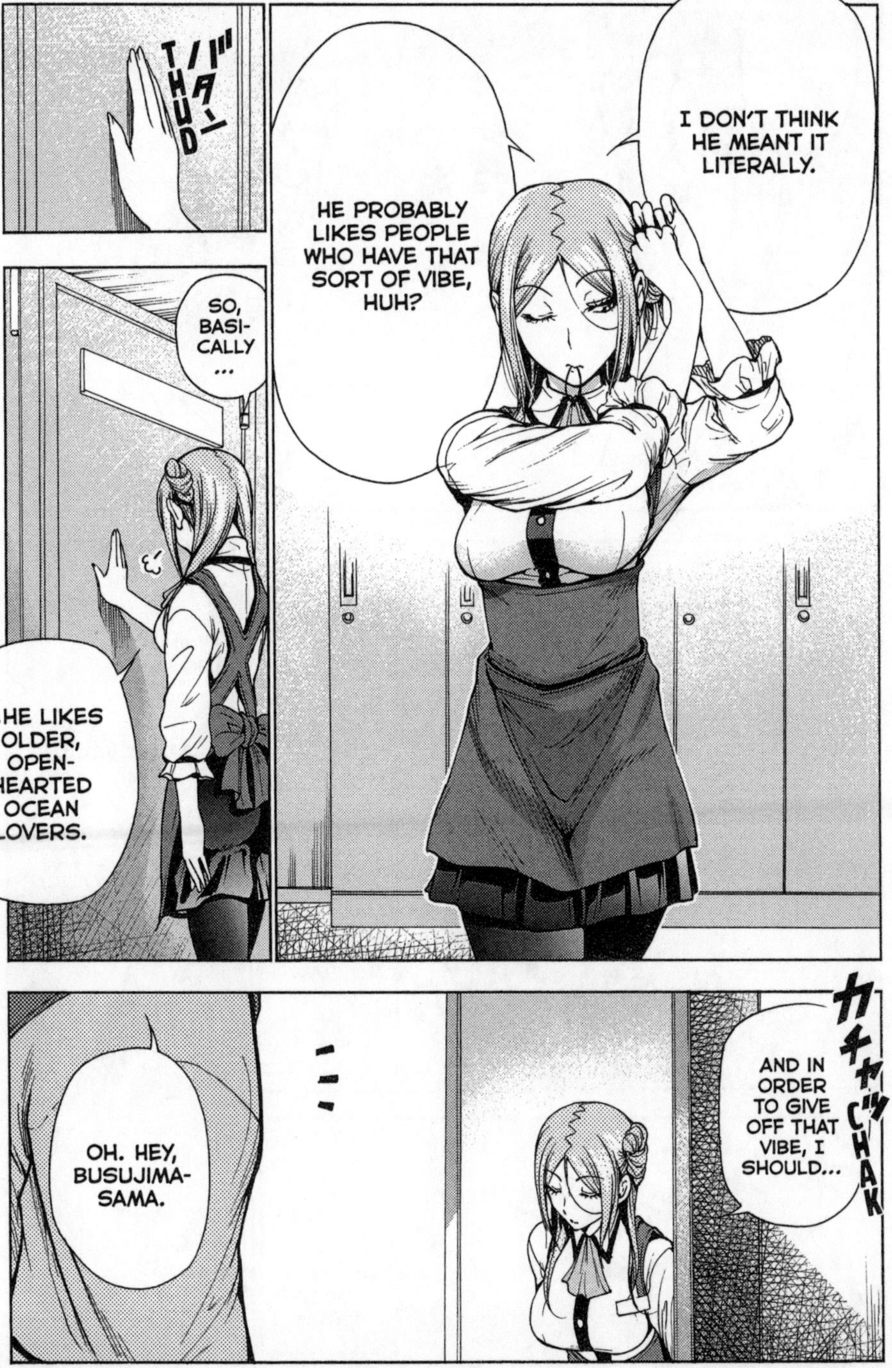
I DON'T THINK HE MEANT IT LITERALLY.
HE PROBABLY LIKES PEOPLE WHO HAVE THAT SORT OF VIBE, HUH?
バターン
THUD
SO, BASI-CALLY ...
...HE LIKES OLDER, OPEN-HEARTED OCEAN LOVERS.
カチャッ
CHAK
AND IN ORDER TO GIVE OFF THAT VIBE, I SHOULD...
OH. HEY, BUSUJIMA-SAMA.

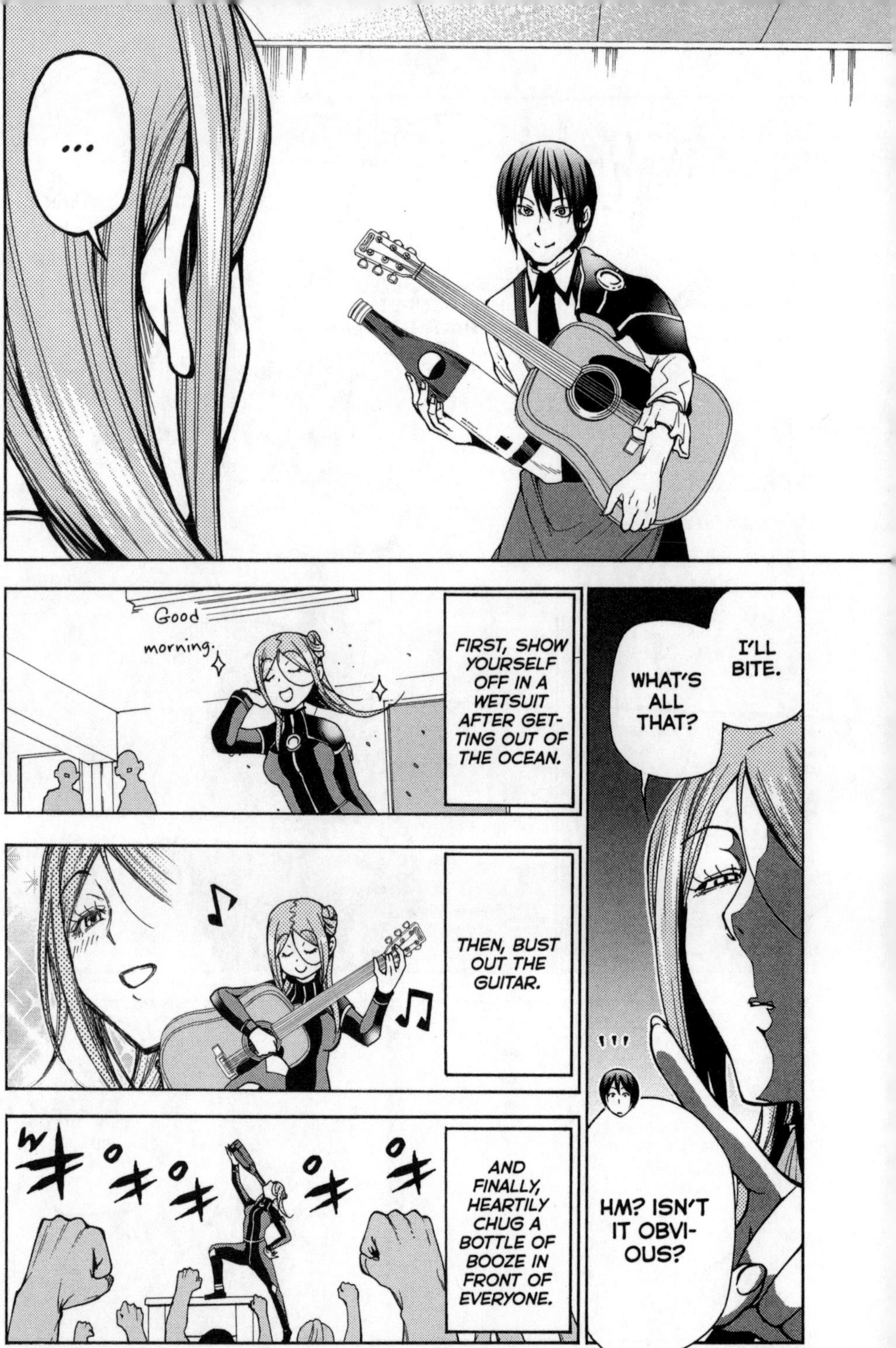
...
I'LL BITE. WHAT'S ALL THAT?
HM? ISN'T IT OBVIOUS?
FIRST, SHOW YOURSELF OFF IN A WETSUIT AFTER GETTING OUT OF THE OCEAN.
Good morning.
THEN, BUST OUT THE GUITAR.
AND FINALLY, HEARTILY CHUG A BOTTLE OF BOOZE IN FRONT OF EVERYONE.

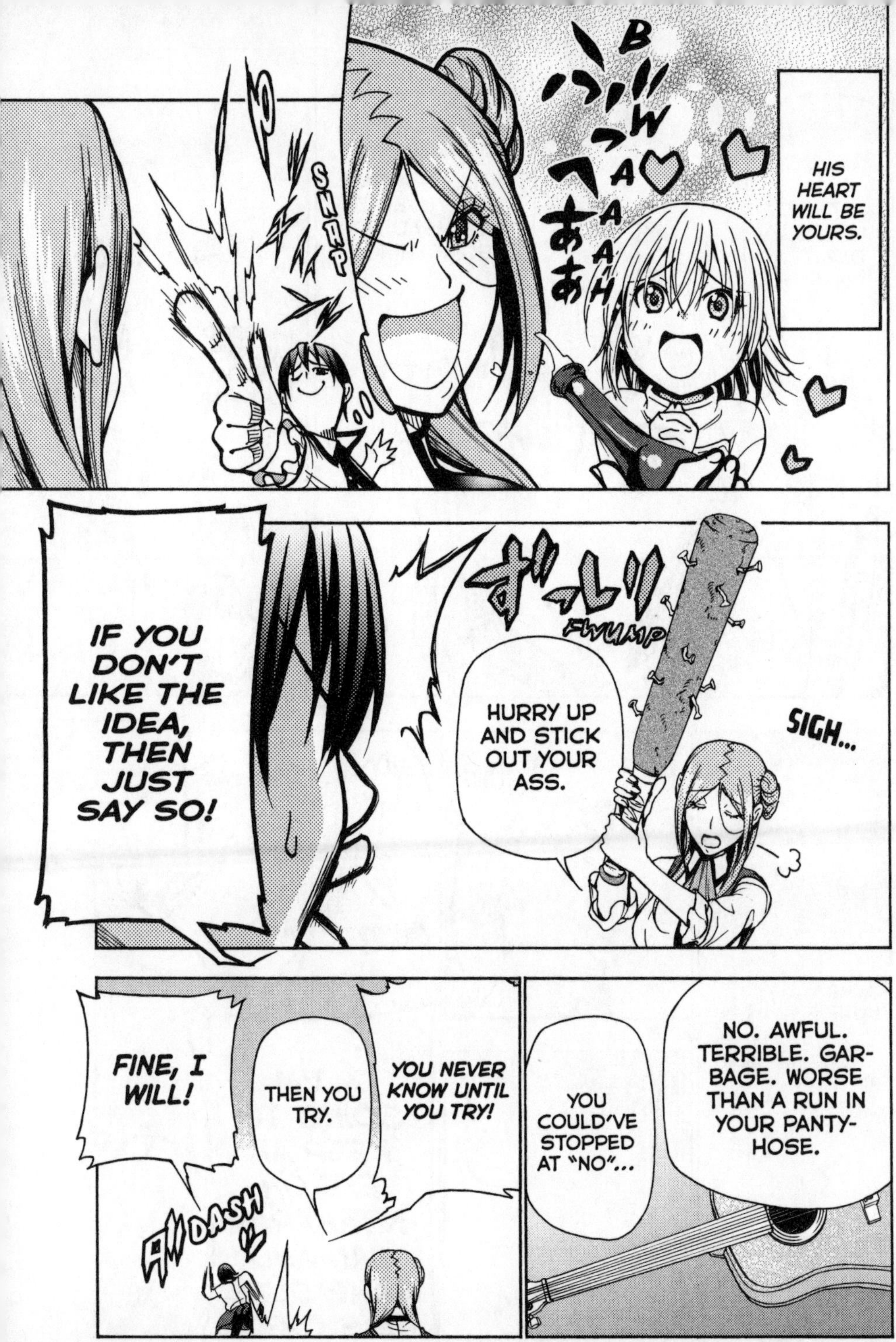

HIS HEART WILL BE YOURS.
BWAAAH
SNAP
SIGH...
HURRY UP AND STICK OUT YOUR ASS.
FWUMP
IF YOU DON'T LIKE THE IDEA, THEN JUST SAY SO!
NO. AWFUL. TERRIBLE. GARBAGE. WORSE THAN A RUN IN YOUR PANTYHOSE.
YOU COULD'VE STOPPED AT "NO"...
YOU NEVER KNOW UNTIL YOU TRY!
THEN YOU TRY.
FINE, I WILL!
DASH

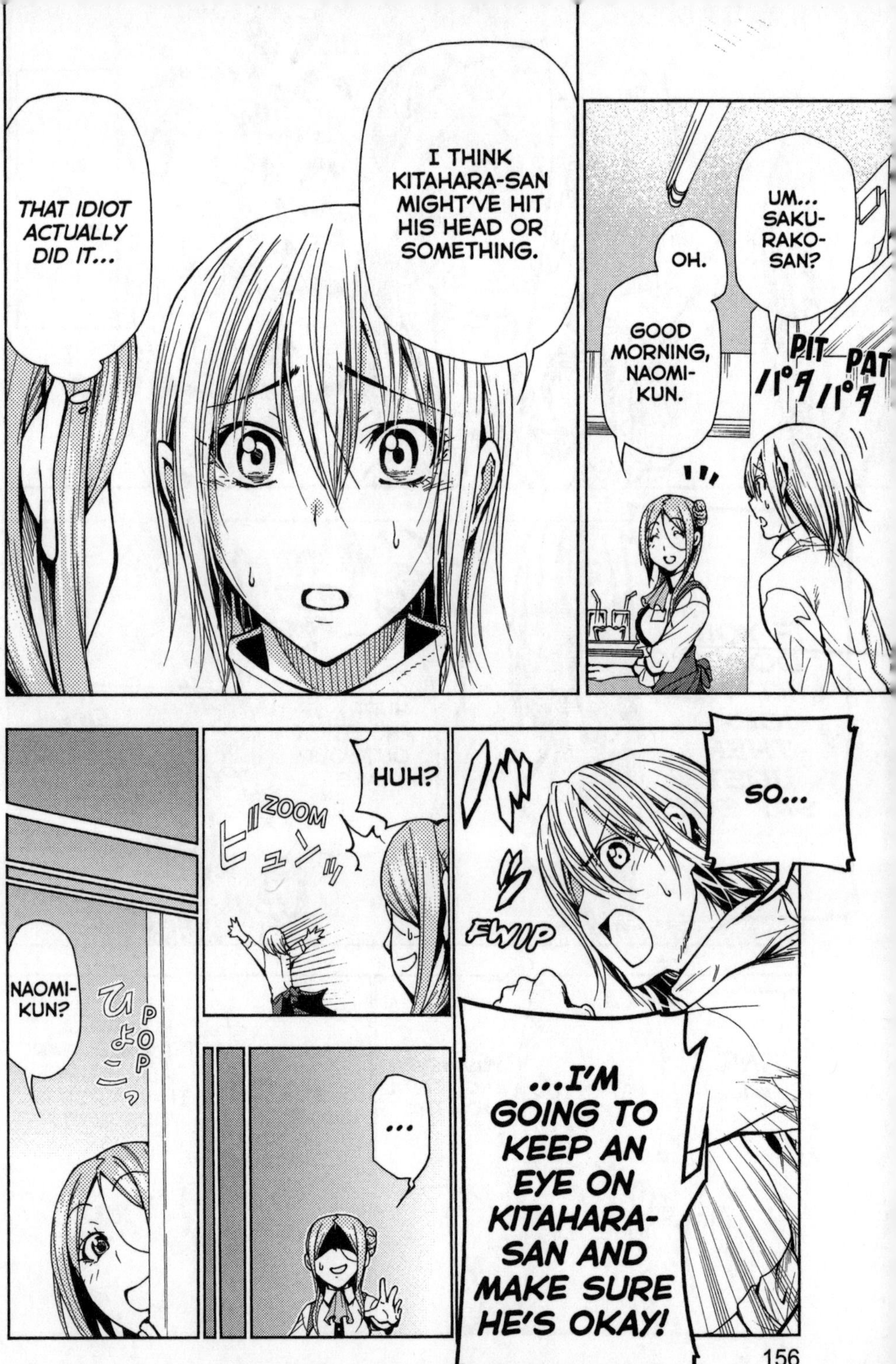
UM... SAKU-RAKO-SAN?
PIT PAT
パタパタ
OH.
GOOD MORNING, NAOMI-KUN.
I THINK KITAHARA-SAN MIGHT'VE HIT HIS HEAD OR SOMETHING.
THAT IDIOT ACTUALLY DID IT...
SO...
FWIP
...I'M GOING TO KEEP AN EYE ON KITAHARA-SAN AND MAKE SURE HE'S OKAY!
HUH?
ZOOM
ビュンッ
...
NAOMI-KUN?
POP
ひょこっ

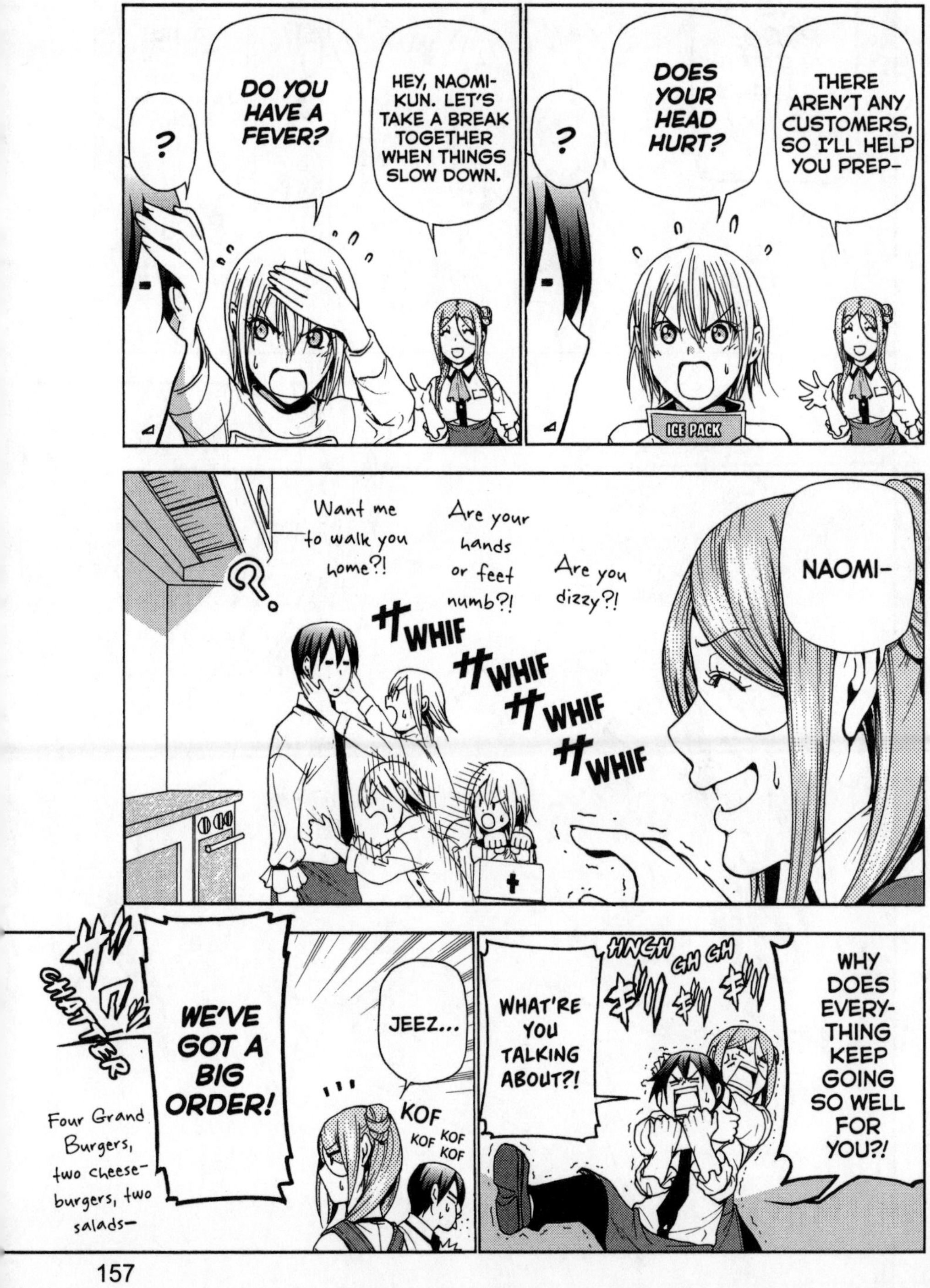
THERE AREN'T ANY CUSTOMERS, SO I'LL HELP YOU PREP-
DOES YOUR HEAD HURT?
?
ICE PACK
HEY, NAOMI-KUN. LET'S TAKE A BREAK TOGETHER WHEN THINGS SLOW DOWN.
DO YOU HAVE A FEVER?
?
NAOMI-
Are you dizzy?!
Are your hands or feet numb?!
Want me to walk you home?!
WHIF
WHIF
WHIF
WHIF
WHY DOES EVERY-THING KEEP GOING SO WELL FOR YOU?!
GH GH
HNGH
WHAT'RE YOU TALKING ABOUT?!
JEEZ...
...
KOF
KOF KOF
KOF
WE'VE GOT A BIG ORDER!
CHATTER
Four Grand Burgers, two cheese-burgers, two salads—

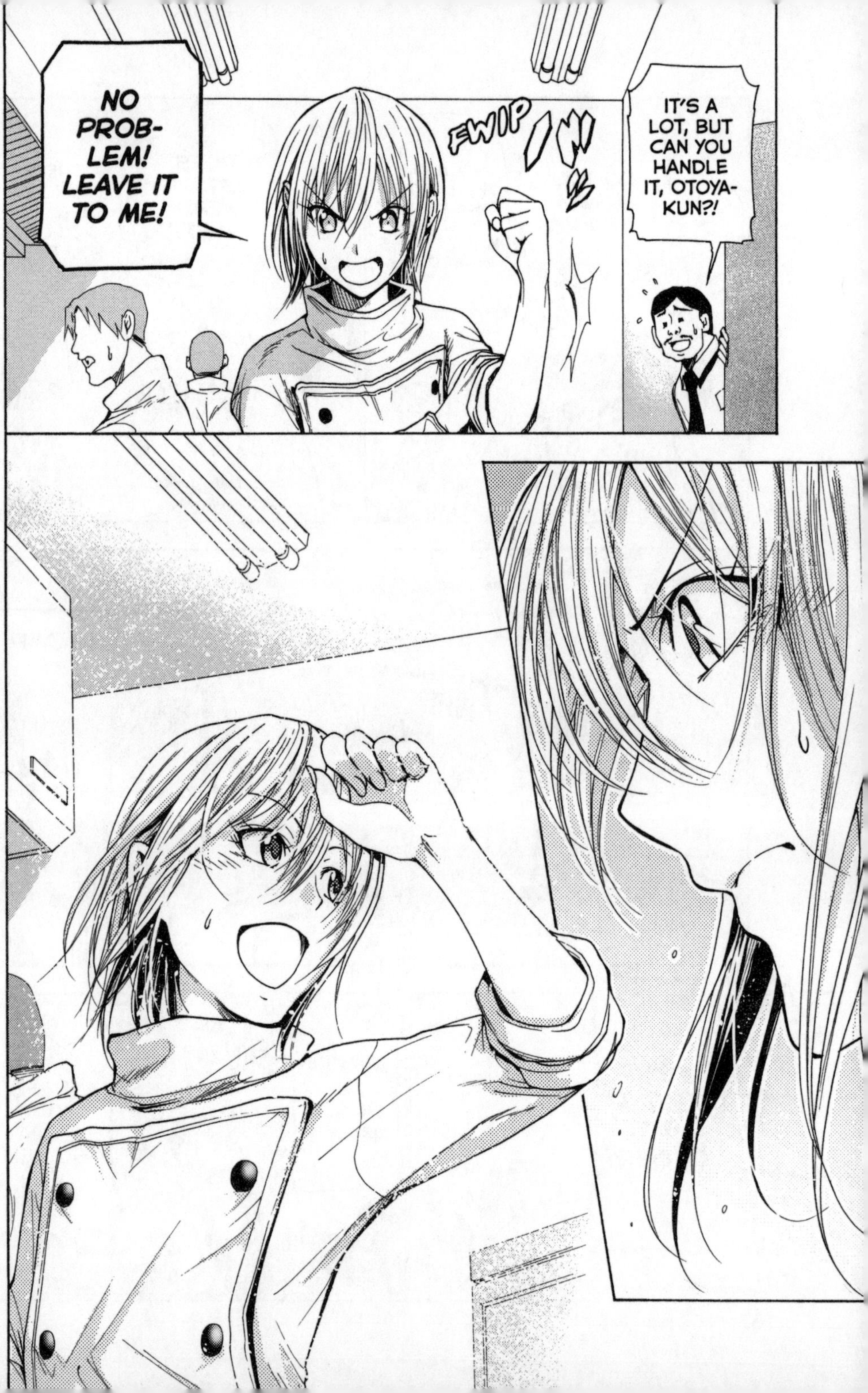
IT'S A LOT, BUT CAN YOU HANDLE IT, OTOYA-KUN?!
FWIP
NO PROB-LEM! LEAVE IT TO ME!

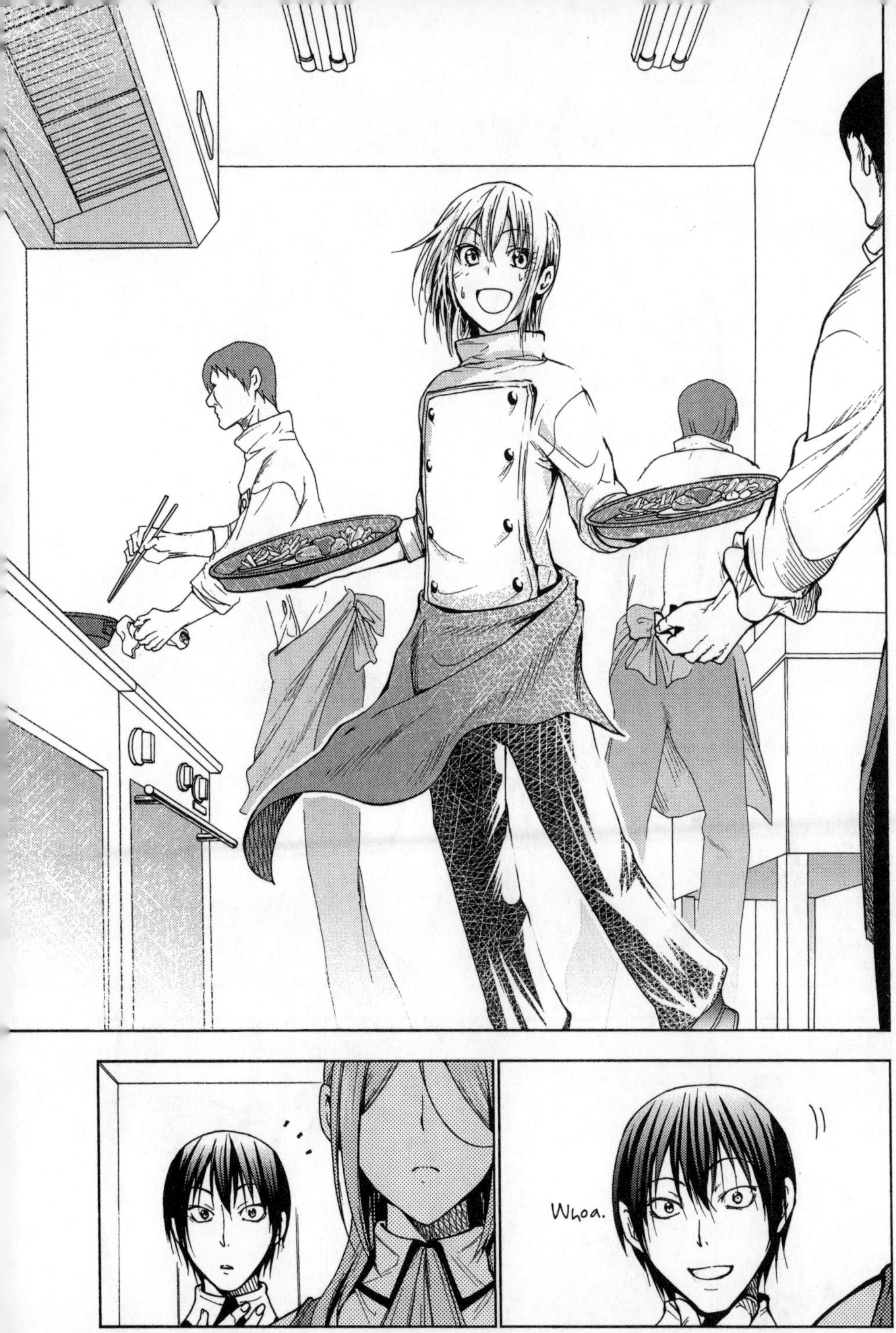
Whoa.

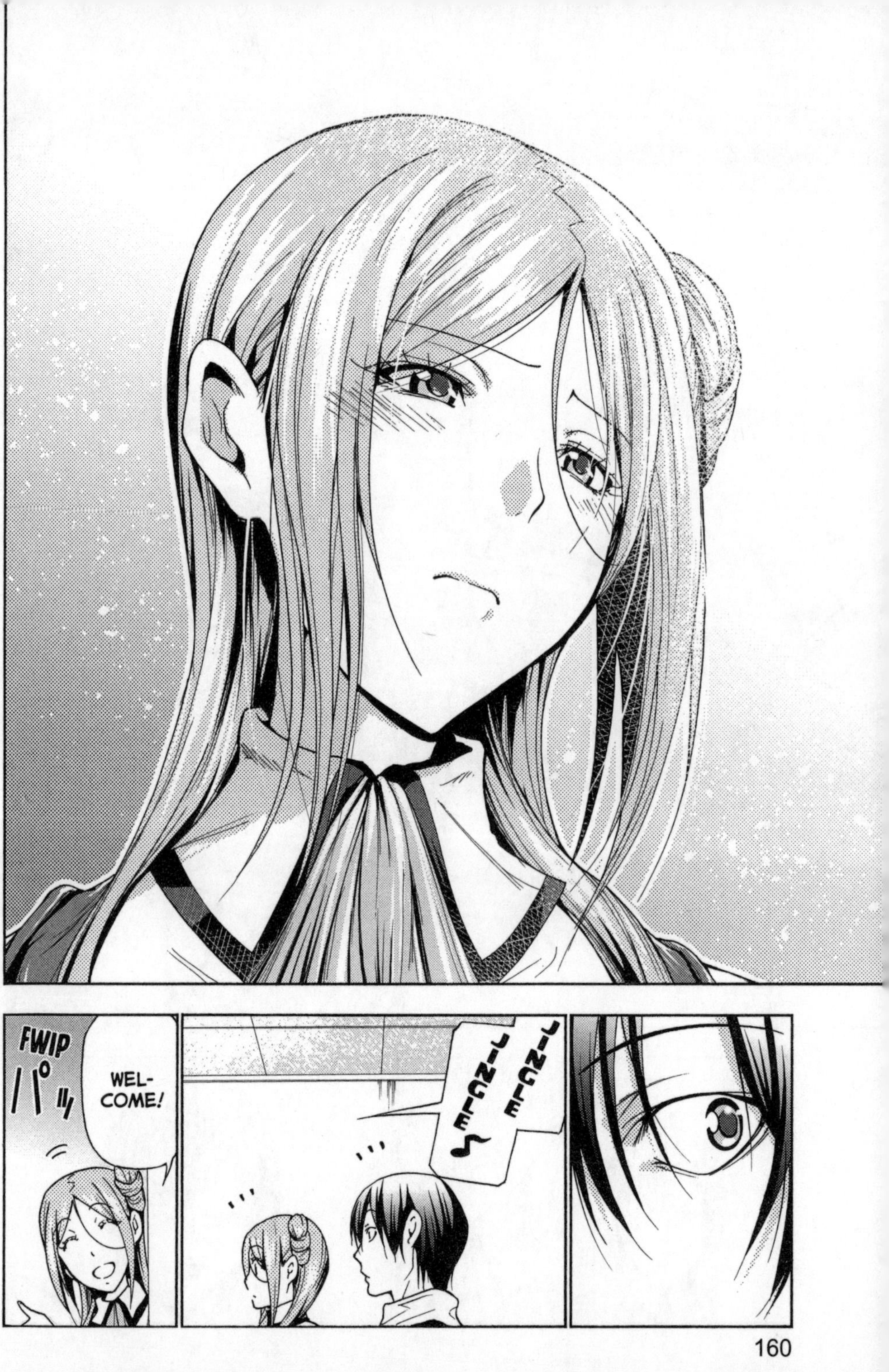
JINGLE JINGLE♪
...
...
FWIP
パッ
WEL-COME!

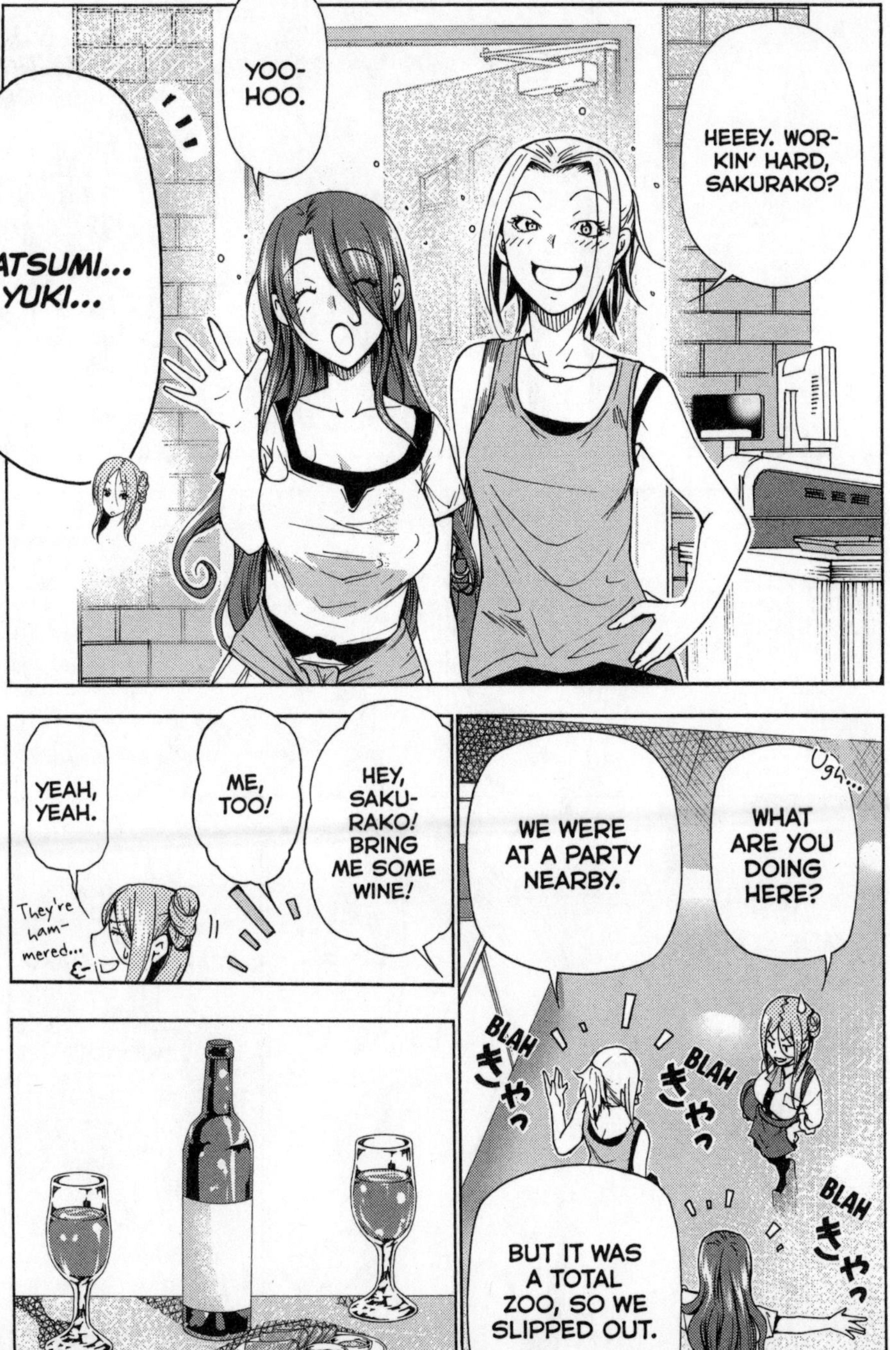
HEEEY. WORKIN' HARD, SAKURAKO?
YOO-HOO.
!!
NATSUMI... YUKI...
Ugh...
WHAT ARE YOU DOING HERE?
WE WERE AT A PARTY NEARBY.
BLAH きゃっ
BLAH きゃっ
BLAH きゃっ
BUT IT WAS A TOTAL ZOO, SO WE SLIPPED OUT.
HEY, SAKURAKO! BRING ME SOME WINE!
ME, TOO!
YEAH, YEAH.
They're hammered...

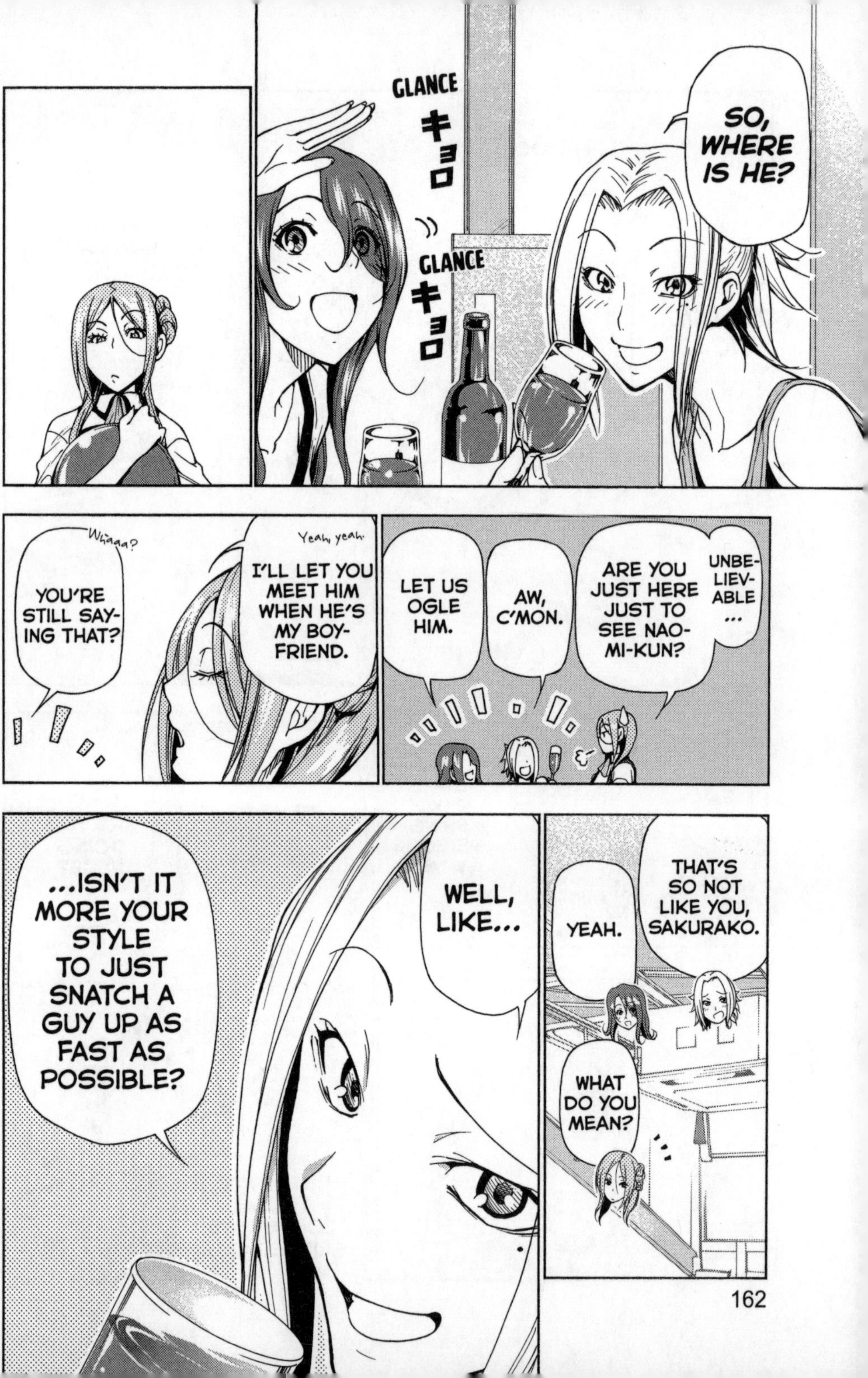
SO, WHERE IS HE?
GLANCE
キョロ
GLANCE
キョロ
UNBE-LIEV-ABLE...
ARE YOU JUST HERE JUST TO SEE NAO-MI-KUN?
AW, C'MON.
LET US OGLE HIM.
Yeah, yeah.
I'LL LET YOU MEET HIM WHEN HE'S MY BOY-FRIEND.
Whaaa?
YOU'RE STILL SAY-ING THAT?
THAT'S SO NOT LIKE YOU, SAKURAKO.
YEAH.
WHAT DO YOU MEAN?
WELL, LIKE...
...ISN'T IT MORE YOUR STYLE TO JUST SNATCH A GUY UP AS FAST AS POSSIBLE?

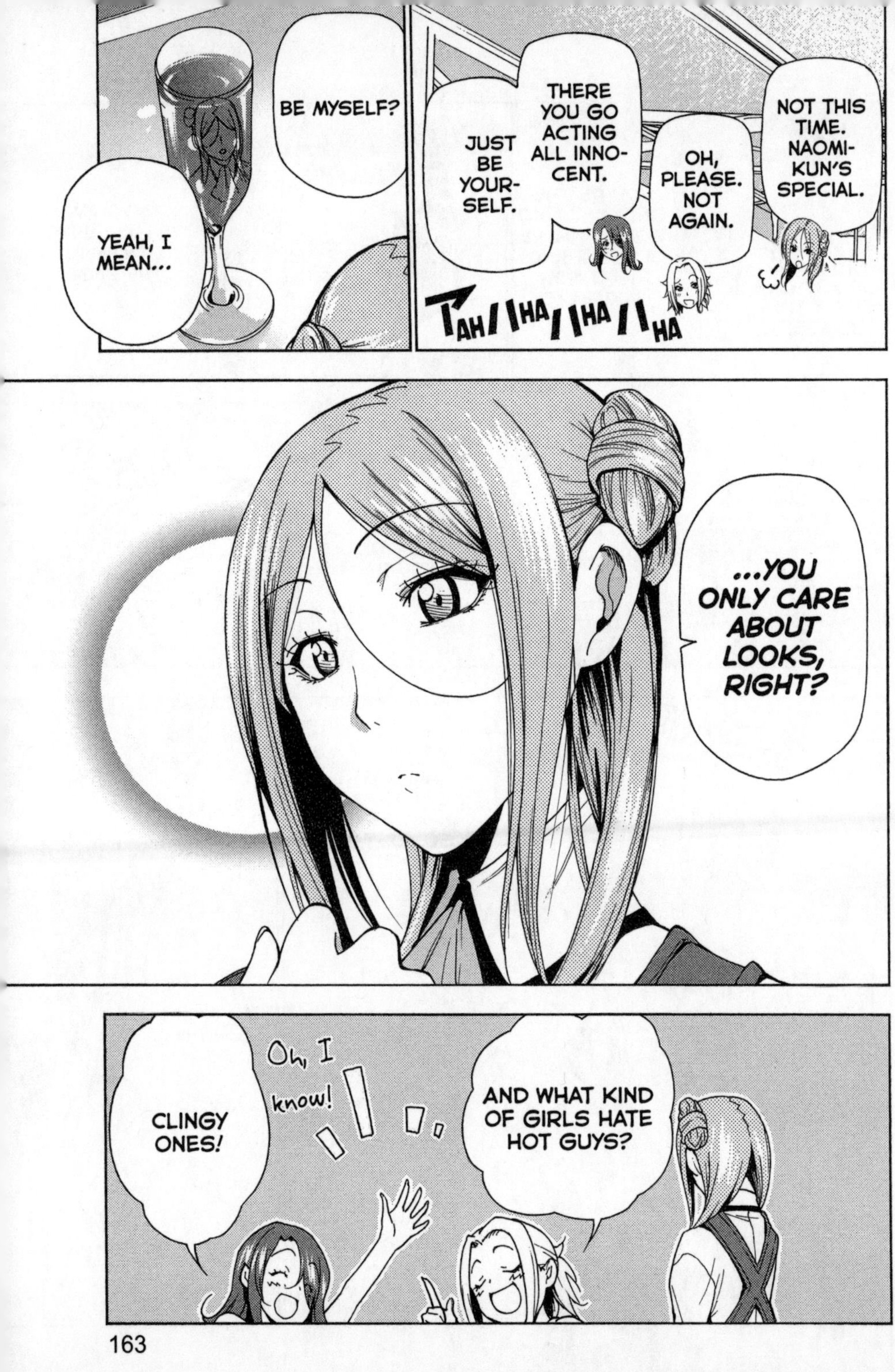
NOT THIS TIME. NAOMI-KUN'S SPECIAL.
OH, PLEASE. NOT AGAIN.
THERE YOU GO ACTING ALL INNO-CENT.
JUST BE YOUR-SELF.
AH HA HA HA
BE MYSELF?
YEAH, I MEAN...
...YOU ONLY CARE ABOUT LOOKS, RIGHT?
AND WHAT KIND OF GIRLS HATE HOT GUYS?
Oh, I know!
CLINGY ONES!

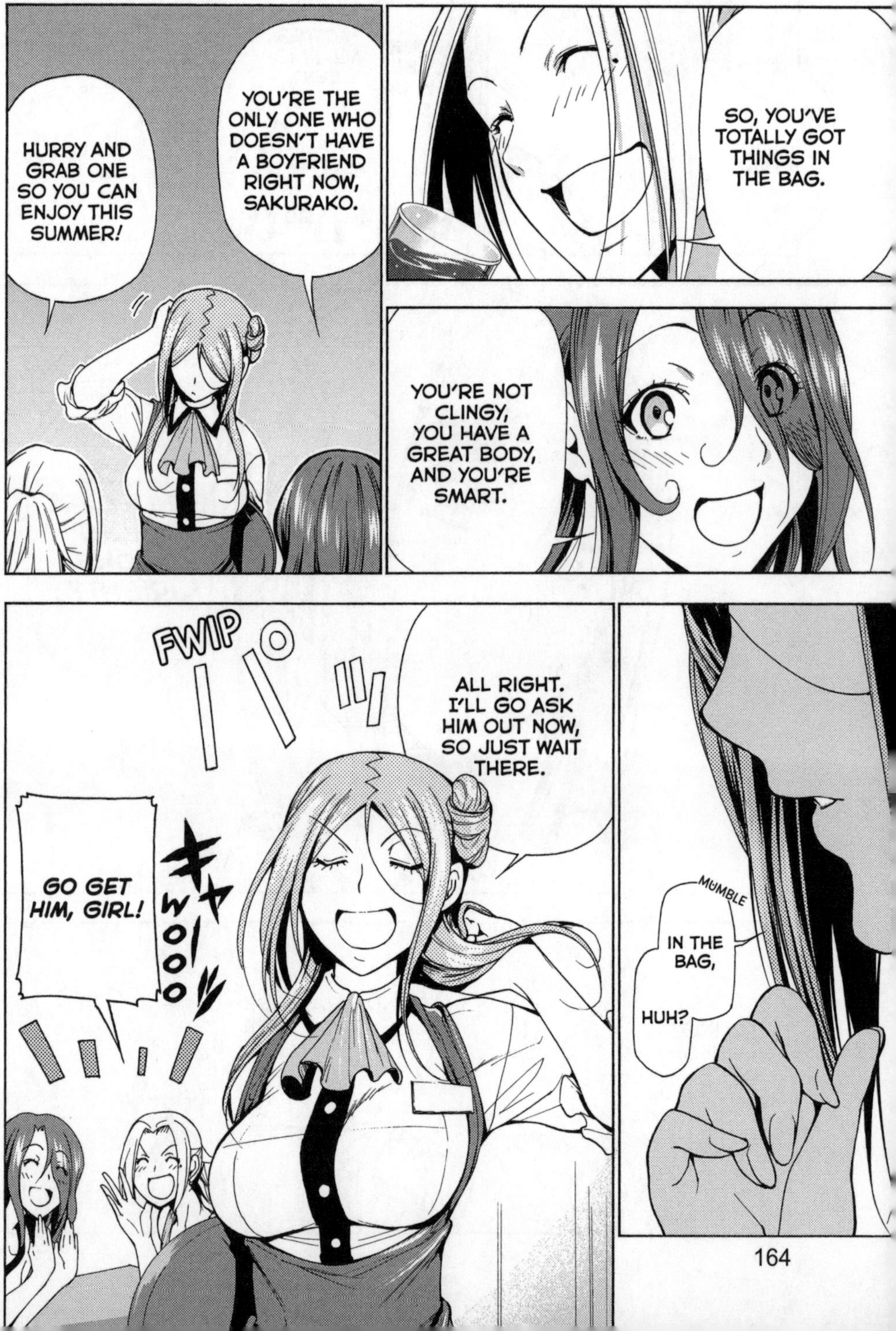
SO, YOU'VE TOTALLY GOT THINGS IN THE BAG.
YOU'RE NOT CLINGY, YOU HAVE A GREAT BODY, AND YOU'RE SMART.
YOU'RE THE ONLY ONE WHO DOESN'T HAVE A BOYFRIEND RIGHT NOW, SAKURAKO.
HURRY AND GRAB ONE SO YOU CAN ENJOY THIS SUMMER!
MUMBLE
IN THE BAG,
HUH?
ALL RIGHT. I'LL GO ASK HIM OUT NOW, SO JUST WAIT THERE.
FWIP
GO GET HIM, GIRL!
WOOO

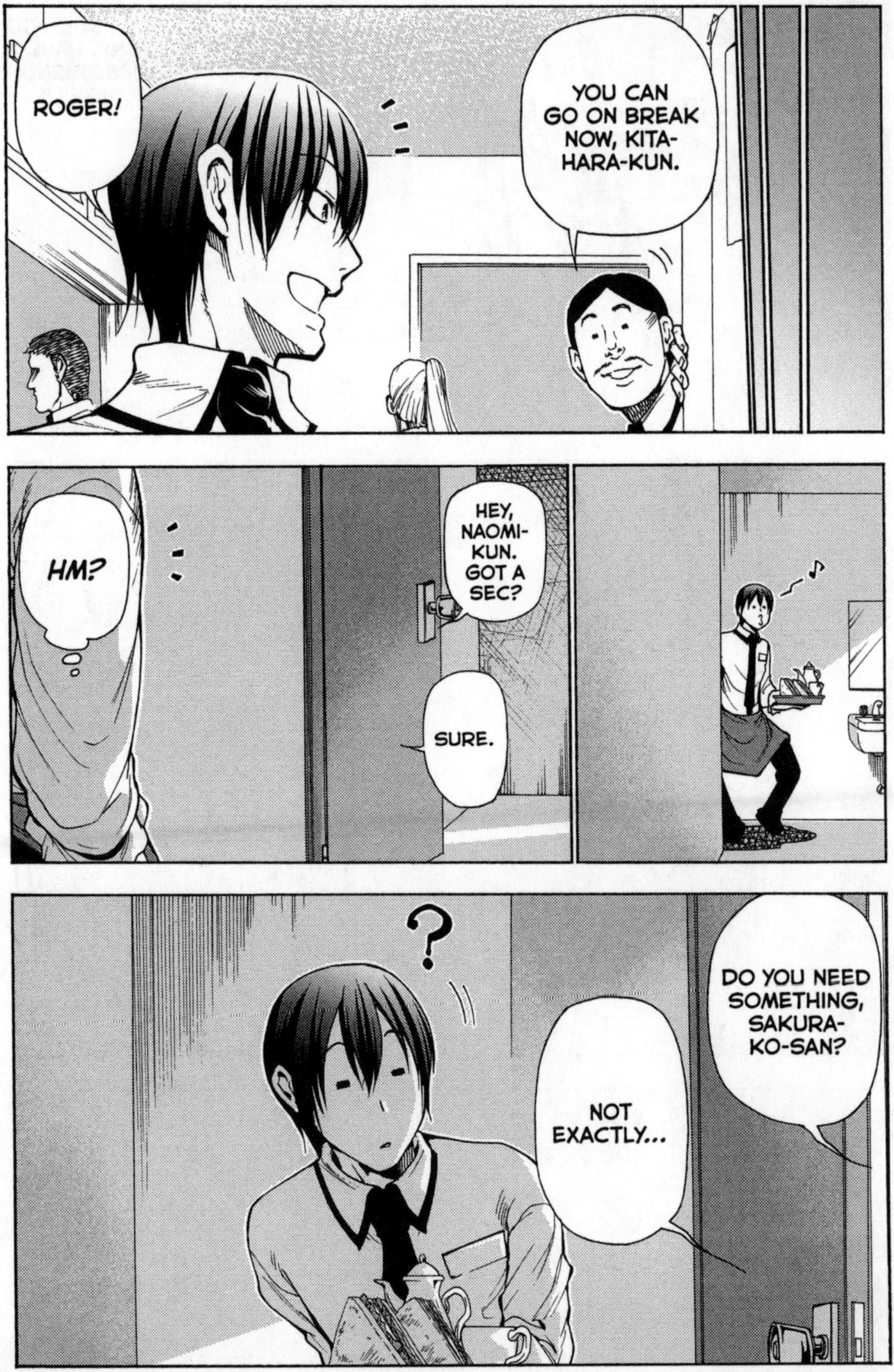
YOU CAN GO ON BREAK NOW, KITA-HARA-KUN.
ROGER!
HEY, NAOMI-KUN. GOT A SEC?
SURE.
HM?
DO YOU NEED SOMETHING, SAKURA-KO-SAN?
NOT EXACTLY...

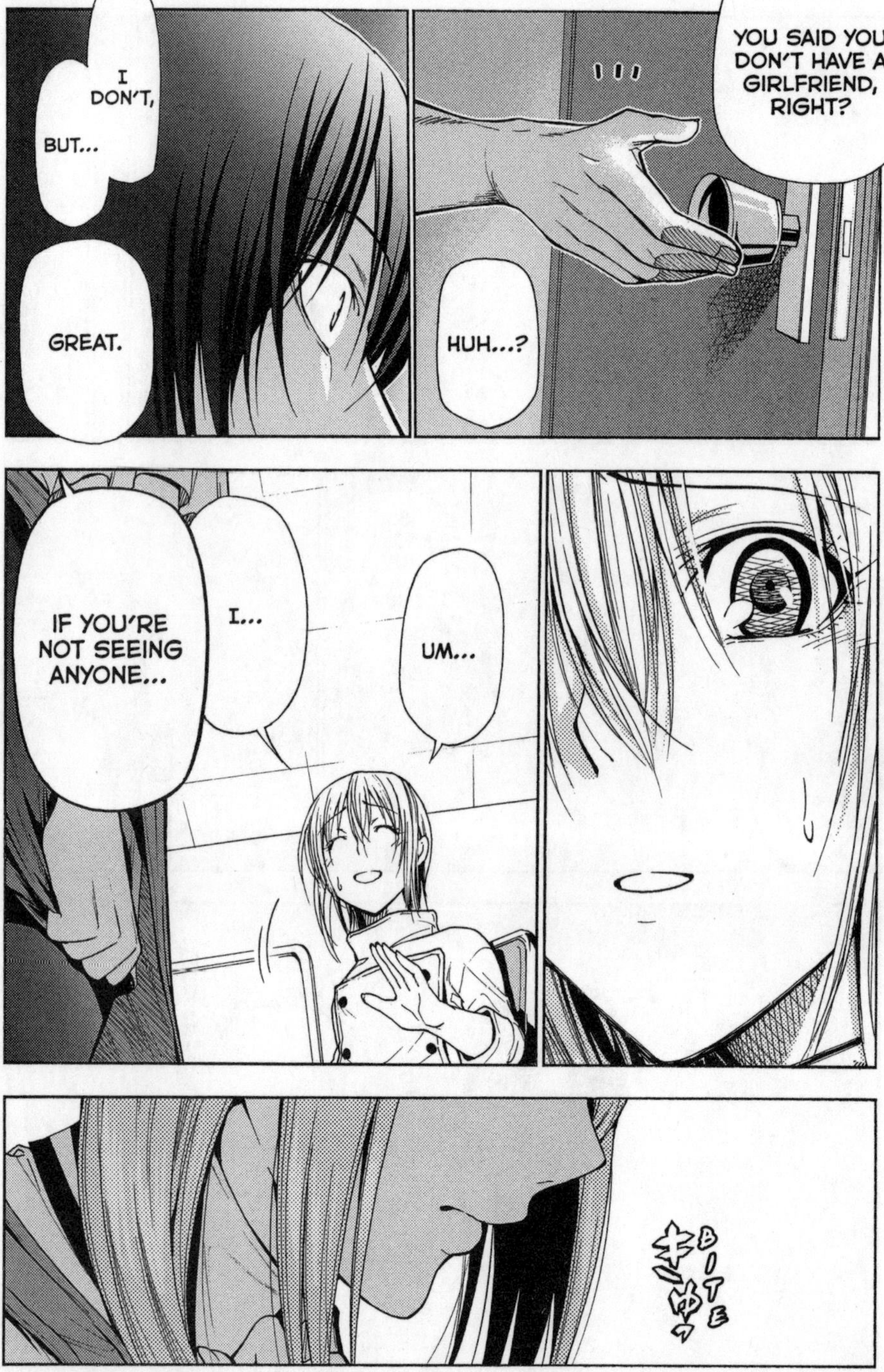
YOU SAID YOU DON'T HAVE A GIRLFRIEND, RIGHT?
HUH...?
I DON'T,
BUT...
GREAT.
UM...
I...
IF YOU'RE NOT SEEING ANYONE...
BITE

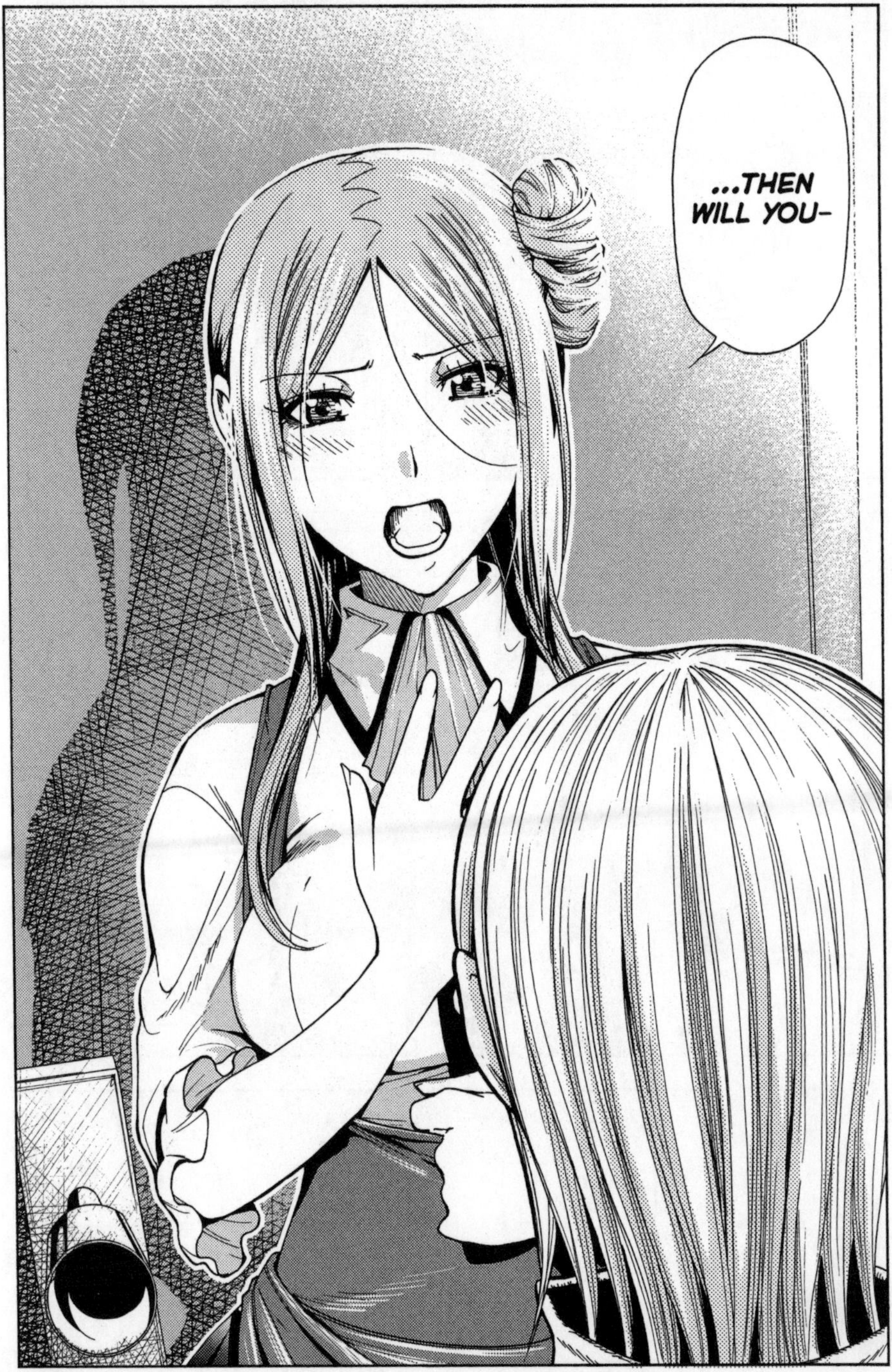
...THEN WILL YOU-

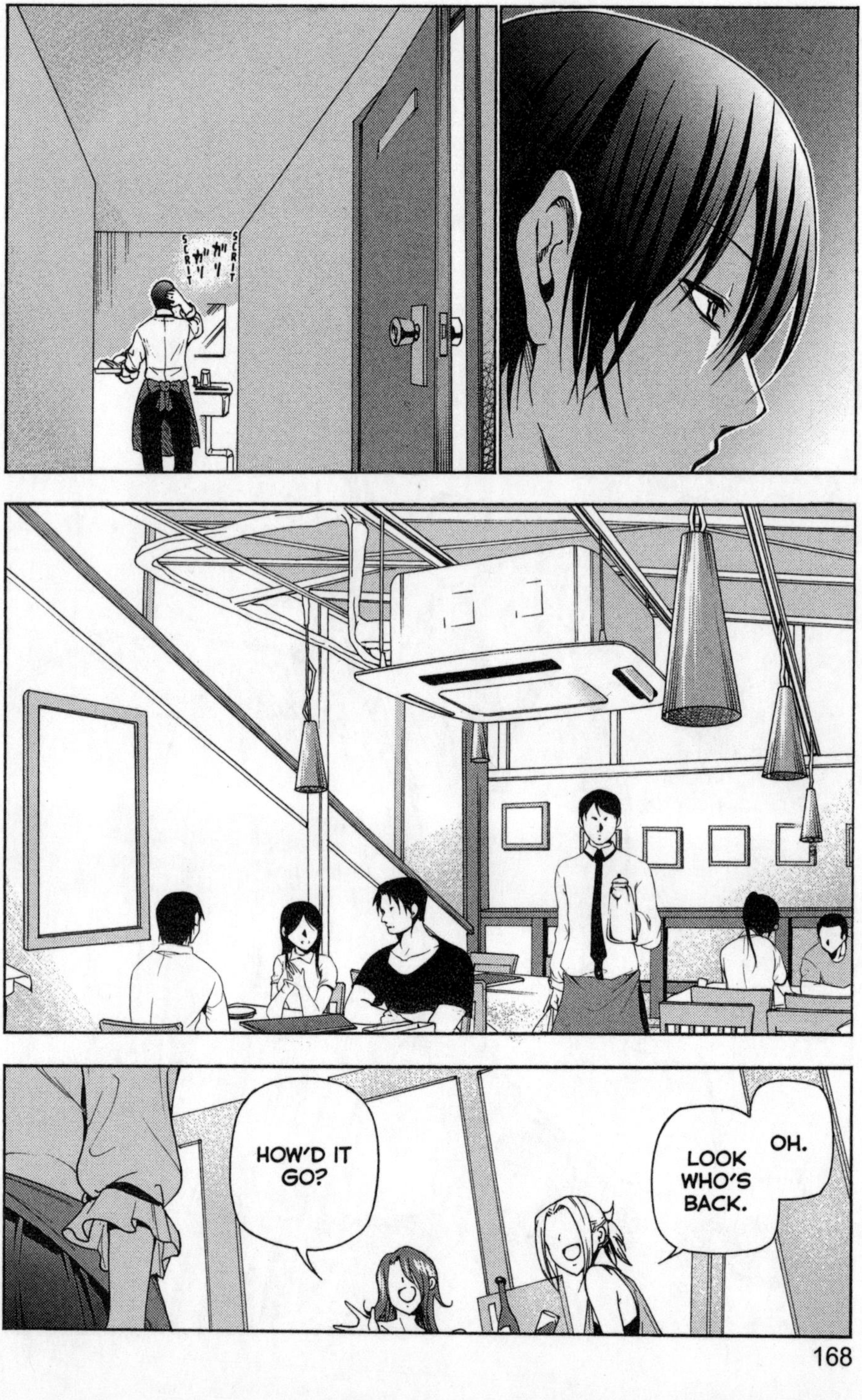
SCRIT ガリ ガリ SCRIT
OH.
LOOK WHO'S BACK.
HOW'D IT GO?

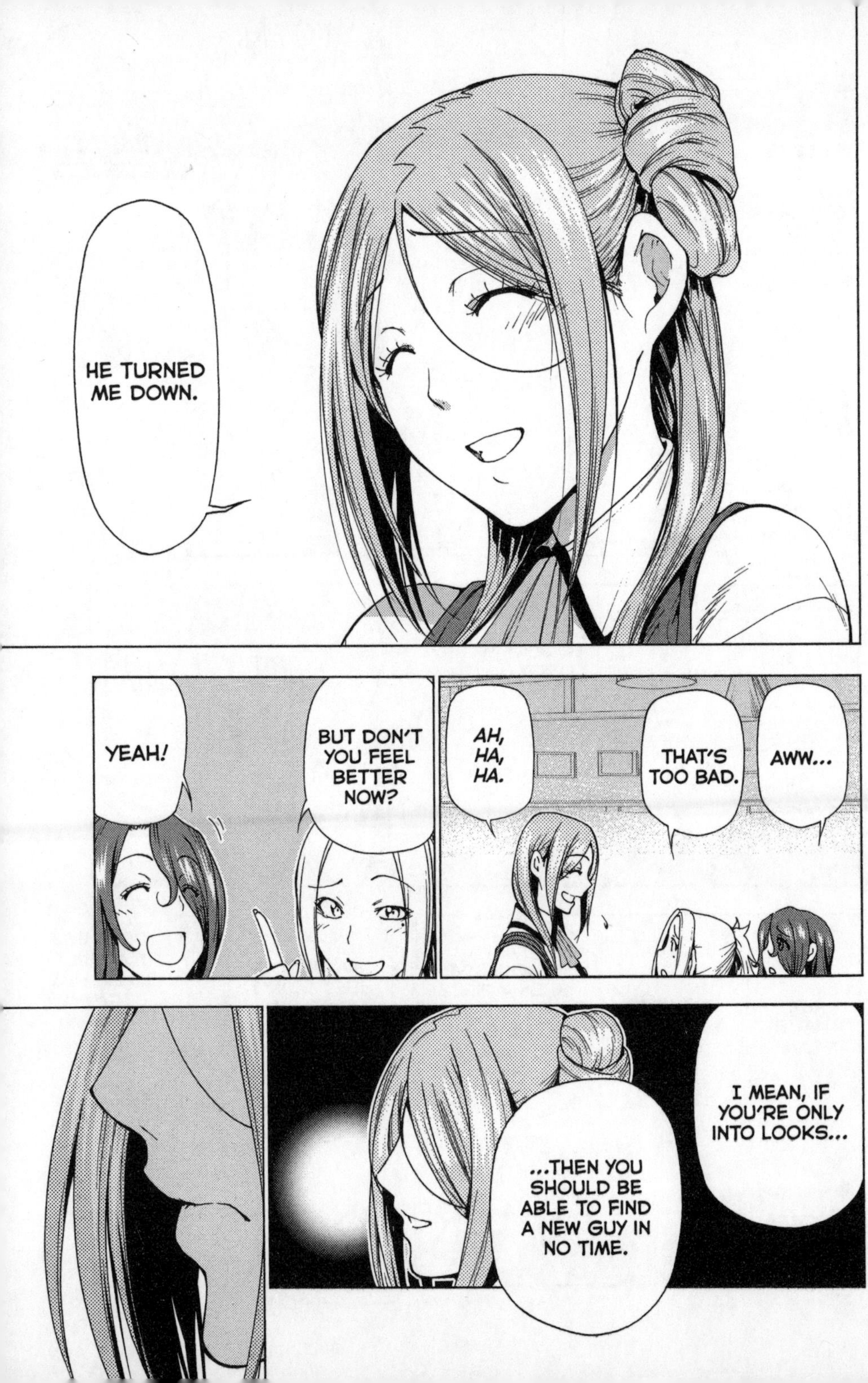
HE TURNED ME DOWN.
AWW...
THAT'S TOO BAD.
AH, HA, HA.
BUT DON'T YOU FEEL BETTER NOW?
YEAH!
I MEAN, IF YOU'RE ONLY INTO LOOKS...
...THEN YOU SHOULD BE ABLE TO FIND A NEW GUY IN NO TIME.

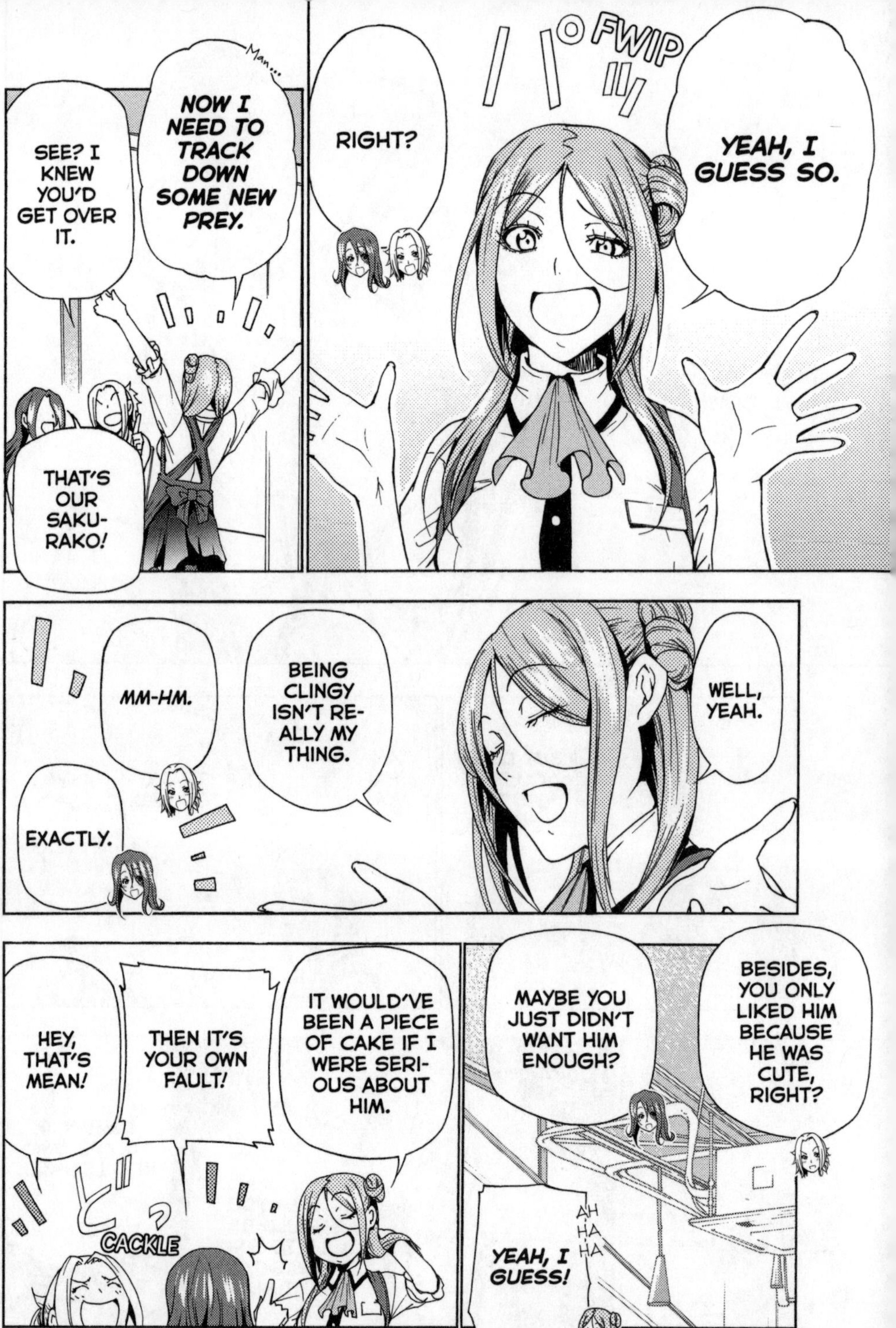
FWIP
YEAH, I GUESS SO.
RIGHT?
NOW I NEED TO TRACK DOWN SOME NEW PREY.
Man...
SEE? I KNEW YOU'D GET OVER IT.
THAT'S OUR SAKURAKO!
WELL, YEAH.
BEING CLINGY ISN'T REALLY MY THING.
MM-HM.
EXACTLY.
BESIDES, YOU ONLY LIKED HIM BECAUSE HE WAS CUTE, RIGHT?
MAYBE YOU JUST DIDN'T WANT HIM ENOUGH?
AH HA HA
YEAH, I GUESS!
IT WOULD'VE BEEN A PIECE OF CAKE IF I WERE SERIOUS ABOUT HIM.
THEN IT'S YOUR OWN FAULT!
HEY, THAT'S MEAN!
CACKLE

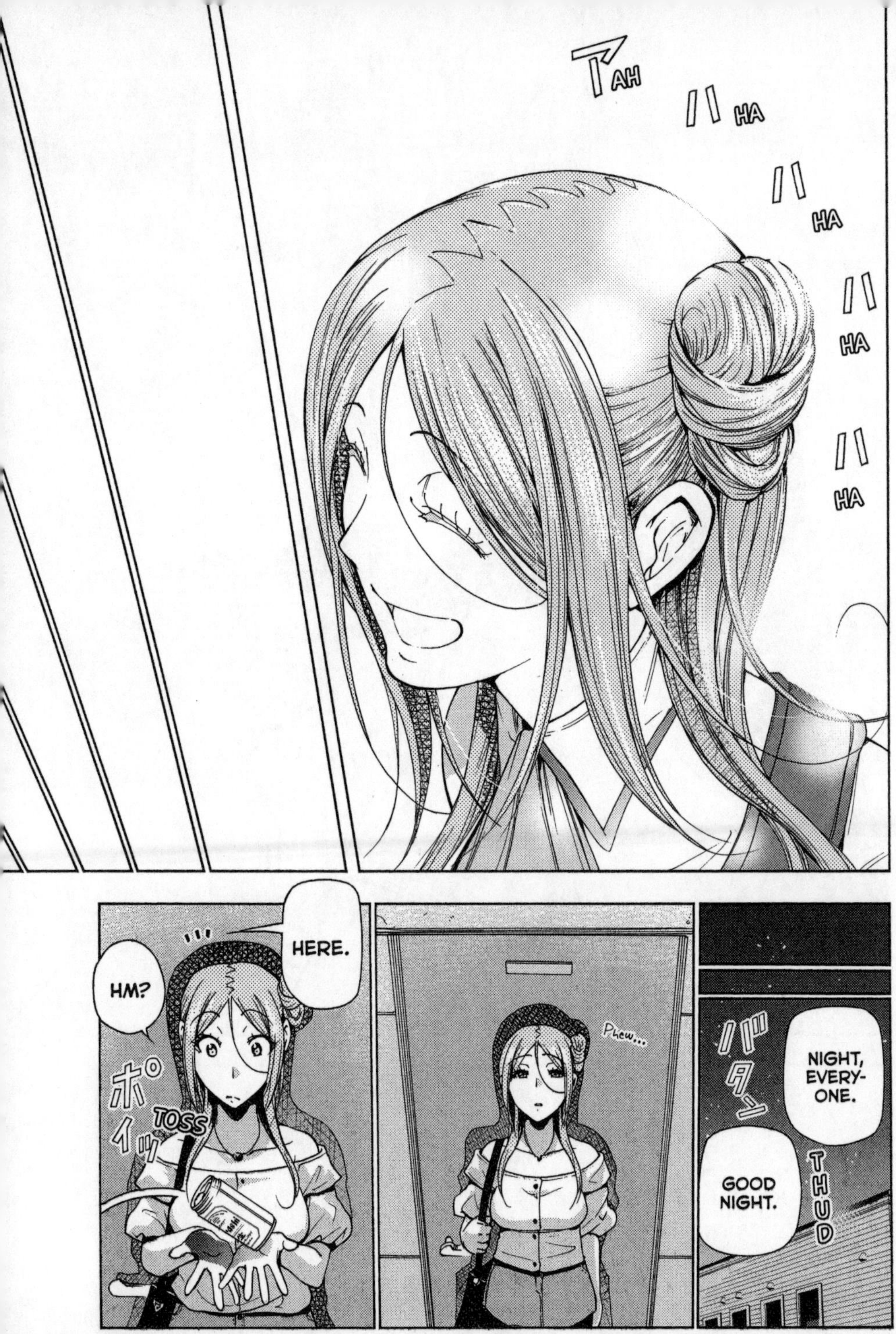
ア
AH
ハ
HA
ハ
HA
ハ
HA
ハ
HA
バタン
THUD
NIGHT, EVERY-ONE.
GOOD NIGHT.
Phew...
HERE.
HM?
ポイッ
TOSS

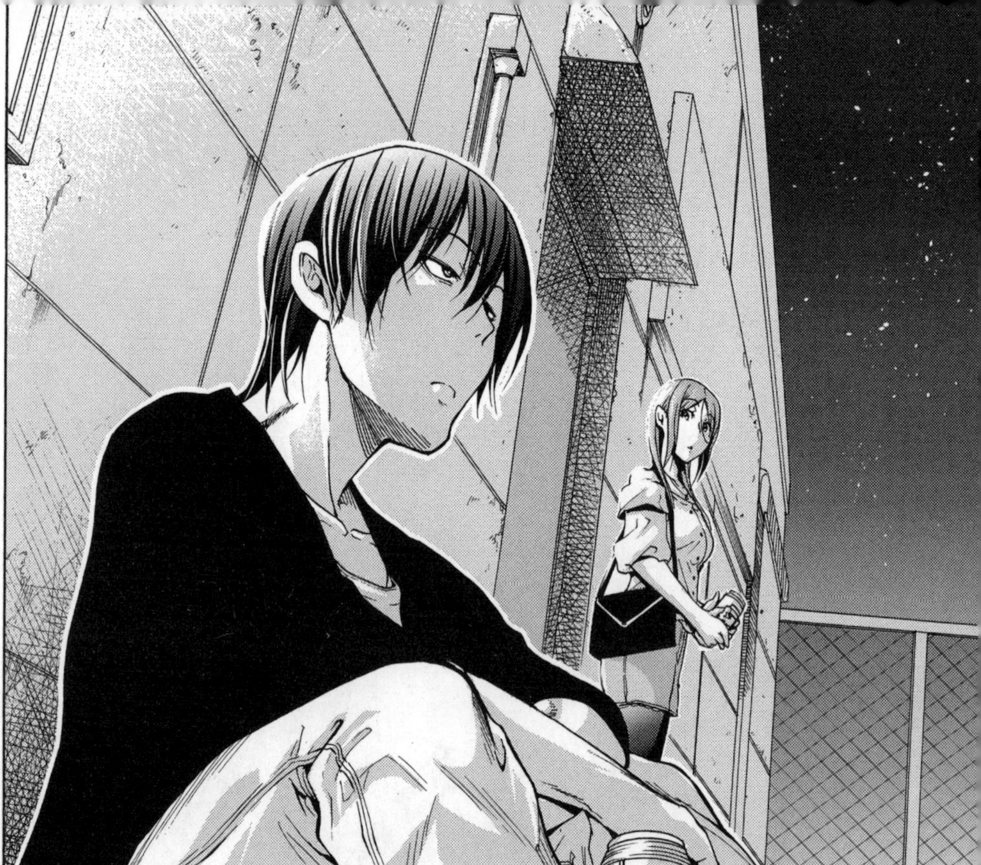

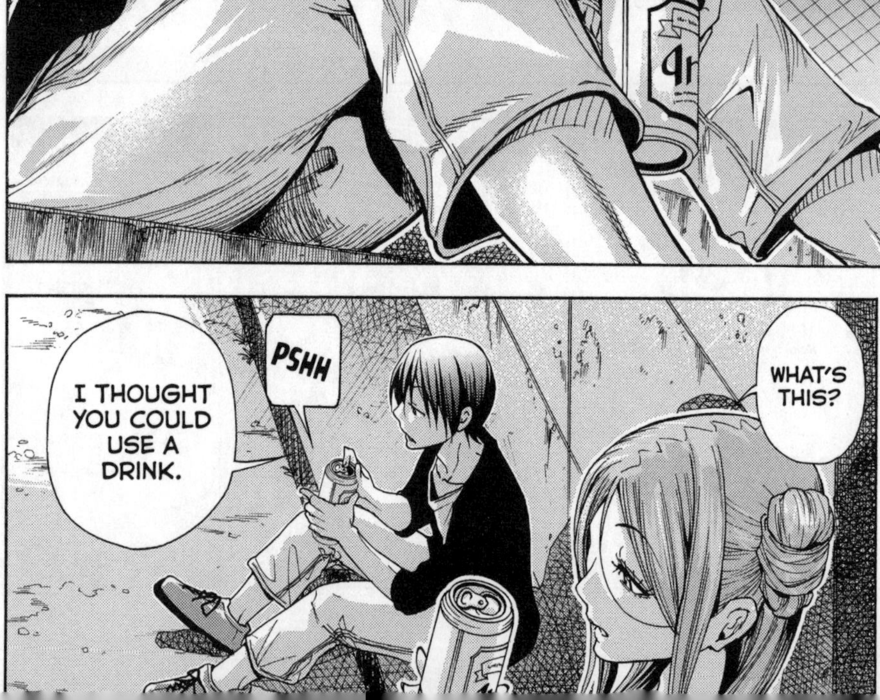
WHAT'S THIS?
PSHH
I THOUGHT YOU COULD USE A DRINK.

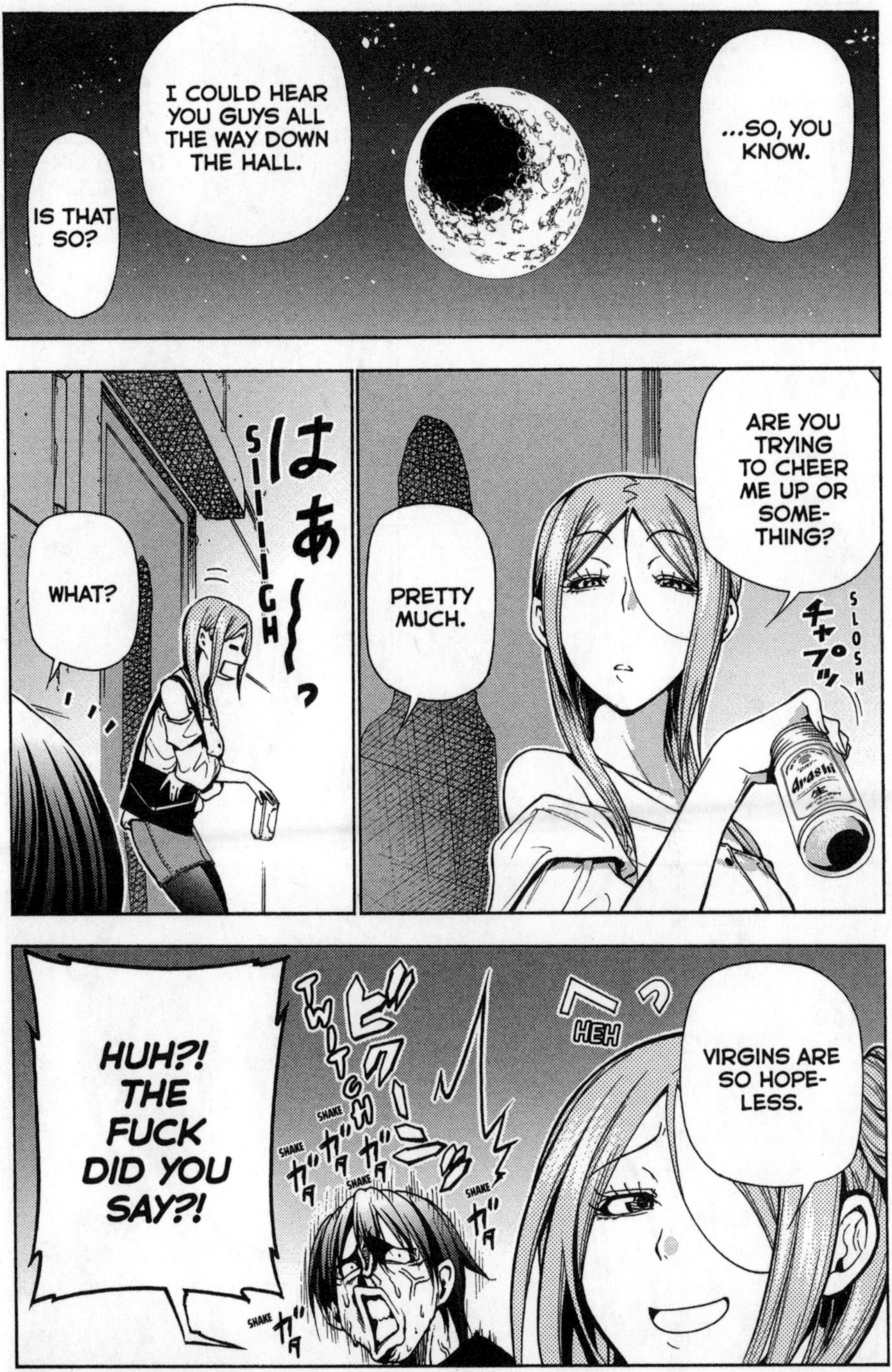
...SO, YOU KNOW.
I COULD HEAR YOU GUYS ALL THE WAY DOWN THE HALL.
IS THAT SO?
ARE YOU TRYING TO CHEER ME UP OR SOME-THING?
チャプッ SLOSH
PRETTY MUCH.
はぁ~っ SIIIIGH
WHAT?
VIRGINS ARE SO HOPE-LESS.
へっ HEH
ビクーンッ TWITCH
ガタ SHAKE
ガタ SHAKE
ガタ SHAKE
ガタ SHAKE
ガタ SHAKE
HUH?! THE FUCK DID YOU SAY?!

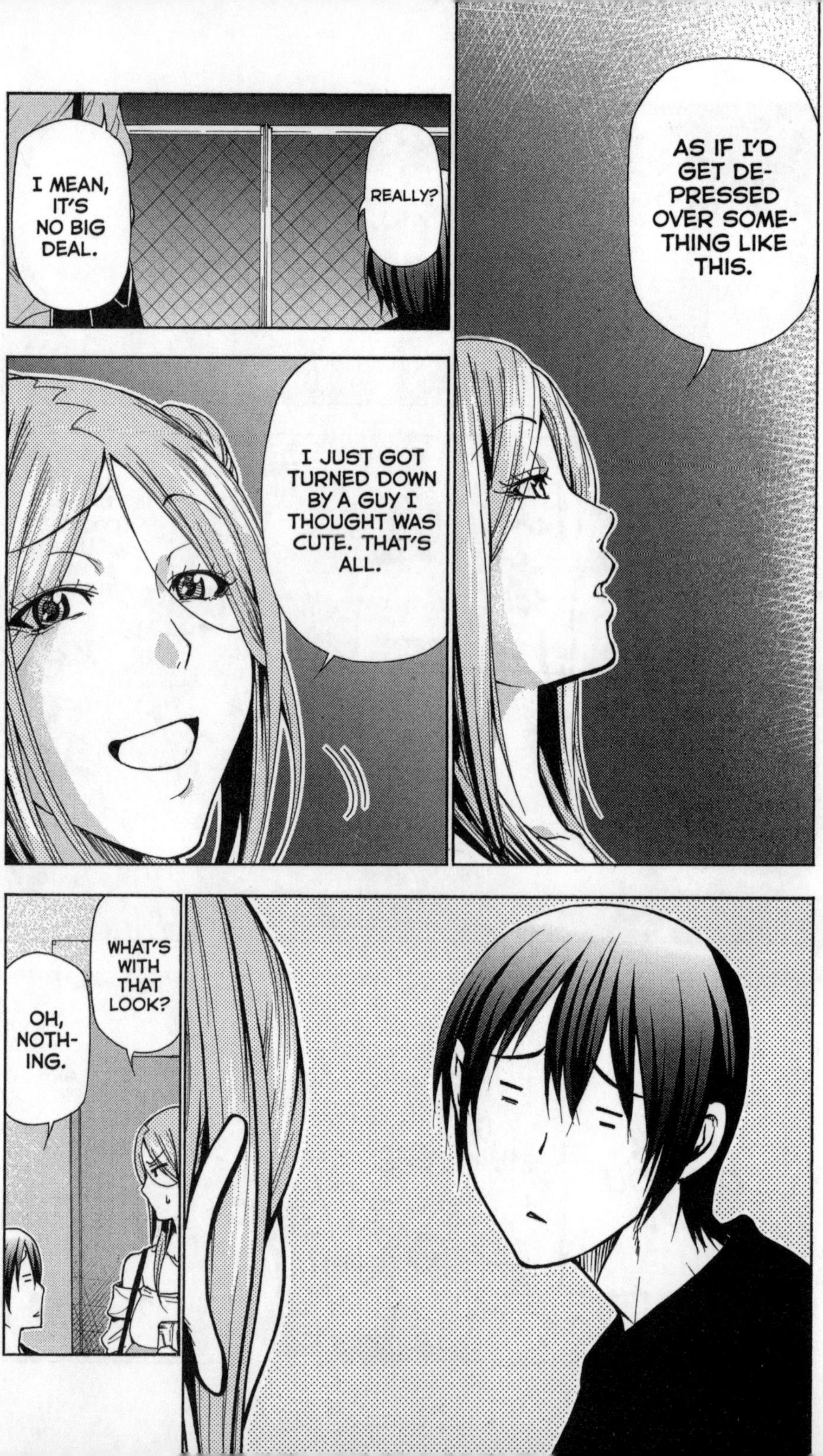
AS IF I'D GET DEPRESSED OVER SOMETHING LIKE THIS.
REALLY?
I MEAN, IT'S NO BIG DEAL.
I JUST GOT TURNED DOWN BY A GUY I THOUGHT WAS CUTE. THAT'S ALL.
WHAT'S WITH THAT LOOK?
OH, NOTHING.

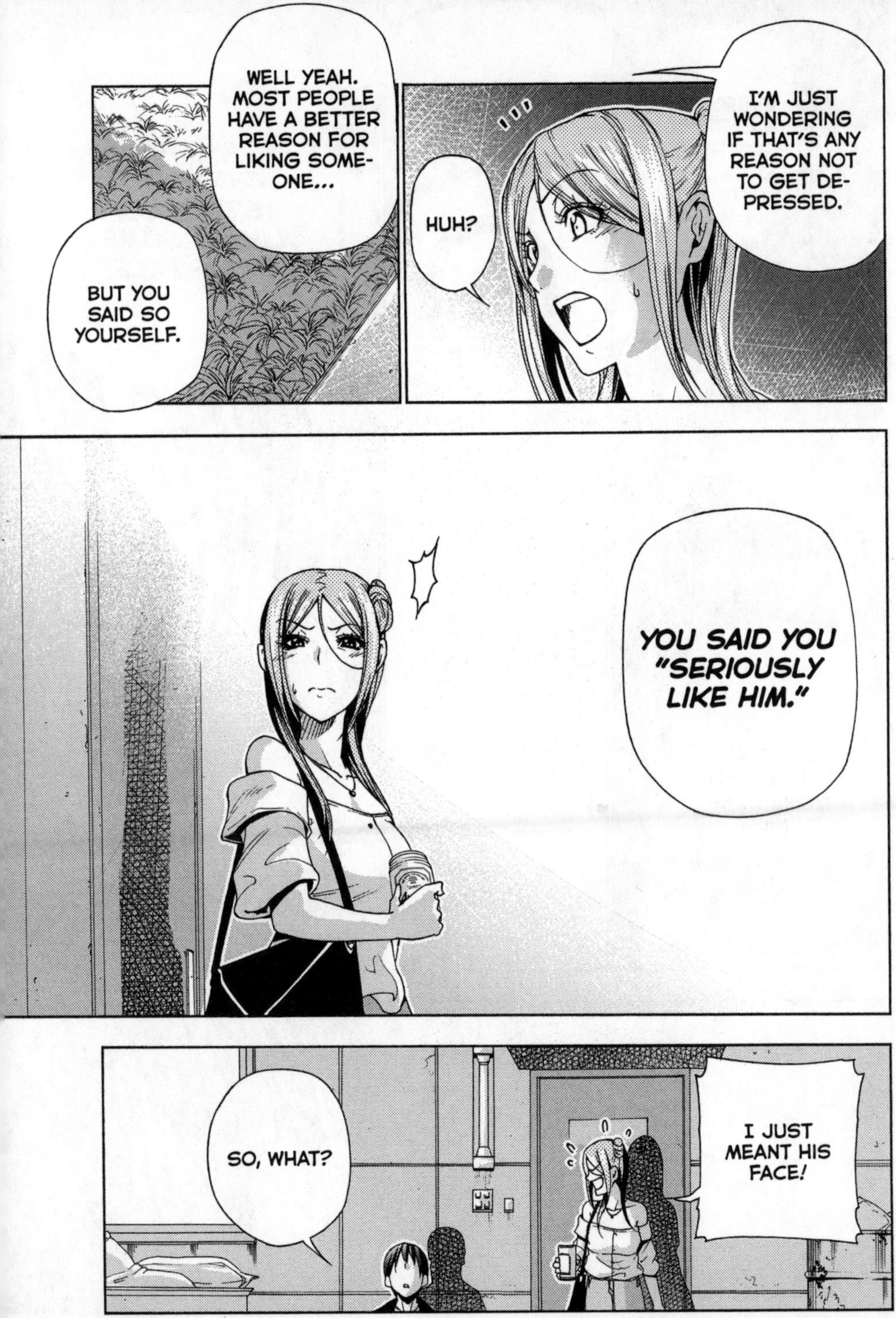
I'M JUST WONDERING IF THAT'S ANY REASON NOT TO GET DEPRESSED.
HUH?
WELL YEAH. MOST PEOPLE HAVE A BETTER REASON FOR LIKING SOMEONE...
BUT YOU SAID SO YOURSELF.
YOU SAID YOU "SERIOUSLY LIKE HIM."
I JUST MEANT HIS FACE!
SO, WHAT?

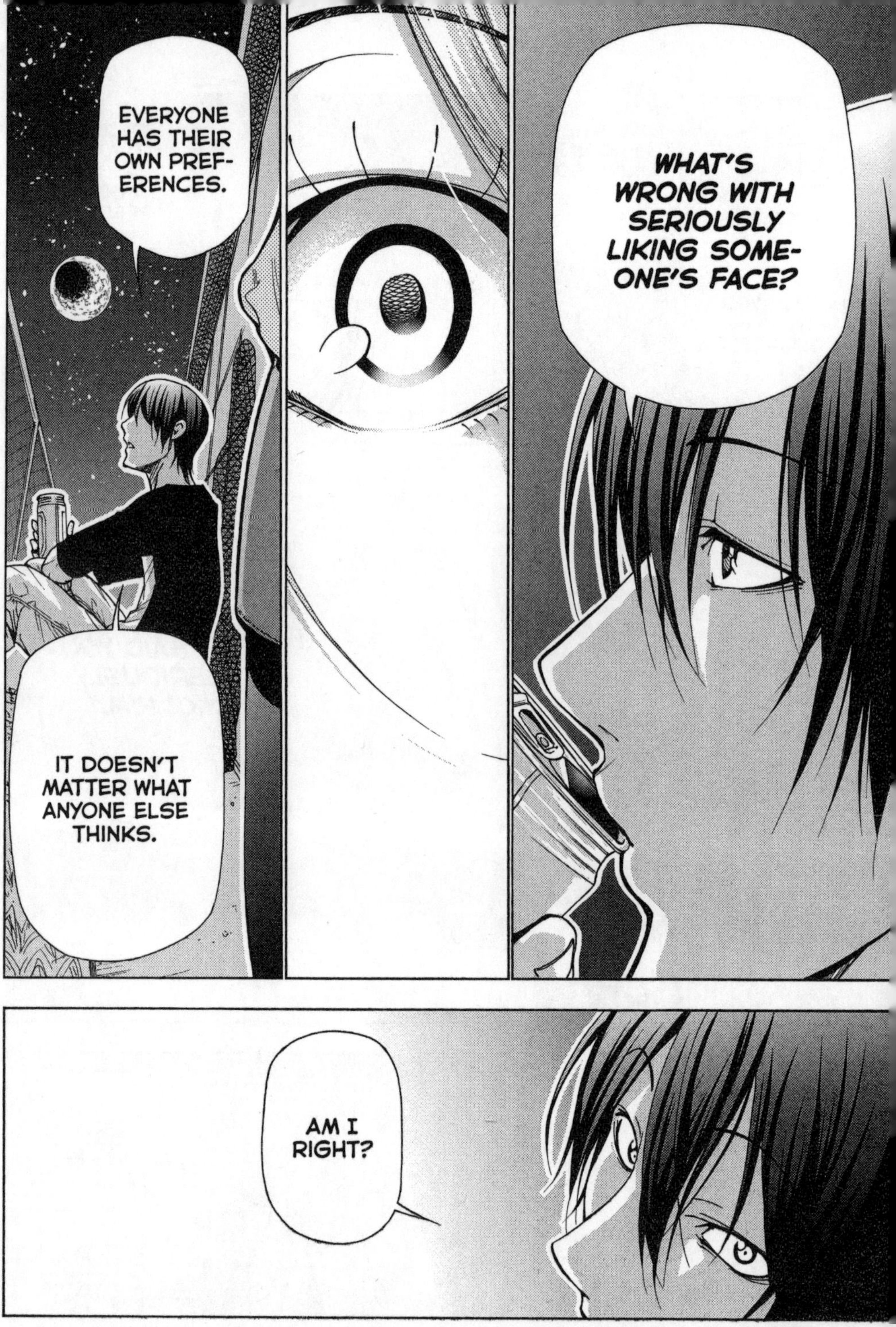
WHAT'S WRONG WITH SERIOUSLY LIKING SOMEONE'S FACE?
EVERYONE HAS THEIR OWN PREFERENCES.
IT DOESN'T MATTER WHAT ANYONE ELSE THINKS.
AM I RIGHT?

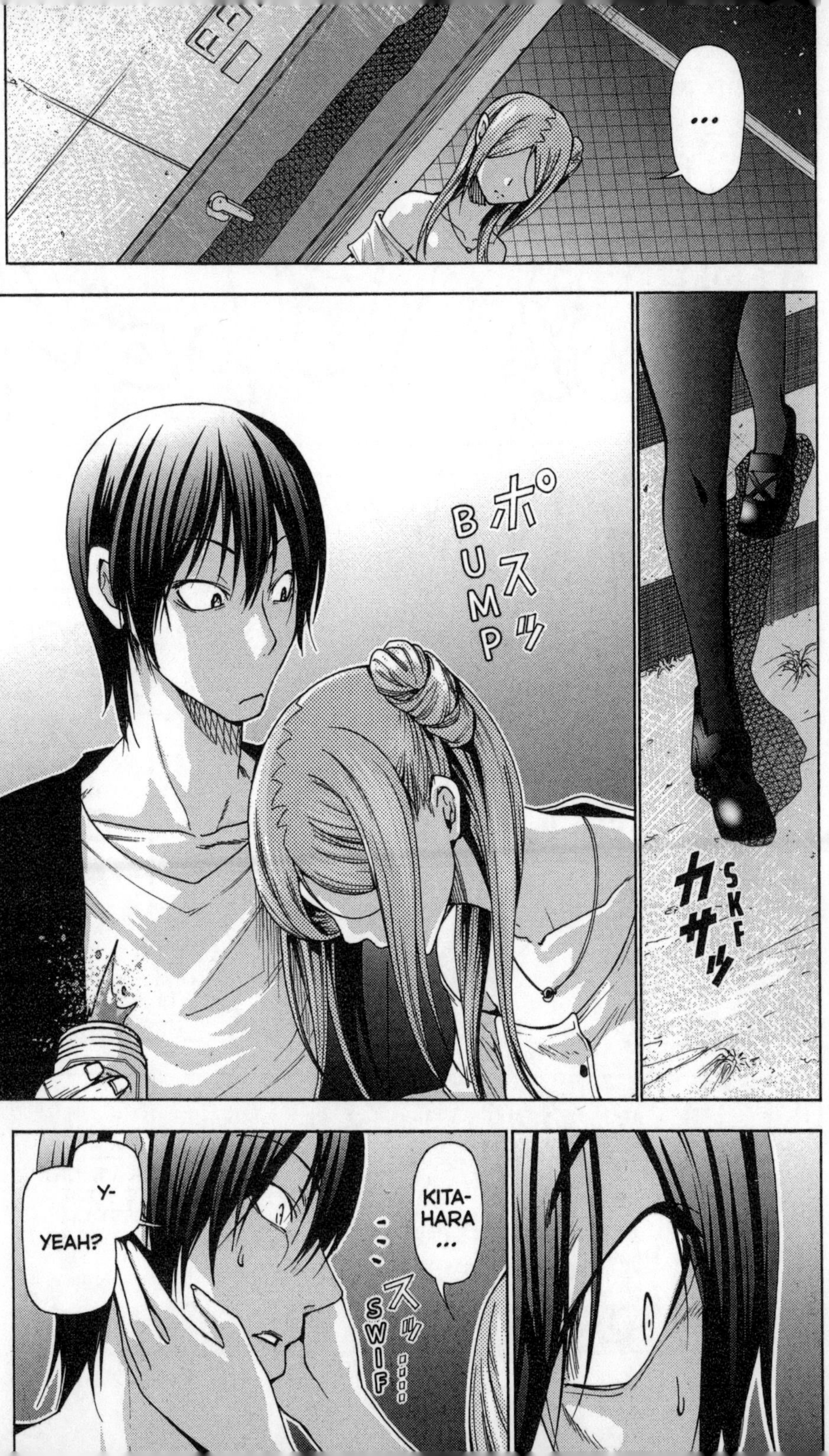
...
カサッ
SKF
ポスッ
BUMP
KITA-HARA...
スッ
SWIF
Y- YEAH?

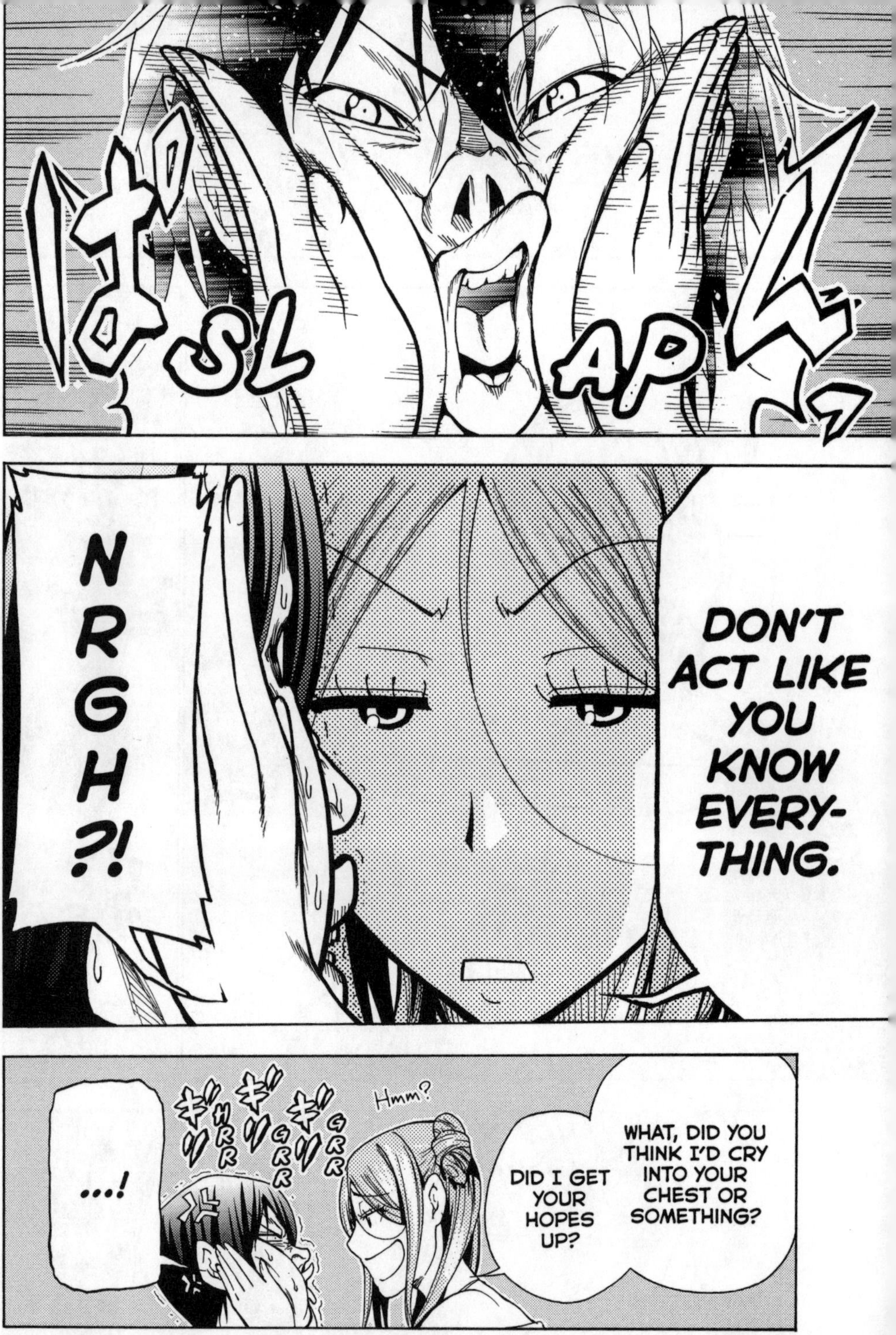
SLAP
DON'T ACT LIKE YOU KNOW EVERY-THING.
NRGH?!
WHAT, DID YOU THINK I'D CRY INTO YOUR CHEST OR SOMETHING?
DID I GET YOUR HOPES UP?
Hmm?
GRR
GRR
HRR
...!

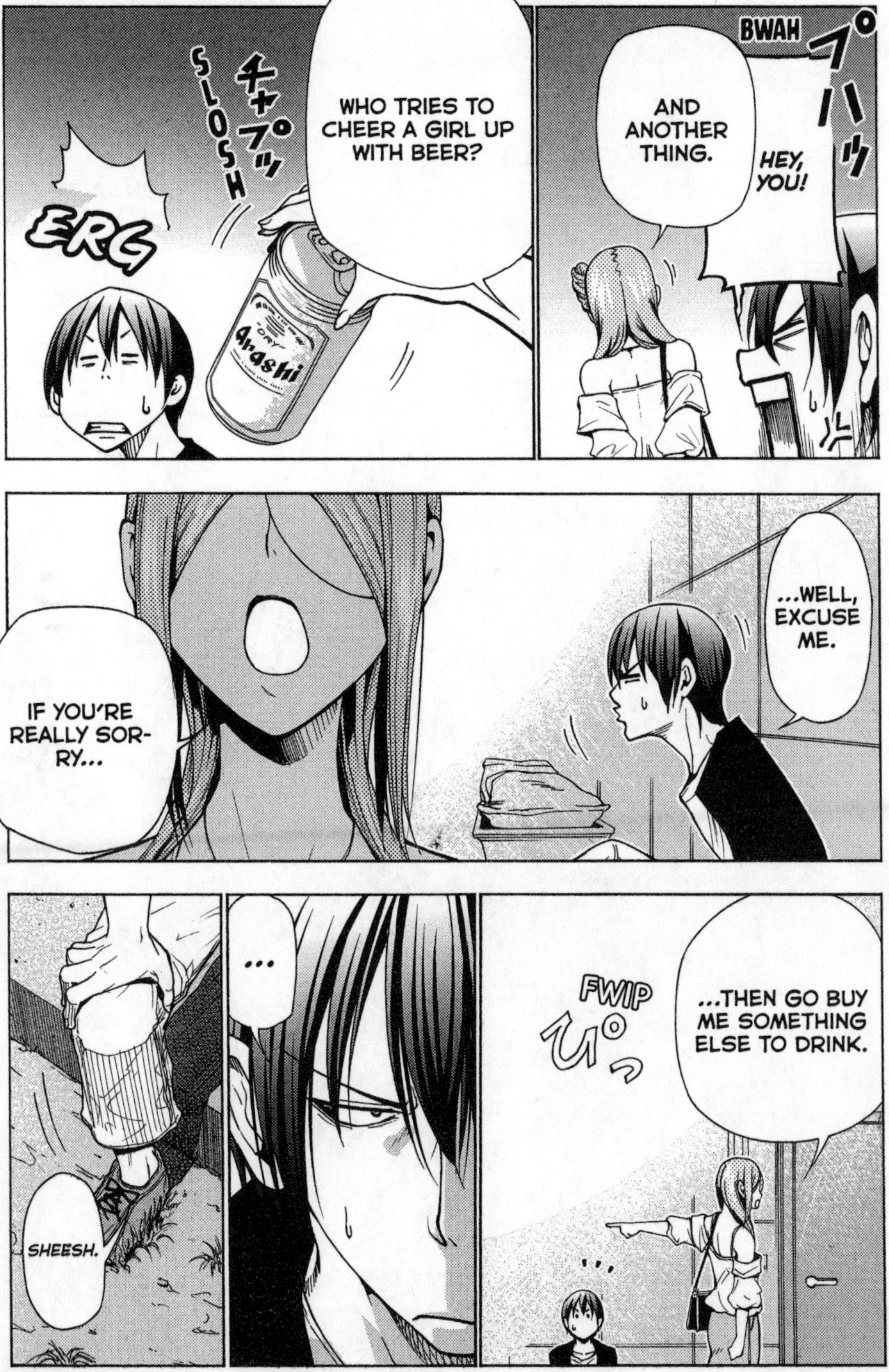
BWAH
プハーッ
HEY, YOU!
AND ANOTHER THING.
WHO TRIES TO CHEER A GIRL UP WITH BEER?
チャプッ
SLOSH
ERG
Arashi
...WELL, EXCUSE ME.
IF YOU'RE REALLY SOR-RY...
...THEN GO BUY ME SOMETHING ELSE TO DRINK.
FWIP
ぴっ
...
SHEESH.

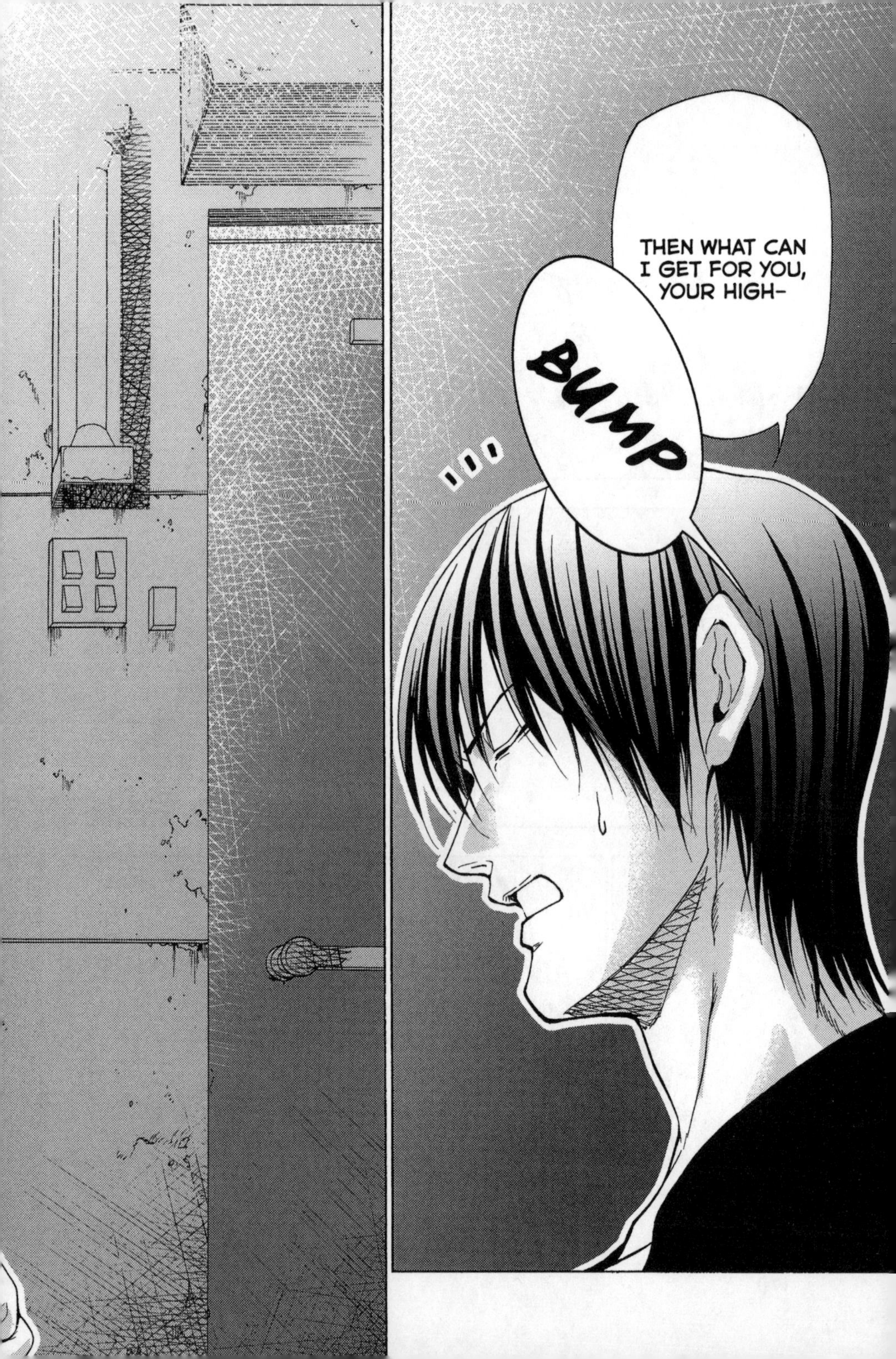
THEN WHAT CAN I GET FOR YOU, YOUR HIGH-
BUMP

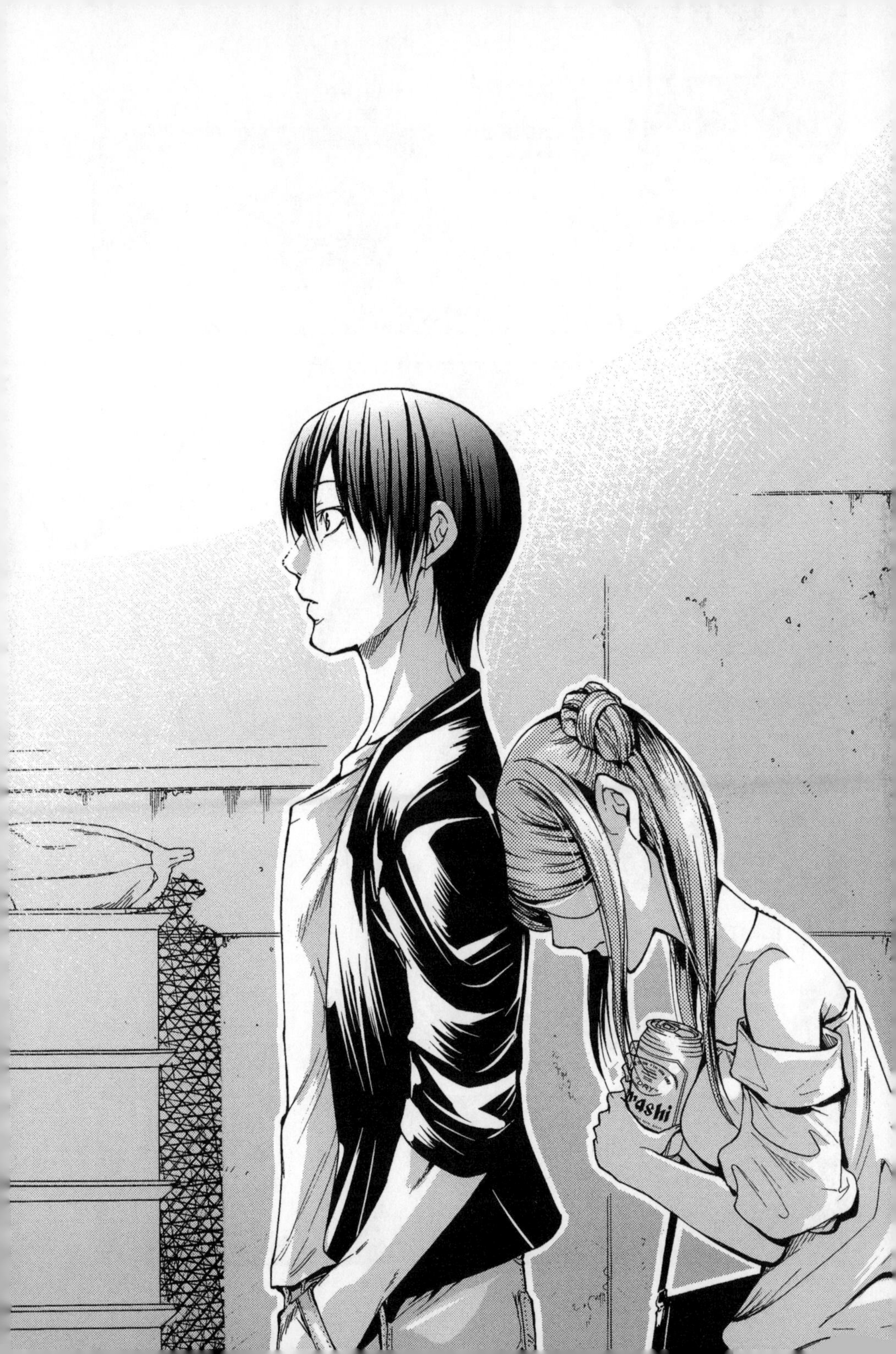

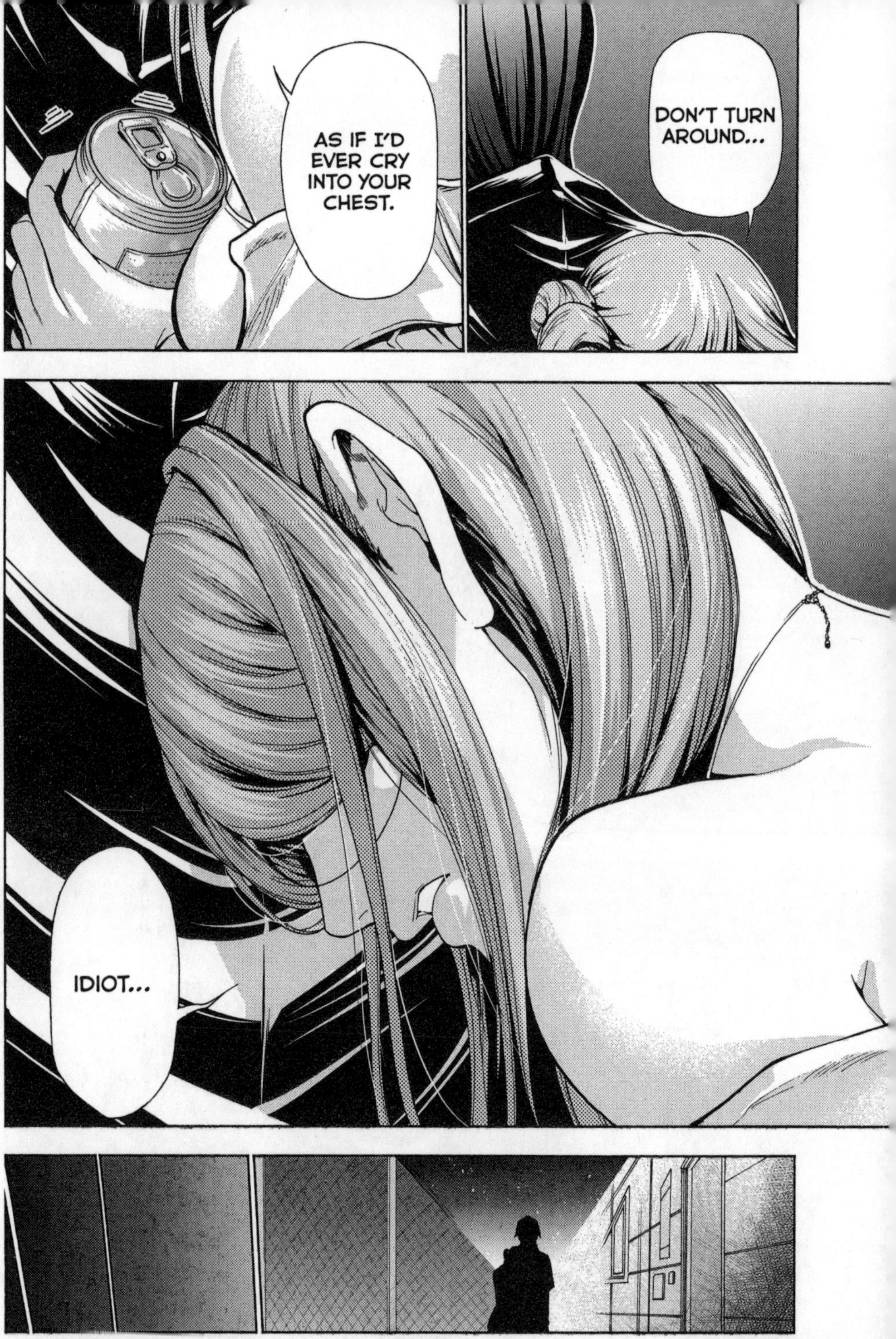
DON'T TURN AROUND...
AS IF I'D EVER CRY INTO YOUR CHEST.
IDIOT...

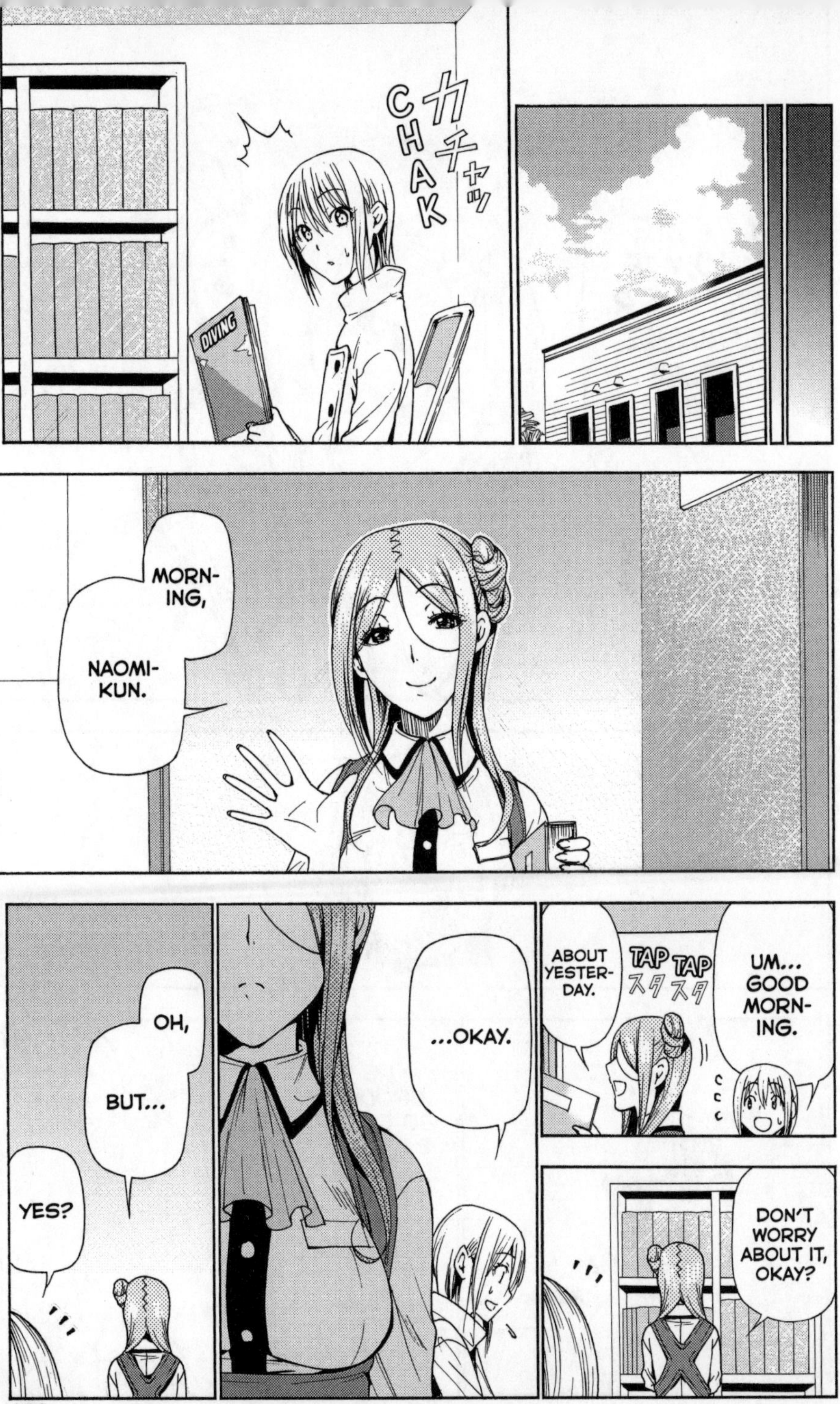
カチャッ
CHAK
MORNING, NAOMI-KUN.
UM... GOOD MORNING.
TAP TAP
スタスタ
ABOUT YESTERDAY.
DON'T WORRY ABOUT IT, OKAY?
...OKAY.
OH, BUT...
YES?

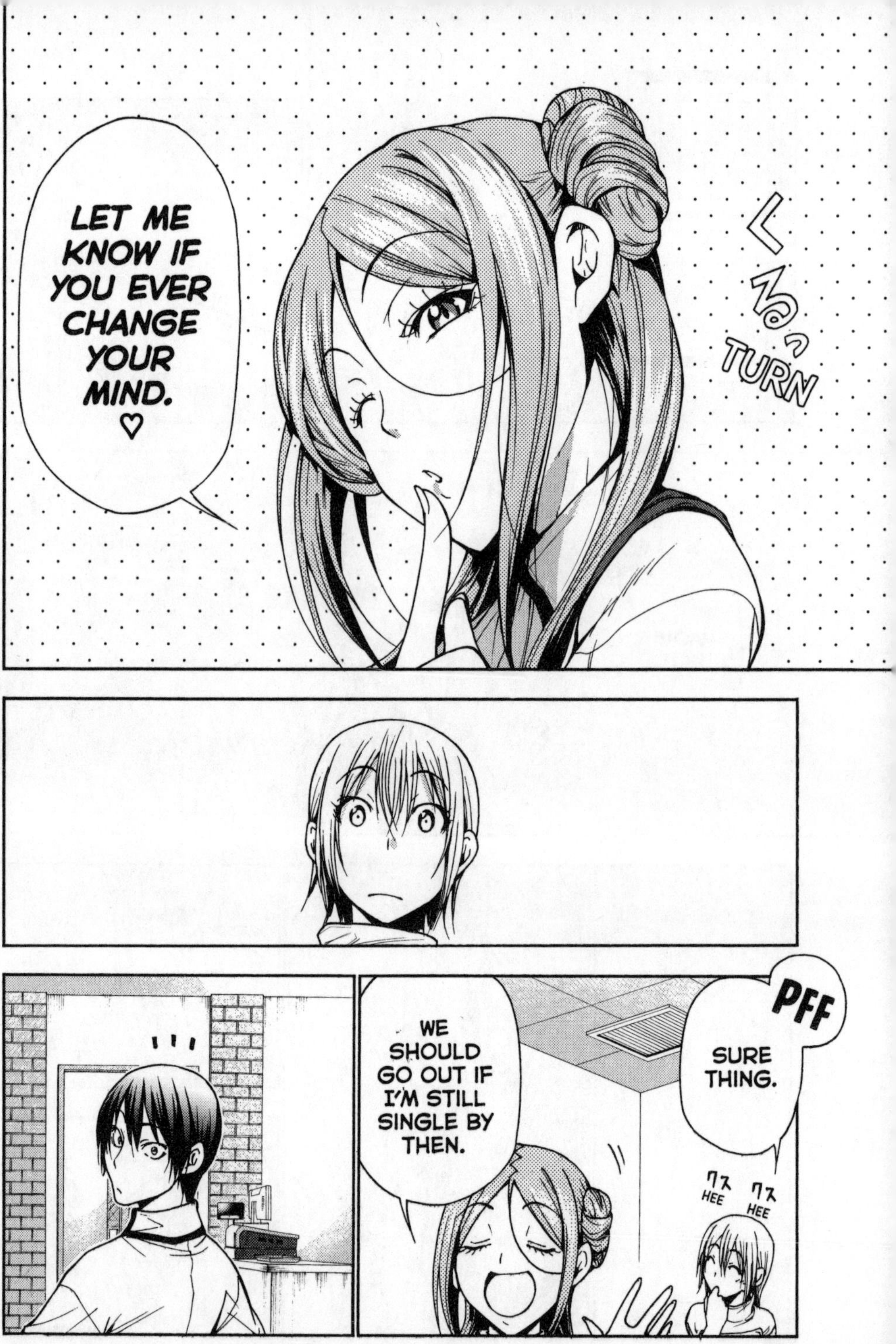
くるっ
TURN
LET ME KNOW IF YOU EVER CHANGE YOUR MIND. ♡
PFF
SURE THING.
WE SHOULD GO OUT IF I'M STILL SINGLE BY THEN.
クス HEE
クス HEE

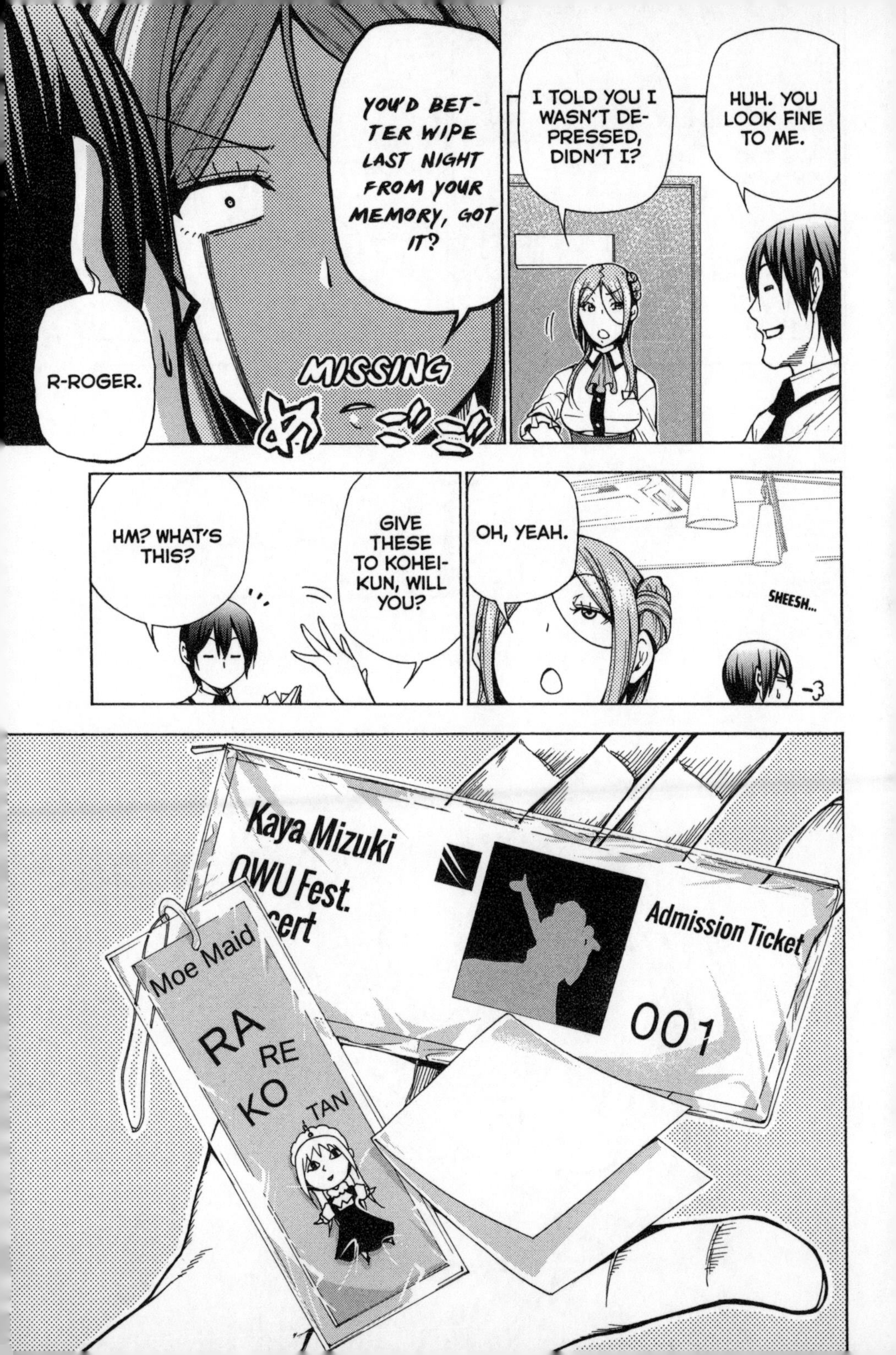
HUH. YOU LOOK FINE TO ME.
I TOLD YOU I WASN'T DE-PRESSED, DIDN'T I?
YOU'D BET-TER WIPE LAST NIGHT FROM YOUR MEMORY, GOT IT?
MISSING
R-ROGER.
OH, YEAH.
SHEESH...
GIVE THESE TO KOHEI-KUN, WILL YOU?
HM? WHAT'S THIS?
Kaya Mizuki
OWU Fest.
cert
Admission Ticket
001
Moe Maid
RA RE KO TAN

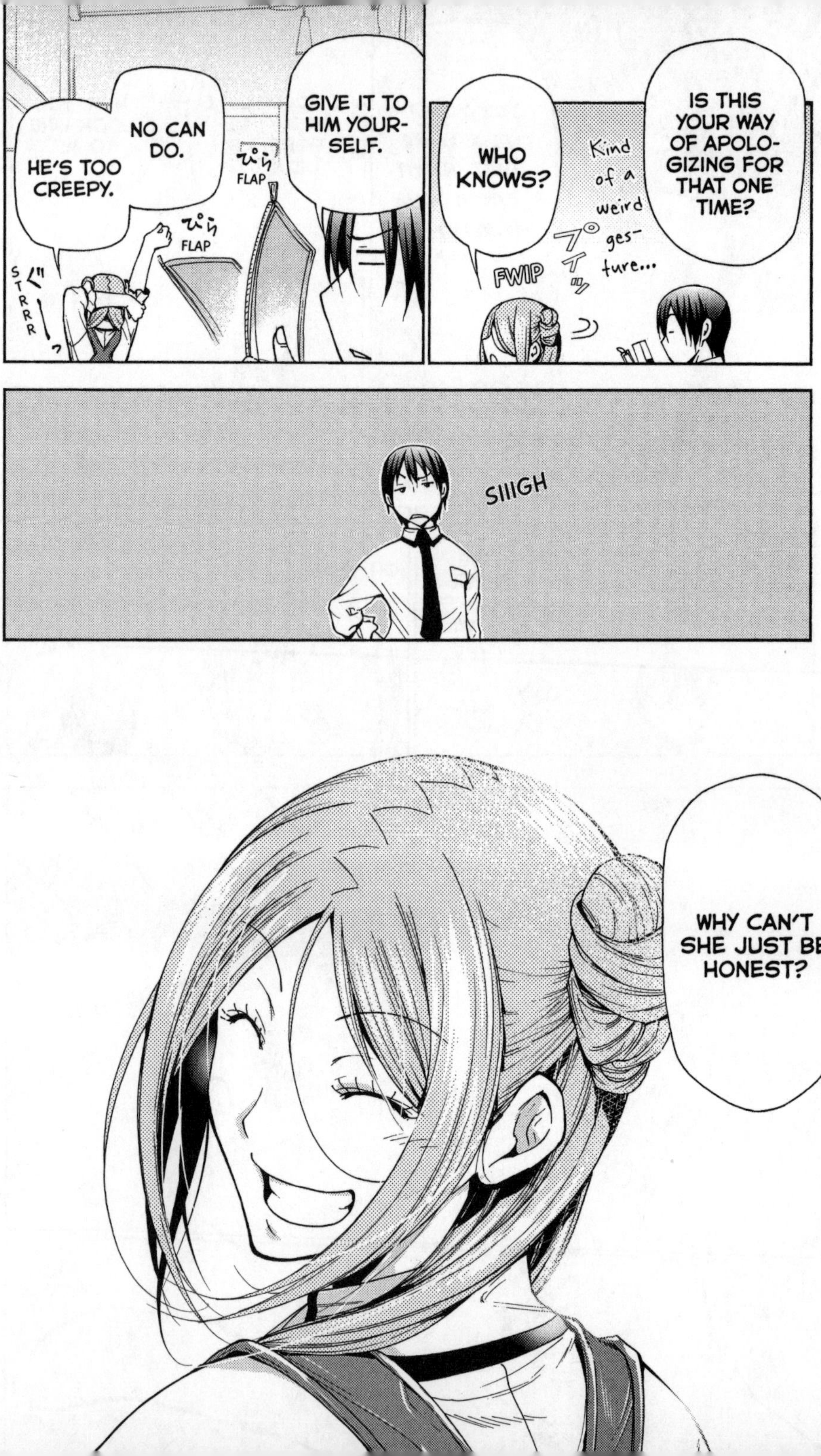
IS THIS YOUR WAY OF APOLO-GIZING FOR THAT ONE TIME?
Kind of a weird ges-ture...
WHO KNOWS?
プイッ
FWIP
GIVE IT TO HIM YOUR-SELF.
ぴら
FLAP
NO CAN DO.
HE'S TOO CREEPY.
ぴら
FLAP
STRRR
SIIIGH
WHY CAN'T SHE JUST BE HONEST?

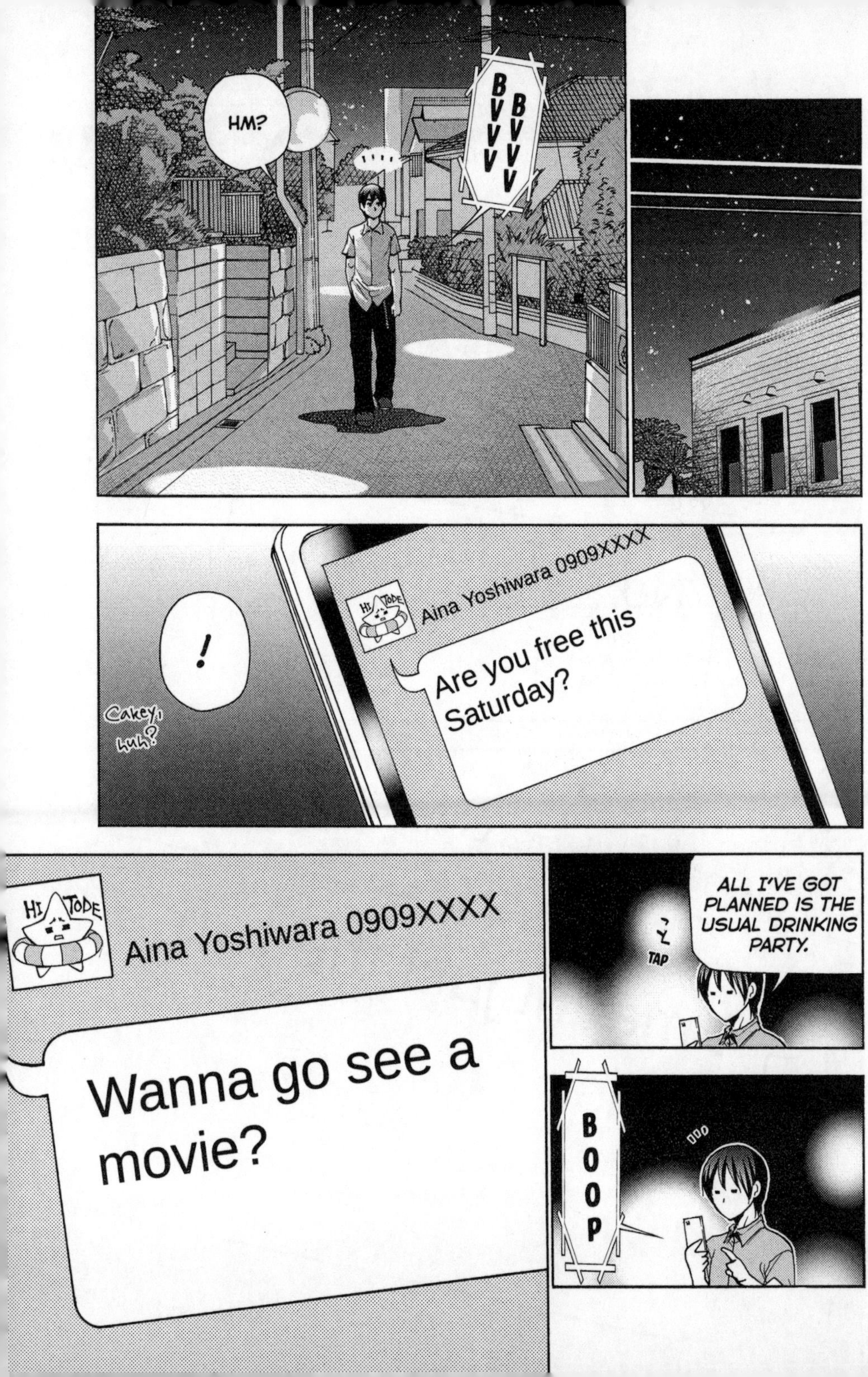
HM?
BVVV BVVV
!
Cakey, huh?
Aina Yoshiwara 0909XXXX
Are you free this Saturday?
ALL I'VE GOT PLANNED IS THE USUAL DRINKING PARTY.
TAP
BOOP
Aina Yoshiwara 0909XXXX
Wanna go see a movie?

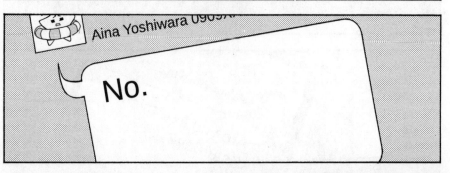

BOOP
OK! KAME
HAVE YOU ASKED CHISA AND KOHEI YET?
TAP ポチポチっと TAP
BOOP BOOP
Aina Yoshiwara
No.
Aina Yoshiwara 0909XXXX
TODE
I meant just the two of us.
CH.37 / End

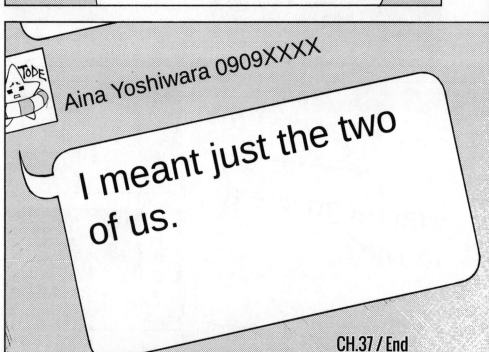

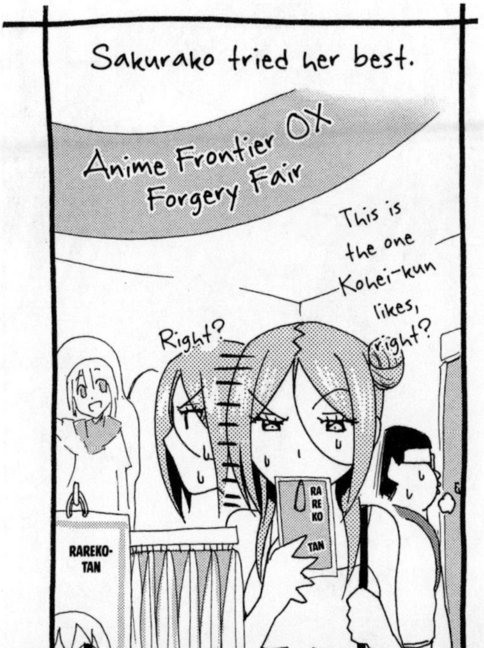
Sakurako tried her best.
Anime Frontier OX Forgery Fair
This is the one Kohei-kun likes, right?
Right?
RA RE KO TAN
RAREKO-TAN

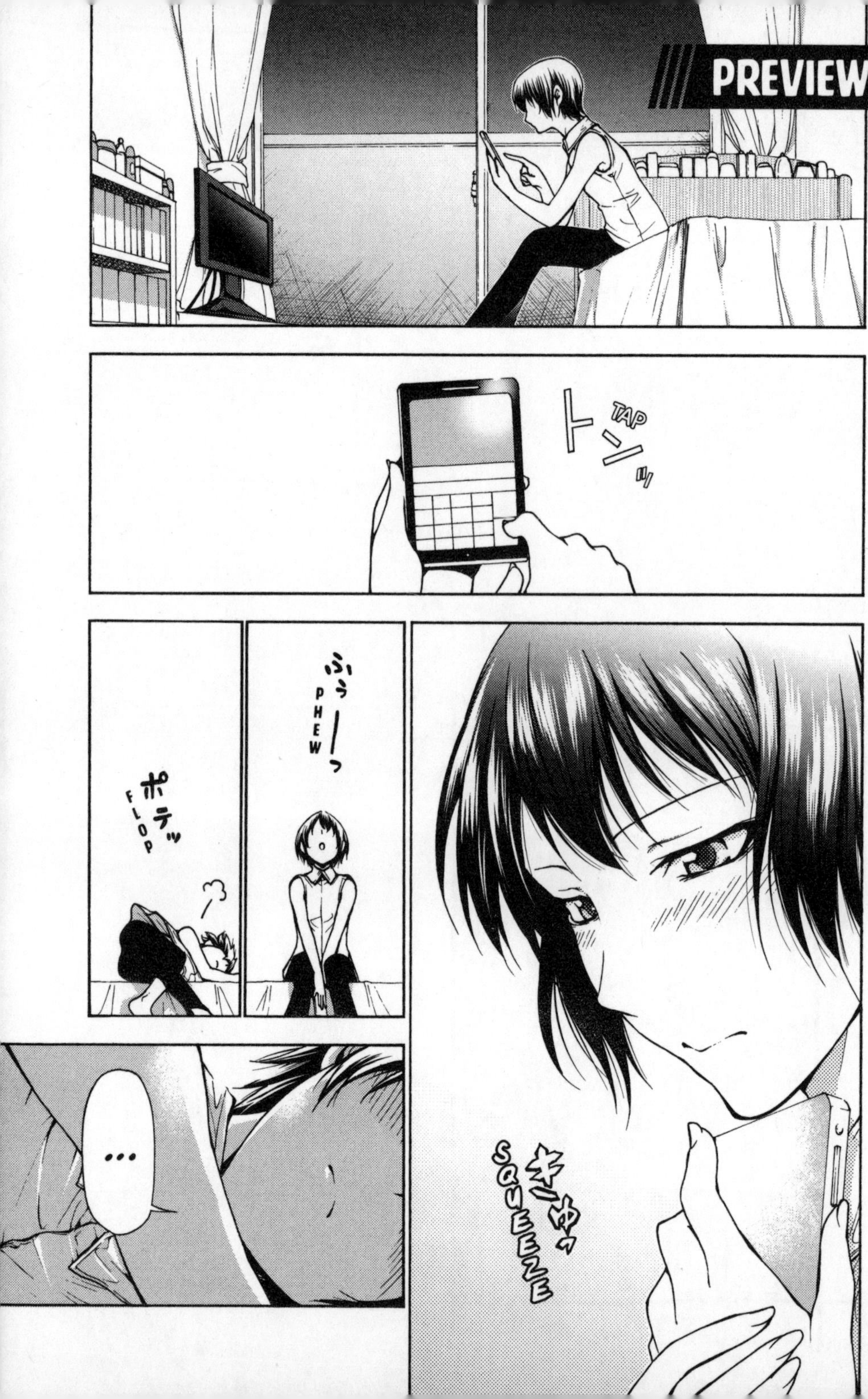
PREVIEW
トンッ
TAP
キゅっ
SQUEEZE
ふぅーっ
PHEW
ポテッ
FLOP
...

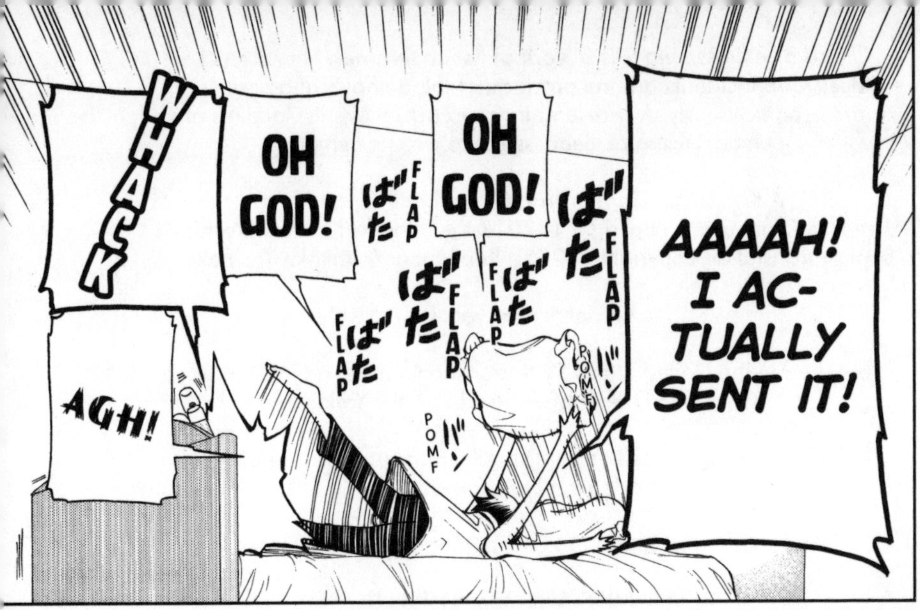
AAAAH! I AC-TUALLY SENT IT!
POMF
POMF
ばた FLAP
ばた FLAP
ばた FLAP
ばた FLAP
ばた FLAP
OH GOD!
OH GOD!
WHACK
AGH!

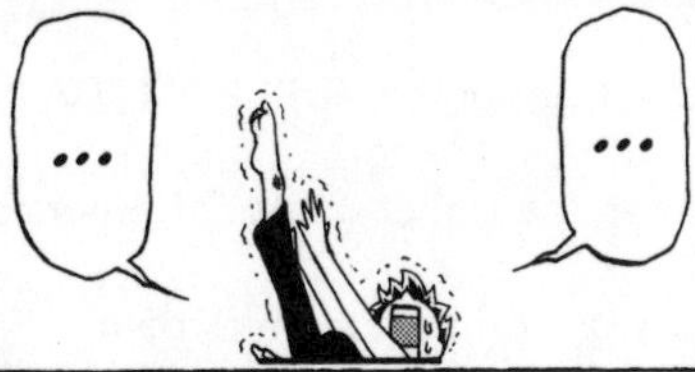
...
...

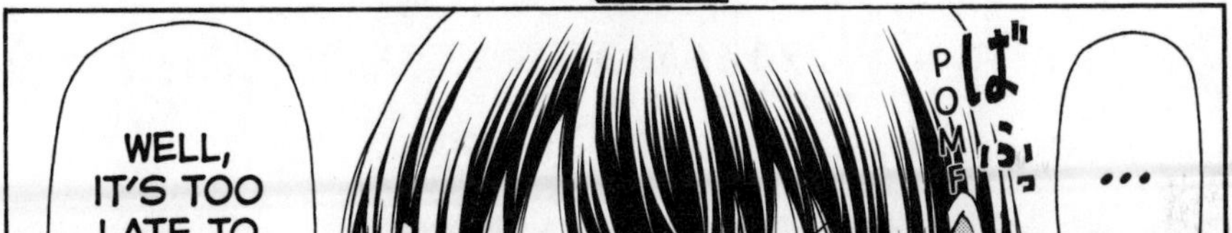
...
ばふっ POMF
WELL, IT'S TOO LATE TO BE EMBAR-RASSED NOW.

Grand Blue Dreaming 10

TO BE CONTINUED IN...

A Kodansha Comics Trade Paperback Original
Grand Blue Dreaming 9 copyright © 2017 Kenji Inoue/Kimitake Yoshioka
English translation copyright © 2020 Kenji Inoue/Kimitake Yoshioka

Published in the United States by Kodansha Comics, an imprint of Kodansha USA Publishing, LLC, New York.

Publication rights for this English edition arranged through Kodansha Ltd., Tokyo.

First published in Japan in 2017 by Kodansha Ltd., Tokyo.

ISBN 978-1-63236-812-6

Original cover design by YUKI YOSHIDA (futaba)

Printed in the United States of America.

www.kodanshacomics.com

9 8 7 6 5 4 3 2
Translation: Adam Hirsch
Lettering: Jan Lan Ivan Concepcion
Editing: Sarah Tilson and Nathaniel Gallant
Additional Layout: Sara Linsley
Editorial Assistance: YKS Services LLC/SKY Japan, INC.
Kodansha Comics edition cover design by Phil Balsman

Publisher: Kiichiro Sugawara
Managing editor: Maya Rosewood
Vice president of marketing & publicity: Naho Yamada

Director of publishing services: Ben Applegate
Associate director of operations: Stephen Pakula
Publishing services managing editor: Noelle Webster
Assistant production manager: Emi Lotto